U.S. and CANADA LITERATURE

GW00690711

NAME: ____________________

COMPANY: ____________________

ADDRESS: ____________________

CITY: ____________________ STATE: __________ ZIP: __________

COUNTRY: ____________________

PHONE NO.: (   ) ____________________

ORDER NO.	TITLE	QTY.	PRICE	TOTAL
		____ ×	____ =	____
		____ ×	____ =	____
		____ ×	____ =	____
		____ ×	____ =	____
		____ ×	____ =	____
		____ ×	____ =	____
		____ ×	____ =	____
		____ ×	____ =	____
		____ ×	____ =	____
		____ ×	____ =	____

Subtotal ________

Must Add Your Local Sales Tax ________

Postage: add 10% of subtotal → Postage ________

Total ________

Pay by check, money order, or include company purchase order with this form ($100 minimum).We also accept VISA, MasterCard or American Express. Make payment to Intel Literature Sales. Allow 2-4 weeks for delivery.

☐ VISA ☐ MasterCard ☐ American Express Expiration Date ____________

Account No. ____________________

Signature ____________________

Mail To: Intel Literature Sales
P.O. Box 7641
Mt. Prospect, Il 60056-7641

International Customers outside the U.S. and Canada should use the International order form or contact their local Sales Office or Distributor.

For phone orders in the U.S. and Canada
Call Toll Free: (800) 548-4725

Prices good until 12/31/90.

Source HB

INTERNATIONAL LITERATURE ORDER FORM

NAME: ____

COMPANY: ____

ADDRESS: ____

CITY: ______________________ STATE: __________ ZIP: __________

COUNTRY: ____

PHONE NO.: (   ) ______________________________________

ORDER NO.	TITLE	QTY.	PRICE	TOTAL
		____ ×	____ =	____
		____ ×	____ =	____
		____ ×	____ =	____
		____ ×	____ =	____
		____ ×	____ =	____
		____ ×	____ =	____
		____ ×	____ =	____
		____ ×	____ =	____
		____ ×	____ =	____
		____ ×	____ =	____

Subtotal __________

Must Add Your Local Sales Tax __________

Total __________

PAYMENT

Cheques should be made payable to your local Intel Sales Office

Other forms of payment may be available in your country. Please contact the Literature Coordinator at your local Intel Sales Office for details.

The completed form should be marked to the attention of the LITERATURE COORDINATOR and returned to your local Intel Sales Office.

intel®

80C186EB/80C188EB USER'S MANUAL

MAY 1990

Additional copies of this manual or other Intel literature may be obtained from:

Intel Corporation
Literature Sales
P.O. Box 7641
Mt. Prospect, IL 60056-7641

CUSTOMER SUPPORT

INTEL'S COMPLETE SUPPORT SOLUTION WORLDWIDE

Customer Support is Intel's complete support service that provides Intel customers with hardware support, software support, customer training, consulting services and network management services. For detailed information contact your local sales offices.

After a customer purchases any system hardware or software product, service and support become major factors in determining whether that product will continue to meet a customer's expectations. Such support requires an international support organization and a breadth of programs to meet a variety of customer needs. As you might expect, Intel's customer support is quite extensive. It can start with assistance during your development effort to network management. 100 Intel sales and service offices are located worldwide—in the U.S., Canada, Europe and the Far East. So wherever you're using Intel technology, our professional staff is within close reach.

HARDWARE SUPPORT SERVICES

Intel's hardware maintenance service, starting with complete on-site installation will boost your productivity from the start and keep you running at maximum efficiency. Support for system or board level products can be tailored to match your needs, from complete on-site repair and maintenance support to economical carry-in or mail-in factory service.

Intel can provide support service for not only Intel systems and emulators, but also support for equipment in your development lab or provide service on your product to your end-user/customer.

SOFTWARE SUPPORT SERVICES

Software products are supported by our Technical Information Service (TIPS) that has a special toll free number to provide you with direct, ready information on known, documented problems and deficiencies, as well as work-arounds, patches and other solutions.

Intel's software support consists of two levels of contracts. Standard support includes TIPS (Technical Information Phone Service), updates and subscription service (product-specific troubleshooting guides and; *COMMENTS Magazine*). Basic support consists of updates and the subscription service. Contracts are sold in environments which represent product groupings (e.g., iRMX® environment).

CONSULTING SERVICES

Intel provides field system engineering consulting services for any phase of your development or application effort. You can use our system engineers in a variety of ways ranging from assistance in using a new product, developing an application, personalizing training and customizing an Intel product to providing technical and management consulting. Systems Engineers are well versed in technical areas such as microcommunications, real-time applications, embedded microcontrollers, and network services. You know your application needs; we know our products. Working together we can help you get a successful product to market in the least possible time.

CUSTOMER TRAINING

Intel offers a wide range of instructional programs covering various aspects of system design and implementation. In just three to ten days a limited number of individuals learn more in a single workshop than in weeks of self-study. For optimum convenience, workshops are scheduled regularly at Training Centers worldwide or we can take our workshops to you for on-site instruction. Covering a wide variety of topics, Intel's major course categories include: architecture and assembly language, programming and operating systems, BITBUS™ and LAN applications.

NETWORK MANAGEMENT SERVICES

Today's networking products are powerful and extremely flexible. The return they can provide on your investment via increased productivity and reduced costs can be very substantial.

Intel offers complete network support, from definition of your network's physical and functional design, to implementation, installation and maintenance. Whether installing your first network or adding to an existing one, Intel's Networking Specialists can optimize network performance for you.

CUSTOMER SUPPORT

Table of Contents

Table of Contents (continued)

Table of Contents (continued)

Table of Contents (continued)

Table of Contents (continued)

Introduction 1

CHAPTER 1
INTRODUCTION

The 80C186EB is the third generation addition to the Intel's 80186 family of embedded microprocessors. Intel's advanced CHMOS IV semiconductor fabrication technology has allowed the integration of many of today's most used peripherals with a high performance, low-power, 8086 compatible CPU core. The 80C186EB is the first choice in portable office and communication equipment due to its low power and high integration. The flexible power management strategy of the 80C186EB allows for low-power applications that do not sacrifice performance.

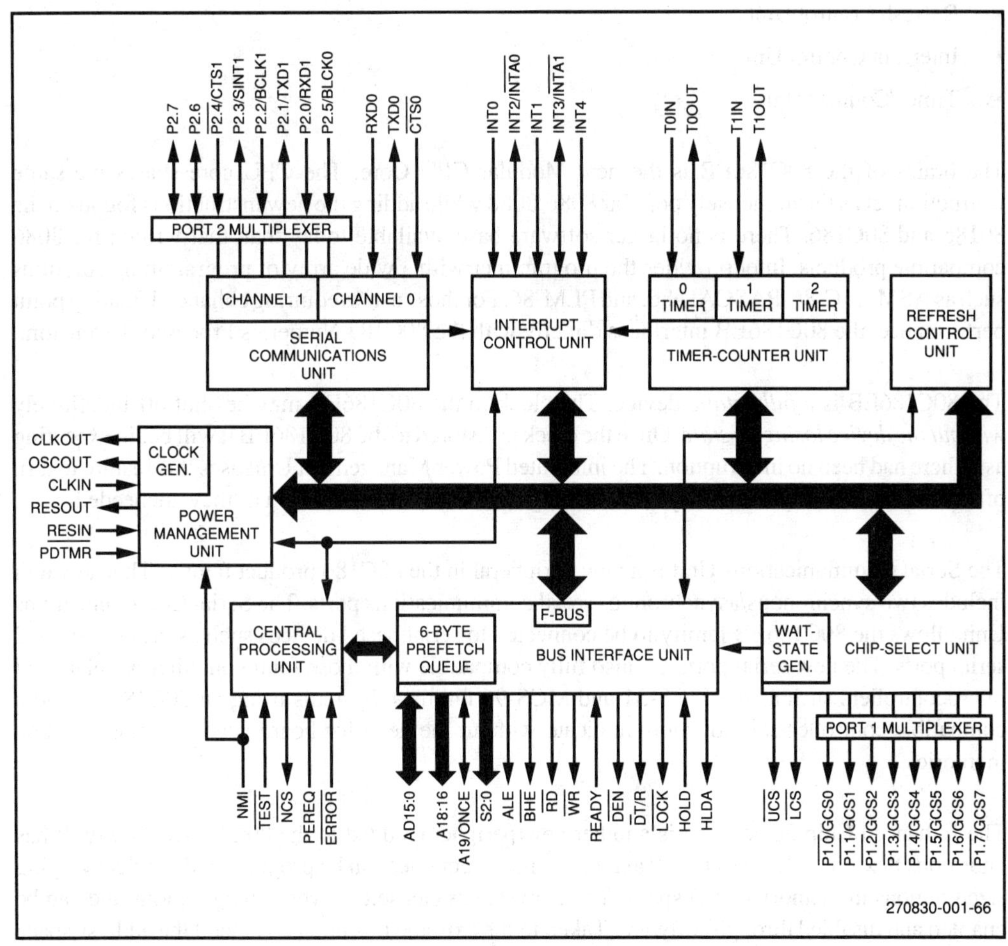

Figure 1.1. 80C186EB Block Diagram

The 80C186EB maintains full code compatibility with it's older relatives the 80186 and 80C186, but adds a new, and enhanced, feature set:

- Low Power/Static CMOS Modular CPU core
- Power Management Unit
- Serial Communications Unit
- Input/Output Port Unit
- Enhanced Chip Select Unit
- Refresh Control Unit
- Interrupt Control Unit
- Timer/Counter Unit

The brains of the 80C186EB is the new Modular CPU Core. The CPU core shares the same instruction set as the immensely popular 8086/8088 while adding the new instructions found on the 80186 and 80C186. There is no larger software base available today than that written for 8086 compatible products. Intel provides the programmer with a wide array of programming solutions such as ASM86, C-86, PASCAL-86, and PLM-86. For those users requiring enhanced floating point performance, the 80C186EB interfaces directly with the 80C187 Numerics Processor Extension.

The 80C186EB is a *fully static* device. The clock to the 80C186EB may be shut off indefinitely *without the device losing its state*. Once the clock is restored to the 80C186EB it will begin executing as if there had been no interruption. The integrated Power Management Unit uses this feature to turn off sections of the chip while they are not being used and re-awaken them as they are needed.

The Serial Communications Unit is a new peripheral in the 80C186 product family. This new unit includes two synchronous/asynchronous serial communications ports. The Serial Communications Unit allows the 80C186EB family to be connected to serial based devices such as printers and PC serial ports. The new serial ports are also fully compatible with those found on other popular Intel microcontrollers such as the MCS-51 and MCS-96 families. Systems using an 80C186EB and a compatible controller can now communicate without the need for board space robbing mailbox memories.

The Enhanced Chip Select Unit is another new peripheral added to the 80C186EB family. It has enormous flexibility. Each of the 10 available chip select lines can be programmed to select varying sized regions in memory or I/O space. The chip selects can select overlapping regions and can be enabled and disabled through software. Taken to the extreme this unit can extend the address space of the 80C186EB to **10 megabytes** of software paged memory.

Some customers may not need all the pin functions available on the 80C186EB. The Input/Output port unit was added to allow the user to swap unused internal peripheral pins for input and output ports. For example, eight of the ten chip select pins may be converted, via software, into output ports.

The Refresh Control Unit has been provided to simplify the design of dynamic memory systems. At programmable intervals, the 80C186EB will run dummy read cycles to refresh the dynamic RAM.

The Interrupt Control Unit handles the 80C186EB interrupt duties. The Interrupt Controller handles interrupt requests from all internal sources as well as the 5 external interrupt pins. If more than five external interrupts are required, the Interrupt Unit can be cascaded to external 82C59 controllers increasing the handling capacity to 129 interrupts.

Many systems require the handling of time related events. The Timer/Counter Unit provides a flexible solution for this system need. The Timer/Counter unit contains three sixteen bit timers that can be configured to perform many tasks including: real time clock, event counter, programmable one shot.

The introduction of the 80C186EB signals a new direction for the successful 80186 family. The 80C186EB story began over a decade ago with the introduction of Intel's first 16-bit microprocessor, the 8086.

1.1 THE 80186 FAMILY LEGACY

The 8086 microprocessor was first introduced in 1978 and gained rapid support as the microcomputer engine of choice. There are literally millions of 8086/8088 based systems in the world today. The amount of software written for the 8086/8088 microprocessor can be rivaled by no other architecture.

The 8086, however, required dozens of support chips to implement even a moderately complex system. Intel recognized the need to integrate commonly used system peripherals onto the same silicon die as the CPU. In 1982 Intel addressed this need by introducing the 80186/80188 family of embedded microprocessors. The 80186 integrated the following peripherals with the CPU: Chip Select Unit, Interrupt Unit, Clock Generator, DMA Unit, Interrupt Unit, and a Timer Counter Unit. In addition to the new integrated peripherals, the CPU was enhanced by adding new instructions and reducing the time required to perform all memory access instructions.

As technology advanced and turned towards small geometry CMOS processes, it became clear that a new 80186 was needed. In 1987 Intel announced the second generation of the 80186 family: the 80C186. The 80C186 is pin compatible with the 80C186 while adding an enhanced feature set including a power save unit, a refresh control unit, and a direct 80C187 interface. The high performance CHMOS III process allowed the 80C186 to run at twice the clock rate of the NMOS 80186.

In the past 5 years the size of personal computing equipment has shrunk dramatically. Computers that once took up half the desk now sit comfortably on your lap during a long flight. Portable phones, once a bulky and expensive luxury, are now commonplace. The FAX machine, a now critical piece of office equipment, is now venturing into the automobile.

Intel saw the need for highly integrated yet low power solutions for these and many other computing applications. Once again, the 80186 architecture was the answer.

The 80C186EB is the first member of the 80C186 Modular Core family. In following with the electronics industry trend towards application specific products, the CPU of the 80C186 was redesigned to be a stand alone, proliferatable, core. The core was given an internal interface bus to which a wide array of integrated peripherals could be attached.

The entire system was designed to be static. When the clock is disabled, while waiting for a relatively slow human to touch the keyboard for instance, the chip will shut off and consume almost no power. This kind of power management is critical in portable applications.

A new and enhanced feature set was added to the 80C186 Modular Core. This new feature set exchanges the DMA controller for 2 serial ports and enhances the capabilities of the original peripherals.

The 80C186EB is the direct result of eight years of 80186 family development. It offers the designer the peace of mind of a well established architecture with benefits of state of the art technology.

1.2 HOW TO USE THIS MANUAL

Throughout this manual you will come across phrases such as "80C186 Modular Core Family" or "80C186EB family". Each of these terms refers to a *specific set of 80C186EB products*. The phrases and the products they refer to are as follows:

80C186 Modular Core Family: This phrase refers to any product that uses the embedded 80C186 CPU core architecture. At this time these are the 80C186EB and 80C188EB. Most discussions that refer to the Modular Core Family are also true of the 80186 and 80C186 CPU's.

80C186 Modular Core: Without the *family*, this refers to just the 16-bit bus members of the modular core family.

80C188 Modular Core: This phrase refers to the 8-bit bus products.

80C186EB Family: This phrase refers specifically to the 80C186EB and the 80C188EB; both the Modular CPU core *and* the specific peripheral set.

80C186EB: This refers to just the 80C186EB (16-bit bus) version of the 80C186EB family.

80C188EB: The 8-bit bus member of the 80C186EB family.

Each chapter covers a specific section of the device beginning with the CPU core. In the appendices you will find information regarding the differences among family members, instruction set references, and special topics.

This user's guide is intended to be a supplement to the device data sheet. Specific timing values are not discussed in this guide; they can be found in the data sheet.

Overview of the 80C186 Family Modular Microprocessor Core Architecture 2

CHAPTER 2
OVERVIEW OF THE 80C186 FAMILY MODULAR MICROPROCESSOR CORE ARCHITECTURE

The 80C186 Modular Microprocessor Core shares a common base architecture with the 8086, 8088, 80186, 80188, 80286, i386™, and i486™ processors. The 80C186 Modular Core maintains full object code compatibility with the well-known 8086/8088 family of 16-bit microprocessors, while adding additional hardware and software performance enhancements. Most instructions require fewer clocks to execute on the 80C186 Modular Core because of hardware enhancements in the Bus Interface Unit and the Execution Unit. In addition, there are a number of additional instructions which simplify programming and reduce code size (see Appendix A.7).

This section describes the base architecture of the 80C186 Modular Core family. Those readers already familiar with the 8086/8088 architecture will find this section to be, for the most part, a review and may wish to read Appendix A ("Differences Between the 80C186 Modular Core Family and the 8086/8088") instead.

2.1 ARCHITECTURAL OVERVIEW

The 80C186 Modular Microprocessor Core incorporates two separate processing units: an Execution Unit (EU) and a Bus Interface Unit (BIU). The EU is functionally identical among all family members. In the 80C186 Core the BIU is configured for a 16-bit external data bus and in the 80C188 Core the BIU is configured for an 8-bit external data bus. The two units are connected by an instruction prefetch queue.

The EU executes instructions and the BIU fetches instructions, reads operands, and writes results. Whenever the EU requires another opcode byte, it takes the byte out of the prefetch queue. The two units can operate independently of one another and are able, under most circumstances, to extensively overlap instruction fetches and execution.

The 80C186 Modular Core family has a 16-bit Arithmetic Logic Unit (ALU) which performs 8-bit or 16-bit arithmetic and logical operations. It provides for data movement among registers, memory and I/O space. In addition, the CPU allows for high speed data transfer from one area of memory to another using string move instructions, and to or from an I/O port and memory using block I/O instructions. Finally, the CPU provides many conditional branch and control instructions.

This architecture features 14 basic registers which are grouped as general registers, segment registers, pointer registers, and status and control registers. The four 16-bit general purpose registers (AX, BX, CX, and DX) may be used as operands in most arithmetic operations in either 8- or 16-bit units. The four 16-bit pointer registers (SI, DI, BP, and SP) may be used both in arithmetic operations and in accessing memory-based variables. Four 16-bit segment registers (CS, DS, SS, and ES) allow simple memory partitioning to aid modular programming. The status and control registers consist of an instruction pointer (IP) and a status word register containing flag bits.

Figure 2.1 is a simplified CPU block diagram.

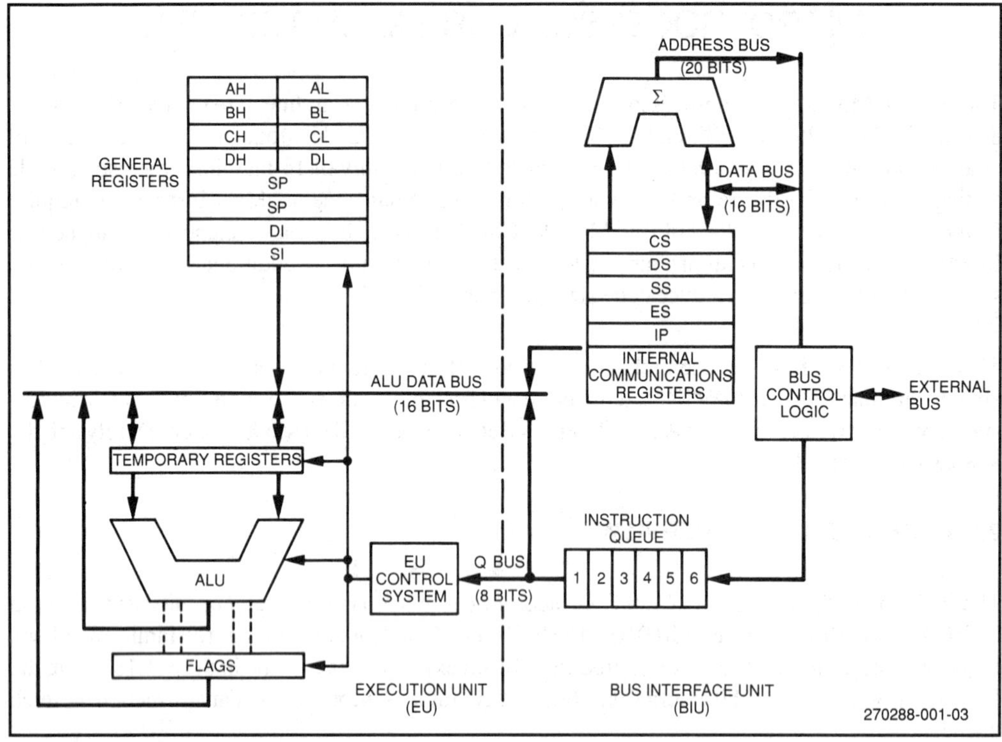

Figure 2.1. Simplified Functional Block Diagram of the 80C186 Modular Core Family CPU

2.1.1 EXECUTION UNIT

The EU is responsible for the execution of all instructions, for providing data and addresses to the BIU, and for manipulating the general registers and the flag register. A 16-bit ALU in the EU maintains the CPU status and control flags, and manipulates the general registers and instruction operands. All registers and data paths in the EU are 16 bits wide for fast internal transfers.

The EU does not connect directly to the system bus. It obtains instructions from a queue maintained by the BIU. Likewise, when an instruction requires access to memory or to a peripheral device, the EU requests the BIU to obtain and store the data. All addresses manipulated by the EU are 16 bits wide. The BIU, however, performs an address calculation that gives the EU access to the full megabyte of memory space.

When the EU is ready to execute an instruction, it fetches the instruction object code byte from the BIU's instruction queue and then executes the instruction. If the queue is empty when the EU is ready to fetch an instruction byte, the EU waits for the instruction byte to be fetched. If a memory location or I/O port must be addressed during the execution of an instruction, the EU requests the BIU to perform the required bus cycle.

2.1.2 BUS INTERFACE UNIT

The 80C186 Core and 80C188 Core BIUs are functionally identical, but are implemented differently to match the structure and performance characteristics of their respective system buses. Data is transferred between the CPU and memory or peripheral devices upon demand from the EU. The BIU executes all external bus cycles. This unit consists of the segment registers, the instruction pointer, the instruction code queue, and several miscellaneous registers. The BIU transfers data to and from the EU on the ALU data bus.

The BIU generates 20-bit physical addresses in a dedicated adder. The adder shifts a 16-bit segment value left 4 bits and then adds an offset value derived from combinations of the pointer registers, the instruction pointer, and immediate values (see Figure 2.2). Any carry of this addition is ignored.

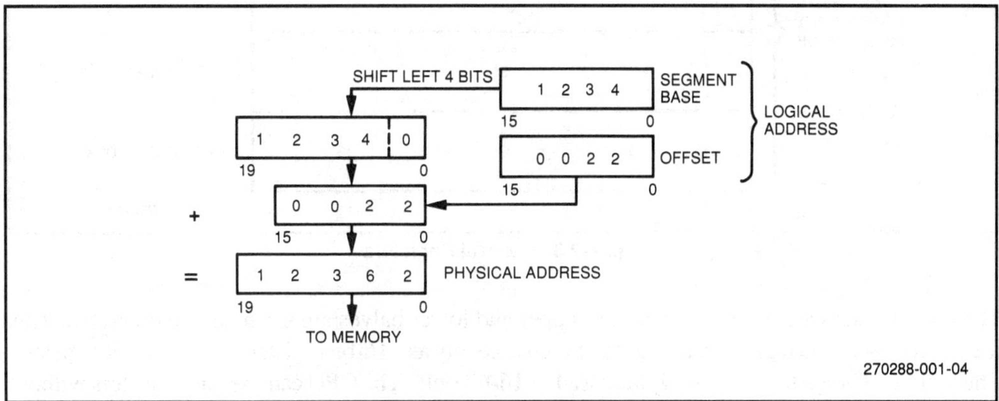

Figure 2.2. Physical Address Generation

During periods when the EU is busy executing instructions, the BIU "looks ahead" and prefetches more instructions from memory. As long as the prefetch queue is partially full, the EU can quickly retrieve instructions upon demand.

2.1.3 GENERAL REGISTERS

80C186 Modular Core family CPUs have eight 16-bit general registers (see Figure 2.3). The general registers are subdivided into two sets of four registers each. These are the data registers (also called the H & L group for high and low), and the pointer and index registers (also called the P & I group).

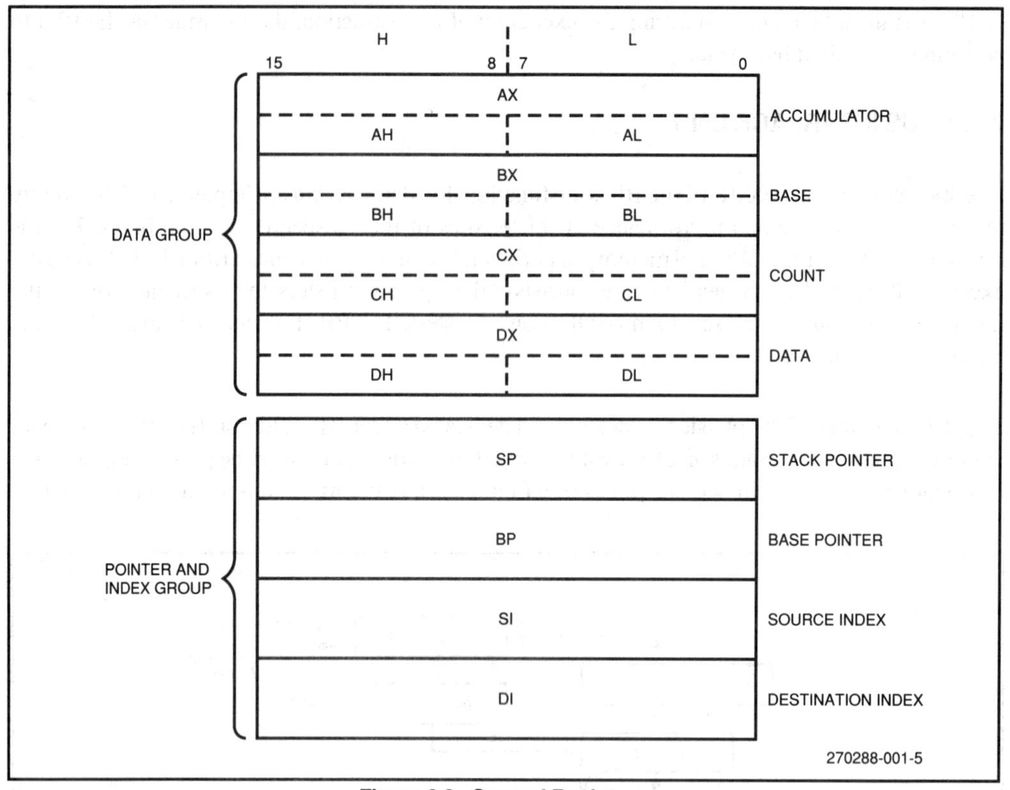

Figure 2.3. General Registers

The data registers are unique in that their upper and lower halves are separately addressable. This means that each data register can be used interchangeably as a 16-bit register or as two 8-bit registers. The other CPU registers are always accessed as 16-bit only. The CPU can use data registers without constraint in most arithmetic and logic operations. Most arithmetic and logic operations can also use the pointer and index registers. Additionally, some instructions use certain registers implicitly (see Table 2.1), therefore allowing compact yet powerful encoding.

Table 2.1. Implicit Use of General Registers

REGISTER	OPERATIONS
AX	Word Multiply, Word Divide, Word I/O
AL	Byte Multiply, Byte Divide, Byte I/O, Translate, Decimal Arithmetic
AH	Byte Multiply, Byte Divide
BX	Translate
CX	String Operations, Loops
CL	Variable Shift and Rotate
DX	Word Multiply, Word Divide, Indirect I/O
SP	Stack Operations
SI	String Operations
DI	String Operations

The state of any of the general registers is undefined at RESET.

2.1.4 SEGMENT REGISTERS

The 80C186 Modular Core family memory space (up to one megabyte) is divided into logical segments of up to 64 Kbytes each. The CPU has direct access to four segments at a time. The base addresses (starting locations) of these memory segments are contained in the segment registers (see Figure 2.4). The CS register points to the current code segment. Instructions are fetched from the CS segment. The SS register points to the current stack segment. Stack operations are performed on locations in the SS segment. The DS register points to the current data segment. The data segment generally contains program variables. The ES register points to the current extra segment, which also is typically used for data storage. The segment registers are accessible to programs and can be manipulated with several instructions.

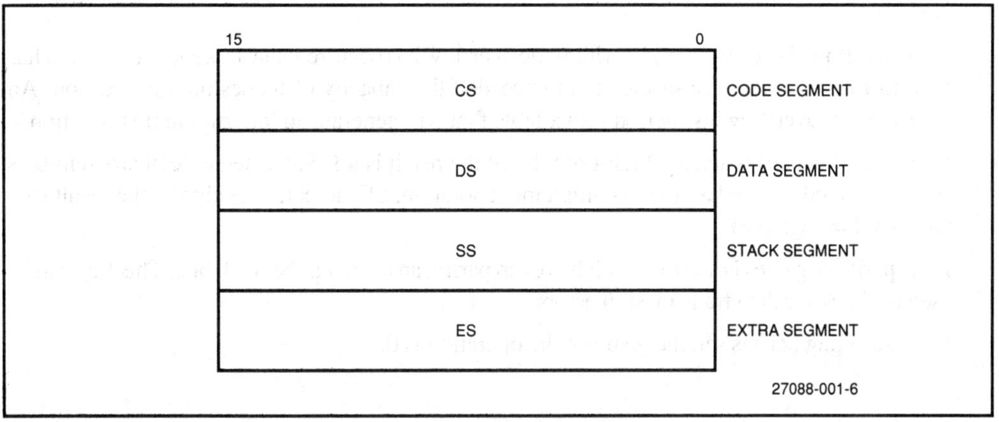

Figure 2.4. Segment Registers

Upon RESET, the CS register is initialized to 0FFFFH, and the DS, ES, and SS register are all initialized to zero.

2.1.5 INSTRUCTION POINTER

The BIU updates a 16-bit instruction pointer (IP) register so that it contains the offset (distance in bytes) of the next instruction from the beginning of the current code segment. In other words, the IP register points to the next instruction. During normal execution, the instruction pointer contains the offset of the next instruction to be **fetched** by the BIU. Whenever the IP register is saved on the stack, however, it is first automatically adjusted to point to the next instruction to be **executed**. Programs do not have direct access to the instruction pointer, but it may change, be saved, or be restored as a result of program execution.

RESET initializes the instruction pointer to 0000H. The concatenation of CS and IP values comprises a starting execution address of 0FFFF0H (see Section 2.1.8 for a description of address formation).

2.1.6 FLAGS

The 80C186 Core family has six one-bit status flags (see Figure 2.5) that the EU posts as the result of an arithmetic or logic operation. Program branch instructions allow a program to alter its execution depending on conditions flagged by prior operation. Different instructions affect the status flags differently, generally reflecting the following states:

- If the auxiliary flag (AF) is set, there has been a carry out from the low nibble into the high nibble or a borrow from the high nibble into the low nibble of an 8-bit quantity (low-order byte of a 16-bit quantity). This flag is used by decimal arithmetic instructions.
- If the carry flag (CF) is set, there has been a carry out of, or a borrow into, the high-order bit of the instruction result (8- or 16-bit). The flag is used by instructions that add and subtract multibyte numbers. Rotate instructions can also isolate a bit in memory or a register by placing it in the carry flag.
- If the overflow flag (OF) is set, an arithmetic overflow has occurred; that is, a significant digit has been lost because the size of the result exceeded the capacity of its destination location. An Interrupt On Overflow instruction is available that will generate an interrupt in this situation.
- If the sign flag (SF) is set, the high-order bit of the result is a 1. Since negative binary numbers are represented in standard two's complement notation, SF indicates the sign of the result (0 = positive, 1 = negative).
- If the parity flag (PF) is set, the result has even parity, an even number of 1-bits. This flag can be used to check for data transmission errors.
- If the zero flag (ZF) is set, the result of the operation is 0.

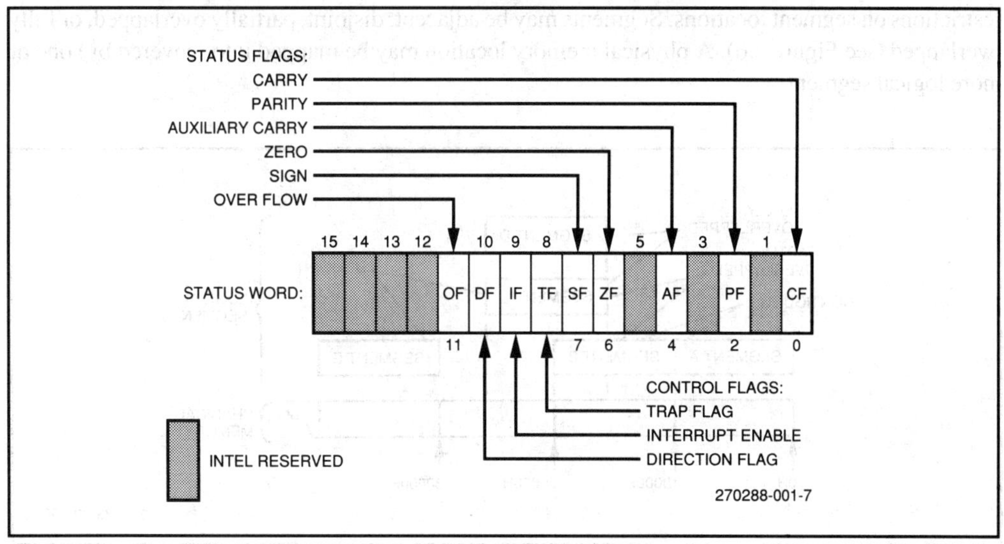

Figure 2.5. Status Word Format

The additional control flags (see Figure 2.5) can be set and cleared by programs to alter processor operations:

- Setting the direction flag (DF) causes string instructions to auto-decrement; that is, to process strings from the high address to the low address, or "right to left". Clearing DF causes string instructions to auto-increment, or process strings "left to right."
- Setting the interrupt-enable flag (IF) allows the CPU to recognize maskable external or internal interrupt requests. Clearing IF disables these interrupts. The interrupt-enable flag has no effect upon software interrupts or non-maskable externally generated interrupts.
- Setting the trap flag (TF) puts the processor into single-step mode for debugging. In this mode, the CPU automatically generates an internal interrupt after each instruction, allowing a program to be inspected as it executes instruction by instruction.

Both the status and control flags are contained in a 16-bit status word (see Figure 2.5). The RESET condition of the status word is OF000H.

2.1.7 MEMORY SEGMENTATION

Programs for the 80C186 Modular Core family view the one megabyte memory space as a group of segments that are user-defined according to application. A segment is a logical unit of memory that may be up to 64 Kbytes long. Each segment if made up of contiguous memory locations and is an independent, separately-addressable unit. Software assigns every segment a base address (starting location) in memory space. All segments begin on 16-bit memory boundaries. There are no other restrictions on segment locations. Segments may be adjacent, disjoint, partially overlapped, or fully overlapped (see Figure 2.6). A physical memory location may be mapped into (covered by) one or more logical segments.

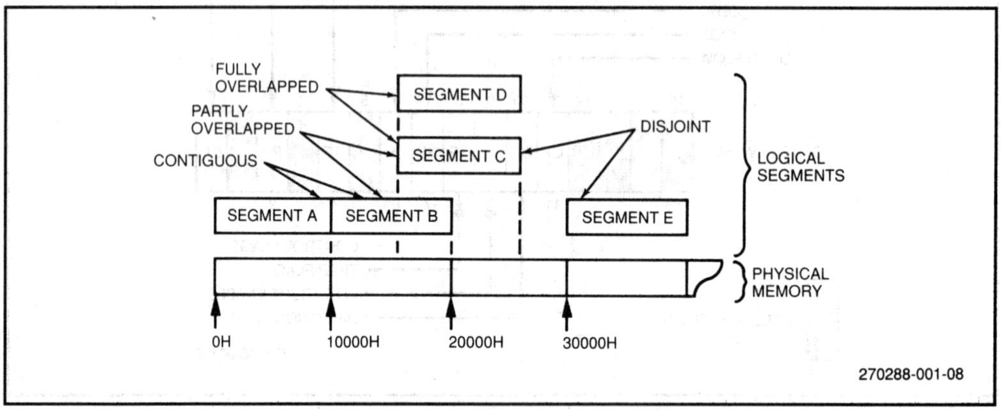

Figure 2.6. Segment Locations in Physical Memory

The four segment registers point to four "currently addressable" segments (see Figure 2.7). The currently addressable segments provide a work space consisting of 64 Kbytes for code, a 64K stack, and 128K of data storage. Programs obtain access to code and data in other segments by changing the segment registers to point to the desired segments.

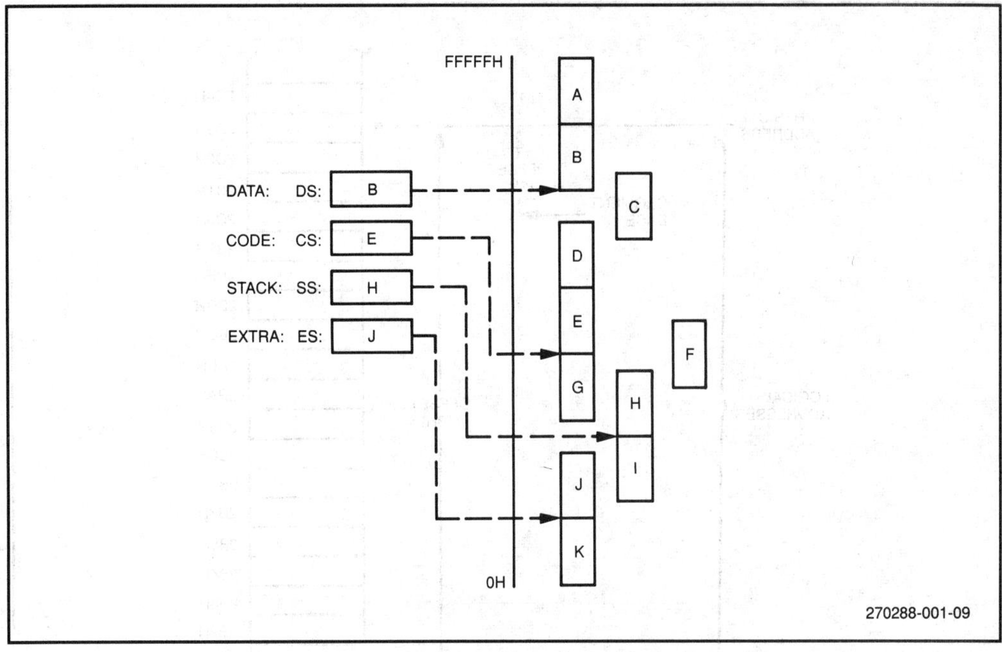

Figure 2.7. Currently Addressable Segments

The segmented memory structure of the 80C186 Modular Core family is a hardware provision to encourage modular programming. Every program will use segmentation differently. Smaller applications tend to initialize the segment registers and then simply forget them. Larger applications give careful consideration to segment definition and use.

2.1.8 LOGICAL ADDRESSES

It is useful to think of every memory location as having two kinds of addresses, physical and logical. A physical address is a 20-bit value that identifies each unique byte location in the memory space. Physical addresses range from 0H to FFFFFH. All exchanges between the CPU and memory components use a physical address.

Programs deal with logical, rather than physical addresses. Program code can be developed without prior knowledge of where the code is to be located in memory; in larger applications, dynamic management of memory resources is a necessity. A logical address consists of a segment base value and an offset value. For any given memory location, the segment base value locates the first byte of the segment and the offset value is the distance, in bytes, of the target location from the beginning of the segment. Segment base and offset values are unsigned 16-bit quantities. Many different logical addresses can map to the same physical location. In the example (see Figure 2.8), physical memory location 2C3H is contained in two different overlapping segments, one beginning at 2B0H and the other at 2C0H.

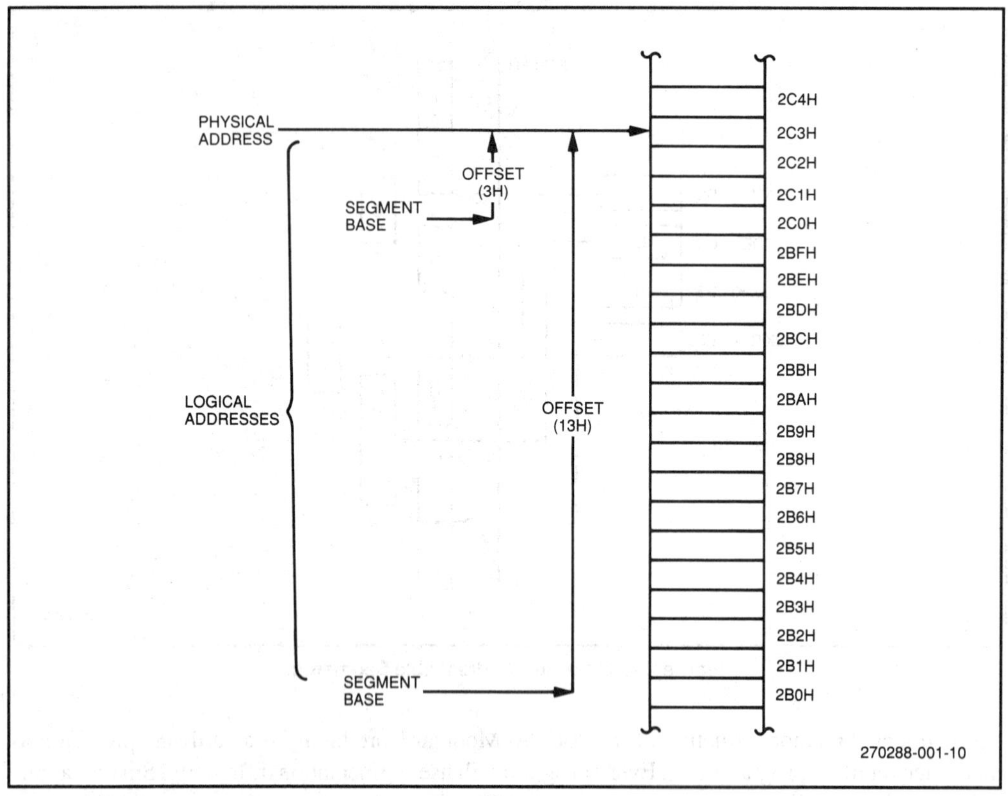

Figure 2.8. Logical and Physical Address

If left alone, the processor automatically assigns segments based on the specific addressing needs of the program. The segment register to be selected is automatically chosen according to the rules in Table 2.2. All information in one segment type generally shares the same logical attributes (e.g., code or data), leading to programs which are shorter, faster, and better structured.

To generate a physical address, the BIU must first obtain the logical address. The logical address of a memory location can come from different sources, depending on the type of reference that is being made (see Table 2.2).

Table 2.2. Logical Address Sources

TYPE OF MEMORY REFERENCE	DEFAULT SEGMENT BASE	ALTERNATE SEGMENT BASE	OFFSET
Instruction Fetch	CS	NONE	IP
Stack Operation	SS	NONE	SP
Variable (except following)	DS	CS, ES, SS	Effective Address
String Source	DS	CS, ES, SS	SI
String Destination	ES	NONE	DI
BP Used As Base Register	SS	CS, DS, ES	Effective Address

Segment base addresses are always held in the segment registers. The BIU conveniently assumes which segment register contains the base address according to the type of memory reference made. However, it is possible for a programmer to explicitly direct the BIU to access a variable in any of the currently addressable segments (except for the destination operand of a string instruction). In assembly language, this is done by preceding an instruction with a segment override prefix.

Instructions are always fetched from the current code segment; the IP register contains the offset of the target instruction from the beginning of the segment. Stack instructions always operate on the current stack segment; the SP (stack pointer) register contains the offset of the top of the stack. Most variables (memory operands) are assumed to reside in the current data segment, but a program can instruct the BIU to override this assumption. Often, the offset of a memory variable is not directly available and must be calculated at execution time. This calculation is based on the addressing mode (see Section 2.2.2) specified in the instruction; the result is called the operand's effective address (EA).

Strings are addressed differently than other variables. The source operand of a string instruction is assumed to lie in the current data segment, but the program may use another currently addressable segment. The operand's offset is taken from the SI (source index) register. The destination operand of a string instruction always resides in the current extra segment; its offset is taken from the DI (destination index) register. The string instructions automatically adjust the SI and DI registers as they process the strings one byte or word at a time.

When register BP, the base pointer register, is designated as a base register in an instruction, the variable is assumed to reside in the current stack segment. Therefore, register BP provides a convenient way to address data on the stack. However, the BP register can also be used to access data in any of the other currently addressable segments.

2.1.9 DYNAMICALLY RELOCATABLE CODE

The segmented memory structure of the 80C186 Modular Core family makes it possible to write programs that are position-independent, or dynamically relocatable. Dynamic relocation allows a multiprogramming or multitasking system to make particularly effective use of available memory. The processor can write inactive programs to a disk and reallocate the space they occupied to other programs. If a disk-resident program is needed later, it can be read back into any available memory location and restarted. Similarly, if a program needs a large contiguous block of storage, and the total amount is only available in non-adjacent fragments, other program segments can be compacted to free up a continuous space. This process is illustrated graphically in Figure 2.9.

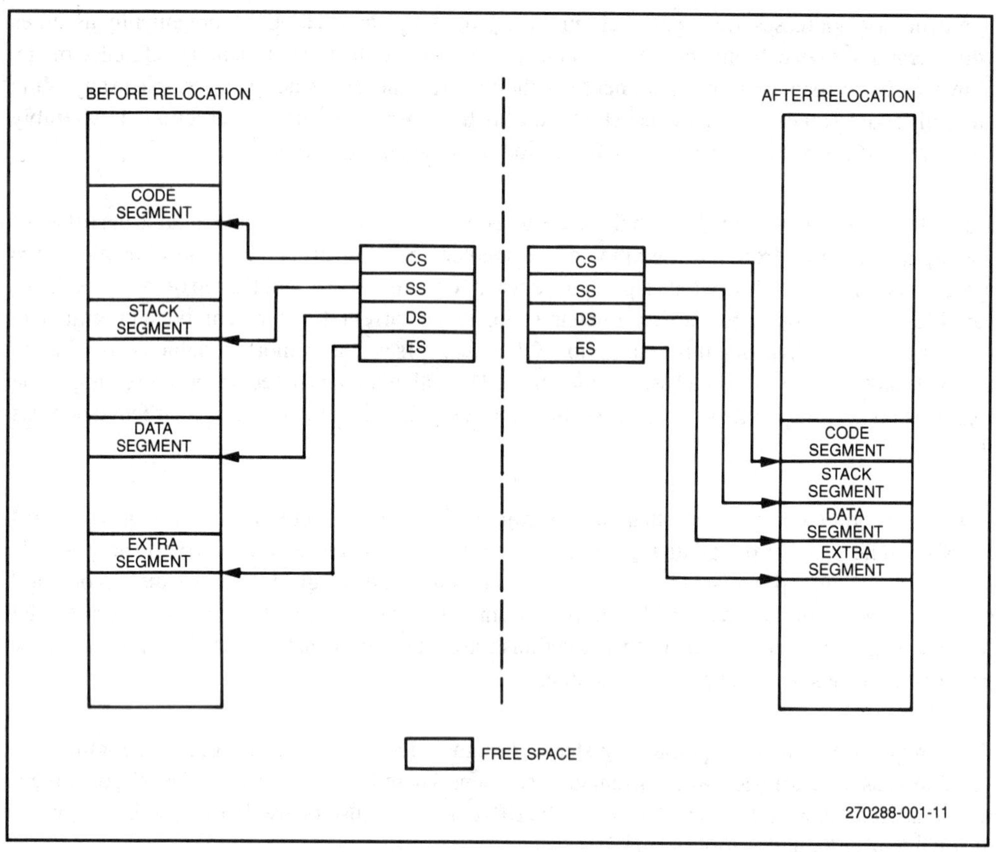

Figure 2.9. Dynamic Code Relocation

To be dynamically relocatable, a program must not load or alter its segment registers and must not transfer directly to a location outside the current code segment. In other words, all offsets in the program must be relative to fixed values contained in the segment registers. This allows the program to be moved anywhere in memory as long as the segment registers are updated to point to the new base addresses.

2.1.10 STACK IMPLEMENTATION

Stacks in the 80C186 Modular Core family are implemented in memory and are located by the stack segment register (SS) and the stack pointer (SP). A system may have numerous stacks, and a stack may be up to 64 Kbytes long, the maximum length of a segment. An attempt to grow a stack beyond 64K overwrites the beginning of the segment. Only one stack is directly addressable at a time. The SS register contains the base address of the current stack; however, the base address is not the origination point of the stack. The SP register contains an offset which points to the top of stack (TOS).

Stacks are 16 bits wide; instructions that operate on a stack add and remove stack elements one word at a time. An element is pushed onto the stack (see Figure 2.10) by first **decrementing** the SP register by 2 and then writing the data word. An element is popped off the stack by copying it from the TOS and then **incrementing** the SP register by 2. In other words, the stack goes **down** in memory toward its base address. Stack operations never move elements on the stack, nor do they erase them. The top of the stack changes only as a result of updating the stack pointer.

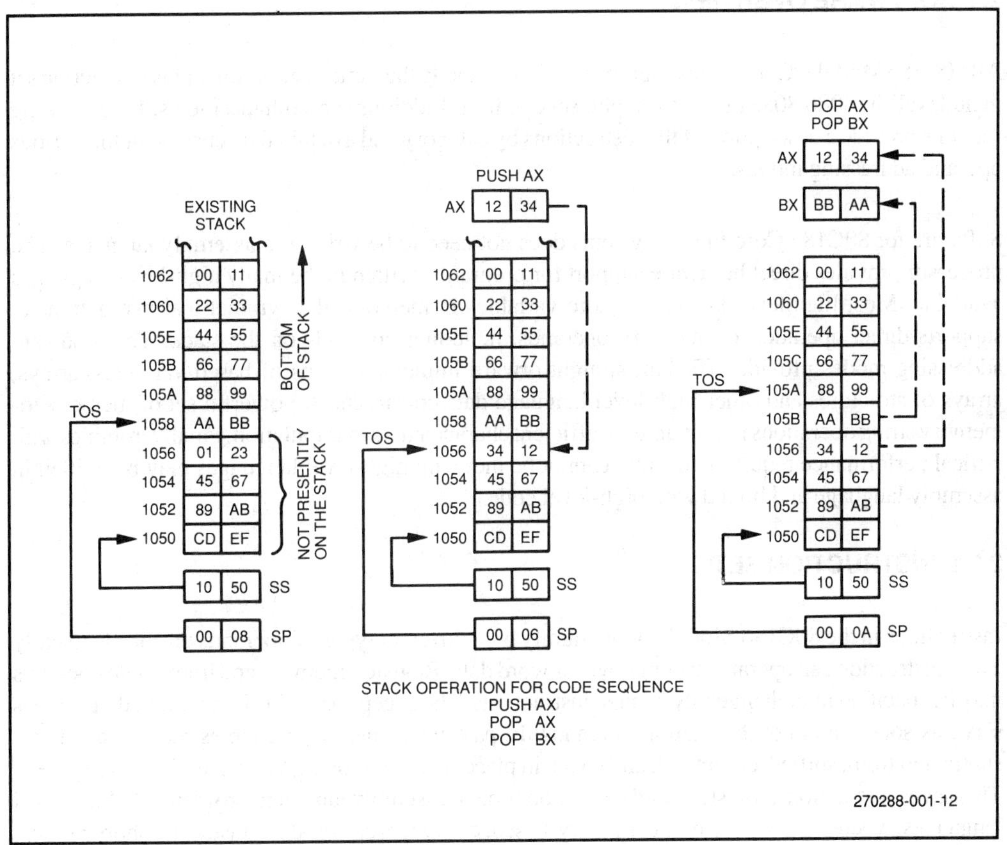

Figure 2.10. Stack Operation

2.1.11 RESERVED MEMORY AND I/O SPACE

Two specific areas in memory and one area in I/O space are reserved in the 80C186 Core family.

- Locations 0H through 3FFH in low memory are reserved for interrupt vectors.
- Locations 0FFFF0H through 0FFFFFH in high memory are reserved for system reset code since the processor begins execution at 0FFFF0H.
- Locations 0F8H through 0FFH in I/O space are reserved for communication with other Intel

hardware products. On the 80C186 Core, these addresses are used as I/O ports for the 80C187 numerics processor extension.

The peripheral control block (see Section 5.0) may reside in memory or I/O space. All unused locations in the peripheral control block are also reserved.

2.2 SOFTWARE OVERVIEW

All 80C186 Modular Core family members execute exactly the same instructions. This instruction set includes all the 8086/8088 instructions plus several useful additions and enhancements. The following sections provide a description of the instructions by category and a detailed discussion of the various operand addressing modes.

Software for 80C186 Core family systems does not need to be written in assembly language. The processor provides direct hardware support for programs written in the many high-level languages available. Most high-level languages store variables in memory; the symmetrical instruction set supports direct operation on memory operands, including operands on the stack. The hardware addressing modes provide efficient, straightforward implementations of based variables, arrays, arrays of structures and other high-level language data constructs. A powerful set of memory-to-memory string operations is available for efficient character data manipulation. Finally, routines with critical performance requirements that cannot be met with high-level languages may be written in assembly language and linked with high-level code.

2.2.1 INSTRUCTION SET

Instructions in the 80C186 Modular Core family treat different types of operands uniformly. Nearly every instruction can operate on either byte or word data. Register, memory and immediate operands may be specified interchangeably in most instructions. The exception to this is that immediate values serve as source and not destination operands. In particular, memory variables may be added to, subtracted from, shifted, compared, and so on, in place, without moving them in and out of registers. This saves instructions, registers, and execution time in assembly language programs. In high-level languages, where most variables are memory-based, compilers can produce faster and shorter object programs.

The 80C186 Core family instruction set can be viewed as existing on two levels. One is the assembly level and the other is the machine level. To the assembly language programmer, the 80C186 Core family appears to have a repertoire of about 100 instructions. One MOV (data move) instruction, for example, transfers a byte of a word from a register of a memory location or an immediate value to either a register or a memory location. The 80C186 Modular Core family CPUs, however, recognize 28 different machine versions of the MOV instruction.

The two levels of instruction set address two different requirements: efficiency and simplicity. The approximately 300 forms of machine-level instructions make very efficient use of storage. For example, the machine instruction that increments a memory operand is three or four bytes long because the address of the operand must be encoded in the instruction. To increment a register, however, does not require as much information, so the instruction can be shorter. The 80C186 Core family has eight different machine-level instructions that increment a different 16-bit register. Each of these instructions is only one byte long.

The assembly level instructions simplify the programmer's view of the instruction set. The programmer writes one form of an INC (increment) instruction and the assembler examines the operand to determine which machine level instruction to generate. The following paragraphs provide a functional description of the assembly-level instructions.

2.2.1.1 DATA TRANSFER INSTRUCTIONS

The instruction set contains 14 data transfer instructions. These instructions move single bytes and words between memory and registers, and also move single bytes and words between the AL or AX registers and I/O ports. Table 2.3 lists the four types of data transfer instructions and their functions.

Table 2.3. Data Transfer Instructions

GENERAL PURPOSE	
MOV	Move byte or word
PUSH	Push word onto stack
POP	Pop word off stack
PUSHA	Push registers onto stack
POPA	Pop registers off stack
XCHG	Exchange byte or word
XLAT	Translate byte
INPUT/OUTPUT	
IN	Input byte or word
OUT	Output byte or word
ADDRESS OBJECT AND STACK FRAME	
LEA	Load effective address
LDS	Load pointer using DS
LES	Load pointer using ES
ENTER	Build stack frame
LEAVE	Tear down stack frame
FLAG TRANSFER	
LAHF	Load AH register from flags
SAHF	Store AH register in flags
PUSHF	Push flags onto stack
POPF	Pop flags off stack

Table 2.4. Arithmetic Instructions

ADDITION	
ADD	Add byte or word
ADC	Add byte or word with carry
INC	Increment byte or word by 1
AAA	ASCII adjust for addition
DAA	Decimal adjust for addition
SUBTRACTION	
SUB	Subtract byte or word
SBB	Subtract byte or word with borrow
DEC	Decrement byte or word by 1
NEG	Negate byte or word
CMP	Compare byte or word
AAS	ASCII adjust for subtraction
DAS	Decimal adjust for subtraction
MULTIPLICATION	
MUL	Multiply byte or word unsigned
IMUL	Integer multiply byte or word
AAM	ASCII adjust for multiply
DIVISION	
DIV	Divide byte or word unsigned
IDIV	Integer divide byte or word
AAD	ASCII adjust for division
CBW	Convert byte to word
CWD	Convert word to doubleword

Table 2.5. Arithmetic Interpretation of 8-Bit Numbers

HEX	BIT PATTERN	UNSIGNED BINARY	SIGNED BINARY	UNPACKED DECIMAL	PACKED DECIMAL
07	0 0 0 0 0 1 1 1	7	+7	7	7
89	1 0 0 0 1 0 0 1	137	-119	invalid	89
C5	1 1 0 0 0 1 0 1	197	-59	invalid	invalid

Data transfer instructions are categorized as general purpose, input/output, address object, and flag transfer. The stack manipulation instructions which are used for transferring flag contents, and the instructions for loading segment registers are also included in this group. Figure 2.11 shows the flag storage formats. The address object instructions manipulate the addresses of variables instead of the contents of values of the variables. This is useful for list processing, based variable, and string operations.

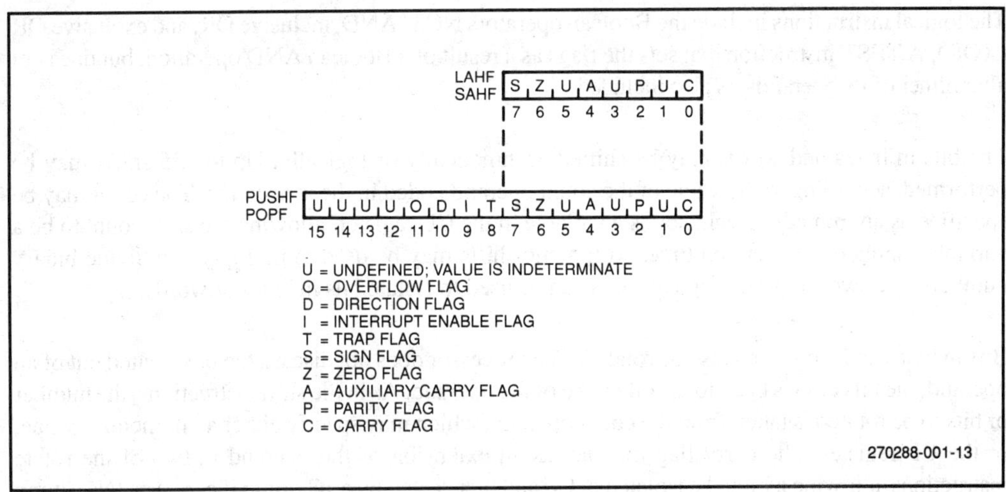

Figure 2.11. Flag Storage Format

2.2.1.2 ARITHMETIC INSTRUCTIONS

The arithmetic instructions (see Table 2.4) operate on four types of numbers:

1. Unsigned binary.
2. Signed binary (integers).
3. Unsigned packed decimal.
4. Unsigned unpacked decimal.

Table 2.5 shows the interpretations of various bit patterns according to each number type.

Binary numbers may be 8 or 16 bits long. Decimal numbers are stored in bytes, two digits per byte for packed decimal and one digit per byte for unpacked decimal. The processor always assumes that the operands specified in arithmetic instructions contain data that represent valid numbers for the instruction being performed. Invalid data may produce unpredictable results. The processor analyzes arithmetic results and posts certain characteristics of the operation to six flags.

2.2.1.3 BIT MANIPULATION INSTRUCTIONS

There are three groups of instructions for manipulating bits within both bytes and word. These three groups are logical, shifts and rotates. Table 2.6 lists these three groups of bit manipulation instructions with their functions.

The logical instructions include the Boolean operators NOT, AND, inclusive OR, and exclusive OR (XOR). A TEST instruction that sets the flags as a result of a Boolean AND operation, but does not alter either of its operands, is also included.

The bits in bytes and words may be shifted arithmetically or logically. Up to 255 shifts may be performed, according to the value of the count operand coded in the instruction. The count may be specified as an immediate value or as a variable in the CL register, allowing the shift count to be a variable supplied at execution time. Arithmetic shifts may be used to multiply and divide binary numbers by powers of two. Logical shifts can be used to isolate bits in bytes or words.

Bits in bytes and words can also be rotated. The processor does not discard the bits rotated out of an operand; the bits circles back to the other end of the operand. As in the shift instructions, the number of bits to be rotated is taken from the count operand, which may specify either an immediate value, or the CL register. The carry flag may act as an extension of the operand in two of the rotate instructions, allowing a bit to be isolated in CF and then tested by a JC (jump if carry) or JNC (jump if not carry) instruction.

2.2.1.4 STRING INSTRUCTIONS

Five basic string operations allow strings of bytes or words to be operated on, one element (byte or word) at a time. Strings of up to 64 Kbytes may be manipulated with these instructions. Instructions are available to move, compare and scan for a value, as well as moving string elements to and from the accumulator. Table 2.7 lists the string instructions. These basic operations may be preceded by a special one-byte prefix that causes the instruction to be repeated by the hardware, allowing long strings to be processed much faster than would be possible with a software loop. The repetitions can be terminated by a variety of conditions, and repeated operations may be interrupted and resumed.

The string instructions operate similarly in many respects (refer to Table 2.8). A string instruction may have a source operand, a destination operand, or both. The hardware assumes that a source string resides in the current data segment. A segment prefix may be used to override this assumption. A destination string must be in the current extra segment. The assembler checks the attributes of the operands to determine if the elements of the strings are bytes or words. However, the assembler does not use the operand names to address strings. Instead, the contents of register SI (source index) are used as an offset to address the current element of the source string. Also, the contents of register DI (destination index) are taken as the offset of the current destination string element. These registers must be initialized to point to the source/destination strings before executing the string instructions. The LDS, LES and LEA instructions are useful in performing this function.

String instructions automatically update the SI or DI register or both prior to processing the next string element. Setting the direction flag (DF) determines whether the index registers are auto-incremented (DF = 0) or auto-decremented (DF = 1). The processor adjusts the DI or SI register or both by one if byte strings are being processed. The adjustment is two for word strings.

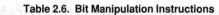

Table 2.6. Bit Manipulation Instructions

LOGICALS	
NOT	"Not" byte or word
AND	"And" byte or word
OR	"Inclusive or" byte or word
XOR	"Exclusive or" byte or word
TEST	"Test" byte or word
SHIFTS	
SHL/SAL	Shift logical/arithmetic left byte or word
SHR	Shift logical right byte or word
SAR	Shift arithmetic right byte or word
ROTATES	
ROL	Rotate left byte or word
ROR	Rotate right byte or word
RCL	Rotate through carry left byte or word
RCR	Rotate through carry right byte or word

Table 2.7. String Instructions

REP	Repeat
REPE/REPZ	Repeat while equal/zero
REPNE/REPNZ	Repeat while not equal/not zero
MOVS	Move byte or word string
MOVSB/MOVSW	Move byte or word string
INS	Input byte or word string
OUTS	Output byte or word string
CMPS	Compare byte or word string
SCAS	Scan byte or word string
LODS	Load byte or word string
STOS	Store byte or word string

Table 2.8. String Instruction Register and Flag Use

SI	Index (offset) for source string
DI	Index (offset) for destination string
CX	Repetition counter
AL/AX	Scan value Destination for LODS Source for STOS
DF	0 = auto-increment SI, DI 1 = auto-decrement SI, DI
ZF	Scan/compare terminator

Table 2.9. Program Transfer Instructions

UNCONDITIONAL TRANSFERS	
CALL	Call procedure
RET	Return from procedure
JMP	Jump
CONDITIONAL TRANSFERS	
JA/JNBE	Jump if above/not below nor equal
JAE/JNB	Jump if above or equal/ not below
JB/JNAE	Jump if below/not above nor equal
JBE/JNA	Jump if below or equal/ not above
JC	Jump if carry
JE/JZ	Jump if equal/zero
JG/JNLE	Jump if greater/not less nor equal
JGE/JNL	Jump if greater or equal/ not less
JL/JNGE	Jump if less/not greater nor equal
JLE/JNG	Jump if less or equal/ not greater
JNC	Jump if not carry
JNE/JNZ	Jump if not equal/not zero
JNO	Jump if not overflow
JNP/JPO	Jump if not parity/parity odd
JNS	Jump if not sign
JO	Jump if overflow
JP/JPE	Jump if parity/parity even
JS	Jump if sign
ITERATION CONTROLS	
LOOP	Loop
LOOPE/LOOPZ	Loop if equal/zero
LOOPNE/LOOPNZ	Loop if not equal/not zero
JCXZ	Jump if register CX=0
INTERRUPTS	
INT	Interrupt
INTO	Interrupt if overflow
BOUND	Interrupt if out of array bounds
IRET	Interrupt return

If a repeat prefix has been coded, then register CX (the count register) is decremented by one after each repetition of the string instruction. The CX register must be initialized to the number of repetitions desired before the string instruction is executed. If the CX register is 0, the string instruction is not executed and control goes to the following instruction.

2.2.1.5 PROGRAM TRANSFER INSTRUCTIONS

The sequence in which instructions are executed in the 80C186 Modular Core family is determined by the contents of the CS and IP registers. The CS register contains the base address of the current code segment. The IP register points to the memory locations from which the next instruction is to be fetched. In most operating conditions, the next instruction to be executed will have already been fetched and is waiting in the CPU instruction queue. The program transfer instructions operate on the instruction pointer and on the CS register; changing the content of these causes normal sequential operation to be altered. When a program transfer occurs, the queue no longer contains the correct instruction. When the BIU obtains the next instruction from memory using the new IP and CS values, it passes the instruction directly to the EU and begins refilling the queue from the new location.

Four groups of program transfers are available with the 80C186 Core family processors. See Table 2.9. These are unconditional transfers, conditional transfers, iteration control instructions, and interrupt-related instructions.

The unconditional transfer instructions may transfer control to a target instruction within the current code segment (intrasegment transfer) or to a different code segment (intersegment transfer). The assembler terms an intrasegment transfer SHORT or NEAR and an intersegment transfer FAR. The transfer is made unconditionally any time the instruction is executed.

The conditional transfer instructions are jumps that may or may not transfer control depending on the state of the CPU flags at the time the instruction is executed. These 18 instructions (see Table 2.10) each test a different combination of flags for a condition. If the condition is logically TRUE then control is transferred to the target specified in the instruction. If the condition is FALSE then control passes to the instruction that follows the conditional jump. All conditional jumps are SHORT, that is, the target must be in the current code segment and within -128 to +127 bytes of the first byte of the next instruction. For example, JMP 00H causes a jump to the first byte of the next instruction. Since jumps are made by adding the relative displacement of the target to the instruction pointer, all conditional jumps are self-relative and are appropriate for position-independent routines.

Table 2.10. Interpretation of Conditional Transfers

MNEMONIC	CONDITION TESTED	"JUMP IF ..."
JA/JNBE	(CF or ZF)=0	above/not below nor equal
JAE/JNB	CF=0	above or equal/not below
JB/JNAE	CF=1	below/not above nor equal
JBE/JNA	(CF or ZF)=1	below or equal/not above
JC	CF=1	carry
JE/JZ	ZF=1	equal/zero
JG/JNLE	((SF xor OF) or ZF) = 0	greater/not less nor equal
JGE/JNL	(SF xor OF)=0	greater or equal/not less
JL/JNGE	(SF xor OF)=1	less/not greater nor equal
JLE/JNG	((SF xor OF) or ZF)=1	less or equal/not greater
JNC	CF=0	not carry
JNE/JNZ	ZF=0	not equal/not zero
JNO	OF=0	not overflow
JNP/JPO	PF=0	not parity/parity odd
JNS	SF=0	not sign
JO	OF=1	overflow
JP/JPE	PF=1	parity/parity equal
JS	SF=1	sign

Note: "above" and "below" refer to the relationship of two unsigned values;
"greater" and "less" refer to the relationship of two signed values.

The iteration control instructions can be used to regulate the repetition of software loops. These instructions use the CX register as a counter. Like the conditional transfers, the iteration control instructions are self-relative and may only transfer to targets that are within -128 to +127 bytes of themselves, i.e., they are SHORT transfers.

The interrupt instructions allow interrupt service routines to be activated by programs as well as by external hardware devices. The effect of software interrupts is similar to hardware-initiated interrupts. However, the processor cannot execute an interrupt acknowledge bus cycle if the interrupt originates in software or with an NMI (Non-Maskable Interrupt).

2.2.1.6 PROCESSOR CONTROL INSTRUCTIONS

The processor control instructions (see Table 2.11) allow programs to control various CPU functions. One group of instructions updates flags, and another group is used primarily for synchronizing the microprocessor to external events. A final instruction causes the CPU to do nothing. Except for the flag operations, none of the processor control instructions affects the flags.

Table 2.11. Processor Control Instructions

FLAG OPERATIONS	
STC	Set carry flag
CLC	Clear carry flag
CMC	Complement carry flag
STD	Set direction flag
CLD	Clear direction flag
STI	Set interrupt enable flag
CLI	Clear interrupt enable flag
EXTERNAL SYNCHRONIZATION	
HLT	Halt until interrupt or reset
WAIT	Wait for $\overline{\text{TEST}}$ pin active
ESC	Escape to external processor
LOCK	Lock bus during next instruction
NO OPERATION	
NOP	No operation

2.2.2 ADDRESSING MODES

An 80C186 Modular Core family member accesses instruction operands in many different ways. Operands may be contained in registers, within the instruction itself, in memory, or at I/O ports. Also, the addresses of memory and I/O port operands can be calculated in several different ways. These addressing modes greatly extend the flexibility and convenience of the instruction set. The following paragraphs briefly describe the register and immediate modes of operand addressing, and then provide a detailed description of the memory and I/O addressing modes.

2.2.2.1 REGISTER AND IMMEDIATE OPERAND ADDRESSING MODES

Instructions that specify only register operands are usually the most compact and fastest executing of the operand addressing forms. This is because the register operand addresses are encoded in instructions in just a few bits, and because these operands are performed entirely within the CPU (no bus cycles are run). Registers may serve as source operands, destination operands, or both.

Immediate operands are constant data contained in an instruction. The data may be either 8 or 16 bits in length. Immediate operands can be accessed quickly because they are available directly from the instruction queue. Like the register operand, no bus cycles need to be run to get an immediate operand. The limitations on immediate operands are that they may only serve as source operands and that they are constant in value.

2.2.2.2 MEMORY ADDRESSING MODES

Although the EU has direct access to register and immediate operands, memory operands must be transferred to and from the CPU over the bus. When the EU needs to read or write a memory operand, it must pass an offset value to the BIU. The BIU adds the offset to the shifted contents of a segment register producing a 20-bit physical address and then executes the bus cycle or cycles needed to access the operand.

The offset that the EU calculates for memory operand is called the operand's effective address or EA. This address is an unsigned 16-bit number that expresses the operand's distance in bytes from the beginning of the segment in which it resides. The EU can calculate the effective address in several ways. Information encoded in the second byte of the instruction tells the EU how to calculate the effective address of each memory operand. A compiler or assembler derives this information from the statement or instruction written by the programmer. Assembly language programmers have access to all addressing modes.

The EU calculates the EA by summing a displacement, the content of a base register and the content of an index register (see Figure 2.12). Any combination of these three components may be present in a given instruction. This allows a variety of memory addressing modes.

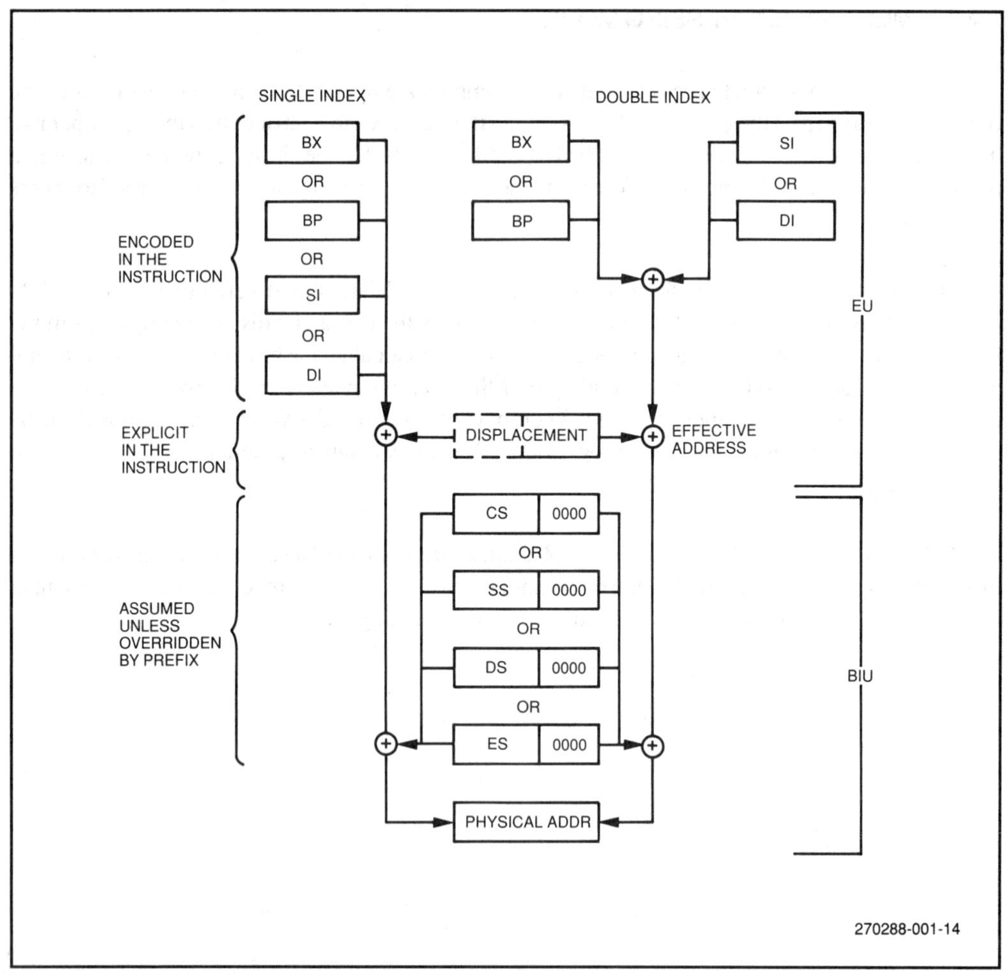

Figure 2.12. Memory Address Computation

The displacement element is an 8-bit or 16-bit number that is contained in the instruction. The displacement generally is derived from the position of the operand name (a variable or label) in the program. The programmer can also modify this value or explicitly specify the displacement.

A programmer may specify that either the BX or BP register is to serve as a base register whose content is to be used in the EA computation.

Similarly, either the SI or DI register may be specified as the index register. The displacement value is a constant. The contents of the base and index registers may change during execution. This allows one instruction to access different memory locations as determined by the current values in the base or base and index registers. Effective address calculations with the BP register are made using the SS register, by default, although either the DS or the ES register may be specified instead.

Direct addressing is the simplest memory addressing mode (see Figure 2.13). No registers are involved and the EA is taken directly from the displacement of the instruction. The programmer typically uses direct addressing to access scaler variables.

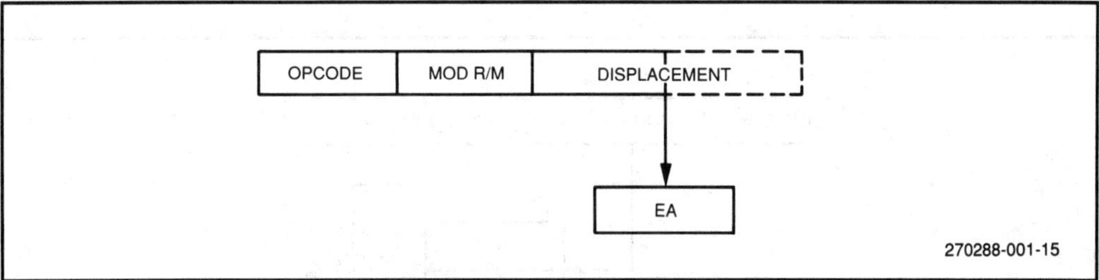

Figure 2.13. Direct Addressing

With register indirect addressing, the effective address of a memory operand may be taken directly from one of the base or index registers (see Figure 2.14). One instruction can operate on many different memory locations if the value in the base or index register is updated appropriately. Any 16-bit general register may be used for register indirect addressing with the JMP or CALL instructions.

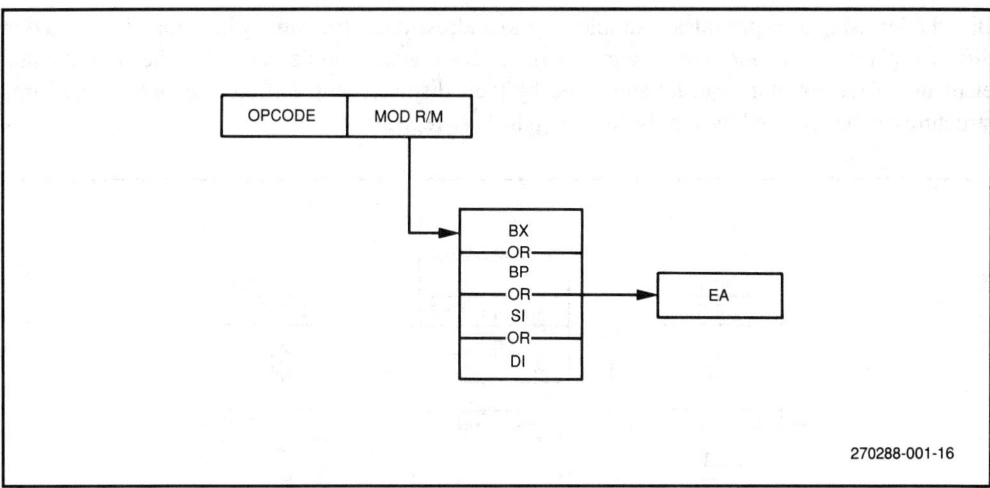

Figure 2.14. Register Indirect Addressing

In based addressing (see Figure 2.15), the effective address is the sum of a displacement value and the content of register BX or BP. Specifying register BP as a base register directs the BIU to obtain the operand from the current stack segment (unless a segment override prefix is present). This makes based addressing with the BP register a very convenient way to access stack data.

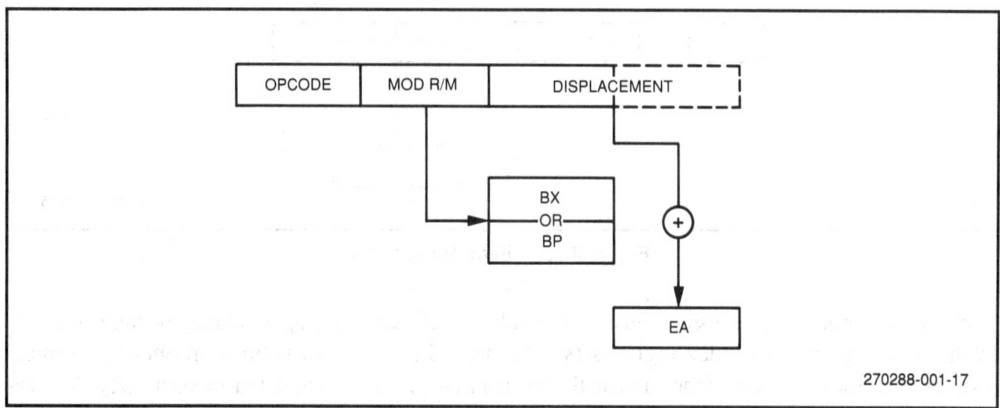

Figure 2.15. Based Addressing

Based addressing also provides a simple way to address data structures which may be located at different places in memory (see Figure 2.16). A base register can be pointed at the structure and elements of the structure can be addressed by their displacement. Different copies of the same structure can be accessed by simply changing the base register.

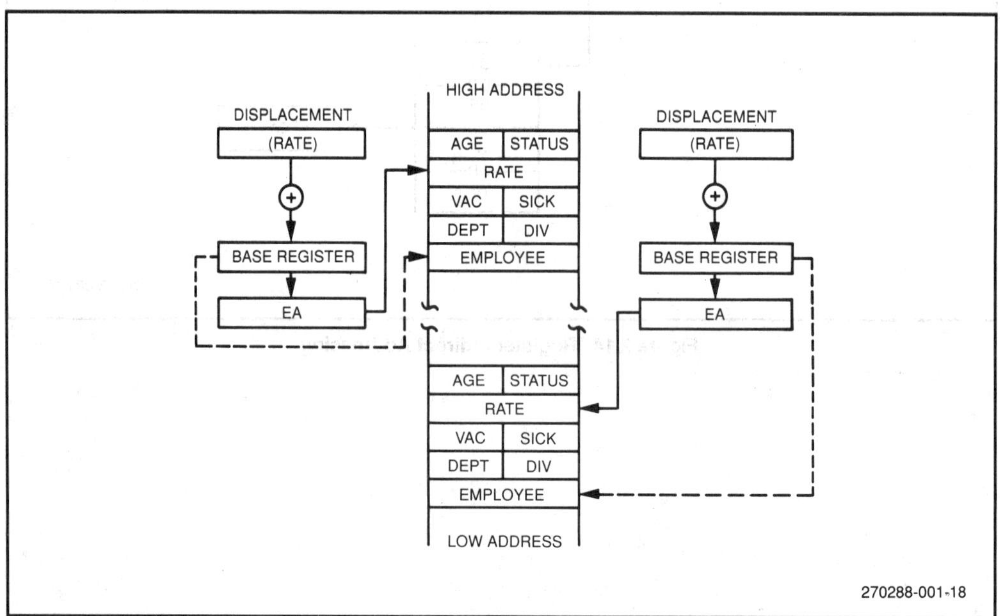

Figure 2.16. Accessing a Structure with Based Addressing

With indexed addressing, the effective address is calculated from the sum of a displacement plus the content of an index register (SI or DI). See Figure 2.17. Indexed addressing is often used to access elements in an array (see Figure 2.18). The displacement locates the beginning of the array, and the value of the index register selects one element. If the index register contains 0000H, the processor selects the first element. Since all array elements are the same length, simple arithmetic on the register may select any element.

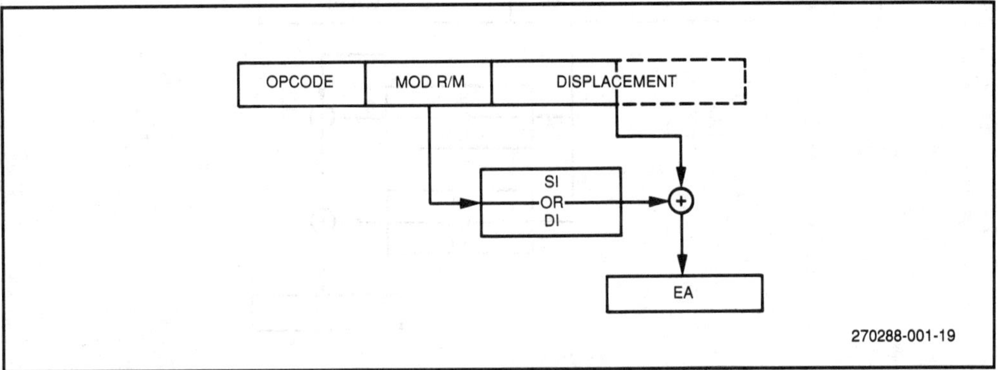

Figure 2.17. Indexed Addressing

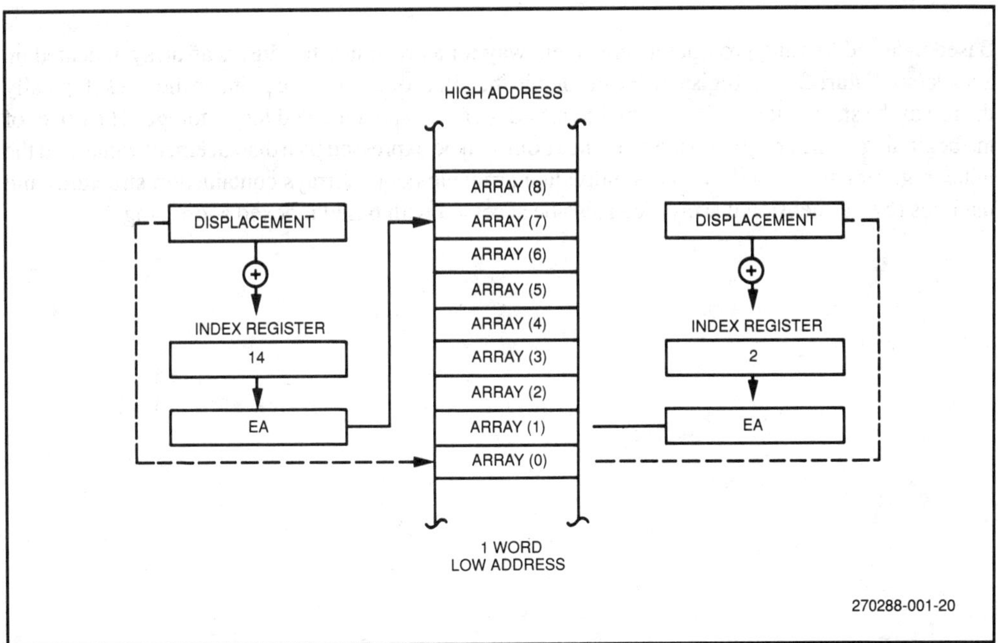

Figure 2.18. Accessing an Array with Indexed Addressing

Based index addressing generates an effective address that is the sum of a base register, an index register, and a displacement (see Figure 2.19). This mode of addressing is very flexible because the values of two address components can be determined at execution time.

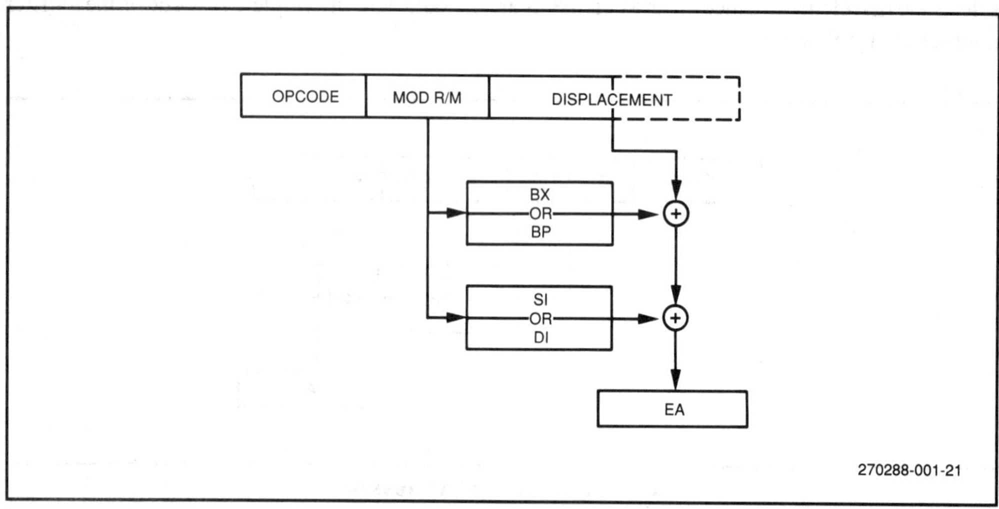

Figure 2.19. Based Index Addressing

Based index addressing provides a convenient way for a procedure to address an array allocated on a stack (see Figure 2.20). Register BP can contain the offset of a reference point on the stack, typically the top of the stack after the procedure has saved registers and allocated local storage. The offset of the beginning of the array from the reference point can be expressed by a displacement value, and the index register can be used to access individual array elements. Arrays contained in structures and matrices (two-dimensional arrays) can also be accessed with based indexed addressing.

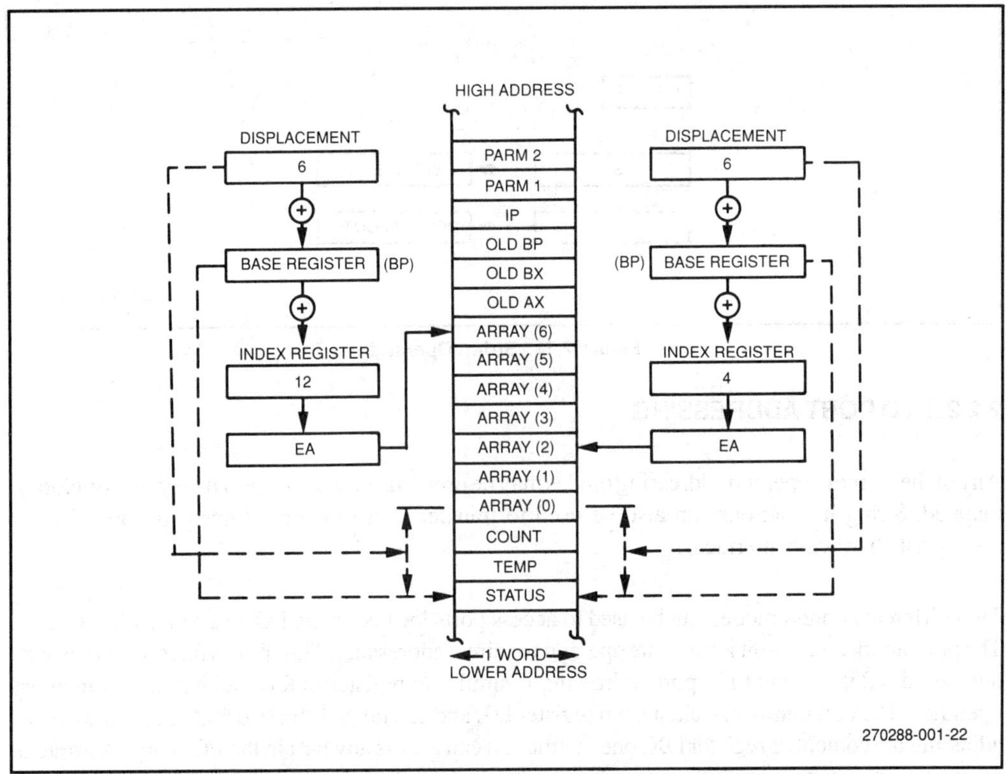

Figure 2.20. Accessing a Stacked Array with Based Index Addressing

String instructions do not use the normal memory addressing modes to access operands. Instead, the index registers are used implicitly (see Figure 2.21). When a string instruction is executed, the SI register is assumed to point to the first byte or word of the source string. The DI register is assumed to point to the first byte or word of the destination string. In a repeated string operation, the CPU will automatically adjust the SI and DI registers to obtain subsequent bytes or words. Note that for string instructions the DS register is the default segment register for the SI register and the ES register is the default segment register for the DI register. This allows string instructions to easily operate on data located anywhere within the one megabyte address space.

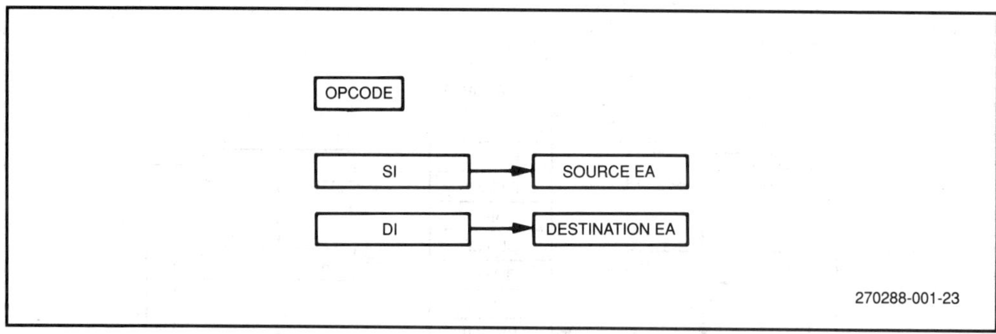

Figure 2.21. String Operand

2.2.2.3 I/O PORT ADDRESSING

Any of the memory operand addressing modes may be used to access an I/O port if the port is memory-mapped. String instructions can also be used to transfer data to memory-mapped ports with an appropriate hardware interface.

Two different address modes can be used to access ports located in the I/O space (see Figure 2.22). The port number is an 8-bit immediate operand for direct addressing. This allows fixed access to ports numbered 0-255. Indirect I/O port addressing is similar to register indirect addressing of memory operands. The port number is taken from register DX and can range from 0 to 65,535. By previously adjusting the content of register DX, one instruction can access any port in the I/O space. A group of adjacent ports can be accessed using a simple software loop that adjusts the value of the DX register.

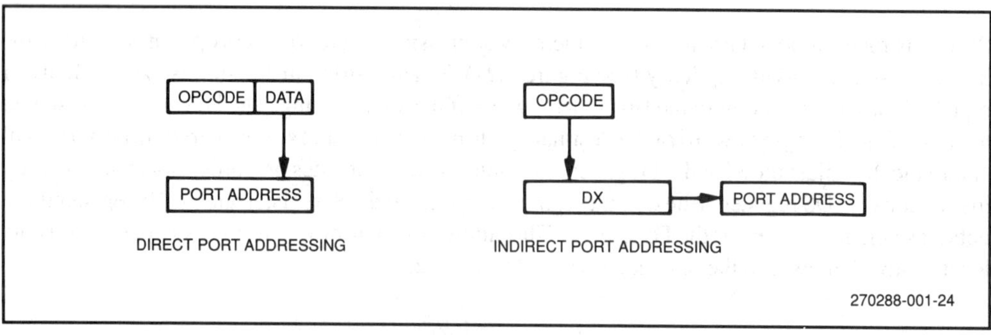

Figure 2.22. I/O Port Addressing

2.2.3 DATA TYPES USED IN THE 80C186 MODULAR CORE FAMILY

The 80C186 Modular Core family supports the following data types:

- Integer - A signed binary numeric value contained in an 8-bit byte or a 16-bit word. All operations assume a 2's complement representation. Signed 32-and 64-bit integers are directly supported with the addition of an 80C187 Numerics Processor Extension to an 80C186 Modular Core system. The 80C188 Modular Core does not support the 80C187.
- Ordinal - An unsigned binary numeric value contained in an 8-bit byte or a 16-bit word.
- Pointer - A 16- or 32-bit quantity, composed of a 16-bit offset component or a 16-bit segment base component in addition to a 16-bit offset component.
- String - A contiguous sequence of bytes of words. A string may contain from one byte to 64 Kbytes.
- ASCII - A byte representation of alphanumeric and control characters using the ASCII standard.
- BCD - A byte (unpacked) representation of the decimal digits 0-9.
- Packed BCD - A byte (packed) representation of two decimal digits (0-9). One digit is stored in each nibble (4 bits) of the byte.
- Floating Point - A signed 32-, 64-, or 80-bit real number representation. Floating point operands are directly supported with the addition of an 80C187 Numerics Processor Extension to an 80C186 Modular Core system. The 80C188 Modular Core does not support the 80C187.

In general, individual data elements must fit within defined segment limits. Figure 2.23 graphically represents the data types supported by the 80C186 Modular Core family.

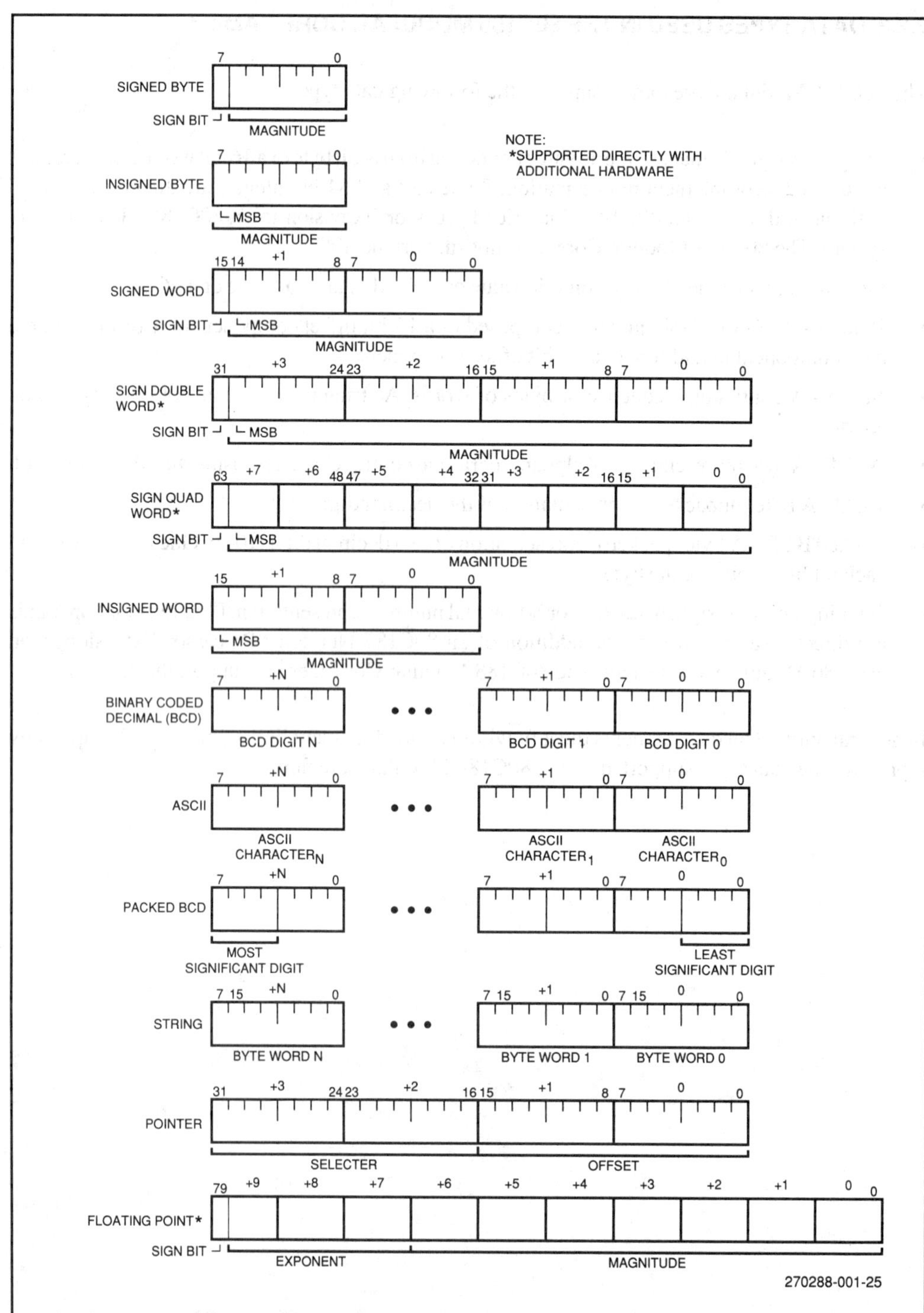

Figure 2.23. 80C186 Modular Core Family Supported Data Types

Bus Interface Unit 3

CHAPTER 3
BUS INTERFACE UNIT

The 80C186 Modular Core family products are true 16-bit embedded microprocessors with 16-bit internal data paths, one megabyte (2^{20}) of memory address space, and a separate 64 Kbyte (2^{16}) I/O address space. The CPU communicates with its external environment via a twenty-bit, time-multiplexed address and data bus. There also exists a command and status bus (see Table 3.1). This communication is managed by the Bus Interface Unit. To understand the operation of the address/data bus requires an understanding of the BIU's bus cycles.

Table 3.1. 80C186 Family Bus Signals

Function	Signal Name
address/data	AD15:0
address	A19:16
coprocessor interface	$\overline{\text{TEST}}$/BUSY, PEREQ, $\overline{\text{ERROR}}$, $\overline{\text{NCS}}$
local bus arbitration	HOLD, HLDA
local bus control	ALE, $\overline{\text{RD}}$, $\overline{\text{WR}}$, DT/$\overline{\text{R}}$, $\overline{\text{DEN}}$
multi-master bus	$\overline{\text{LOCK}}$
ready interface	READY
status information	$\overline{\text{S2:0}}$

3.1 T-STATES

To transfer data or fetch instructions the CPU executes a bus cycle. A bus cycle consists of a minimum of four CPU clock cycles or T-states plus any number of wait states necessary to accommodate the access time limitations of external memory or peripheral devices. T-states are numbered sequentially T_1, T_2, T_3, T_4, and T_W. Additional idle T-states (T_i) can occur between T_4 and T_1 when the processor requires no bus activity. The beginning of a T-state is signaled by a HIGH-to-LOW transition of the CPU clock. Each T-state is divided into two phases, phase 1 (the LOW phase) and phase 2 (the HIGH phase). Figure 3.1 illustrates an 80C186 Modular Core family clock cycle.

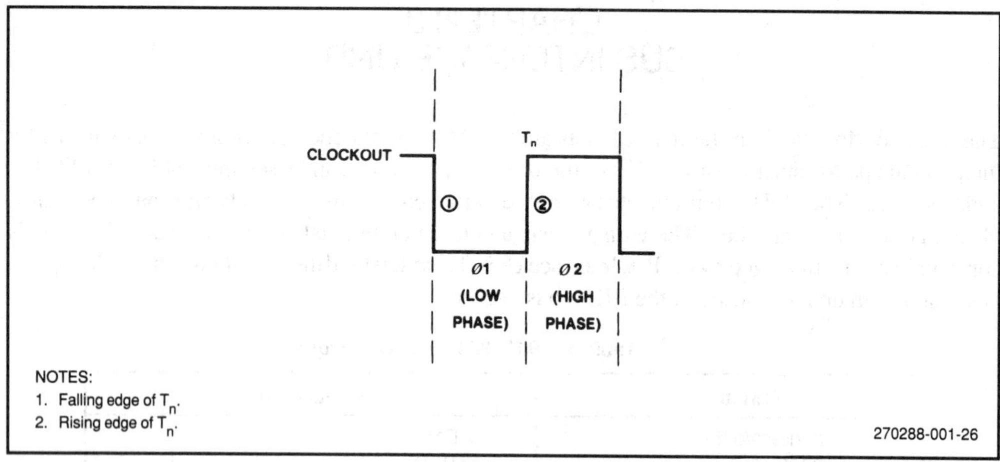

Figure 3.1. T-State in a 80C186 Modular Core Family Processor

Different types of bus activity occur for all of the T-states (see Figure 3.2). Address generation information occurs during T_1, and data generation occurs during T_2, T_3, T_W and T_4. The beginning of a bus cycle is signaled by the status lines of the processor going from a passive state (all HIGH) to an active state in the middle of the T-state immediately before T_1 (either a T_4 or a T_i). Information concerning an impending bus cycle appears during the T-state immediately before the first T-state of the cycle itself. Two different types of T_4 and T_i can be generated, one where the T-state is immediately followed by a bus cycle, and one where the T-state is immediately followed by an idle T-state.

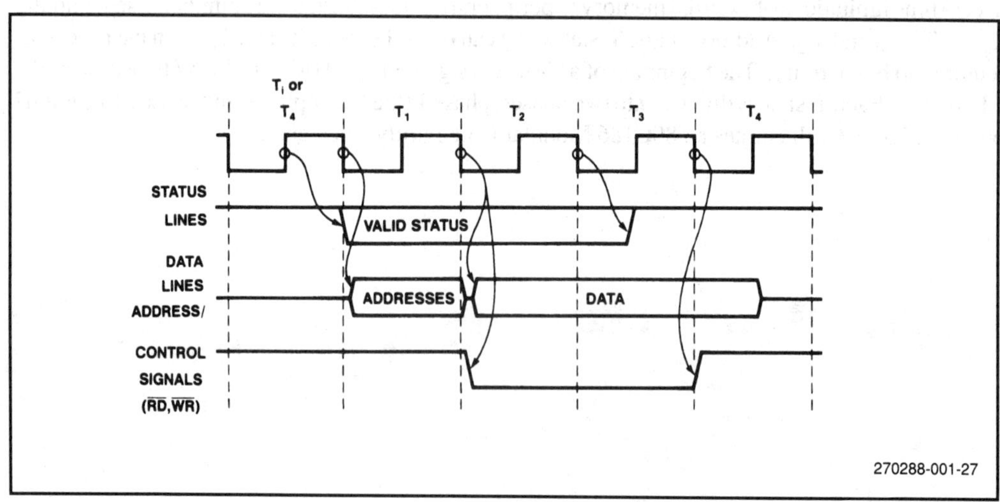

Figure 3.2. Example Bus Cycle of the 80C186 Core Family

During the first type of T_4 or T_i, the processor generates status information concerning the impending bus cycle. This information will be available no later than T_{CHOV} after the LOW-to-HIGH transition of the processor's CLKOUT in the middle of the T-state. During the second type of T_4 or T_i, the status outputs remain inactive because no bus cycle will follow. The decision on which type T_4 or T_i state to present is made at the beginning of the T-state preceding the T_4 or T_i state (see Figure 3.3). This determination has an effect on bus latency (see Section 3.8.2).

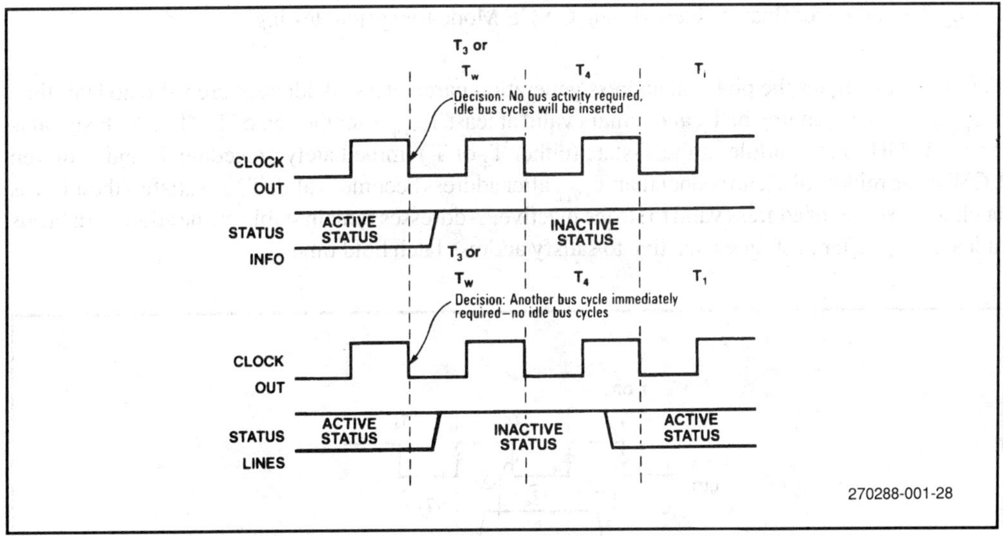

Figure 3.3. Active-Inactive Status Transitions in 80C186 Core Family Processor

The READY signal controls the number of wait states (T_W) inserted in each bus cycle. The maximum number of wait states is unbounded.

The bus may remain idle for several T-states (T_i) between accesses initiated by an 80C186 Modular Core family processor. This situation occurs under the following diverse conditions:

- When the prefetch queue is full.
- When the processor is running a type of bus cycle which always includes idle states (interrupt acknowledge, for example).
- When an instruction forces idle states (LOCK, for example).

During idle states, the processor may not necessarily float the bus; however, if the processor does drive the bus, no control strobes are active.

3.2 PHYSICAL ADDRESS GENERATION

Physical addresses are generated by 80C186 Modular Core family processors during T_1 of a bus cycle. Since the address and data lines are multiplexed, addresses must be latched during T_1 if they are required to remain stable for the duration of the bus cycle. To facilitate latching of the physical address, 80C186 Modular Core family processors generate an active-HIGH ALE (Address Latch Enable) signal which can be directly connected to the strobe input of a transparent latch. ALE is active for all bus cycles and never floats (except during ONCE Mode for system testing).

Figure 3.4 illustrates the physical address generation parameters. Addresses are valid no later than T_{CLOV} after the beginning of T_1, and remain valid at least T_{CLOF} after the end of T_1. The ALE signal is driven HIGH in the middle of the T-state (either T_4 or T_i) immediately preceding T_1 and is driven LOW in the middle of T_1, no sooner than T_{AVLL} after address becomes valid. T_{AVLL} satisfies the address latch set-up times of address valid to strobe inactive. Addresses remain stable on the address/data bus at least T_{LLAX} after ALE goes inactive to satisfy address latch hold times.

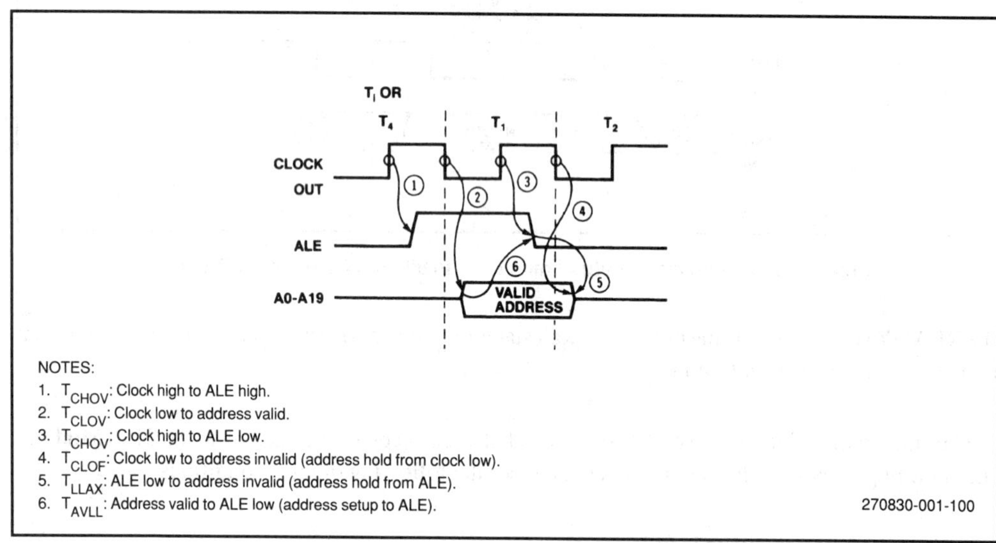
T_i OR
T_4
T_1
T_2
CLOCK
OUT
ALE
A0-A19
VALID
ADDRESS
1
2
3
4
5
6
NOTES:
1. T_CHOV: Clock high to ALE high.
2. T_CLOV: Clock low to address valid.
3. T_CHOV: Clock high to ALE low.
4. T_CLOF: Clock low to address invalid (address hold from clock low).
5. T_LLAX: ALE low to address invalid (address hold from ALE).
6. T_AVLL: Address valid to ALE low (address setup to ALE).
270830-001-100

Figure 3.4. Address Generation Timing

Because ALE goes HIGH before addresses become valid, the delay through the address latches will be the propagation delay through the latch rather than the delay from the latch strobe.

A typical circuit for latching physical addresses is shown in Figure 3.4. This circuit uses 3 transparent non-inverting latches to demultiplex the 20 address bits provided on all 80C186 Modular Core family microprocessors. Typically, the upper 4 address bits only select among various memory components or subsystems, so when the integrated chip selects (see Chapter 7) are used, these upper bits need not be latched. The worst case address generation time from the beginning of T_1 (including address latch propagation) time for the circuit is:

$$T_{CLOV} + T_{PD}$$

Some memory and peripheral devices do not require addresses to remain stable throughout a data transfer. If a system is constructed wholly with these types of devices, addresses need not be latched.

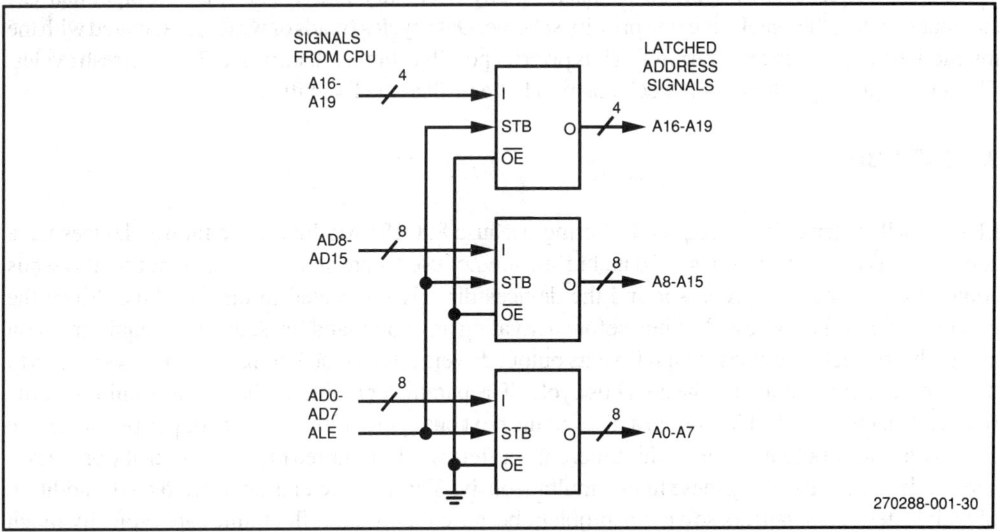

Figure 3.5. Demultiplexing the Address Bus of an 80C186 Modular Core Family Processor Using Transparent Latches.

The 80C186 Core generates one more signal, $\overline{BHE}$ (Bus High Enable), to address memory. $\overline{BHE}$ and A0 are used to enable data transfers on either or both halves of the 16-bit bus. Since A0 only enables devices onto the lower half of the data bus, systems commonly drive address inputs with address bits A1-A19. This provides 512K unique word addresses, or 1M unique byte addresses. $\overline{BHE}$ does not need to be latched. On the 80C188 Core, $\overline{BHE}$ is absent; all data transfers take place across a single byte-wide data bus.

On 80C186 Modular Core family processors, effective (physical) address calculations take place in dedicated hardware. An effective address (EA) calculation may be either fully-pipelined or non-pipelined. The BIU gives no indication when a fully-pipelined address calculation occurs.

Non-pipelined EA calculations are required anytime an instruction has MOD and R/M bits in its opcode. These bits often denote addressing modes which take longer to calculate the EA, such as register-offset or two-register addressing. Here are some assembly code examples which cause non-pipelined EA calculations:

```
MOV   AX, ES:[DI]          ; Uses indirect addressing.
AND   AX, [DI] + 5         ; Uses register-offset addressing.
XCHG  mem_variable, DX     ; Direct offset but has MOD and
                           ; R/M bits.
```

A non-pipelined EA calculation takes four clocks, and occurs during T_3(or T_W)-T_4-T_i-T_i, T_4(or T_i)-T_i-T_i-T_i, cycle sequences. In addition to inserting any necessary idle T-states, a non-pipelined EA calculation alters the usual bus cycle priority scheme. Data cycles (reads or writes) associated with the instruction temporarily take the highest bus priority possible, higher than even DRAM refresh cycles. The altered priority scheme is a mechanism to better utilize the Execution Unit.

3.3 DATA BUS

Many small systems do not require buffering because 80C186 Modular Core family devices have adequate bus drive capabilities. If data buffers are not used, care should be taken not to allow bus contention between the processor and the devices directly connected to the data bus. Since the processor floats the address/data bus before activating any command lines, the only requirement on a directly connected device is that it float its output drivers after a read before the processor begins to drive address information for the next bus cycle. The parameter of interest here is the minimum time from $\overline{RD}$ inactive until addresses go active for the next bus cycle. If the memory or peripheral device cannot disable its output drivers in this time, data buffers will be required to prevent both the processor and the device from driving these lines simultaneously. This parameter is unaffected by the addition of wait states. Data buffers solve this problem because their output float times are typically much faster than the required minimum.

3.3.1 80C186 MODULAR CORE DATA BUS OPERATION

Throughout T_2, T_3, T_W and T_4 of a bus cycle the multiplexed address/data bus becomes a 16-bit data bus. Data transfers on this bus may be either bytes or words. All memory is byte addressable (see Figure 3.6).

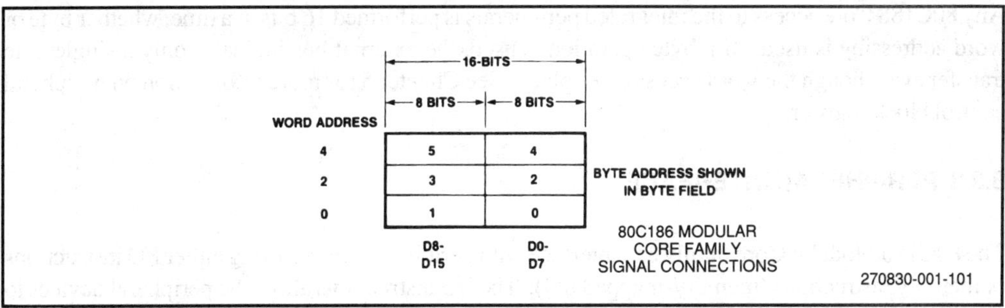

Figure 3.6. Physical Memory Byte/Word Addressing in 80C186 Modular Core Family Microprocessors

All bytes with even addresses (A0 = 0) reside on the lower 8 bits of the data bus, while all bytes with odd addresses (A0 = 1) reside on the upper 8 bits of the data bus. Whenever an access is made to only the even byte, A0 is driven LOW, $\overline{BHE}$ is driven HIGH, and the data transfer occurs on D0-D7 of the data bus. Whenever an access is made to only the od d byte, $\overline{BHE}$ is driven LOW, A0 is driven HIGH, and the data transfer occurs on D8-D15 of the data bus. Finally, if a word access is performed to an even address, both A0 and $\overline{BHE}$ are driven LOW and the data transfer occurs on D0-D15 of the data bus.

Word accesses are made to the addressed byte and to the next higher numbered byte. If a word access is performed to an odd address, two byte accesses must be performed, the first to access the odd byte at the first word address on D8-D15, the second to access the even byte at the next sequential word address on D0-D7. For example, in Figure 3.6, byte 0 and byte 1 can be individually accessed in two separate bus cycles to byte address 0 and 1 at word address 0. They may also be accessed together in a single bus cycle to word address 0. However, if a word access is made to address 1, two bus cycles will be required, the first to access byte 1 at word address 0 (byte 0 will not be accessed), and the second to access byte 2 at word address 2 (byte 3 will not be accessed). This is why all word data should be located at even addresses to increase processor performance.

When byte reads are made, the data returned on the unused half of the data bus is ignored. When byte writes are made, the data driven on the unused half of the data bus is indeterminate.

The 80C186 Core always fetches the instruction stream in words from even addresses except that the first fetch after a program transfer to an odd address obtains a byte. The processor disassembles the instruction stream inside the processor; so instruction alignment will not materially affect the performance of most systems.

3.3.2 80C188 MODULAR CORE DATA BUS OPERATION

Because the 80C188 core externally has only an 8-bit data bus, the above discussion about upper and lower bytes of the data bus does not apply. No performance improvement will occur if word data is placed on even boundaries in memory space. All word accesses require two bus cycles, the first to access the lower byte of the word and the second to access the upper byte of the word.

Any 80C188 Core access to the integrated peripherals is performed 16 bits at a time, whether byte or word addressing is used. If a byte operation is used, the external bus indicates only a single byte transfer even though the word access takes place. See Chapter 5 for more information on peripheral control block registers.

3.3.3 PERIPHERAL INTERFACE

The 80C186 Modular Core family can interface with peripheral devices using either I/O instructions or memory instructions (memory-mapped I/O). The I/O instructions allow the peripheral devices to reside in a separate I/O address space while memory-mapped I/O allows the full power of the instruction set to be used for peripheral operations. Up to 64 Kbytes of I/O address space may be defined for system peripherals. To the programmer, the separate I/O address space is only accessible with IN and OUT commands, which transfer data between peripheral devices and the AX register (or AL for 8-bit data). The first 256 bytes of I/O space (0 to 255) are directly addressable while the entire 64K is only accessible via register indirect addressing through the DX register. The latter technique is particularly desirable for service procedures that handle more than one peripheral by allowing the desired device address to be passed to the procedure as a parameter. Peripherals may be connected to the local CPU bus or a buffered system bus.

On the 80C186 Modular Core, 8-bit peripherals may be connected to either the upper or lower half of the data bus. Assigning an equal number of devices to the upper and lower halves of the bus will distribute the bus loading. If a device is connected to the upper half of the data bus, all I/O addresses assigned to the device must be odd (A0 = 1). If the device is on the lower half of the bus, its addresses must be even (A0 = 0). The address assignment directs the 8-bit transfer to the upper (odd) or lower (even) half of the 16-bit data bus. Since A0 will always be a one or zero for a specific device, A0 cannot be used as an address input to select registers within a specific device. If a device on the upper half of the bus and one on the lower half are assigned addresses that differ only in A0 (adjacent odd and even address), A0 and $\overline{BHE}$ must be conditions of chip select decode to prevent a write to one device from erroneously performing a write to the other.

16-bit peripheral devices should be assigned even addresses for reasons of efficient bus utilization and simplicity of device selection. To guarantee the device is selected only for word operations, A0 and $\overline{BHE}$ should be conditions of chip select decode.

3.4 BUS CONTROL SIGNALS

80C186 Modular Core family processors directly provide the control signals $\overline{RD}$, $\overline{WR}$, $\overline{LOCK}$, and $\overline{TEST}$. In addition, the processors provide the status signals $\overline{S0}$-$\overline{S2}$ from which other required bus control signals can be generated.

3.4.1 $\overline{RD}$ AND $\overline{WR}$

The $\overline{RD}$ and $\overline{WR}$ signals strobe data from or to memory or I/O space.

The $\overline{RD}$ signal is driven LOW at the beginning of T_2 during all memory and I/O reads (see Figure 3.7). $\overline{RD}$ will not become active until the microprocessor ceases driving address information on the address/data bus. Data is sampled into the processor at the beginning of T_4. $\overline{RD}$ will not go inactive until the processor's data hold time has been satisfied.

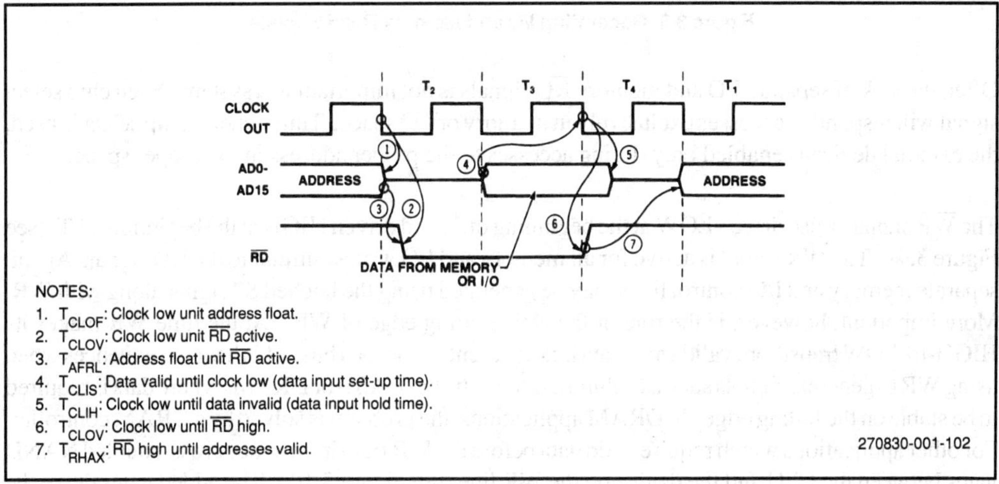

Figure 3.7. Read Cycle Timing of 80C186 Family Microprocessors

Note that 80C186 Modular Core family processors do not provide separate I/O and memory $\overline{RD}$ signals. If separate I/O read and memory read signals are required, they can be synthesized using the $\overline{S2}$ signal (LOW for I/O operations and HIGH for memory operations) and the $\overline{RD}$ signal (see Figure 3.8). If this approach is used, the $\overline{S2}$ signal will require latching, since the $\overline{S2}$ signal (like $\overline{S0}$ and $\overline{S1}$) goes to an inactive state well before the beginning of T_4 (where $\overline{RD}$ goes inactive). If S2 was directly used for this purpose, the type of read command (I/O or memory) could change just before T_4 as $\overline{S2}$ goes to the inactive state (HIGH). The status signals may be latched using ALE.

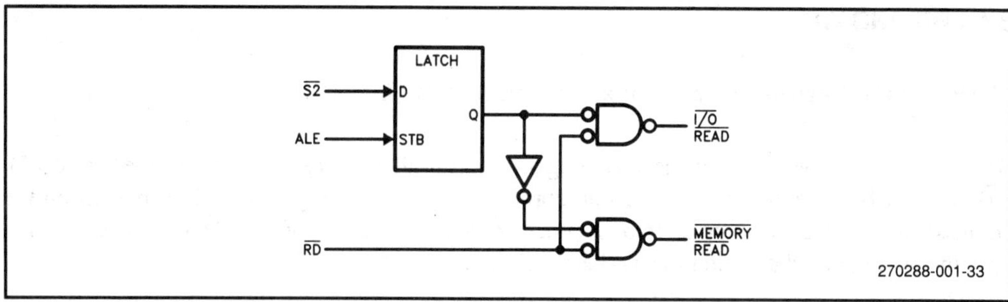

Figure 3.8. Generating I/O and Memory Read Signals

Often the lack of separate I/O and memory RD signals is not important in a system. Each chip select signal will respond to accesses exclusively in memory or I/O space. Thus, when a chip select is used, the external device is enabled only during accesses to the proper address in the proper space.

The WR signal is also driven LOW at the beginning of T_2 and driven HIGH at the beginning of T_4 (see Figure 3.9). The WR signal is active for all memory and I/O writes, similar to the RD signal. Again, separate memory and I/O control lines may be generated using the latched S2 signal along with WR. More important, however, is the role of the active-going edge of WR. At the time WR makes its HIGH-to-LOW transition, valid write data is not present on the data bus. This has consequences when using WR to generate signals such as column address strobe (CAS) for DRAMs where data is required to be stable on the falling edge. In DRAM applications, the problem is solved by a DRAM controller. For other applications which require valid data before the WR transition, place cross-coupled NAND gates between the CPU and the device on the WR line (see Figure 3.10). The added gates delay the active-going edge of WR to the device by one clock phase, at which time valid data is driven on the bus by the microprocessor.

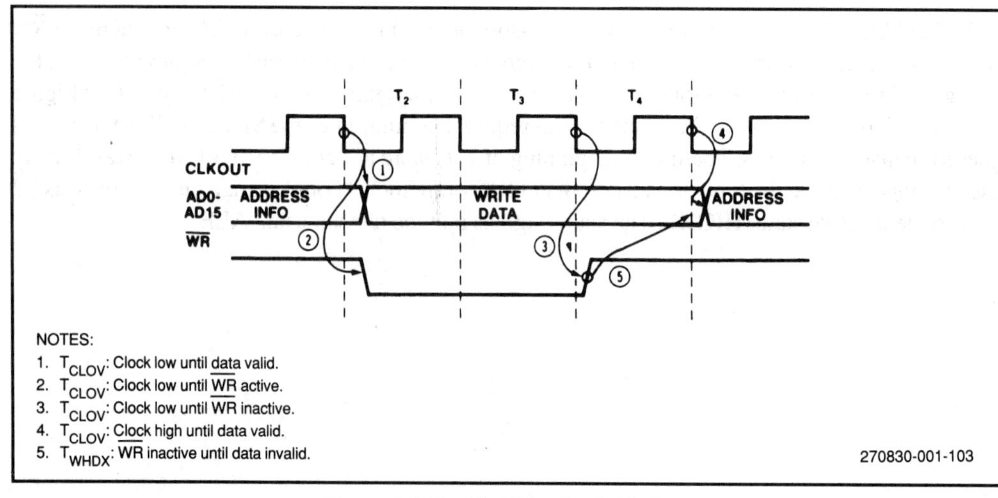

Figure 3.9. Family Write Cycle Timing

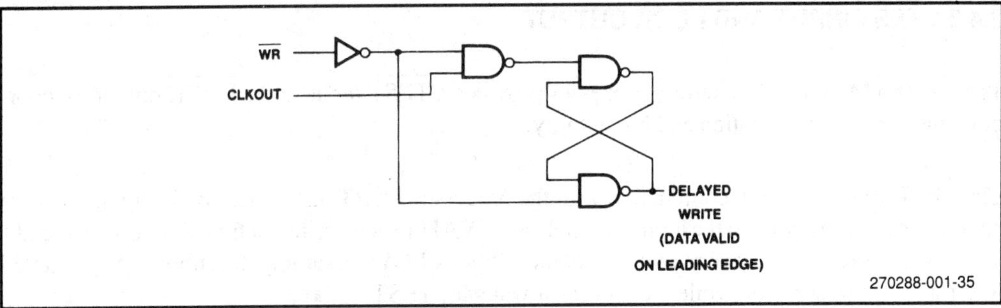

Figure 3.10. Synthesizing a Delayed Write Signal

3.4.2 STATUS LINES

An 80C186 Modular Core family processor provides three status outputs which indicate the type of bus cycle in progress. These signals go from an inactive state (all HIGH) to one of seven possible active states during the T-state immediately preceding T_1 of a bus cycle (see Figure 3.3). The possible status line encodings are given in Table 3.2. The status lines are driven inactive in the T_3 or T_W state immediately preceding T_4 of the current bus cycle.

Table 3.2. Status Line Interpretation

$\overline{S2}$	$\overline{S1}$	$\overline{S0}$	Operation
0	0	0	interrupt acknowledge
0	0	1	read I/O
0	1	0	write I/O
0	1	1	halt
1	0	0	instruction fetch
1	0	1	read memory
1	1	0	write memory
1	1	1	passive

The status lines may be directly connected to an 82C88 Bus Controller, which provides local bus control signals or MULTIBUS™ control signals. Use of the 82C88 Bus Controller does not preclude the use of the CPU-generated $\overline{RD}$, $\overline{WR}$ and ALE signals, however. The processor-generated signals can provide local bus control signals, while an 82C88 can provide MULTIBUS control signals.

3.4.3 SOFTWARE-INITIATED BUS CONTROL

The programmer may control the progress of 80C186 Modular Core family execution-related bus activity by using the WAIT (or FWAIT), LOCK, and HLT instructions.

3.4.3.1 TEST INPUT AND LOCK OUTPUT

The 80C186 Modular Core family processor provides a TEST input and a LOCK output for coordinating instruction execution and bus activity.

The TEST input is used in conjunction with the processor WAIT instruction, typically in a system containing a coprocessor. If the input is HIGH when WAIT executes, instruction execution suspends. TEST will be resampled every five clocks until it goes LOW, resuming execution. Any enabled interrupts will be serviced while the processor waits for TEST.

The LOCK output is driven LOW whenever the data cycles of a LOCKed instruction are executed. A LOCKed instruction is generated whenever the LOCK prefix occurs immediately before an instruction. The LOCK prefix is active for the single instruction immediately following the LOCK prefix. The LOCK signal indicates to a bus arbiter (e.g., the 8289) that an atomic (uninterruptible) bus operation is occurring. The bus arbiter should under no circumstances release the bus while LOCKed transfers are occurring. An 80C186 Modular Core family processor will not recognize a bus HOLD during LOCKed operations. LOCKed transfers are typically used in multiprocessor systems to access memory-based semaphore variables which control access to shared system resources.

On 80C186 Modular Core family devices, the LOCK signal will go active during T1 of the first data cycle of the LOCKed transfer. It is driven inactive at the end of T4 of the last data cycle of the LOCKed transfers independent of the number of wait states.

The LOCK output is also driven LOW during interrupt acknowledge cycles when the integrated Interrupt Controller is connected to an external interrupt controller (i.e. 82C59A).

80C186 Modular Core family processors drive LOCK HIGH for one clock during RESET. Then, the pin floats until the start of the first bus cycle. LOCK also floats during HOLD.

3.4.3.2 PROCESSOR HALT

A HALT bus cycle signifies that the CPU has executed the HLT (HALT) instruction. It differs from a regular bus cycle in two ways.

The first way a HALT bus cycle differs is that neither RD nor WR will be driven active. Address and data information will not be driven by the processor. The second way a HALT bus cycle differs is that the S0-S2 status lines go to their inactive state (all HIGH) during T_2 of the bus cycle, well before they go to their inactive state during a regular bus cycle.

Like a normal bus cycle, however, ALE is driven active. Since no valid address information is present, the information strobed into the address latches should be ignored. This ALE pulse can be used, however, to latch the HALT status from the S0-S2 status lines. READY is ignored during HALT cycles.

The HALTed state of the processor does not interfere with the operation of any of the 80C186 Modular Core family integrated peripheral units. After the processor HALTs, a HOLD input can elicit HLDA and release of the bus by the processor as usual.

Activation of $\overline{\mathrm{RESIN}}$, an NMI request, or a non-masked interrupt request from the integrated Interrupt Controller forces the processor out of the HALT state.

Exiting from the HALT state is also dependent on the power management mode that the 80C186 Modular Core family device is operating in. Please see the Power Management chapter of this user's guide for more details.

3.5 TRANSCEIVER CONTROL SIGNALS

If data buffers are required, the 80C186 Modular Core family processor provides $\overline{\mathrm{DEN}}$ (Data ENable) and DT/$\overline{\mathrm{R}}$ (Data Transmit/Receive) signals to simplify buffer interfacing. The $\overline{\mathrm{DEN}}$ and DT/$\overline{\mathrm{R}}$ signals are activated during all bus cycles, including transfers between the 80C186 core and 80C187.

The $\overline{\mathrm{DEN}}$ signal is driven LOW whenever the processor is either ready to receive data (during a read) or when the processor is ready to send data (during a write). In other words, $\overline{\mathrm{DEN}}$ is LOW during any active bus cycle when address information is not being generated on the address/data pins. In most systems, the $\overline{\mathrm{DEN}}$ signal should not be directly connected to the $\overline{\mathrm{OE}}$ inputs of a buffer, since unbuffered devices (or other buffers) may be directly connected to the processors's address/data pins. If $\overline{\mathrm{DEN}}$ were directly connected to several buffers, contention would occur during read cycles, as many devices attempt to drive the processor bus. Rather, it should be a factor along with the chip selects in generating the output enable. $\overline{\mathrm{DEN}}$ is HIGH whenever DT/$\overline{\mathrm{R}}$ changes state.

The DT/$\overline{\mathrm{R}}$ signal determines the direction of data through the bi-directional buffers. It is HIGH whenever data is being written from the processor, and is LOW whenever data is being read into the processor. Unlike the $\overline{\mathrm{DEN}}$ signal, it may be directly connected to bus buffers, since this signal does not usually enable the output drivers of the buffer. Figure 3.11 shows an example data bus subsystem supporting both buffered and unbuffered devices. Note that the A side of the buffer is connected to the 80C186 Modular Core family device, the B side to the external device. The DT/$\overline{\mathrm{R}}$ signal can directly drive the T (transmit) signal of a typical buffer since it has the correct polarity.

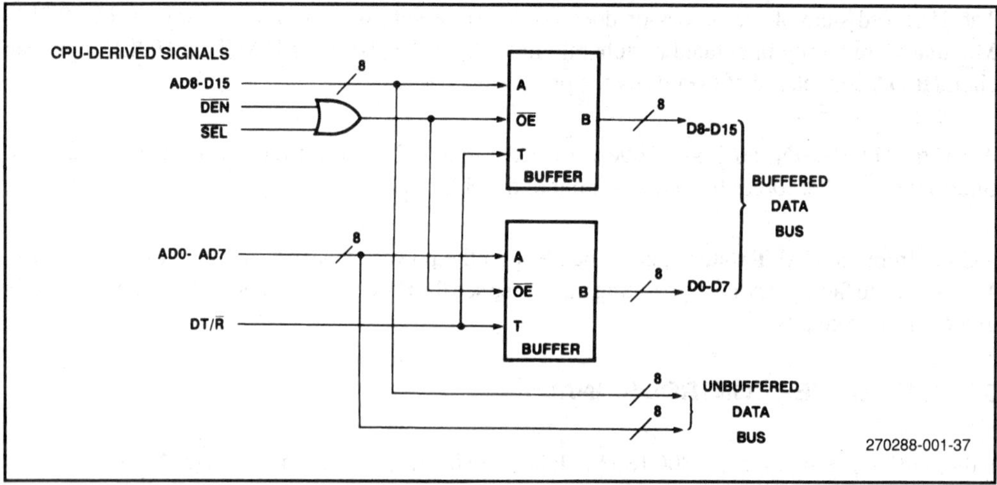

Figure 3.11. Example Buffered/Unbuffered Data Bus

The processor drives the DT/$\overline{R}$ and $\overline{DEN}$ pins HIGH for one clock during RESET. Then the pins float until the first bus cycle.

3.6 READY INTERFACING

80C186EB family devices provide a READY line to allow the connection of slower memory and peripheral devices to the system bus. This line signals the Bus Interface Unit to insert wait states (T_W) into a CPU bus cycle, allowing slower devices to respond to bus activity. Wait states will only be inserted when READY is LOW. Any number of wait states may be inserted into a bus cycle. The processor will ignore the READY input during any accesses to the integrated peripheral registers and to any area where the chip select READY bits indicate that the external READY should be ignored.

The READY line is synchronized (see Appendix D) by the CPU before presentation to the rest of the bus control logic. As shown in Figure 3.12, the first flip-flop is used to resolve the asynchronous transition of the READY line. It will achieve a definite HIGH or LOW level before its output is latched into the second flip-flop. When latched HIGH, it passes along the level present on the READY line; when latched LOW, it forces Not READY to be passed along to the rest of the circuit. With this design, note that only the rising edge of READY is fully synchronized; the falling edge of READY must be externally synchronized to the processor clock. Any asynchronous transition on the READY line when the processor is not sampling the input does not matter.

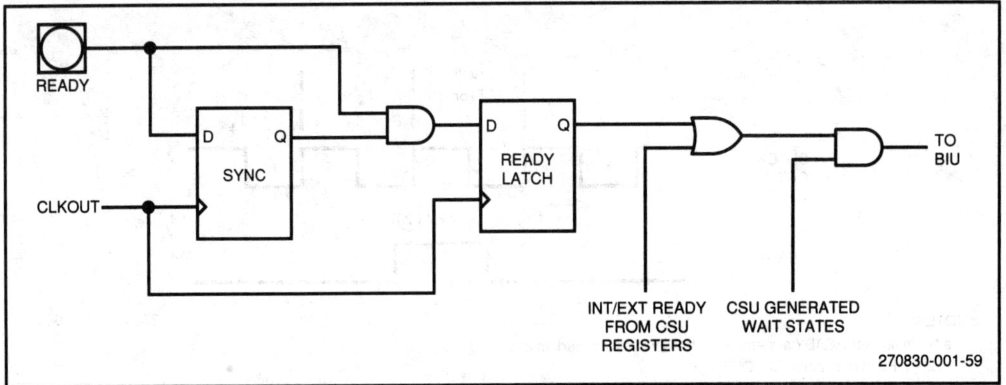

Figure 3.12. 80C186 Core Family READY Circuitry

Figure 3.13 depicts activity for Normally-READY and Normally-Not-READY configurations of external logic.

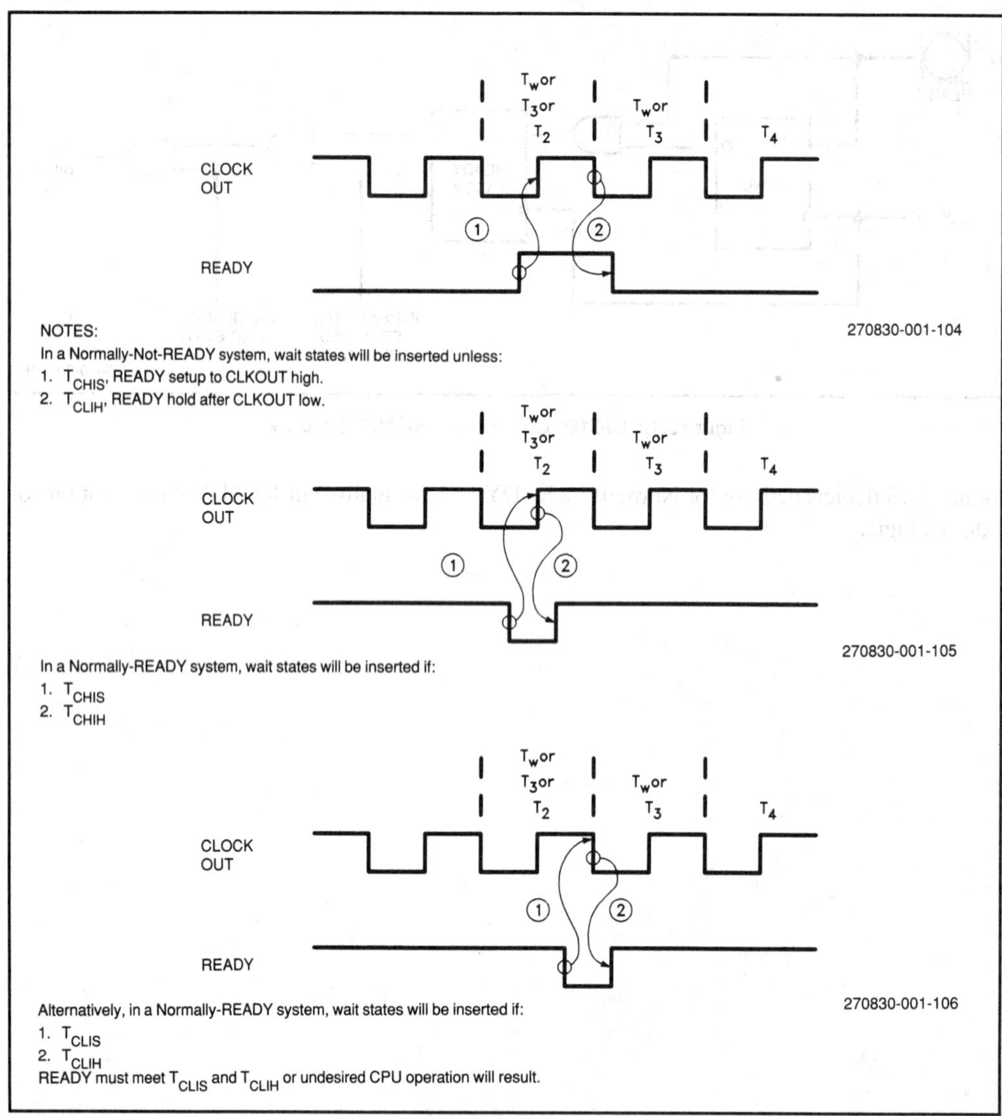

Tw or T3 or T2
Tw or T3
T4
CLOCK OUT
READY
NOTES:
In a Normally-Not-READY system, wait states will be inserted unless:
1. T_{CHIS}, READY setup to CLKOUT high.
2. T_{CLIH}, READY hold after CLKOUT low.
270830-001-104
In a Normally-READY system, wait states will be inserted if:
1. T_{CHIS}
2. T_{CHIH}
270830-001-105
Alternatively, in a Normally-READY system, wait states will be inserted if:
1. T_{CLIS}
2. T_{CLIH}
READY must meet T_{CLIS} and T_{CLIH} or undesired CPU operation will result.
270830-001-106

Figure 3.13. READY Transitions

In a Normally-Not-READY implementation the setup and hold times of **both** the resolution flip-flop **and** the READY latch must be satisfied. The READY pin must go active at least T_{CHIS} before the rising edge of T_2, T_3 or T_W, and stay active until T_{CLIH} after the falling edge of T_3 or T_W to stop generation of wait states and terminate the bus cycle. If READY goes active after the falling edge of T_3 there will be no wait state inserted.

In a Normally-READY implementation the setup and hold times of **either** the resolution flip-flop or the READY latch must be met. If the external hardware does not meet this requirement, the CPU will not function properly. Wait states will be generated if READY goes inactive T_{CHIS} before the rising edge of T_2 and stays inactive a minimum of T_{CHIH} after the edge, or if READY goes inactive at least T_{CLIS} before the falling edge of T_3 and stays inactive a minimum of T_{CLIH} after the edge. The READY circuitry performs this way to allow a slow device the maximum amount of time to respond with a Not READY after it has been selected.

3.7 EXECUTION UNIT/BUS INTERFACE UNIT RELATIONSHIP

The 80C186 Modular Core family employs a pipelined architecture that allows instructions to be prefetched during spare bus cycles. The Bus Interface Unit (BIU) fetches instructions from memory and loads them into a prefetch queue. The Execution Unit (EU) executes instructions from the prefetch queue while other instructions are prefetched. The process of fetching new instructions while executing the current instruction is invisible to the user.

3.7.1 PREFETCH QUEUE AND BUS PERFORMANCE

The prefetch queue is six bytes long on the 80C186 Core. When two or more bytes are empty and the EU does not require the BIU to perform a bus cycle, the BIU executes instruction fetch cycles to refill the queue. Figure 3.14 shows how instruction fetches are interleaved with EU-initiated bus cycles. The chosen queue size allows the BIU to keep the EU supplied with prefetched instructions under most conditions without monopolizing the system bus. Recall that the 80C186 Core BIU normally accesses two bytes (one word) of opcode per bus cycle. If a program transfer forces fetching from an odd address, the 80C186 Core automatically reads one byte from the odd address and then resumes fetching words from the subsequent even addresses.

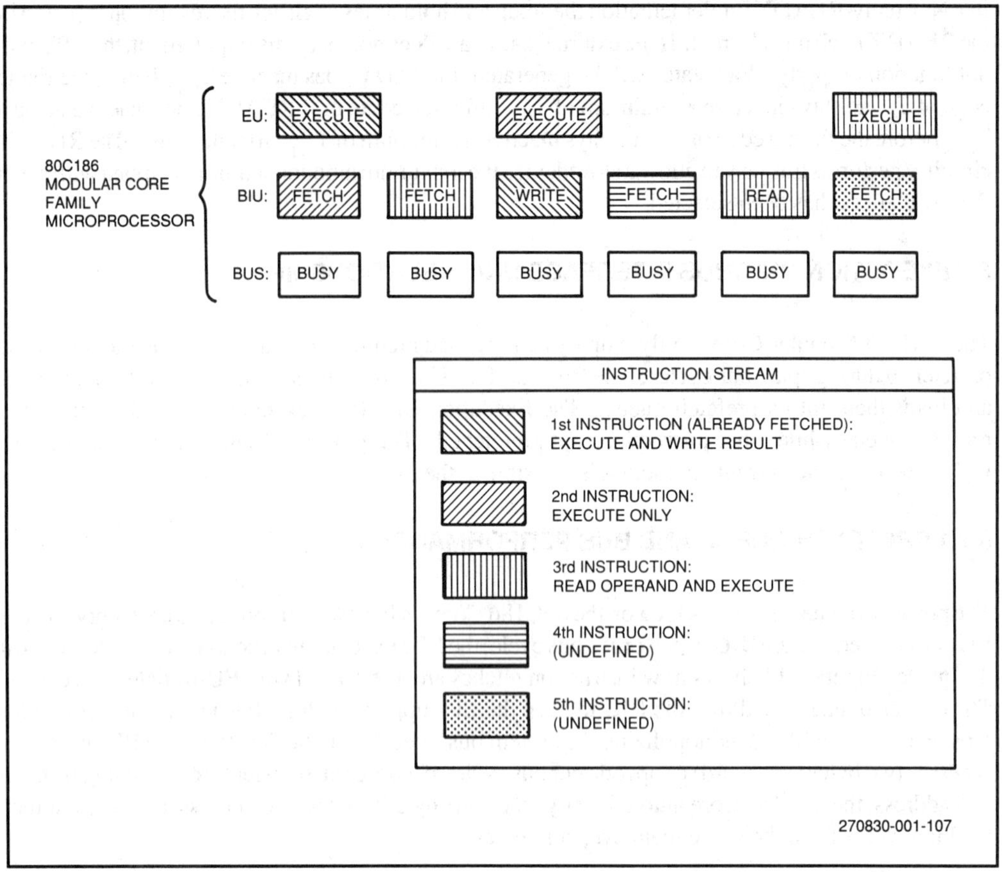

Figure 3.14. Overlapped Instruction Fetch and Execution

The prefetch queue is four bytes long on the 80C188 Core. When one or more bytes are empty, the processor attempts to refill the queue. With an 8-bit data bus, the 80C188 Core BIU accesses one byte of opcode per bus cycle.

In most circumstances the queues contain at least one byte of the instruction stream and the EU does not have to wait for instructions to be fetched. The queue holds instructions from memory locations just above the source of the current instruction. That is, they are the next logical instructions so long as execution proceeds serially. If the EU executes an instruction that transfers control to another location, the BIU resets the queue, fetches the instruction from the new address, passes it immediately to the EU, and then begins refilling the queue from the new location. In addition, the BIU suspends instruction fetching whenever the EU requests a memory or I/O read or write, except for a fetch already in progress.

Bus cycles occur sequentially, but do not necessarily follow immediately one after another. Since the CPU prefetches up to six bytes of the instruction stream for storage and execution from an internal instruction queue, the relationship between **prefetching** and instruction **execution** may be skewed in time and separated by additional instruction fetch bus cycles. In general, if the BIU fetches an instruction into the processor's internal instruction queue, it may also fetch several additional instructions before the EU removes the instruction from the queue and executes it. If the EU executes a jump or other control transfer instruction from the queue, it ignores any instructions remaining in the queue; the CPU discards these instructions with no effect on operation. The bus activity observed during execution of a specific instruction depends on the preceding instructions; the activity, however, may always be determined within a specific sequence.

3.7.2 BUS PERFORMANCE AND CPU PERFORMANCE

Overall performance of a system based on an 80C186 Modular Core family member system depends on both the bus bandwidth and execution rate.

The number of clock cycles required to execute an instruction varies from two clocks for a register to register move to 67 clocks for an integer divide. If a program contains many long instructions, program execution will be CPU-limited, i.e., the prefetch queue will be full most of the time. If a program contains mainly short instructions or data move instructions, execution will be bus-limited. Here the processor will be required to wait often for an instruction to be fetched before it continues its operation.

With an 8-bit external data bus, the 80C188 Modular Core can provide an opportunity for significant system cost savings over its 16-bit counterpart, the 80C186 Modular Core. In applications which manipulate only 8-bit quantities, the performance of the 80C188 Core can approach that of the 80C186 Core. The same is true for applications that are highly CPU-intensive (but not memory-intensive) since all 80C186 Modular Core family CPUs are internally 16-bit.

Typical 80C186 Modular Core family applications are more data-intensive than computation-intensive. The processor with an 8-bit bus must not only move data around eight bits at a time but also fetch instructions eight bits at a time. A sufficient number of prefetched bytes may not reside in the prefetch queue much of the time. In many cases, the performance degradation of an 8-bit bus will be significant.

Adding up instruction clock counts given in 80C186 Modular Core family data sheets and reference manuals yields only a rough approximation of execution time. Published clock counts assume that all the necessary opcode bytes reside in the prefetch queue, frequently not the case for the 80C188 Core. A conservative rule of thumb for the 80C188 Core is to add 100 per cent to the calculated clock count. The correction for the 80C186 Core is typically about five to seven per cent. If there is any doubt of the performance capabilities of either the 80C186 Core or the 80C188 Core, we suggest the use of a performance analyzer on critical code sections early in the design process.

3.7.3 WAIT STATES AND CPU PERFORMANCE

Because an 80C186 Modular Core family processor contains separate Bus Interface and Execution Units, the actual performance of the processor will not degrade at a constant rate as wait states are added to the memory cycle time from the processor. Shown below are two disparate ASM186 assembly language routines, and the actual execution time for the two procedures as wait states are added to the memory system of the processor (CLKOUT = 8 MHz). The percentage degradation from each wait state level to the following wait state level is also indicated. The actual rate of performance degradation is not as important as the conclusion that wait state degradation will depend on the type and mix of instructions encountered in the user's program.

Example 1

```
$mod186
name                    example_wait_state_performance
;
;   This file contains two programs which demonstrate the 80186 family processor
;           performance degradation as wait states are inserted. Procedure Bench1
;           performs a transformation betrween two types of of characters sets, then
;           copies the transformed characters back to the original buffer (which is
;           64 bytes long. Procedure Bench_2 performs the same type of
;           transformation, however instead of performing a table lookup, it
;           multiplies each number in the original 32 word buffer by a constant 3
;           (note the use of the integer immediate multiply instruction). Program
;           nothing_is used to measure the call and the return time from the
;           driver program only.
;
cgroup          group   code
dgroup          group   data
data            segment public_data_.

t_table         db      256 dup (?)
t_string        db      64 dup (?)
m_array         dw      32 dup(?)
data            ends

code            segment public'code'
                assume  CS:cgroup,DS:dgroup
                public  bench_1, bench_2, nothing_,wait state_, set_timer_.
bench_1         proc    near                    ;save registers used
                push    SI
                push    CX
                push    BX
                push    AX

                mov     CX,64                   ;translate 64 bytes
                mov     SI,0
                mov     BH,0

loop_back:
                mov     BL,t_string             ;get the byte
                mov     AL,t_table[BX]          ;and store it
                mov     t_string[SI],AL         ;and store it
                inc     SI                      ;increment index
                loop    loop_back               ;do the next byte

                pop     AX
                pop     BX
                pop     CX
                pop     SI
bench_1         endp

bench_2         proc    near
                puxh    AX                      ;save registers used
                push    SI
                push    CX
```

```
                mov     CX,32                   ;multiply 32 numbers
                mov     SI,offset m_array
loop_back_2:
                imul    AX,wordptr [si],3       ;immediate multiply
                mov     word ptr [SI], AX
                inc     SI
                inc     SI
                loop    loop_back_2

                pop     CX
                pop     SI
                pop     AX
                ret
bench_2         endp

nothing_.       proc    near
                ret
nothing_.       endp
;
; Wait_staten sets the 80C186EB family processor LCSST register to the number of
;          wait states (0 to 3) indicated by the parameter n (which is passed on
;          the stack). No other bits of the LCSST register are modified.
;
wait_state_.    proc    near
                enter   0,0                     ; set up stack frame
                push    AX                      ; save registers used
                push    BX
                push    DX

                mov     BX, word ptr [BP+4]     ; get argument
                mov     DX, 0FFA0               ; get current LCSST register
                                                ; contents
                in      AX,DX

                and     AX,0FFF0H               ; and off existing ready bits
                and     BX,3                    ; insure ws count is good
                or      AX,BX                   ;adjust the ready bits
                out     DX,AX                   ; and write to LCSST
                pop     DX
                pop     BX
                pop     AX
                leave                           ; tear downstack frame
wait_state_.    endp
;
; Set_timer ( ) initializes the 80C186EB family processor timers to count
;          microseconds. Timer 2 is set up as a prescaler to timer 0, the
;          register at location FF50H is I/O space.
;
set_timer_.     proc    near
                push    AX
                push    DX
                mov     DX,0ff46H               ; stop timer 2
                mov     AX,4000h
                out     DX,AX

                mov     DX,0ff30H               ;clear timer 0 count
                mov     AX,0
                out     DX,AX

                mov     DX,0ff32H               ;timer 0 counts up to 65536
                mov     AX,0
                out     DX,AX

                mov     DX,0ff36H               ;enable timer 0
                mov     AX,0c009H
                out     DX,AX

                mov     DX,0ff40H               ;clear timer 2 count
                mov     AX,0
                out     DX,AX
```

```
        mov     DX,0ff42H        ;set maximum count of timer 2
        mov     AX,0
        out     DX,AX

        mov     DX,0ff46H        ;re-enable timer 2
        mov     AX,0
        out     DX,AX
```

Table 3.3. Performance Degradation vs. Wait States

# of Wait States	Program 1		Program 2	
	Exec Time (μsec)	Perf Degr	Exec Time (μsec)	Perf Degr
0	505		294	
1	595	18%	311	6%
2	669	12%	337	8%
3	752	12%	347	3%

Procedure Bench_1 is very bus intensive. It performs many memory operations using elaborate addressing modes which also require more opcode bytes. As a result, the Execution Unit must constantly wait for the Bus Interface Unit to fetch and perform the memory cycles to allow it to continue. Thus, the execution time of this type of routine will grow quickly as wait states are added, since the execution time depends mainly on the speed at which the processor can run bus cycles.

Note also that the program execution time calculated by merely summing up the number of clock cycles given in the data sheet will typically be less than the number of clock cycles actually required to run the program. This is true because the numbers quoted in the data sheet assume that the opcode bytes have been prefetched and reside in the prefetch queue for immediate access by the Execution Unit. If the Execution Unit cannot access the opcode bytes immediately upon request, dead clock cycles will be inserted in which the Execution Unit will remain idle, thus increasing the number of clock cycles required to complete execution of the program.

On the other hand, procedure Bench_2 is more CPU intensive. The Bus Interface Unit can fill up the instruction prefetch queue in parallel with the Execution Unit performing integer multiplies. In this program, the Bus Interface Unit can perform bus operations faster than the Execution Unit actually requires them to be run. The performance degradation is much less as wait states are added to the memory interface. The execution time of this program is close to the number calculated by adding the number of cycles per instruction because the Execution Unit does not have to wait for the Bus Interface Unit to place an opcode byte in the prefetch queue as often. Fewer clock cycles are wasted by the Execution Unit lying idle for want of instructions.

3.8 HOLD/HLDA INTERFACE

The 80C186 Modular Core family employs a HOLD/HLDA bus exchange protocol. This protocol allows other asynchronous bus masters (i.e., ones which drive address, data, and control information on the bus) to gain control.

3.8.1 RESPONSE TO HOLD

In the HOLD/HLDA protocol, a device requiring bus control (e.g., a token-ring communications controller) raises the HOLD line. In response to this HOLD request, the processor will raise its HLDA line after it has finished its current bus activity. When the external device is finished with the bus, it drops its bus HOLD request. The processor responds by dropping its HLDA line and resuming bus operation.

When the processor recognizes a bus HOLD by driving HLDA HIGH, it will float many of its signals (see Figure 3.15). AD0-AD15 and $\overline{DEN}$ are floated within T_{CLOF} after the clock edge when HLDA is driven active. A16-A19, $\overline{RD}$, $\overline{WR}$, $\overline{BHE}$, DT/$\overline{R}$, and $\overline{S0}$-$\overline{S2}$ are floated within T_{CHOF} after the clock edge on which HLDA becomes active.

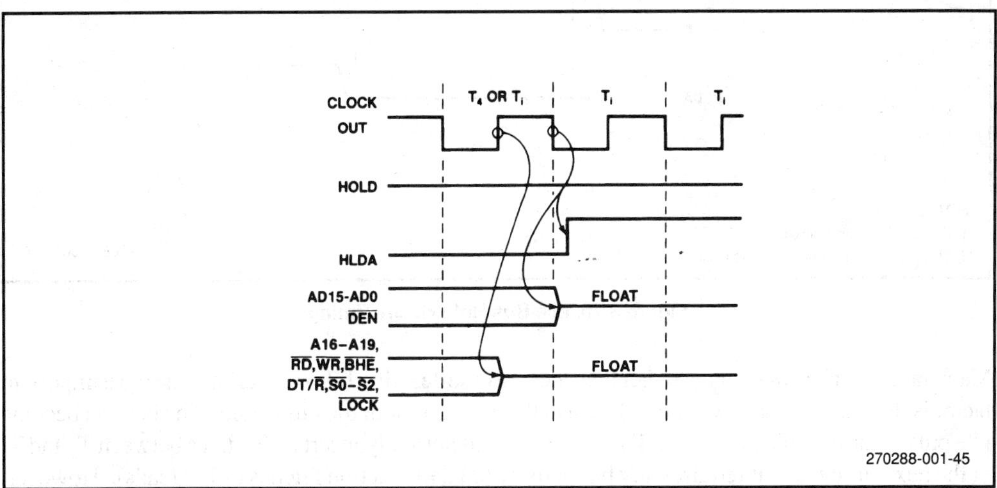

Figure 3.15. Signal Float/HLDA Timing of 80C186 Core Family Processor

Only the above mentioned signals are floated during bus HOLD. Of the signals not floated by the processor, some have to do with peripheral functionality (e.g., timer outputs). Many others either directly or indirectly control bus devices. These signals are ALE and all chip select lines ($\overline{UCS}$, $\overline{LCS}$, $\overline{GCS0-7}$).

3.8.2 HOLD/HLDA TIMING AND BUS LATENCY

The time required between HOLD going active and the microprocessor driving HLDA active is known as bus latency. Many factors affect bus latency, including synchronization delays, bus cycle times, LOCKed transfer times, interrupt acknowledge cycles, and DRAM refresh cycles.

The HOLD request line is internally synchronized by the 80C186 Modular Core family processor, and may therefore be an asynchronous input. To guarantee recognition on a particular falling clock edge, it must satisfy setup and hold times. A full CPU clock cycle is required for synchronization (see Appendix B). If the bus is idle, HLDA will follow HOLD by two CPU clock cycles plus setup and propagation delay time. The first clock cycle synchronizes the input; the second signals the internal circuitry to initiate a bus HOLD (see Figure 3.16).

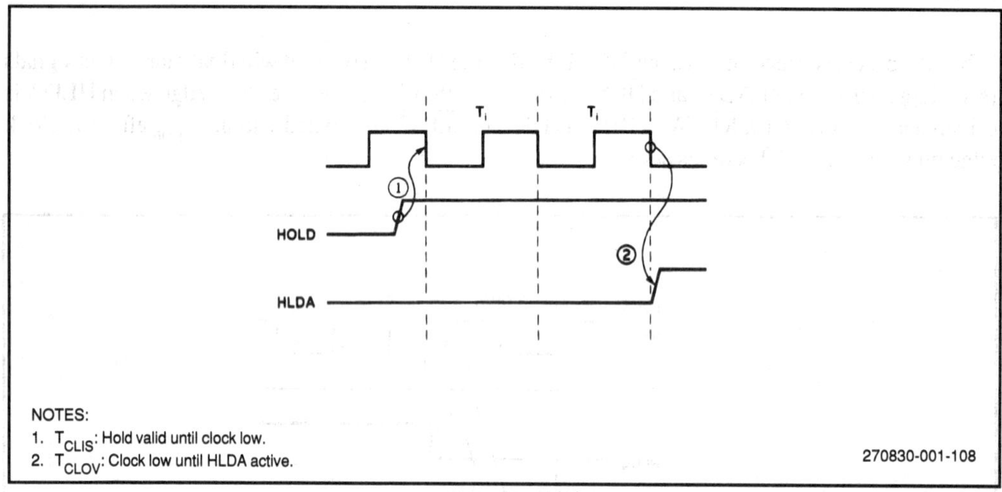
T_i
T_i
①
HOLD
②
HLDA
NOTES:
1. T_{CLIS}: Hold valid until clock low.
2. T_{CLOV}: Clock low until HLDA active.
270830-001-108

Figure 3.16. Idle Bus Hold/HLDA Timing

Many factors make bus latency longer than the best case described above. Perhaps the most important factor is that the processor will not relinquish the local bus until the bus is idle. The bus can become idle only at the end of a bus cycle. The processor will normally insert no T_i states between T_4 and T_1 of the next bus cycle if it requires any bus activity (e.g., instruction fetches or I/O reads). However, the processor may not have an immediate need for the bus after a bus cycle, and will insert T_i states independent of the HOLD input (see Section 3.1).

When the HOLD request is active, the 80C186 Modular Core family BIU will proceed from T_4 to T_i to relinquish the bus. HOLD must go active two T-states before the end of a bus cycle to force the BIU to insert idle T-states after T_4. One T-state is spent synchronizing the request and one T-state is spent signaling the processor that T_4 of the bus cycle will be followed by idle T-states (see Section 3.1). After the bus cycle has ended, the HOLD will be immediately acknowledged. If, however, the processor has already determined that an idle T-state will follow T_4 of the current bus cycle, HOLD needs to go active only two T-states before the end of the bus cycle to force the microprocessor to relinquish the bus. Figure 3.17 shows these processes. Also, if HOLD is asserted during RESET, the processor releases the bus prior to the first fetch.

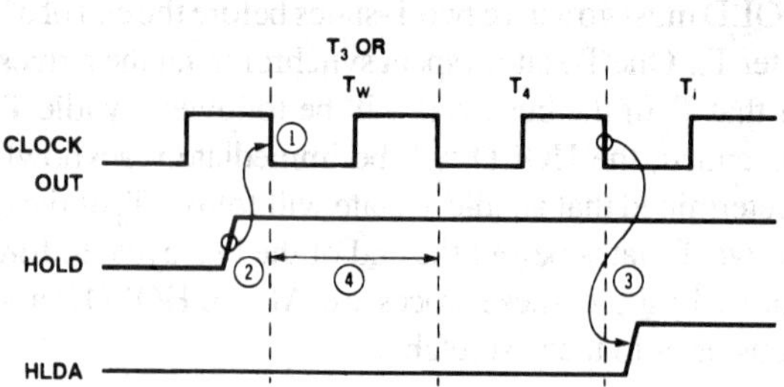

NOTES:

1. Decision: No additional internal bus cycles required, idle T-states will be inserted after T_4.
2. Greater than T_{CLIS}.
3. Less than T_{CHOV}.
4. HOLD request internally synchronized.

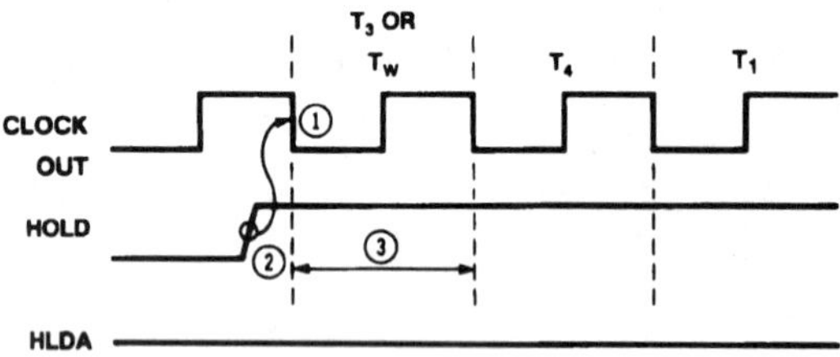

NOTES:

1. Decision: Additional internal bus cycles required, no idle T-states will be inserted, HOLD not active soon enough to force idle T-states.
2. Greater than T_{CLIS}: not required since it will not get recognized anyway.
3. HOLD request internally synchronized.

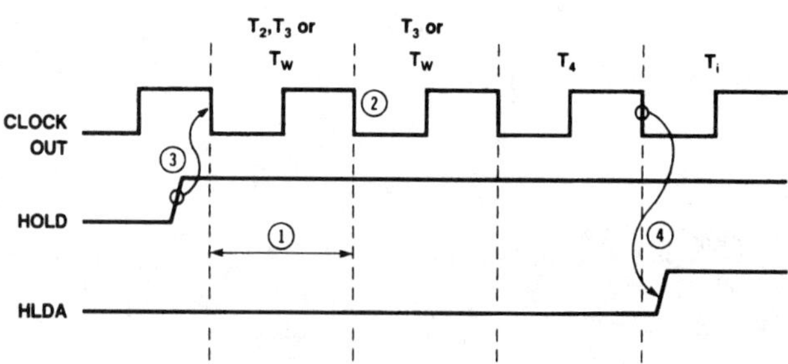

NOTES:

1. HOLD request internally synchronized.
2. Decision: HOLD request active, idle T-states will be inserted at end of current bus cycle.
3. Greater than T_{CLIS}.
4. Less than T_{CLOV}.

Figure 3.17. HOLD/HLDA Timing in the 80C186 Modular Core Family

An external HOLD has higher priority than a CPU bus request. However, an external HOLD will not separate the two cycles needed to perform a word access when the word accessed is located at an odd location (see Section 3.3.1).

Another factor influencing bus latency time is LOCKed transfers. Whenever a LOCKed transfer is occurring, the processor will not recognize external HOLDs. LOCKed transfers are programmed by preceding an instruction with the LOCK prefix. String instructions may be LOCKed. Since string transfers may require thousands of bus cycles, bus latency time will suffer if they are LOCKed.

The final factor affecting bus latency time is interrupt acknowledge cycles. When an external interrupt controller is used the CPU will run two interrupt acknowledge cycles back-to-back. These cycles are automatically LOCKed and will never be separated by bus HOLD.

3.8.3 LEAVING HOLD

When the HOLD input goes inactive, the processor lowers its HLDA line in a single clock as shown in Figure 3.18. If there is pending bus activity, only two T_i states will be inserted after HLDA goes inactive. Status information will go active during the last idle state concerning the bus cycle about to be run (see Section 3.1). If there are no bus cycles to be run by the CPU, it will continue to float all lines until the last Ti before it begins its first bus cycle after the HOLD.

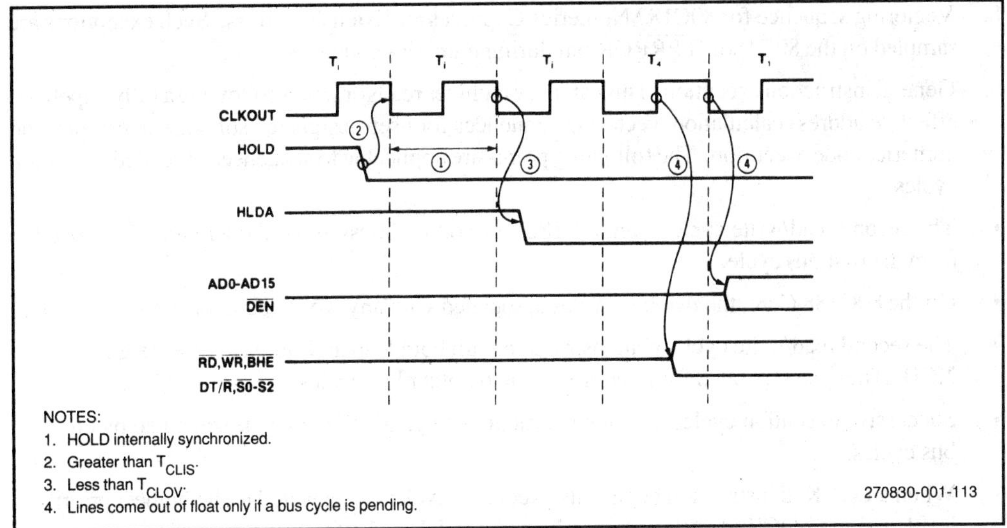
T_i
T_i
T_i
T_4
T_1
CLKOUT
HOLD
HLDA
AD0-AD15
DEN
RD, WR, BHE
DT/R, S0-S2
NOTES:
1. HOLD internally synchronized.
2. Greater than T_{CLIS}.
3. Less than T_{CLOV}.
4. Lines come out of float only if a bus cycle is pending.
270830-001-113

Figure 3.18. 80C186 Modular Core Family

A special mechanism exists on the 80C186/80C188 to provide for DRAM refreshing while the bus is in HOLD. See the chapter of this manual on the Refresh Control Unit for details.

3.9 PRIORITY OF BUS CYCLE TYPES

The 80C186EB family Bus Interface Unit arbitrates requests for bus cycles originating in the integrated peripherals as well as the Execution Unit. Here is a summary of the overall priority for all bus cycle types (highest to lowest):

1. Instruction execution reads or writes following a non-pipelined effective address calculation.
2. DRAM refresh cycles.
3. Bus cycles run by an external bus master during HOLD. The 80C186 Modular Core family signals its need to use the bus for a DRAM refresh cycle by lowering HLDA.
4. Vectoring sequence for the single step interrupt.
5. Vectoring sequence for the NMI interrupt.
6. Vectoring sequence for divide error, breakpoint, overflow, array bounds, unused opcode, and ESCape trap interrupts, according to priority resolution.
7. Vectoring sequence for hardware interrupts from the timers, Serial Communications Unit, and external pins.
8. Vectoring sequence for 80C187 Numerics Coprocessor Extension errors. Such exceptions are sampled on the 80C186EB $\overline{\text{ERROR}}$ pin during numerics code execution.
9. General instruction execution. This category includes reads or writes following a fully-pipelined effective address calculation, vectoring sequences for user-designated software interrupts, and numerics code execution. The following points are applicable to sequences of related execution cycles:

- The second read/write cycle of an 80C186 Core odd-addressed word operation is inseparable from the first bus cycle.
- On the 80C188 Core, the two bus cycles associated with any word operation are inseparable.
- The second read/write cycle of an instruction with both load and store accesses (e.g., XCHG) may be separated from the first cycle by other bus cycles.
- Successive execution cycles of string instructions (e.g., MOVS) may be separated by other bus cycles.
- When a LOCKed instruction begins, its execution cycles are elevated to the highest priority level, making LOCKed cycles inseparable even to DRAM refresh cycles. String operations and 80C186EB/80C187 execution may be LOCKed like any other instructions.

10. Fetches necessary to fill the prefetch queue with opcodes and operands.

Clock Generator 4

CHAPTER 4
CLOCK GENERATOR

The clock generator provides the main clock signal for all integrated components and all CPU synchronous devices in a system based on the 80C186EB family. This clock generator includes a crystal oscillator, divide-by-two counter, RESET circuitry, and power management circuitry. A block diagram of the clock generator is shown in Figure 4.1.

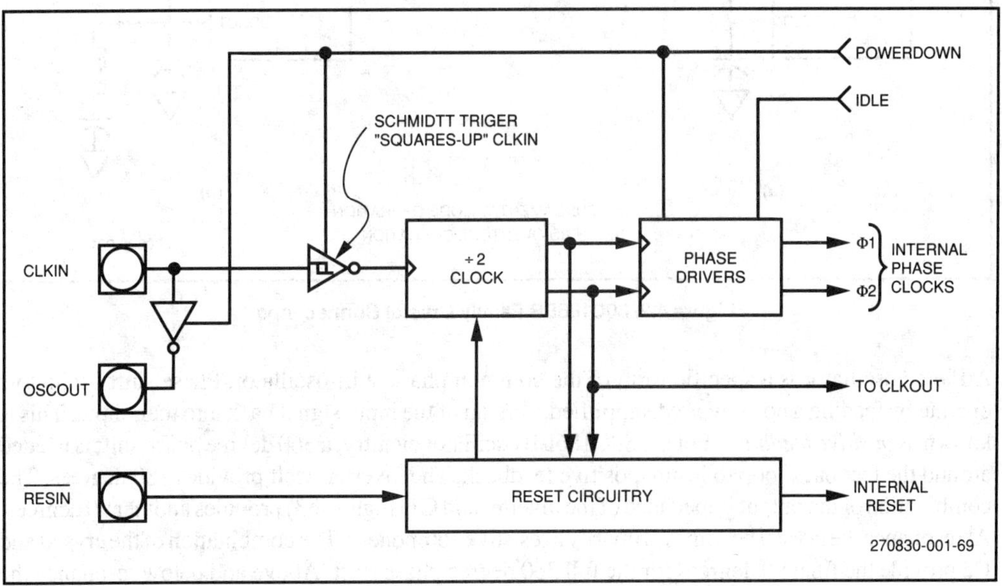

Figure 4.1. Clock Generator

4.1 CRYSTAL OSCILLATOR

80C186EB family microprocessors use a parallel resonant Pierce oscillator. For low frequency 80C186EB family applications, a fundamental mode crystal is appropriate. At higher frequencies, the diminishing thickness of fundamental mode crystals makes a third overtone crystal the appropriate choice. The addition of external capacitors at CLKIN and OSCOUT is always required, and a third overtone crystal also requires an RC tank circuit to select the third overtone frequency over the fundamental frequency (see Figure 4.2).

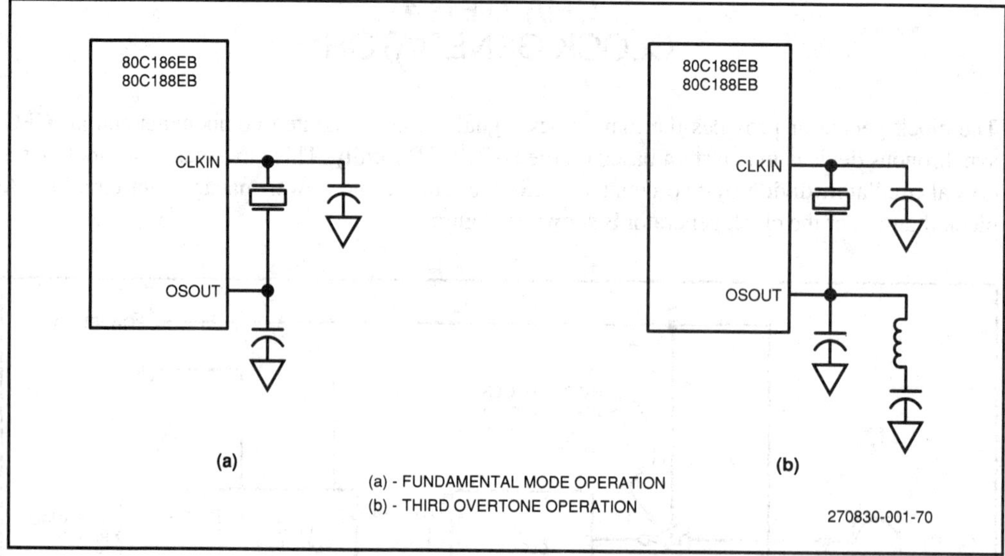

Figure 4.2. 80C186EB Family Crystal Connections

A Pierce oscillator is a specific form of the common phase shift oscillator. Phase shift oscillators operate by feeding a non-inverted, amplified, version of the input signal back into their input. This is known as *positive feedback*. For the 80C186EB oscillator cicuitry, a 360 degree phase shift is needed around the feedback loop to insure positive feedback. The inverter itself provides 180 degrees. The combination of the output impedance of the inverter and C1 (Figure 4.3) provides another 90 degrees. At resonance the crystal becomes primarily a resistive component. The combination of the crystal and C2 provide the final 90 degrees for the full 360 degree phase shift. Above and below resonance the crystal is reactive and tends to force the oscillator back towards the crystal's rated frequency.

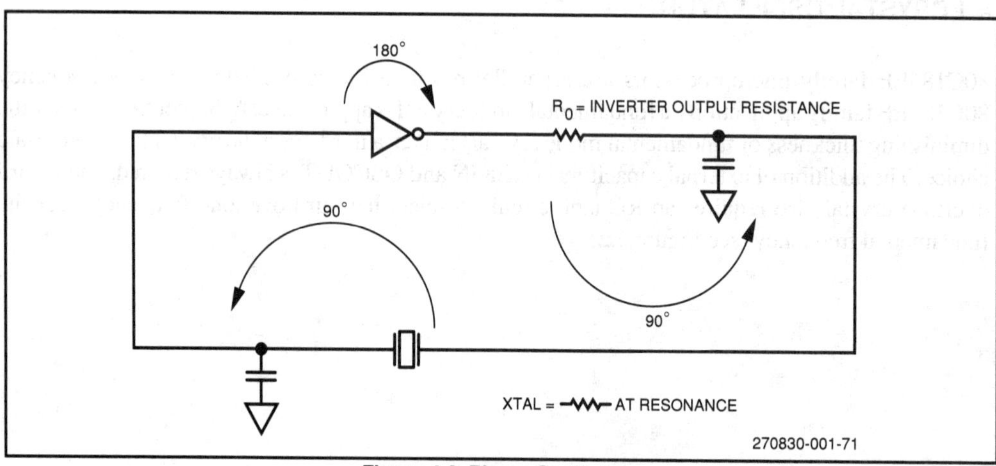

Figure 4.3. Pierce Oscillator

The RC tank circuit, used for third overtone crystals, suppresses oscillation at the fundamental frequency. This is accomplished by preventing the first 90 degree phase shift from occurring. A more detailed analysis of crystal oscillator circuits is beyond the scope of this user's guide. Several excellent articles and texts can be found on the subject of crystal oscillators should more information be necessary.

The recommendations given in 80C186EB family data sheets for the values of the external components should be taken only as rough guidelines, since there are situations which alter typical oscillator characteristics. One example would be the case in which the circuit layout introduces significant stray capacitance to the CLKIN and OSCOUT pins. Another example is at low frequencies (CLKOUT less than 6 MHz) where slightly larger capacitors are desirable. Finally, it is also possible to use ceramic resonators in place of crystals for low cost when precise frequencies are not required.

For assistance in selecting the external oscillator components for unusual circumstances, the best resource is the crystal manufacturer. In general, almost any microprocessor grade crystal will work satisfactorily with any member of the 80C186EB family. The foremost circuit consideration is that the oscillator **start** correctly over the entire voltage and temperature ranges expected in operation.

4.2 USING AN EXTERNAL OSCILLATOR

An external oscillator may be used with the 80C186EB family. The external frequency input (EFI) signal is connected directly to the CLKIN input of the oscillator. **OSCOUT must be left unconnected.** This oscillator input drives an internal divide-by-two counter to generate the CPU clock signal. Thus the external frequency input can be of practically any duty cycle, so long as the minimum HIGH and LOW times for the signal (as stated in the data sheet) are met.

4.3 OUTPUT FROM CLOCK GENERATOR

The output of the crystal oscillator (or the external frequency input) drives a divide-by-two circuit which generates a 50 per cent duty cycle clock for the 80186 family processor system. All processor timing is referenced to this clock, available externally at the CLKOUT pin. CLKOUT changes state on the HIGH-to-LOW transition of the CLKIN signal, and is active during RESET and bus HOLD. CLKOUT is also available during Idle mode but not during Powerdown Mode (see the Chapter 12 for more details).

4.4 RESET

The 80C186EB family clock generator also provides a synchronized RESET signal for the system. This signal is generated from the $\overline{\text{RESIN}}$ input to the device. The clock generator synchronizes this signal to the CLKOUT signal.

A Schmitt trigger in the $\overline{\text{RESIN}}$ input circuit ensures that a voltage difference separates the switch points for logic states 0 and 1. This hysteresis measures approximately 600 mV. An 80C186EB family processor must remain in $\overline{RESET}$ a minimum of four CLKOUT cycles after V_{CC} and CLKOUT stabilize. The hysteresis allows the $\overline{RESIN}$ input to be driven with a simple RC circuit as shown in Figure 4.4. Typical applications can use an RC time constant of approximately 100 ms. $\overline{RESIN}$ must be held LOW upon power-up for correct processor initialization.

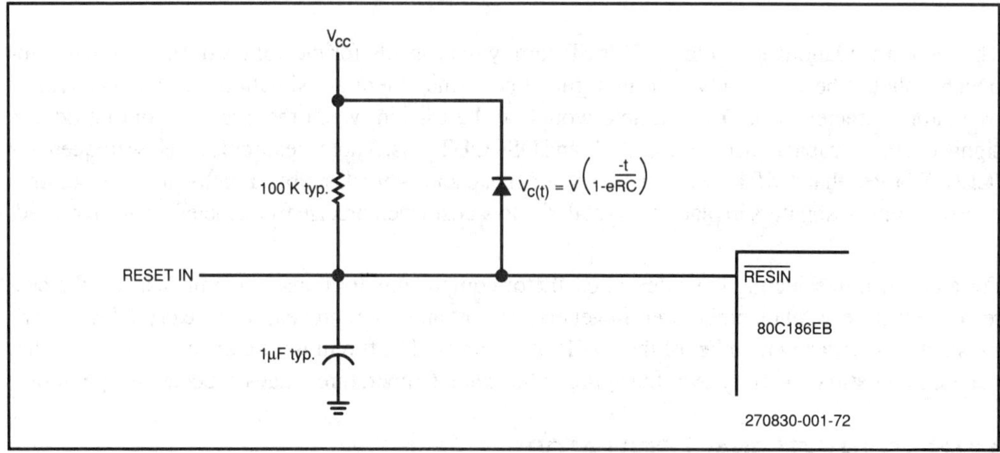

Figure 4.4. Simple RC Circuit for Power Up RESET

There are two types of RESETs than can occur: cold and warm. A cold reset takes place only at powerup (Figure 4.5). The $\overline{RESIN}$ input must be held low during power supply and oscillator startup. The device pins will assume their RESET pin states a maximum of 28 CLKIN periods after CLKIN and VCC have stabilized. $\overline{RESIN}$ must be held low an additional 4 CLKIN periods after the device pins have assumed their RESET state.

A warm RESET takes place when the device is RESET while it is running (Figure 4.6). In this case, $\overline{RESIN}$ must be held low at least 4 CLKOUT periods. The device pins will assume their RESET states on the second falling edge of CLKIN following the assertion of $\overline{RESIN}$.

Exiting RESET is the same in both cases. The rising edge of $\overline{RESIN}$ generates an internal RESYNC pulse (Figure 4.7) that resynchronizes the divide-by-2 internal phase clock. $\overline{RESIN}$ is sampled by the falling edge of CLKIN. If $\overline{RESIN}$ is sampled high while CLKOUT is high, then CLKOUT will be forced low for the next 2 CLKOUT cycles. The clock essentially "skips a beat" to synchronize the internal phases. If $\overline{RESIN}$ is sampled high while CLKOUT is low, CLKOUT will not be affected (it is already in phase).

RESOUT is deasserted on the second falling edge of CLKOUT after the internal clocks have re-synchronized. Bus activity will begin seven CLKOUT periods after $\overline{RESIN}$ goes high. If HOLD is asserted during RESET, the processor will immediately assert HLDA (no instructions will be fetched).

The state of all device pins at RESET can be found in Appendix H "Modal Pin States".

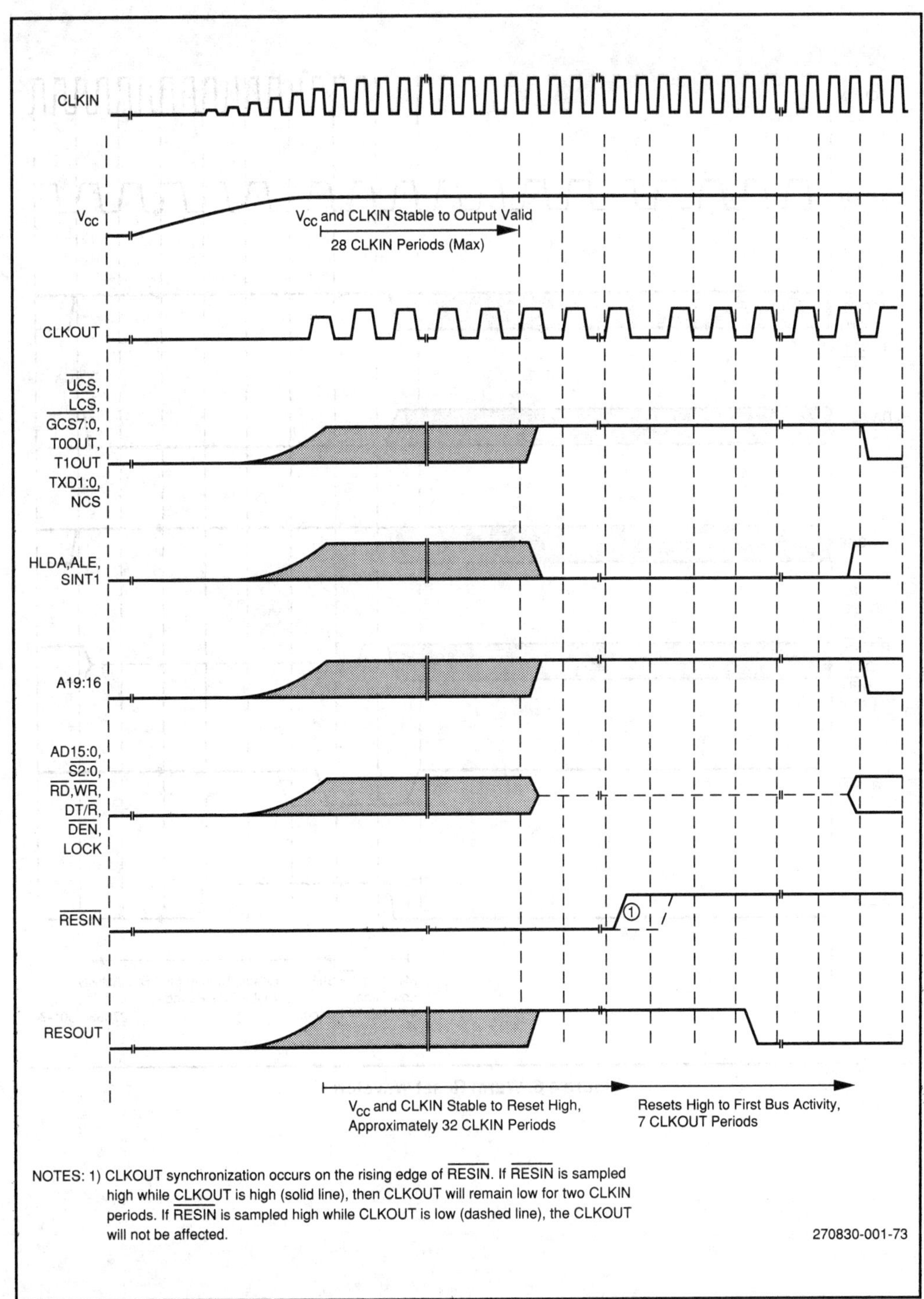

Figure 4.5. Cold Reset Waveform

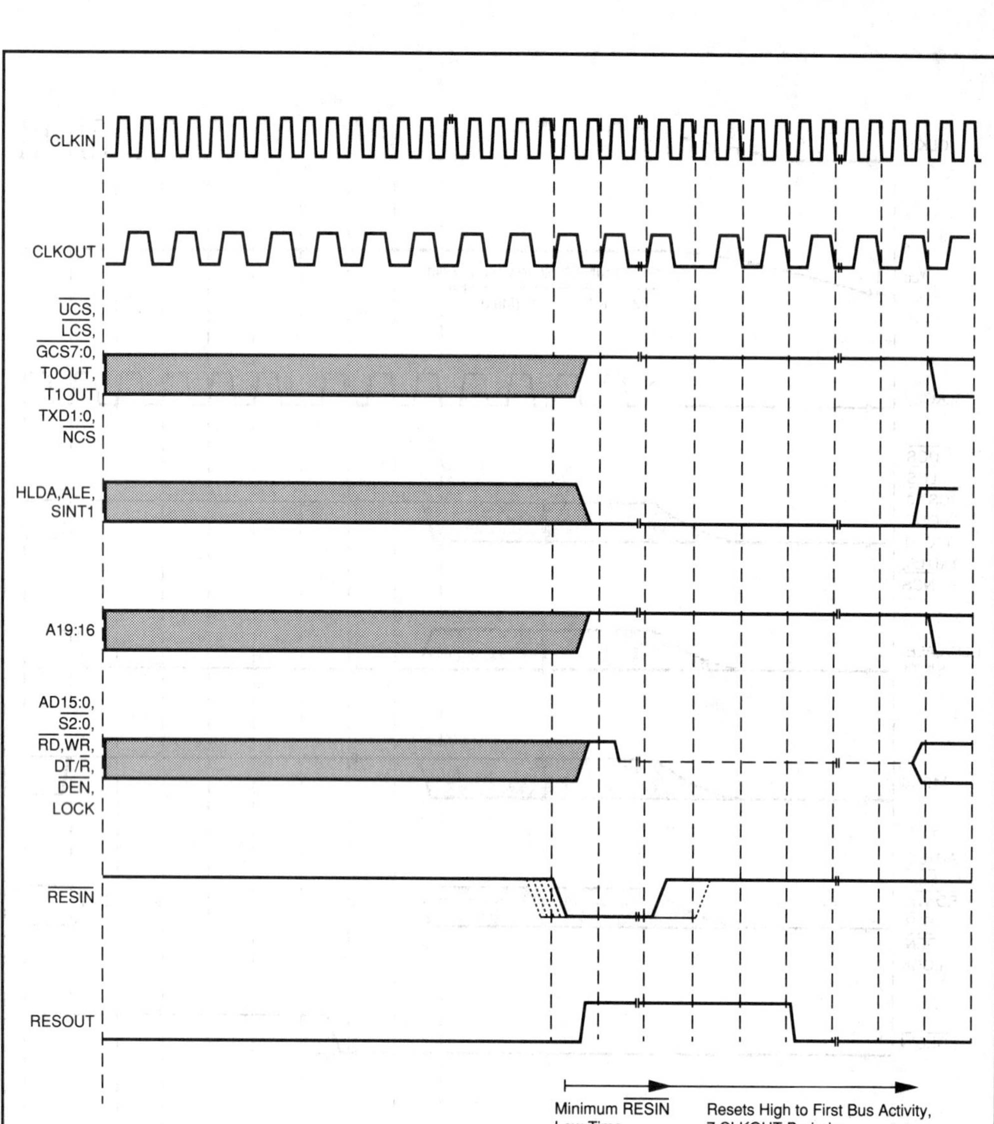

Figure 4.6. Warm Reset Waveform

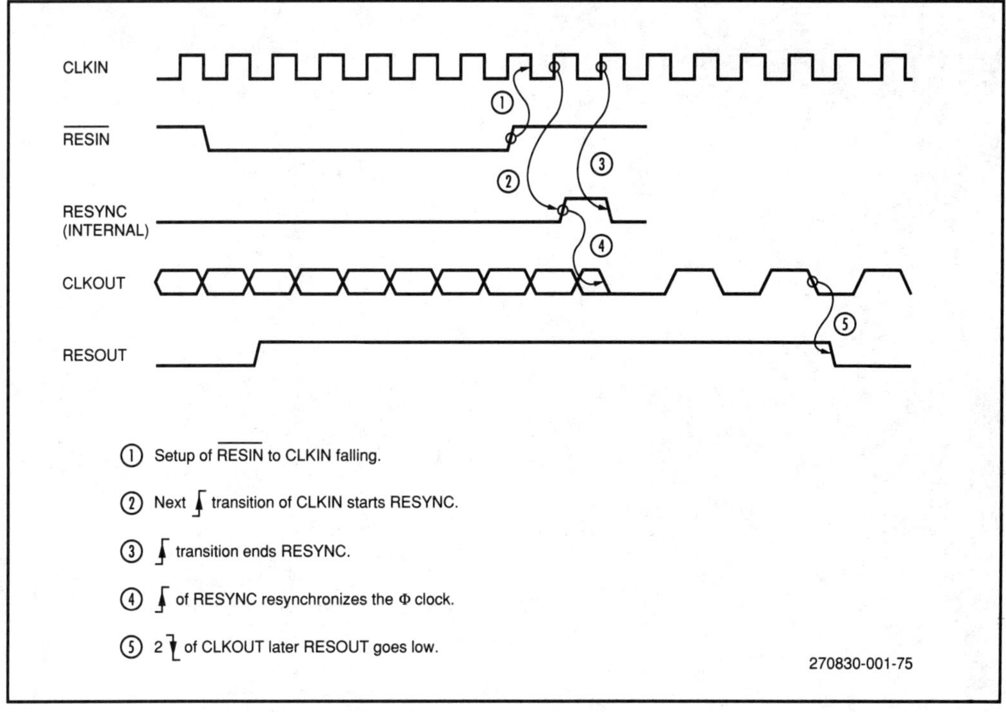

Figure 4.7. Clock Synchronization

Peripheral Control Block 5

CHAPTER 5
PERIPHERAL CONTROL BLOCK

All the integrated peripherals on the 80C186EB/80C188EB are controlled by sets of registers contained within an integrated peripheral control block (PCB). The registers are physically located in the peripheral devices they control, but are addressed as a single block of registers. This set of registers encompasses 256 contiguous bytes and can be located on any 256 byte boundary of the memory or I/O space. Maps of these registers are shown in Figure 5.1. Any unused locations are reserved.

00H	Reserved	40H	T2 Count	80H	GCS0 Start	C0H	Reserved
02H	End Of Interrupt	42H	T2 Compare	82H	GCS0 Stop	C2H	Reserved
04H	Poll	44H	Reserved	84H	GCS1 Start	C4H	Reserved
06H	Poll Status	46H	T2 Control	86H	GCS1 Stop	C6H	Reserved
08H	Interrupt Mask	48H	Reserved	88H	GCS2 Start	C8H	Reserved
0AH	Priority Mask	4AH	Reserved	8AH	GCS2 Stop	CAH	Reserved
0CH	In-Service	4CH	Reserved	8CH	GCS3 Start	CCH	Reserved
0EH	Interrupt Request	4EH	Reserved	8EH	GCS3 Stop	CEH	Reserved
10H	Interrupt Status	50H	PORT1 Direction	90H	GCS4 Start	D0H	Reserved
12H	Timer Control	52H	PORT1 Pin	92H	GCS4 Stop	D2H	Reserved
14H	Serial Control	54H	PORT1 Control	94H	GCS5 Start	D4H	Reserved
16H	INT4 Control	56H	PORT1 Latch	96H	GCS5 Stop	D6H	Reserved
18H	INT0 Control	58H	PORT2 Direction	98H	GCS6 Start	D8H	Reserved
1AH	INT1 Control	5AH	PORT2 Pin	9AH	GCS6 Stop	DAH	Reserved
1CH	INT2 Control	5CH	PORT2 Control	9CH	GCS7 Start	DCH	Reserved
1EH	INT3 Control	5EH	PORT2 Latch	9EH	GCS7 Stop	DEH	Reserved
20H	Reserved	60H	SERIAL0 Baud	A0H	LCS Start	E0H	Reserved
22H	Reserved	62H	SERIAL0 Count	A2H	LCS Stop	E2H	Reserved
24H	Reserved	64H	SERIAL0 Control	A4H	UCS Start	E4H	Reserved
26H	Reserved	66H	SERIAL0 Status	A6H	UCS Stop	E6H	Reserved
28H	Reserved	68H	SERIAL0 RBUF	A8H	RELOCATION	E8H	Reserved
2AH	Reserved	6AH	SERIAL0 TBUF	AAH	Reserved	EAH	Reserved
2CH	Reserved	6CH	Reserved	ACH	Reserved	ECH	Reserved
2EH	Reserved	6EH	Reserved	AEH	Reserved	EEH	Reserved
30H	T0 Count	70H	SERIAL1 Baud	B0H	REFRESH Base	F0H	Reserved
32H	T0 Compare A	72H	SERIAL1 Count	B2H	REFRESH Time	F2H	Reserved
34H	T0 Compare B	74H	SERIAL1 Control	B4H	REFRESH Control	F4H	Reserved
36H	T0 Control	76H	SERIAL1 Status	B6H	REFRESH Address	F6H	Reserved
38H	T1 Count	78H	SERIAL1 RBUF	B8H	POWER Control	F8H	Reserved
3AH	T1 Compare A	7AH	SERIAL1 TBUF	BAH	Reserved	FAH	Reserved
3CH	T1 Compare B	7CH	Reserved	BCH	Stepping ID	FCH	Reserved
3EH	T1 Control	7EH	Reserved	BEH	Reserved	FEH	Reserved

Figure 5.1. PCB Register Map

5.1 SETTING THE BASE LOCATION

In addition to the control registers for each of the integrated peripheral devices, the peripheral control block contains the peripheral control block relocation register. This register allows the PCB to be relocated on any 256 byte boundary within the processor's memory or I/O space. Figure 5.2 shows the layout of this register.

RCB RELOCATION REGISTER: (RELREG)

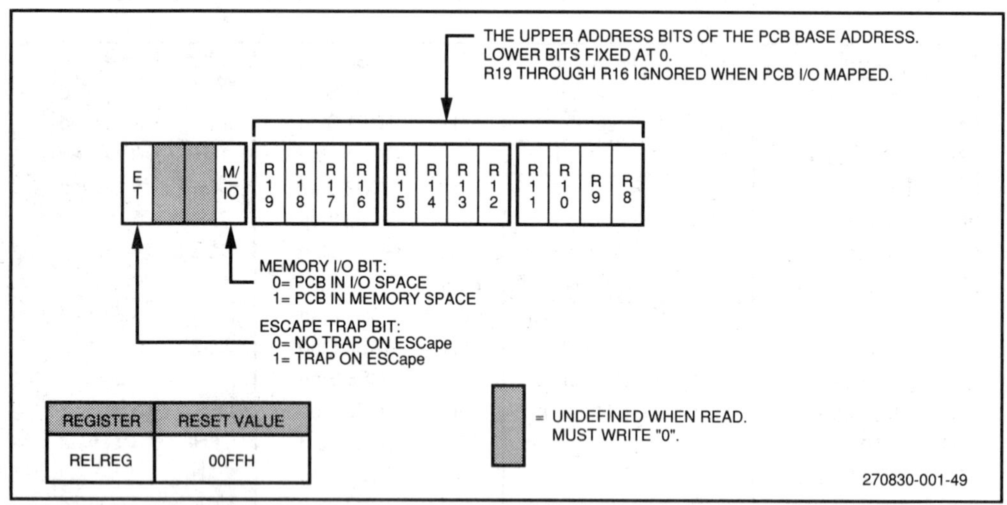

Figure 5.2.

The relocation register is located at offset 0A8H within the PCB. Since it is contained within the peripheral control block, any time the peripheral control block is moved, the relocation register will also move.

In addition to the PCB relocation information, the relocation register contains an additional bit used to force the processor to trap whenever an ESCape (coprocessor) instruction is encountered. The function of this bit is described in greater detail in the "Provisions for Floating Point Math" section of this manual.

The relocation register contains the value 00FFH upon RESET. This means that the peripheral control block will be located at the very top (0FF00H to 0FFFFH) of I/O space. Thus after RESET the relocation register will be located at word location 0FFA8H in I/O space.

To relocate the PCB to the memory range 10000-100FFH, for example, the user programs the relocation register with the value 1100H. Since the relocation register is contained within the peripheral control block, it moves to word location 100A8H.

All communication between the integrated peripherals and the Modular CPU Core takes place over a special bus called the F-Bus. The F-Bus always carries 16 bit data for both the 80C186EB and the 80C188EB.

Whenever mapping the 80C188EB peripheral control block to another location, the programming of the relocation register should be done with a byte write (i.e., OUT DX, AL). Any access to the control block is done 16 bits at a time. Thus, internally, the relocation register will be written with 16 bits of the AX register while externally, the BIU will run only one 8-bit bus cycle. If a word instruction is used (i.e., OUT DX, AX), the relocation register will be written on the first bus cycle. The BIU will then run a second bus cycle which is unnecessary. The address of the second bus cycle will no longer be within the control block (i.e., the control block was moved on the first cycle), and therefore will require the generation of external READY to complete the cycle. For this reason we recommend the use of byte operations for the relocation register. Byte instructions may also be used for the other registers in the control block of a 80C188EB and will eliminate half of the bus cycles required if a word operation had been specified. Byte operations are only valid for even addressed writes to the PCB. A word read (i.e., IN AX, DX) must be performed to read a 16-bit PCB register.

5.2 PERIPHERAL CONTROL BLOCK REGISTERS

Each of the integrated peripherals' control and status registers are located at a fixed location above the programmed base location of the peripheral control block. There are many locations within the peripheral control block which are not assigned to any peripheral. If a write is made to any of these locations, the bus cycle will be run, but the value will not be stored in any internal location. This means that if a subsequent read is made to the same location, the value written will not be read back.

The processor will run an external bus cycle for any memory or I/O cycle which accesses a location within the integrated control block. This means that the address, data, and control information will be driven on the processor external pins just as if an ordinary bus cycle had been run. Any information returned by an external device will be ignored, however, even if the access was to a location which does not correspond to any of the integrated peripheral control registers. The above is true for the 80C188EB except that the word access made to the integrated registers will be performed in two bus cycles.

The processor internally generates a READY signal whenever any of the integrated peripherals are accessed; any external READY signal is ignored. This READY will also be returned if an access is made to a location within the 256 byte area of the peripheral control block which does not correspond to any integrated peripheral control register. The processor will insert no wait states for any access within the integrated peripheral control clock except for accesses to the timer registers. Any access to the timer control and counting registers will incur one wait state. This wait state is required to properly multiplex processor and counter element accesses to the timer control registers.

The F-Bus does not function the same as the external data bus with regards to byte and word accesses. All write transfers on the F-Bus take place as words regardless of how they are encoded. For example, the instruction OUT DX, AL (DX is even) will write the entire AX register to the PCB register at even location [DX]. If DX were an odd location, AL would be placed in [DX] and AH would be placed at [DX-1]. Similarly, a word operation to an odd address would modify [DX] and [DX-1] with the AH and AL bytes swapped. **This is different from normal external bus operation where unaligned word writes would cause the modification of [DX] and [DX+1].**

Aligned word reads work normally, however, unaligned word reads do not. For example, IN AX, DX (DX is odd) will actually transfer [DX] into AL and [DX-1] into AH. Byte reads from either even or odd addresses work normally, however **only a byte will be read**. Unlike the write operation, an IN AL, DX will **not** transfer [DX] into AX (only AL is modified).

No problems will arise if the following recommendations are adhered to. For the 80C186EB:

Word reads: Access only even aligned word with IN AX, DX or MOV <word register>, <even PCB address>.

Byte reads: Work normally. Beware of reading word wide PCB registers that may change value between successive reads (i.e. Timer count value).

Word writes: Always write even aligned words. Writing an odd aligned word will give unexpected results. Use either OUT DX, AX or OUT DX, AL (or MOV <even PCB address>, <word register>).

Byte writes: Do not perform unaligned byte writes. Even aligned byte writes will modify the entire word PCB location.

For the 80C188EB:

Word reads: Access only even aligned words with IN AX, DX or MOV <word register>, <even PCB address>.

Byte reads: Work normally. Beware of reading word wide PCB registers that may change value between successive reads (i.e. Timer count value).

Word writes: Always write even aligned words. Writing an odd aligned word will give unexpected results. Use OUT DX, AL or MOV <even aligned byte PCB address>, <byte register low byte>. Using OUT DX, AX will perform an unnecessary extra bus cycle.

Byte writes: Do not perform unaligned byte writes. Even aligned byte writes will modify the entire word PCB location.

5.3 RESERVED LOCATIONS AND THE NUMERICS INTERFACE

Any location within the 256 byte peripheral control block that are not explicitly used are **reserved.** Reading from these locations yields an undefined result. If reserved registers are written, for example during a block MOVe instruction, they must be set to 0H. **Failure to follow this guideline could result in incompatibilities with future 80C186EB and other 80C186 Modular Core family products.**

Systems using the 80C187 Numeric Processor Extension must not relocate the PCB to location 0H in I/O space. The 80C186EB/80C187 interface uses I/O locations 0F84 through 0FFH. If the PCB were relocated over these locations, the 80C186EB would be communicating with the PCB and **not** the 80C187 interface circuitry. This will cause indeterminate system operation if a numerics instruction is encountered when the escape trap bit is cleared.

Timer/Counter Unit 6

CHAPTER 6
TIMER / COUNTER UNIT

The 80C186EB family includes a Timer/Counter Unit which consists of three independent 16-bit timers (figure 6.1). These timers operate independently of the CPU. Two have input and output pins allowing counting of external events and generation of arbitrary waveforms. The third can be used as a free running timer or as a prescaler for the other timers.

All of the timers can generate internal interrupt requests. Although the three timers share one request, they each have their own vectoring location and have a fixed priority amongst themselves.

Timers 0 and 1 have two maximum count compare registers. Timers 0 and 1 also can be enabled or disabled via a package pin. This allows for convenient measurement of external pulse widths. The timer 0 and 1 in and out pins can also be configured as a digital one-shot.

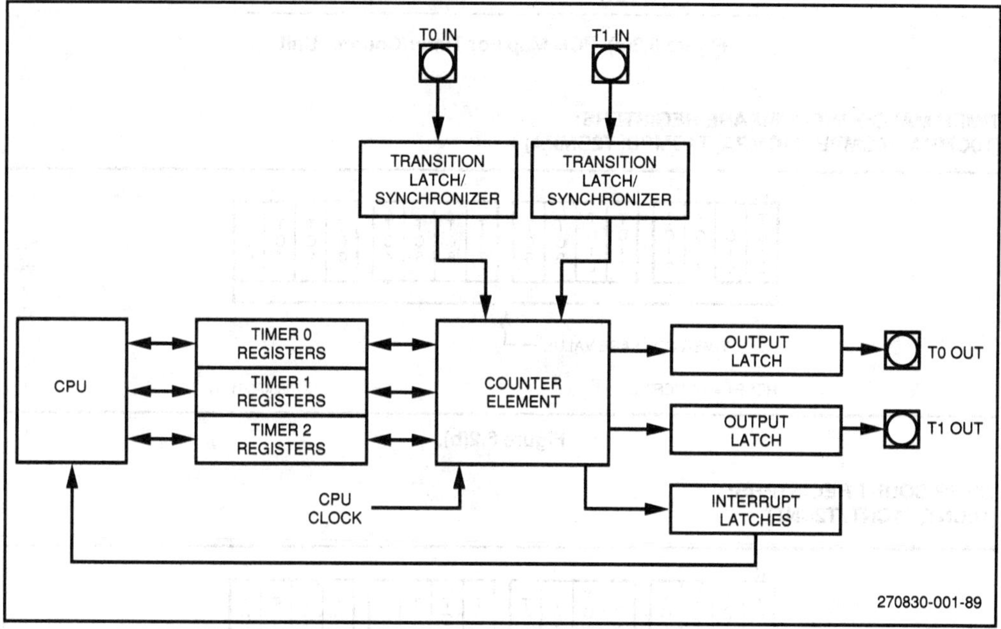

Figure 6.1. Timer/Counter Unit Block Diagram

Three peripheral control block registers are used for each timer: the control register, the count register, and the compare register. Timers 0 and 1 have an additional compare register. The PCB map and summary of operation are shown in figure 6.2.

REGISTER NAME	OFFSET
T0CNT	30H
T0CMPA	32H
T0CMPB	34H
T0CON	36H
T1CNT	38H
T1CMPA	3AH
T1CMPB	3CH
T1CON	3EH
T2CNT	40H
T2CMPA	42H
RESERVED	44H
T2CON	46H

Figure 6.2(a). PCB Map For Timer/Counter Unit

TIMER MAXCOUNT COMPARE REGISTERS:
(T0CMPA, T0CMPB, T1CMPA, T1CMPB, T2CMPA)

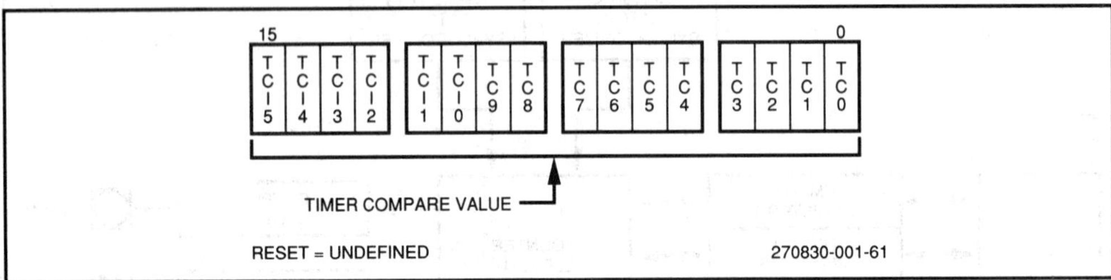

Figure 6.2(b).

TIMER COUNT REGISTERS:
(T0CNT, T1CNT, T2CNT)

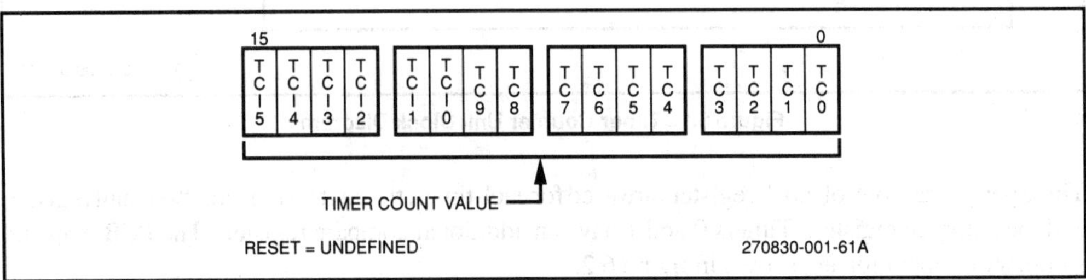

Figure 6.2(c).

TIMER 0 and TIMER 1 CONTROL REGISTERS: (T0CON, T1CON)

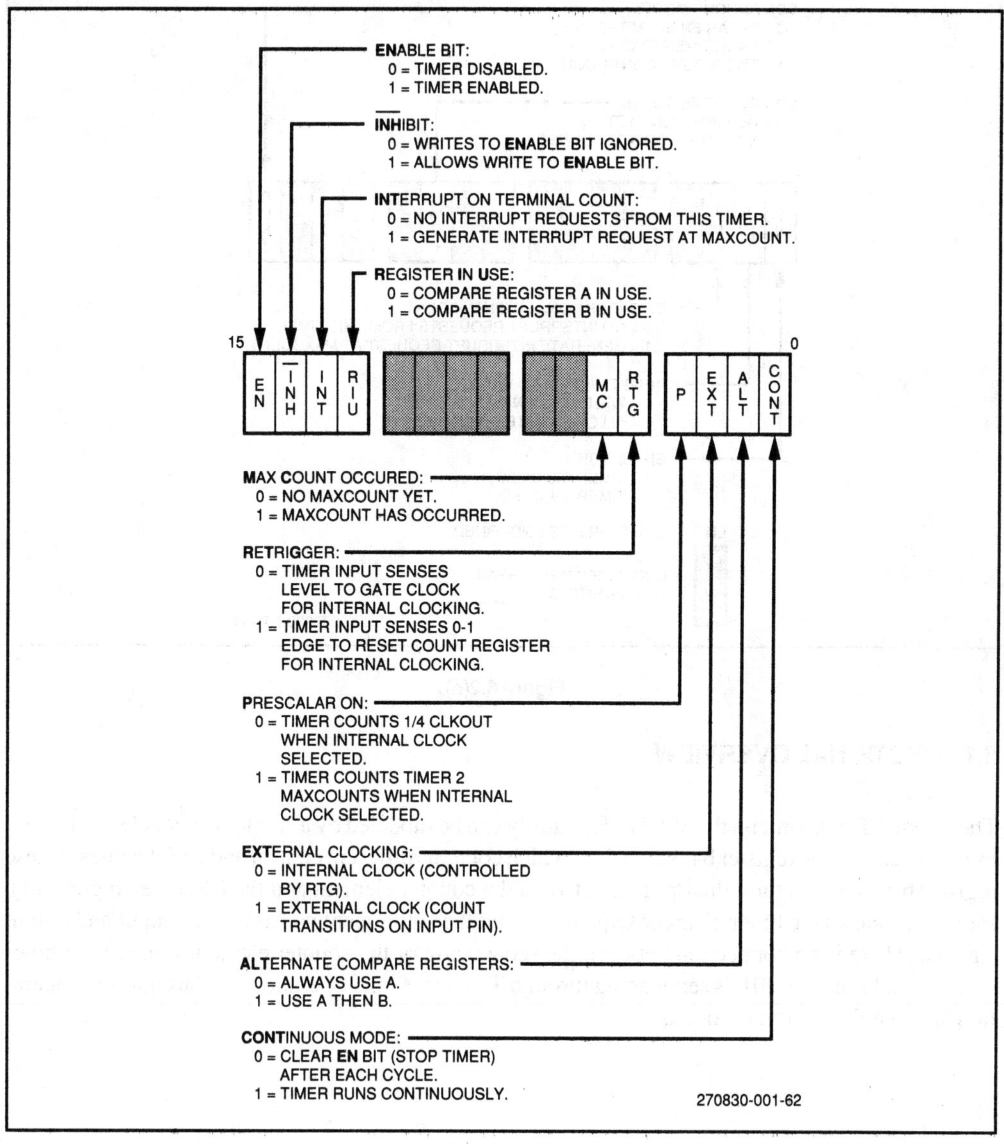

ENABLE BIT:
0 = TIMER DISABLED.
1 = TIMER ENABLED.
INHIBIT:
0 = WRITES TO ENABLE BIT IGNORED.
1 = ALLOWS WRITE TO ENABLE BIT.
INTERRUPT ON TERMINAL COUNT:
0 = NO INTERRUPT REQUESTS FROM THIS TIMER.
1 = GENERATE INTERRUPT REQUEST AT MAXCOUNT.
REGISTER IN USE:
0 = COMPARE REGISTER A IN USE.
1 = COMPARE REGISTER B IN USE.
15
0
EN
INH
INT
RIU
MC
RTG
P
EXT
ALT
CONT
MAX COUNT OCCURED:
0 = NO MAXCOUNT YET.
1 = MAXCOUNT HAS OCCURRED.
RETRIGGER:
0 = TIMER INPUT SENSES LEVEL TO GATE CLOCK FOR INTERNAL CLOCKING.
1 = TIMER INPUT SENSES 0-1 EDGE TO RESET COUNT REGISTER FOR INTERNAL CLOCKING.
PRESCALAR ON:
0 = TIMER COUNTS 1/4 CLKOUT WHEN INTERNAL CLOCK SELECTED.
1 = TIMER COUNTS TIMER 2 MAXCOUNTS WHEN INTERNAL CLOCK SELECTED.
EXTERNAL CLOCKING:
0 = INTERNAL CLOCK (CONTROLLED BY RTG).
1 = EXTERNAL CLOCK (COUNT TRANSITIONS ON INPUT PIN).
ALTERNATE COMPARE REGISTERS:
0 = ALWAYS USE A.
1 = USE A THEN B.
CONTINUOUS MODE:
0 = CLEAR EN BIT (STOP TIMER) AFTER EACH CYCLE.
1 = TIMER RUNS CONTINUOUSLY.
270830-001-62

Figure 6.2(d).

TIMER 2 CONTROL REGISTER:

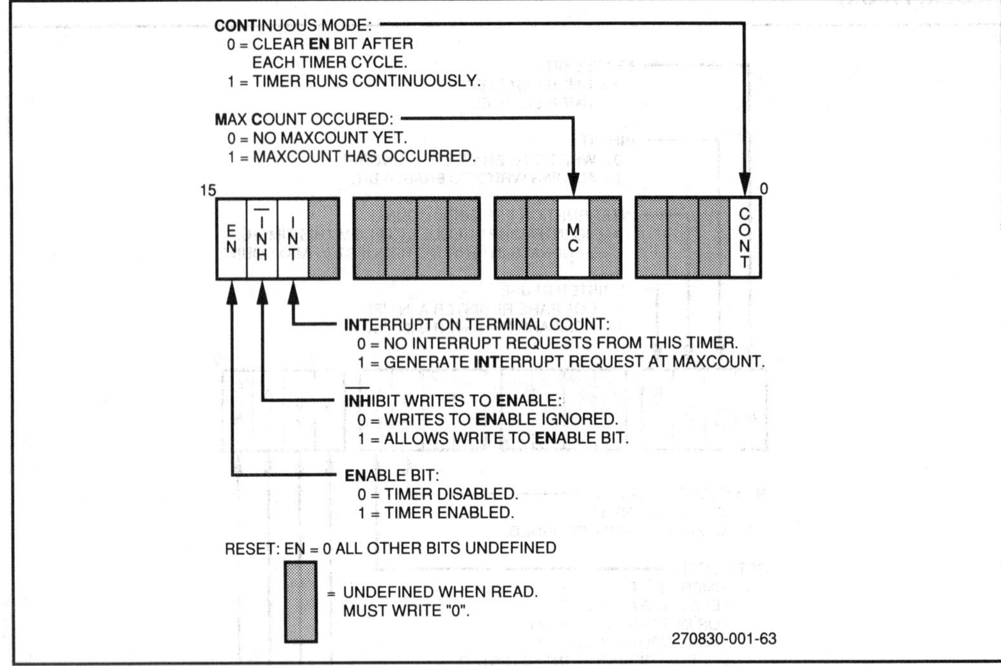

Figure 6.2(e).

6.1 FUNCTIONAL OVERVIEW

The internal Timer Unit on the 80C186EB family can be modeled by a single counter element, time-multiplexed to three register banks, each of which contains different control and count values. These register banks are, in turn, dual-ported between the counter element and the CPU (see Figure 6.1). Figure 6.3 shows the timer element sequencing and the subsequent constraints on input and output signals. There is no connection between the sequencing of the counter element through the timer register banks and the BIU's sequencing through T-states. Timer operation and bus interface operation are completely asynchronous.

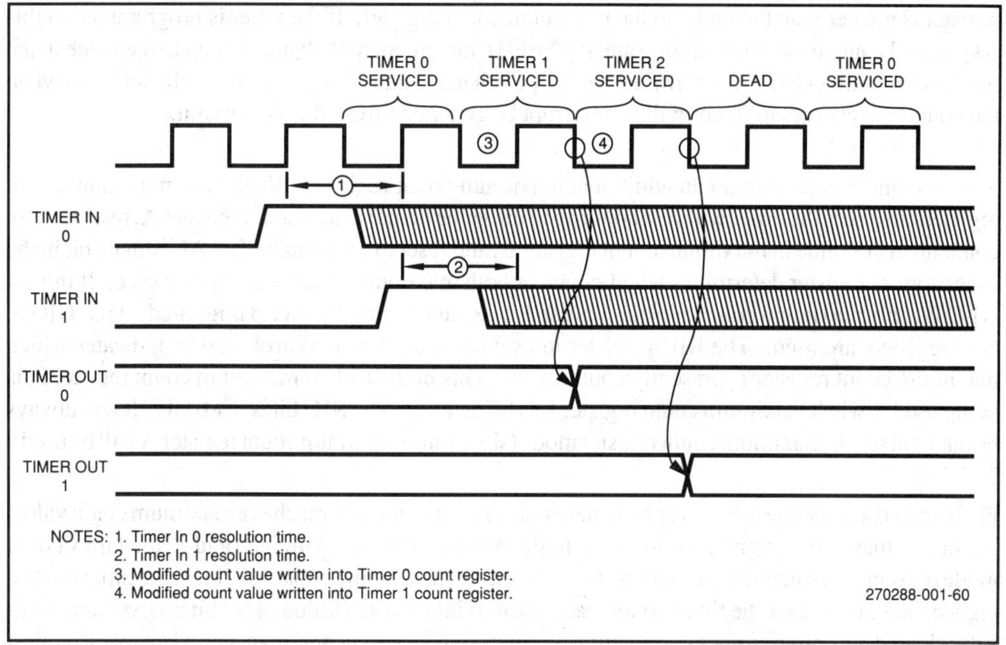

Figure 6.3. Counter Element Multiplexing and Timer Input Synchronization

Each timer is controlled by a register block (see Figure 6.2). Each of these registers can be read or written whether or not the timer is operating. All processor accesses to these registers are synchronized to all counter accesses to these registers, meaning that one will never read a count register in which only half of the bits have been modified.

The Bus Interface Unit automatically inserts one wait state for any access to the timer registers to perform this synchronization. LOCKing accesses to timer registers will not prevent the timer's counter elements from accessing the timer registers.

Each timer has a 16-bit count register which is incremented for each timer event. A timer event can be a LOW-to-HIGH transition on a timer input pin (for Timers 0 and 1), a pulse generated every fourth CPU Clock, or a time out of Timer 2 (for Timers 0 and 1). The count register is 16 bits wide, allowing up to 65536 (2^{16}) events to be counted. Upon RESET, the contents of the count registers are indeterminate and they should be initialized to zero before any timer operation.

Each timer includes a maximum count register. Whenever the timer count register is equal to the maximum count register, the count register resets to zero, so the maximum count value is never stored in the count register. This maximum count value may be written while the timer is operating. A maximum count value of 0 implies a maximum count of 65536, a maximum count value of 1 implies a maximum count of 1, etc. Only equivalence between the count value and the maximum count register value is checked. This means that the count value will not be cleared if the value in the count register is greater than the value in the maximum count register. If the timer is programmed in this way, it will count to the maximum count (0FFFFH), increment to 0, then count up to the value in the maximum count register. The terminal count (TC) bit in the timer control register will not be set when the counter overflows to 0, nor will an interrupt be generated from the Timer Unit.

Timers 0 and 1 each contain an additional maximum count register. When both maximum count registers are used, the timer will first count up to the value in maximum count register A, reset to zero, count up to the value in maximum count register B, and reset to zero again. The ALTernate bit in the timer control register determines whether one or both maximum count registers are used. If this bit is LOW, only maximum count register A is used; maximum count register B is ignored. If it is HIGH, both registers are used. The RIU (register in use) bit in the timer control register indicates which maximum count register is presently counting up. This bit is 0 when maximum count register A is being used, 1 when maximum count register B is being used. The RIU bit is read only. It will always be read 0 in single maximum count register mode (since only maximum count register A will be used).

Each timer can generate an interrupt whenever the timer count value reaches a maximum count value. All timers may use maximum count A in single max count mode. Timers 0 and 1 (dual max count mode) may also use maximum count B. In addition, the maximum count (MC) bit in the timer control register is set whenever the timer count reaches a maximum count value. This bit is never automatically cleared, i.e., programmer intervention is required. If a timer generates a second interrupt request before the first interrupt request has been serviced, the first interrupt request to the CPU will be lost.

Each timer has an ENable bit in the timer control register. The timer will count timer events only when this bit is set. Any write to the timer control register will modify the ENable bit only if the INHibit bit is also set. The INHibit bit in the timer control register allows selective updating of the timer ENable bit. The value of the INHibit bit is not stored in a write to the timer control register; it will always be read as logic zero.

Each timer has a CONTinuous bit in the timer control register. If this bit is cleared, the timer ENable bit will be automatically cleared at the end of each timing cycle. If a single maximum count register is used, the end of a timing cycle occurs when the count value resets to zero after reaching the value in maximum count register A. If dual maximum count registers are used, the end of a timing cycle occurs when the count value resets to zero after reaching the value in maximum count register B. If the CONTinuous bit is set, the ENable bit will never be automatically reset. Thus, after each timing cycle, another timing cycle will automatically begin. For example, in single maximum count register mode, the timer will count up to the value in maximum count register A, reset to zero, ad infinitum. In dual maximum count register mode, the timer will count up to the value in maximum count register A, reset to zero, count up to the value in maximum count register B, reset to zero, and repeat.

A flowchart of timer 0 and 1 operation can be found in Figure 6.4.

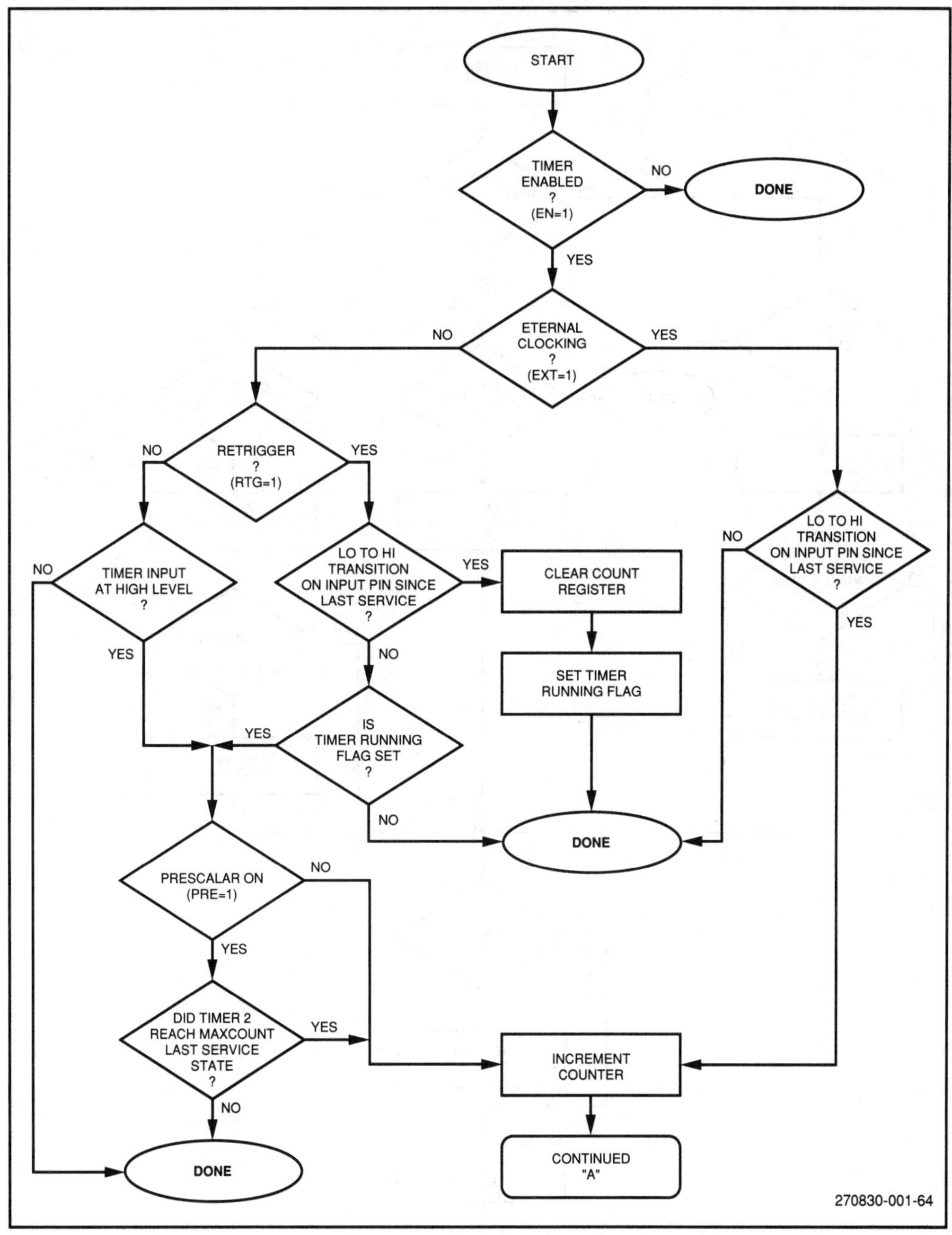

Figure 6.4(a). Timer 0 and 1 Flowchart.

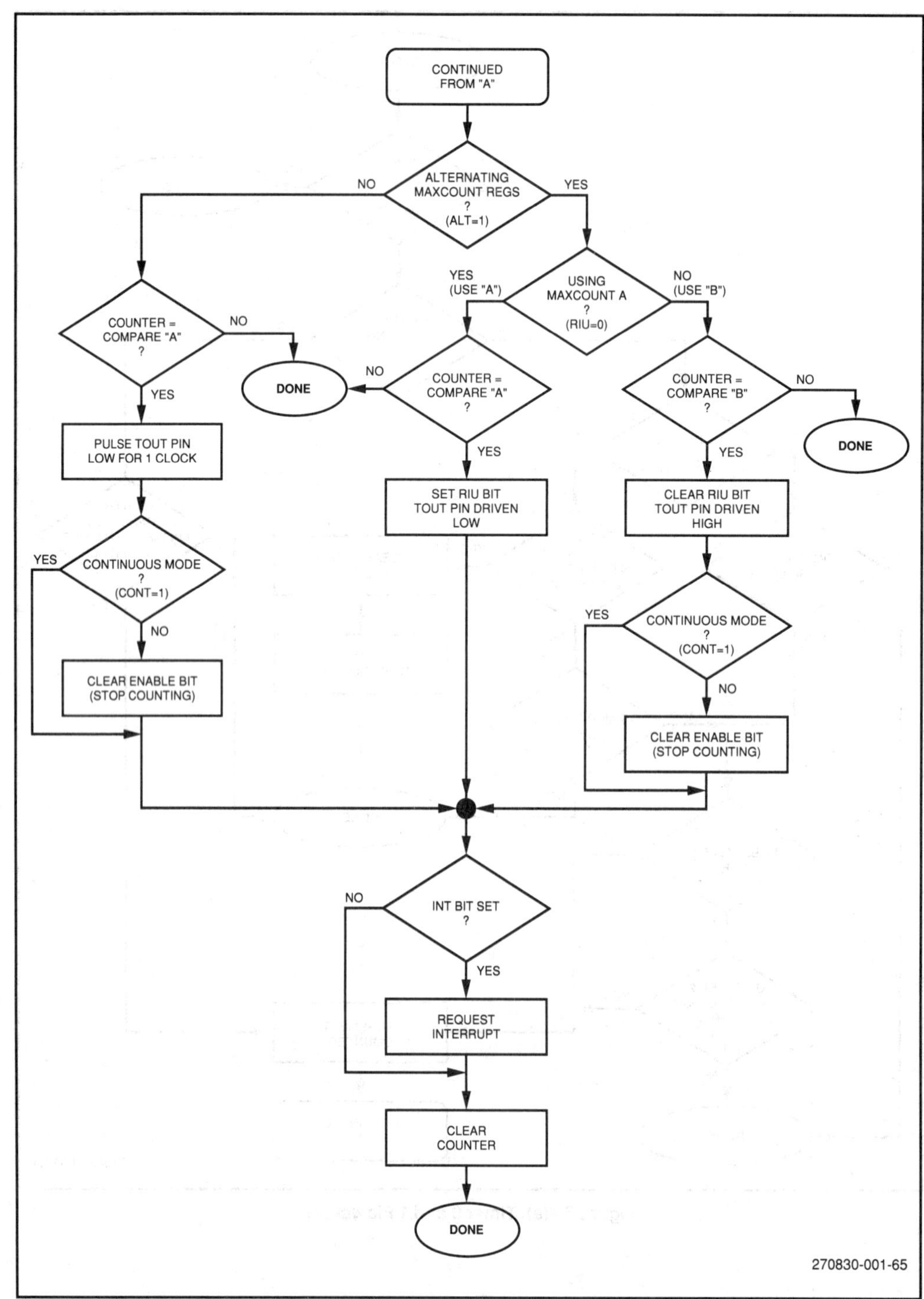

Figure 6.4(b). Timer 0 and 1 Flowchart (continued)

6.2 TIMER EVENTS

Each timer counts events. All timers can use a transition of the CPU clock as an event. If the internal clock is used, the count increments every fourth CPU clock because of timer element multiplexing. For Timer 2, this is the only timer event which can be used. For Timers 0 and 1, this event is selected by clearing the EXTernal and Prescaler bits in the timer control register.

Timers 0 and 1 can use Timer 2 reaching its maximum count as a timer event. This is selected by clearing the EXTernal bit and setting the Prescaler bit in the timer control register. When this is done, the timer will increment whenever Timer 2 resets to zero having reached its own maximum count. Note that Timer 2 must be initialized and running in order to increment the value in the other timer/counter.

Timers 0 and 1 can also be programmed to count LOW-to-HIGH transitions on the external input pin. Each transition on the external pin is synchronized to the 80C186EB family processor clock before it is presented to the timer circuitry (see Appendix B for information on synchronizers). The timer counts transitions on the input pin; the input value must go LOW, then HIGH, to cause the timer to increment. Transitions on this line are latched. The maximum count rate for the timer is 1/4 the CPU clock rate measured at CLKOUT.

6.3 TIMER INPUT PIN OPERATION

Timers 0 and 1 each have individual timer input pins. All LOW-to-HIGH transitions on these input pins are synchronized, latched, and presented to the counter element when the particular timer is being serviced by the counter element.

Signals on this input can affect timer operation in three different ways. The manner in which the pin signals are used is determined by the EXTernal and RTG (retrigger) bits in the timer control register. If the EXTernal bit is set, transitions on the input pin will cause the timer count value to increment if the timer is enabled (that is, the ENable bit in the timer control register is set). Thus, the timer counts external events. If the EXTernal bit is cleared, all timer increments are caused by either the CPU clock or by Timer 2 reaching its maximum count. In this mode, the RTG bit determines whether the input pin will enable timer operation, or whether it will retrigger timer operation.

When the EXTernal bit is LOW and RTG bit is also LOW, the timer will count internal timer events only when the timer input pin is HIGH and the ENable bit in the timer control register is set. Note that in this mode, the pin is level sensitive, not edge sensitive. A LOW-to-HIGH transition on the timer input pin is not required to enable timer operation. If the input is tied HIGH, the timer will be continually enabled. The timer enable input signal is completely independent of the ENable bit in the timer control register. Both must be HIGH for the timer to count. Examples of uses for the timer in this mode would be a real time clock or a baud rate generator.

When the EXTernal bit is LOW and the RTG bit is HIGH, every LOW-to-HIGH transition on the timer input pin causes the timer count register to reset to zero. This mode of operation can be used to generate a retriggerable digital one-shot. After the timer is enabled (i.e., the ENable bit in the timer control register is set), timer operation (counting) will begin only after the first LOW-to-HIGH transition of the timer input pin has been detected. If another LOW-to-HIGH transition occurs on the input pin before the end of the timer cycle, the timer will reset to zero and begin the timer cycle again. A timer cycle is defined as the time the timer is counting from zero to the maximum count (either max count A or max count B). This means that in the dual max count mode, the RIU bit is not set if the timer is reset by the LOW-to-HIGH transition on the input pin. Should a timer reset occur when RIU is set (indicating max count B), the timer will again begin to count up to max count B before resetting the RIU bit. Thus, when the ALTernate bit is set, a timer reset will retrigger (or extend) the duration of the current max count in use (which means that either the LOW or HIGH level of the timer output will be extended). If the CONTinuous bit in the timer control register is cleared, the timer ENable bit will automatically be cleared whenever a timer cycle has been completed (max count is reached). If the CONtinuous bit in the timer control register is set, the timer will reset to zero and begin another timer cycle whenever the current cycle has completed.

6.4 TIMER OUTPUT PIN OPERATION

Timers 0 and 1 each have a timer output pin which can perform two functions. The first is a single pulse indicating the end of a timing cycle. The second is a level indication of the maximum count register being used. The timer outputs operate as outlined below whether internal or external clocking of the timer is used. With external clocking, the time between a transition on the timer input pin and a corresponding transition on the timer output pin varies from 2 1/2 to 6 clocks. The exact timing depends on when the input transition occurs relative to timer service by the counter element.

When the timer is in single maximum count register mode, the timer output pin will go LOW for a single CPU clock one clock after the timer is serviced by the counter element when maximum count is reached (see Figure 6.5).

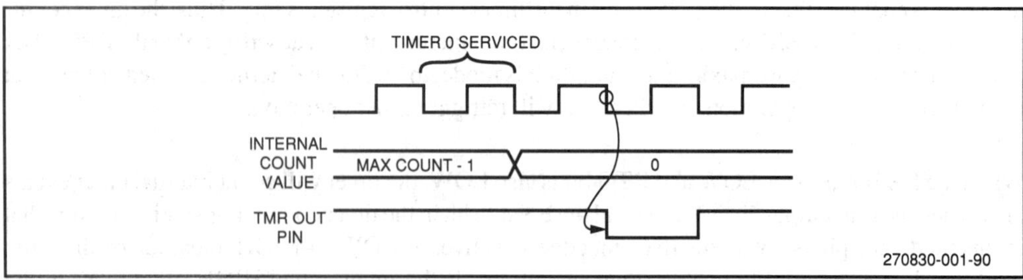

Figure 6.5. TxOUT Signal.

When the timer is programmed in dual maximum count register mode, the timer output pin indicates which maximum count register is being used. It is LOW if maximum count register B is being used and HIGH if maximum count register A is being used. The timer can generate a repetitive waveform if the CONTinuous bit in the timer control register is set. The frequency and duty cycle of this waveform is easily controlled by the programmer. For example, if maximum count register A contains 10, maximum count register B contains 20, and CLKOUT is 12.5 MHz, the timer generates a 33 per cent duty cycle waveform at 104 kHz. If the timer is programmed to halt upon maximum count, the output pin will go HIGH when the timer halts.

The timer output pins do not float during bus HOLD.

6.5 PROGRAMMING THE TIMER/COUNTER UNIT REGISTERS

Each timer is controlled through the use of at least three registers. The Timer Control Registers (T2CON, T1CON, and T0CON) control the functional modes for the timers. The Timer Count Registers (T2CNT, T1CNT, and T0CNT) hold the count value for the timers. The maximum count compare A registers hold the maxcount compare value for each timer (T0CMPA, T1CMPA, and T2CMPA). Timers 0 and 1 add two additional compare registers, T0CMPB and T0CMPA.

The compare and count registers have already been described. The following section describes the control register in detail.

6.5.1 THE TIMER CONTROL REGISTER (T0CON, T1CON, AND T2CON)

The timer 0 and 1 control registers contain 10 fields. Timer 2 uses only 5 fields since it lacks some of the functionality of the other timers.

The ten bit fields are as follows:

ALT:
The ALT bit determines which of two MAX COUNT registers is used for count comparison. If ALT=0, register A for that timer is always used, while if ALT=1, the comparison will alternate between register A and register B when each maximum count is reached. This alternation allows the user to change one MAX COUNT register while the other is being used, and thus provides a method of generating non-repetitive waveforms. Square waves and pulse outputs of any duty cycle are a subset of available signals obtained by not changing the final count registers. The ALT bit also determines the function of the timer output pin. If ALT is zero, the output pin will go LOW for one clock, the clock after the maximum count is reached. If ALT is one, the output pin will reflect the current MAX COUNT register being used (0/1 for B/A).

CONT:
Setting the CONT bit causes the associated timer to run continuously, while resetting it causes the timer to halt upon maximum count. If CONT=0 and ALT=1, the timer will count to the MAX COUNT register A value, reset, count to the register B value, reset, and halt.

EXT:
The external bit selects between internal and external clocking for the timer. The external signal may be asynchronous with respect to the 80C186EB family clock. If this bit is set the timer will count LOW-to-HIGH transitions for the input pin. If cleared, it will count an internal clock while using the input pin for control. In this mode, the function of the external pin is defined by the RTF bit. The maximum input to output transition latency time may be as much as 6 clocks. However, clock inputs may be pipelined as closely together as every 4 clocks without losing clock pulses.

P:
The prescaler bit is ignored unless internal clocking has been selected (EXT=0). If the P bit is a zero, the timer will count at one-forth the internal CPU clock rate. If the P bit is a one, the output of timer 2 will be used as a clock for the timer. Note that the user must initialize and start timer 2 to obtain the prescaled clock.

RTG:
Retrigger bit is only active for internal clocking (EXT=0). In this case it determines the control function provided by the input pin.

If RTG=0, the input level gates the internal clock on and off. If the input pin is HIGH, the timer will count; if the input pin is LOW, the timer will hold its value. As indicated previously, the input signal may be asynchronous with respect to the 80C186EB family clock.

When RTG=1 , the input pin detects LOW-to-HIGH transitions. The first such transition starts the timer running, clearing the timer value to zero on the first clock and then incrementing thereafter. Further transitions on the input pin will again reset the timer to zero, from which it will start counting up again. If CONT=0 when the timer has reached maximum count, the EN bit will be cleared, inhibiting further timer activity.

EN:
The enable bit provides programmer control over the timer's RUN/HALT status. When set, the timer is enabled to increment subject to the input pin constraints in the internal clock mode (discussed previously). When cleared, the timer will be inhibited from counting. All input pin transitions during the time EN is zero will be ignored. If CONT as zero, the EN bit is automatically cleared upon maximum count.

$\overline{\text{INH}}$:
The inhibit bit allows for selective updating of the enable (EN) bit. If $\overline{\text{INH}}$ is a one during the write to mode/control word, then the state of the EN bit will be modified by the write. If $\overline{\text{INH}}$ is a zero during

the write, the EN bit will be unaffected by the operation. This bit is not stored; it will always be a 0 on a read.

INT:
When set, the INT bit enables interrupts from the timer, which will be generated on every terminal count. If the timer is configured in dual MAX COUNT register mode, an interrupt will be generated each time the value in MAX COUNT register A is reached, and each time the value in MAX COUNT register B is reached. If this enable bit is cleared after the interrupt request has been generated, but before a pending interrupt is serviced, the interrupt request will still be in force. (The request is latched in the interrupt Controller.)

MC:
The Maximum Count is set whenever the timer reaches its final maximum count value. If the timer is configured in dual MAX COUNT register mode, this bit will be set each time the value in TxCMPA is reached, and each time the value in the TxCMPB is reached. The MC bit gives the user the ability to monitor timer status through software instead of through interrupts. Programmer intervention is required to clear this bit.

RIU:
The Register in Use bit indicates which MAX COUNT register is currently being used for comparison to the timer count value. A zero value indicates register A. The RIU bit cannot be written, i.e., its value is not affected when the control register is written. It is always cleared when the ALT bit is zero.

The following fields are not used for the T2CON register: ALT, EXT, P, RTG, and RIU. Note that these bits will return a zero when read.

6.6 EXAMPLE TIMER INITIALIZATION CODE

The 80C186EB family timers possess great flexibility. It is easy to program them as baud rate generators, digital one-shots, pulse width modulators, event counters, and pulse width measurement applications.

6.6.1 REAL TIME CLOCK

Example 1 contains sample code to initialize Timer 2 to generate interrupts every millisecond. The CPU then increments memory-based clock variables.

Example 1

```
$mod186
name                example_80186_family_timer_code
;
;   This file contains an example 80186 family timer routine to set
;       up the timer and interrupt controller to cause the timer to
;       generate an interrupt every 10 milliseconds, and to service
;       interrupts to implement a real time clock. Timer 2 is used
;       in this example because no input or output signals are
;       required. The code example assumes that the peripheral
;       control block has not been moved from its reset location
;       (FF00-FFFF in I/O space).
arg1            equ     word ptr [BP + 4]
arg2            equ     word ptr [BP + 6]
arg3            equ     word ptr [BP + 8]
timer_2 nt      equ     19                          ;timer 2 has vector type 19
T2CON       equ     0FF46H
T2CMPA      equ     0FF42H
T2CNT       equ     0FF40H
TCUCON      equ     0FF12H
EOI         equ     0FF02H                          ;interrupt controller reg
INTSTS      equ     0FF10H

data        segment public 'data'
            public  hour_, minute_,second_,mesc_.
mesc_.      db      ?
hour_.      db      ?
minute_.    db      ?
second_.    db      ?
data        ends

cgroup      group   code
dgroup      group   data

code        segment public_code_.
            public  set_time
            assume  cs:code, ds:dgroup
;
;           set_time(hour,minute,second)
;           sets the time variables, initializes timer 2 to pro-
;           vide interrupts every 10 milliseconds, and programs
;           the interrupt vector for timer 2
;
set_time    proc    near                    ;set stack addressability
            enter 0.0                       ;save registers used
            push    AX
            push    DX
            push    SI
            push    DS
            xor     AX,AX                   ;set the interrupt vector
                                            ;the timers have unique
                                            ;interrupt vectors even though
                                            ;they share the same control
                                            ;register
            mov     DS,AX
            mov     SI,4*timer_2int
            mov     word ptr DS:[SI],offset timer_2_interrupt_routine
            inc     SI
            inc     SI
            mov     DS:[SI],CS
            pop     DS

            mov     AX,arg1                 ;set the time values
            mov     hour_,AL
            mov     X,arg2
```

```
          mov     minute_,AL
          mov     AX,arg3
          mov     second_,AL

          mov     msec_,0
          mov     DX,T2CNT                ;clear the
          xor     AX,AX                   ;count
          out     DX,AX                   ;register

          mov     DX,T2CMPA               ;set the max count vlaue
          mov     AX,2000                 ;10mx/500 ns(timer 2 counts
                                          ;at 1/4 the CPU clock rate)
          out     DX,AX
          mov     DX,T2CON                ;set up the control word
          mov     AX,1110000000000001b    ;enable counting,generate
                                          ;interrupts on TC, continuous
                                          ;counting
          out     DX,AX

          mov     dx,TCUCON               ;set up the interrupt
                                          ;controller
          mov     AX,0000b                ;unmask interrupts highest
                                          ;priority interrupt
          out     DX,AX
          sti                             ;enable processor interrupts

          pop     SI
          pop     DX
          pop     AX
          leave
          ret
set_time  endp

timer_2_interrupt_routine   proc  far
                            push  AX
                            push  DX

                            cmp   msec_,99      ;see if one second has
                                                ;passed
                            jae   bump_second   ;if above or equal...
                            inc   mesc_.
                            jmp   reset_int_ctl
bump_second:
                            move  mesc_,0       ;reset millisecond
                            cmp   minute_,59    ;see if one minute has
                                                ;passed
                            jae   bump_minute
                            inc   second_.
                            jmp   reset_int_ctl
bump_minute:
                            move  second_,0
                            cmp   minute_,59    ;see if one hour has
                                                ;passsed
                            jae   bump_hour
                            inc   minute_.
                            jmp   reset_int_ctl
                            pop   DX
                            pop   AX
                            ret
bmp_hour:
                            mov   minute_,0
                            cmp   hour_,12      ;see if 12 hours have
                                                ;passed
                            jae   reset_hour
                            inc   hour_.
                            jmp   reset_int_ctl
```

```
reset_hour:
                                mov    hour_,1
reser_int_ctl:
                                mov    DX,EOI
                                mov    AX,8000h          ;non-specific end of
                                                         ;interrupt
                                out    DX,AX

                                pop    DX
                                pop    AX
                                iret
timer_2_interrupt_routine       endp
code                            ends
                                end
```

270288-001-63

6.6.2 EVENT COUNTER

An 80C186EB family timer can count events using the timer input pins. Sample code for such an application is shown in Example 2.

Example 2

```
$mod186
name                example_80186_family_timer_code
;
;   This file contains an example 80186 family timer routine to set
;       up the timer as an external event counter. In this mode,
;       Timer 1 is used to count transitions on its input pin. After
;       the timer has been set up by the routine, the number of
;       events counted can be directly read from the timer count
;       register. The timer will count a maximum of 65535 timer
;       events before wrapping around to zero. This code example
;       also assumes that the peripheral control block has not been
;       moved from its reset location (FF00-FFFF in I/O space).
;
T1CON       equu    0FF3EH
T1CMPA      equ     0FF3AH
T1CNT       equ     0FF38H

code        segment public'code'
            assume  cs:code
;
;           set_count() initializes the 80186 timer 1 as an event
;           counter
;
set_count   proc    near                    ;save registers used
            push    AX
            push    DX

            mov     DX,T1CMPA               ;set the max count value
            mov     AX,0                    ;allows the timer to count
                                            ;all the way to FFFFH
            out     DX,AX
            mov     DX,T1CON                ;set the control word
            mov     AX,1100000000000101b    ;enable counting
                                            ;no interrupt on TC
                                            ;continuous counting
                                            ;single max count register
                                            ;external clocking
            out     DX,AX
```

```
            xor     DX,T1CNT              ;zero AX
            mov     DX,T1CNT              ;and zero the count in the
                                          ;timer
            out     DX,AX
            pop     DX
            pop     AX
            ret

set_count   endp
code        ends
            end
```

270288-001-65

Chip Select/Ready Logic Unit 7

CHAPTER 7
CHIP SELECT/READY LOGIC UNIT

The 80C186EB contains an integrated Chip Select and Ready Logic Unit capable of supplying chip select signals for up to ten memory and peripheral devices. The Chip Select Unit (CSU) can often eliminate the need for external chip select decoding logic in small to medium sized systems (see Figure 7.1). READY signal generation, needed for slower memory or peripheral devices, is integrated into the CSU.

The CSU is an extremely flexible unit. The ten chip selects are all identical and completely independent in operation. Two PCB registers define the operational characteristics of each channel (20 total registers).

Each chip select is active for a programmable **active range** in either memory or peripheral (I/O) space. The chip selects can be individually disabled under software control. An enabled chip select line becomes active low whenever the Bus Interface Unit accesses a location (memory or I/O) within the channel's active range. Channels configured for memory accesses can select ranges in 1K byte increments from 0 to the full 1 megabyte of physical memory. Those channels configured for I/O accesses can select ranges in 64 byte increments from 0 to the full 64K byte size of I/O space.

Chip select ranges may overlap. Overlapping chip selects will all become active during accesses to their shared ranges. This allows for the easy implementation of shadowed and paged memory. Devices can share the same physical address space and be selectively enabled by software. The user could configure the CSU for up to **ten megabytes** of software paged memory without external paging hardware.

The granularity of the CSU is not fixed as it is with many popular external decoding schemes. Typically, a simple external chip select decoding scheme will select one of several equally sized ranges. The CSU can select **varying** sized ranges. This allows for optimization of the full memory and peripheral space.

Each chip select has integrated programmable READY logic. This logic can automatically insert between 0 and 15 wait states into bus cycles accessing memory or I/O locations within a chip select's range. If greater than 15 waits states are required the READY pin can be used to extend the bus cycle indefinitely.

The integrated chip select unit has advantages beyond reducing the chip count of a system. Externally generated chip selects are delayed from a valid address by the propagation delay of the decoding circuitry. Chip select signals generated by the CSU become active at the same time as the address. This time savings can, in some instances, allow the use of slower memory devices **without** the insertion of wait states.

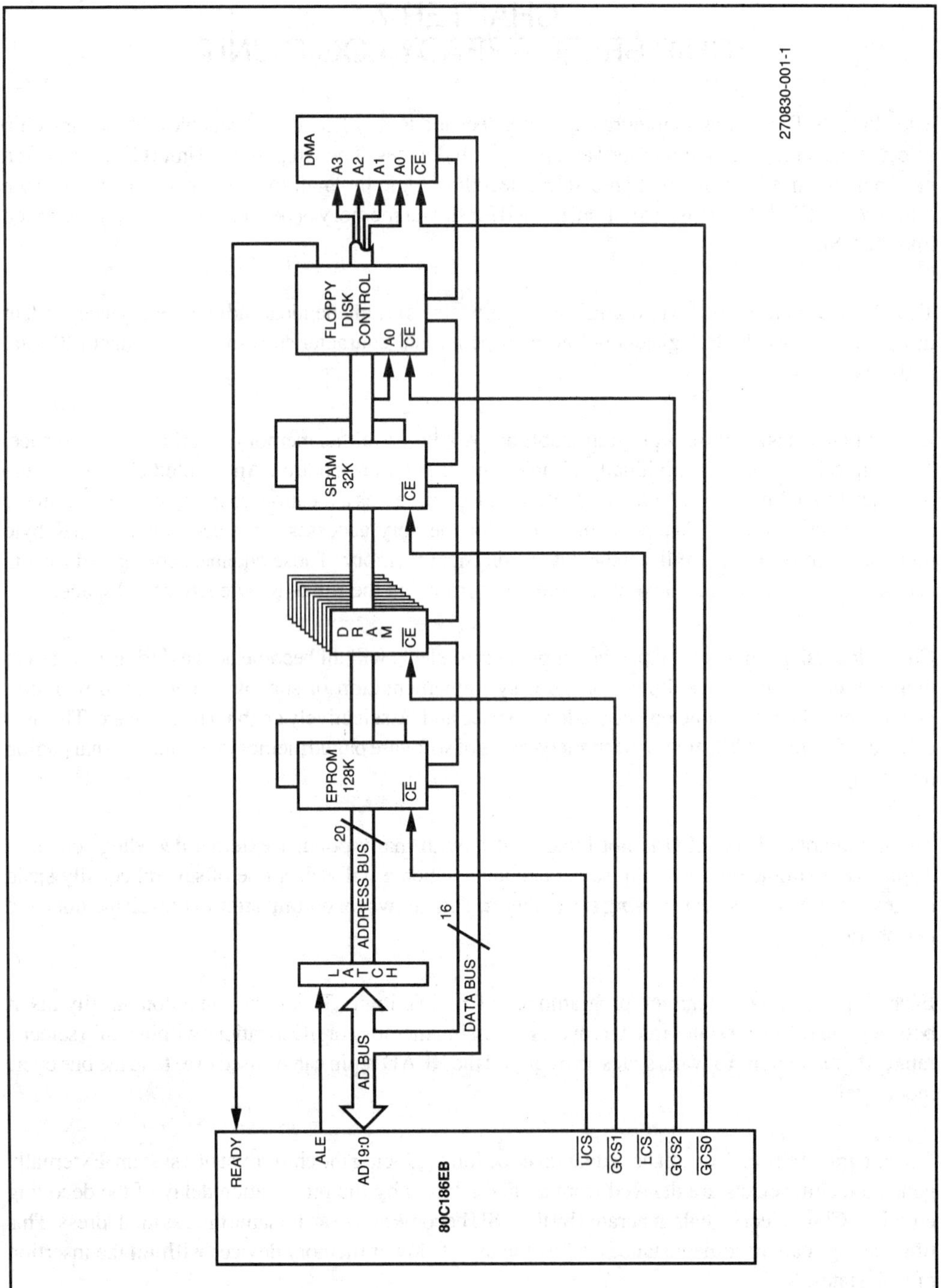

Figure 7.1. Chip Select Unit Typical Application

The Chip Select Unit will generate chip select signals **only** for accesses generated by the CPU (BIU cycles and DRAM refresh cycles). An external bus master must supply its own chip select signals. See Section 7.1.5 below for a discussion of external bus masters.

The Chip Select Unit PCB map and summary of register operation is shown in Figure 7.2.

REGISTER NAME	OFFSET
GCS0ST	80H
GCS0SP	82H
GCS1ST	84H
GCS1SP	86H
GCS2ST	88H
GCS2SP	8AH
GCS3ST	8CH
GCS3SP	8EH
GCS4ST	90H
GCS4SP	92H
GCS5ST	94H
GCS5SP	96H
GCS6ST	98H
GCS6SP	9AH
GCS7ST	9CH
GCS7SP	9EH
LCSST	A0H
LCSSP	A2H
UCSST	A4H
UCSSP	A6H

Figure 7.2(a). PCB Map for Chip Select Unit

CHIP SELECT CHANNEL START REGISTERS: (UCSST, LCSST, GCS0ST through GCS7ST)

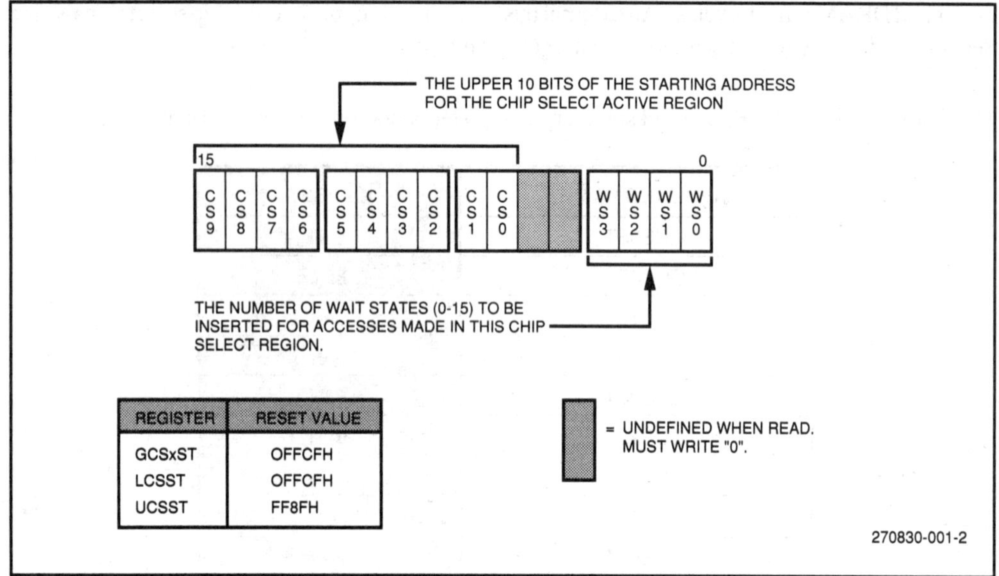

REGISTER	RESET VALUE
GCSxST	OFFCFH
LCSST	OFFCFH
UCSST	FF8FH

Figure 7.2(b).

CHIP SELECT CHANNEL STOP REGISTERS: (UCSSP, LCSSP, GCS0SP through GCS7SP)

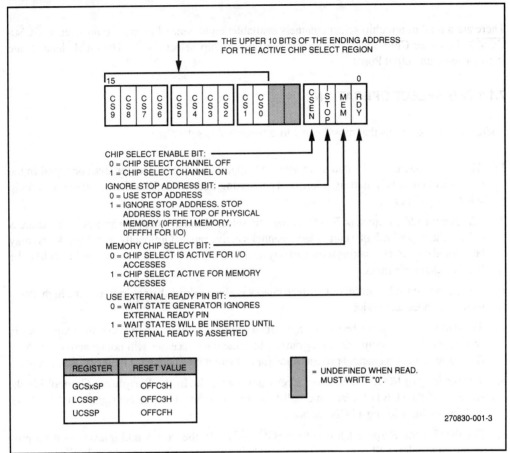

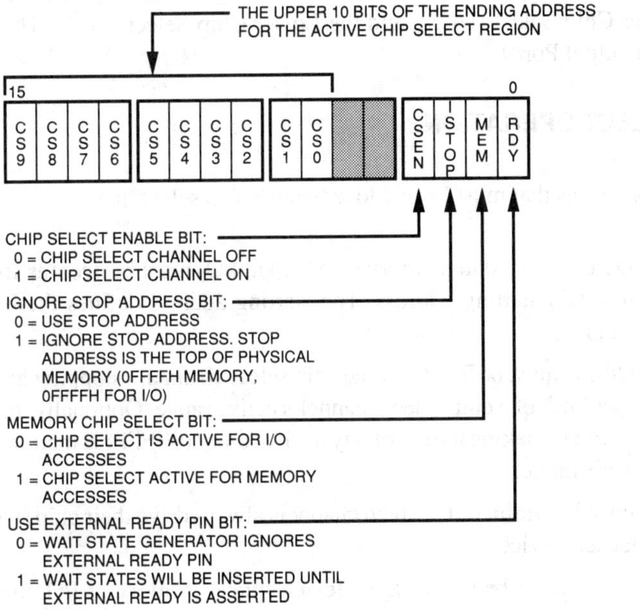

REGISTER	RESET VALUE
GCSxSP	0FFC3H
LCSSP	0FFC3H
UCSSP	0FFCFH

Figure 7.2(c).

7.1 FUNCTIONAL OVERVIEW

There are a total of ten chip select channels available: eight general purpose chip selects ($\overline{GCS0}$-$\overline{GCS7}$), the Upper Chip Select ($\overline{UCS}$), and the Lower Chip Select ($\overline{LCS}$). The $\overline{GCS}$ channels are multiplexed with output Port 1.

7.1.1 CHIP SELECT OPERATION

There are five conditions that must be met to activate a chip select line:

1. The current address (A19:0 in memory or A15:0 in I/O) must be **greater than or equal to** the chip select channel's starting address. The starting address defines the beginning of a chip select's active range.
2. The current address must be **less than** the chip select channel's stopping address. This address defines the upper limit of a chip select channel's active range. Optionally, the stop address may be ignored effectively making the top of physical memory (0FFFFFH memory; 0FFFFH I/O) the end of a channel's range.
3. The channel must be **enabled.** Disabled channels always drive their chip select line high, deselecting the attached device.
4. The current access must be to the same **device space**, memory or I/O, that the chip select is programmed for. A chip select programmed for memory accesses will not be active for IN or OUT instructions; a channel programmed for I/O will not be active for memory accesses.
5. The memory or I/O location being accessed **must not be in the Peripheral Control Block**. Accesses to the PCB take place internally and do not require a chip select signal. All CSU lines will remain high during a PCB access.
6. For the General Purpose Chip Selects ($\overline{GCS7}$-$\overline{GCS0}$), the Port 1 multiplexer must be programmed to select CSU functions (see the I/O Unit section of this manual for details).

Every chip select channel that meets all these criteria will become active for a given 80C186EB bus cycle. Since each channel is independent, it is possible to have more than one channel active at a time. The operation of **overlapping channels** is explained below. A logic block diagram describing chip select operation is shown in Figure 7.3.

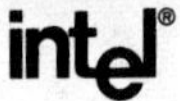

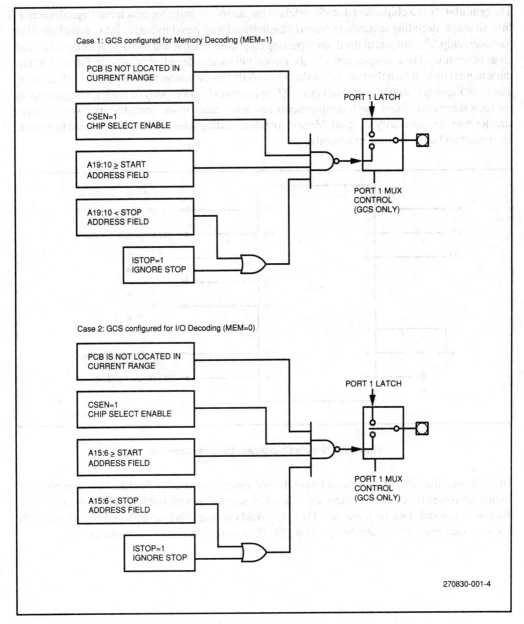

Figure 7.3. CSU Logic Block Diagram

The **granularity** of a chip select decoder refers to the size of the range for which each signal is active. In most simple decoding schemes a portion of the high order address bits are fed into a demultiplexing (decoder) chip. The outputs of the demultiplexing chip would then select one of several equally sized areas of memory. For example, consider the typical chip select decoding scheme in Figure 7.4. The three highest order bits of the memory address bus (A19:17) are connected to a 74138 3 to 8 decoder. The resulting chip selects would result in 8 128K byte ranges (a granularity of 128K). The granularity for such schemes is fixed. Such arrangements can leave holes in the memory map when devices smaller than the granularity are used. More elaborate decoding schemes could be devised to provide for greater and more flexible granularity.

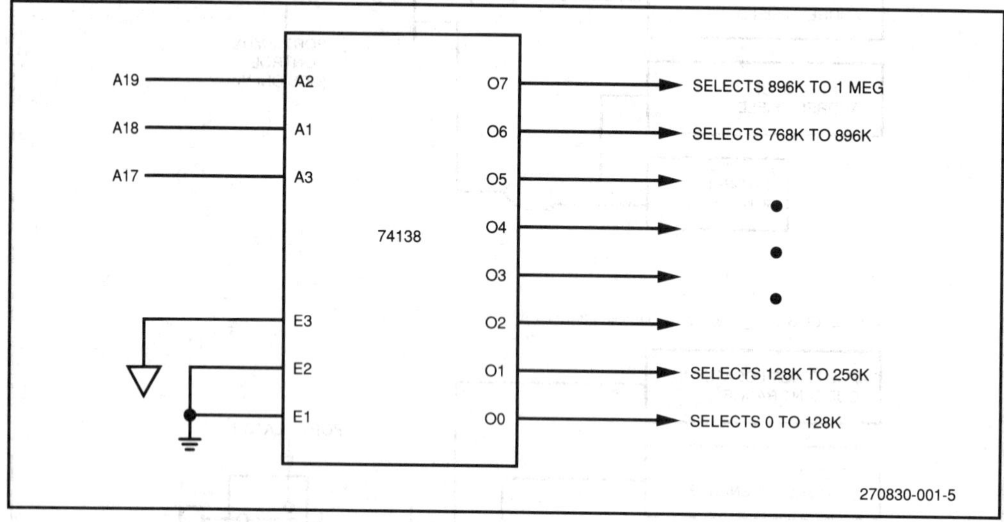

Figure 7.4. Simple Chip Select Decoder Example

The CSU uses the 10 most significant bits of the address to decode each channel. The beginning and ending addresses for each chip select are defined by separate ten bit fields in 2 PCB registers. The lower bits are fixed at zero in hardware. The ten bit field width results in a minimum granularity of 1K bytes for memory accesses and 64 bytes for I/O. The example in Figure 7.5 illustrates this.

EXAMPLE A: MEMORY ADDRESSING

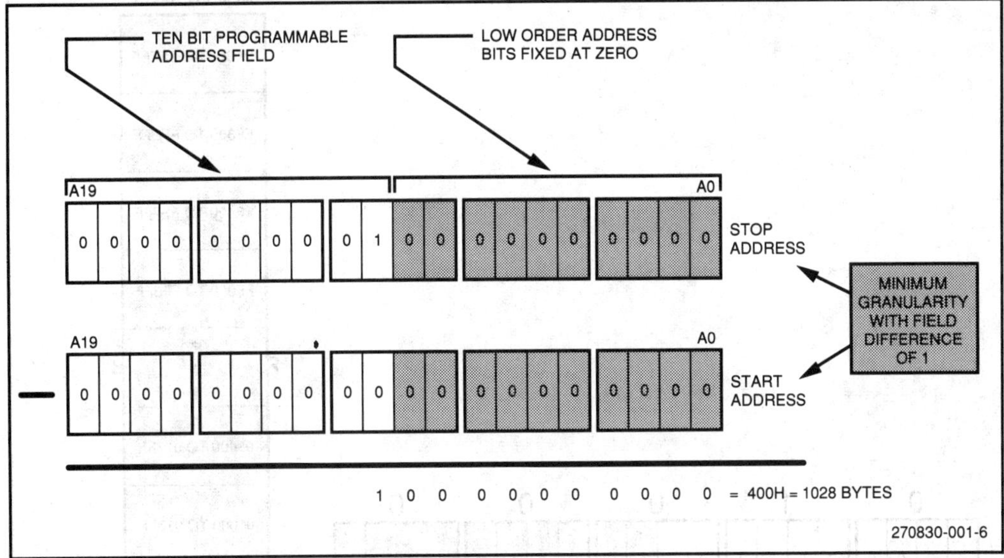

Figure 7.5(a).

EXAMPLE B: PERIPHERAL ADDRESSING

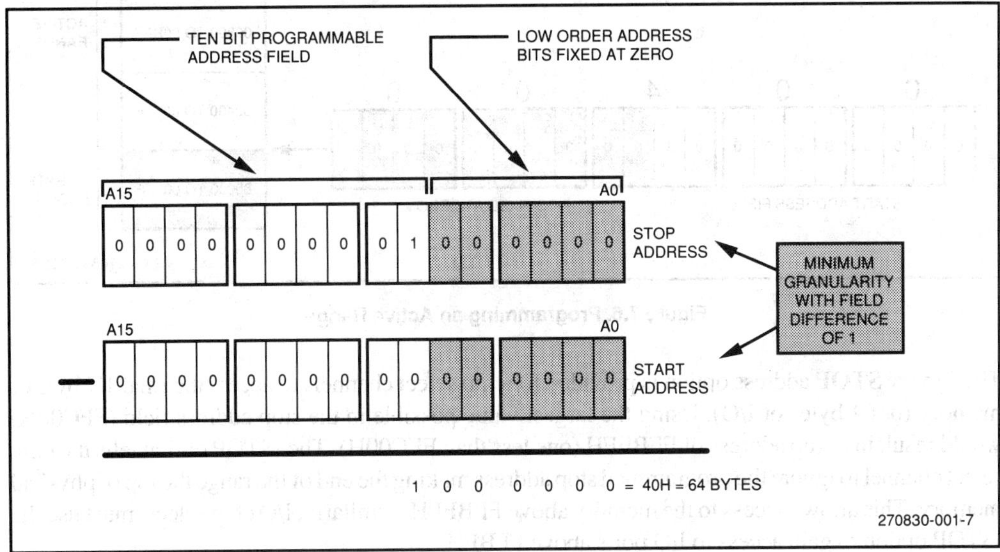

Figure 7.5(b).

Active ranges all begin on modulo 1K boundaries for memory and modulo 64 byte for I/O. The end of a chip select range is one less than the stop address (unless the ignore stop address option is selected). Figure 7.6 illustrates how the starting and stopping address fields are used to select the active range for a chip select.

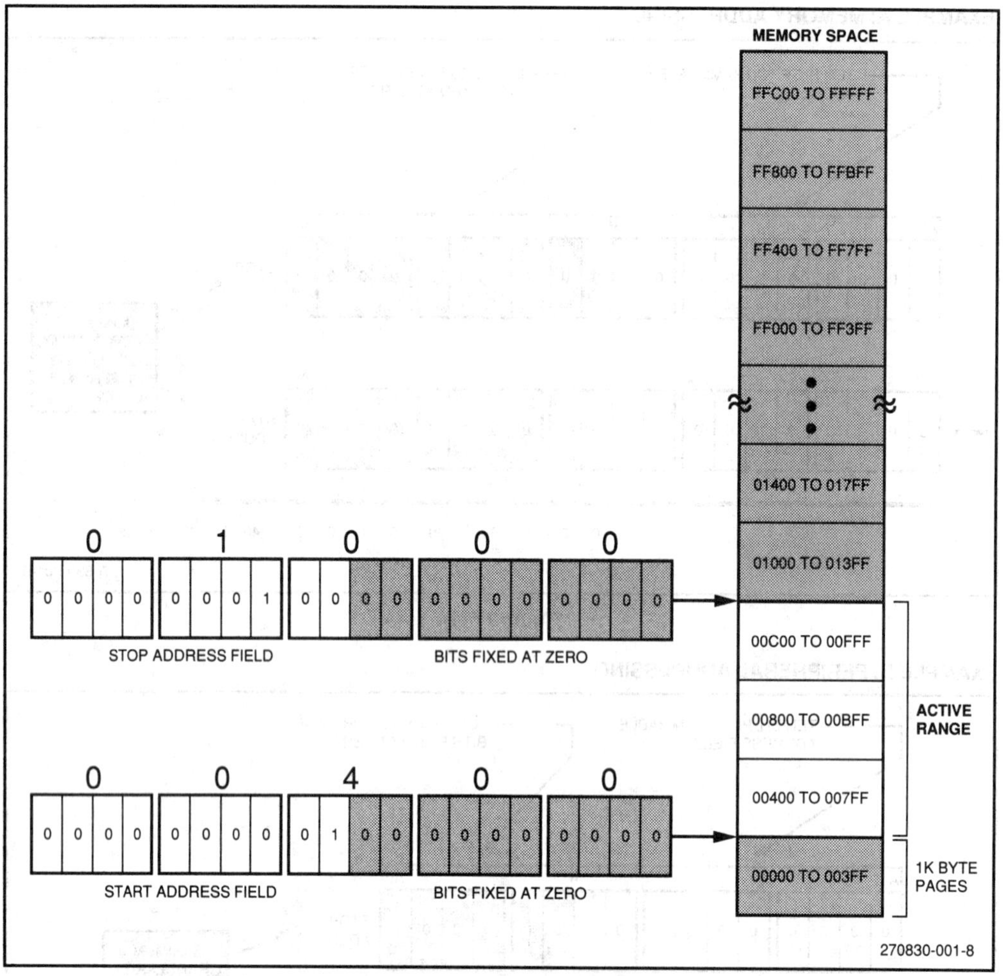

Figure 7.6. Programming an Active Range

The **Ignore STOP** address option is provided for chip select channels to access the final 1K byte of memory (or 64 bytes of I/O). Using the largest value possible in the stop address field (FFC00H) would result in a stop address of FFBFFH (one less than FFC00H). The ISTOP option tells the chip select channel to ignore the programmed stop address making the end of the range the top of physical memory. This allows access to the memory above FFBFFH. Similarly, I/O chip selects must use the ISTOP option to gain access to I/O ports above FFBFH.

7.1.2 READY GENERATION AND WAIT STATE INSERTION

Each channel has an associated wait state/ready logic circuit. For any accesses within a chip select's range, between 0 and 15 wait states will automatically be inserted into the bus cycle. With the READY control **enabled**, the programmed number of wait states will be inserted then control will pass to the

READY pin. Wait states will continue to be inserted until READY is asserted. With READY control **disabled**, only the programmed number of wait states will be inserted; the state of the READY pin is ignored.

Proper READY signal interfacing is explained in the Bus Interface Unit section.

7.1.3 OVERLAPPING RANGES

Chip select channels are permitted to have overlapping active ranges. An access to an overlapping range results in **all** of the **enabled** overlapping chip selects becoming active. If all the overlapping channels ignore external READY, then the **maximum** programmed number of wait states will be inserted by the BIU. If one or more are programmed for external READY control, the **minimum** number of programmed wait states are inserted after which control is passed to the READY signal.

As an example, consider the following three chip selects:

$\overline{\text{UCS}}$:	Active Range = 0 to 0FFFFFH in memory Enabled with 5 wait states, NO external READY
$\overline{\text{GCS0}}$:	Active Range = 01000H to 01400H in memory Enabled with 3 wait states, NO external READY
$\overline{\text{GCS3}}$:	Active Range = 0400H to 01800H in memory Enabled with 1 wait state, NO external READY

Any access to the overlapping region (01000H to 013FFH) will result in all chip selects going active and 5 wait states inserted in the cycle. As a second example, let's assume $\overline{\text{GCS0}}$ required external READY (though still with 3 wait states programmed). In this case an access to the overlapping region would again result in all chip selects going active. This time, however, only **one** wait state is inserted; control then passes to external READY. Once READY is asserted the bus cycle completes.

7.1.4 PORT 1 MULTIPLEXER

$\overline{\text{GCS7}}$ through $\overline{\text{GCS0}}$ are multiplexed with output port 1 functions. The Port 1 Control registers must be properly programmed for the $\overline{\text{GCS}}$ signals to appear at the package pins. Refer to the I/O Ports section of this manual for further information.

7.1.5 EXTERNAL BUS MASTERS

The Chip Select Unit is active **only** for internally generated bus accesses. These include any opcode fetch, memory or I/O access, or DRAM refresh cycle. Any bus cycles generated by an external master will not cause the chip selects to go active. During a bus HOLD sequence the chip selects will not float, but will instead remain in their inactive HIGH state. Systems utilizing external bus masters will require the logic shown in Figure 7.7 to generate the proper chip select signals.

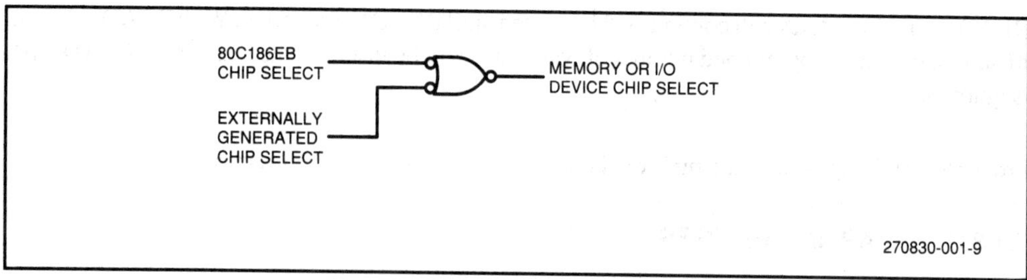

Figure 7.7. CS Generation with External Bus Masters

7.1.6 NUMERICS I/O LOCATIONS (I/O LOCATIONS 00F8H TO 00FFH)

The interface between the 80C186EB and the 80C187 numerics processor extension makes use of the I/O ports located between 00F8H and 00FFH. Programming a chip select with an active range that includes these locations is not recommended.

7.1.7 CSU TIMINGS

The decision to activate a particular chip select is performed just after the effective address calculation is completed. Both of these events occur **before** the address appears on the bus. The address and chip select signals are gated on to the bus simultaneously in T1. The status lines (S2:0) become valid one half a cycle earlier. The status lines can be combined with the chip selects to create early read and write selects for slow memory and peripheral devices.

The relative timings for the address lines, chip selects, and status lines can be found in Figure 7.8.

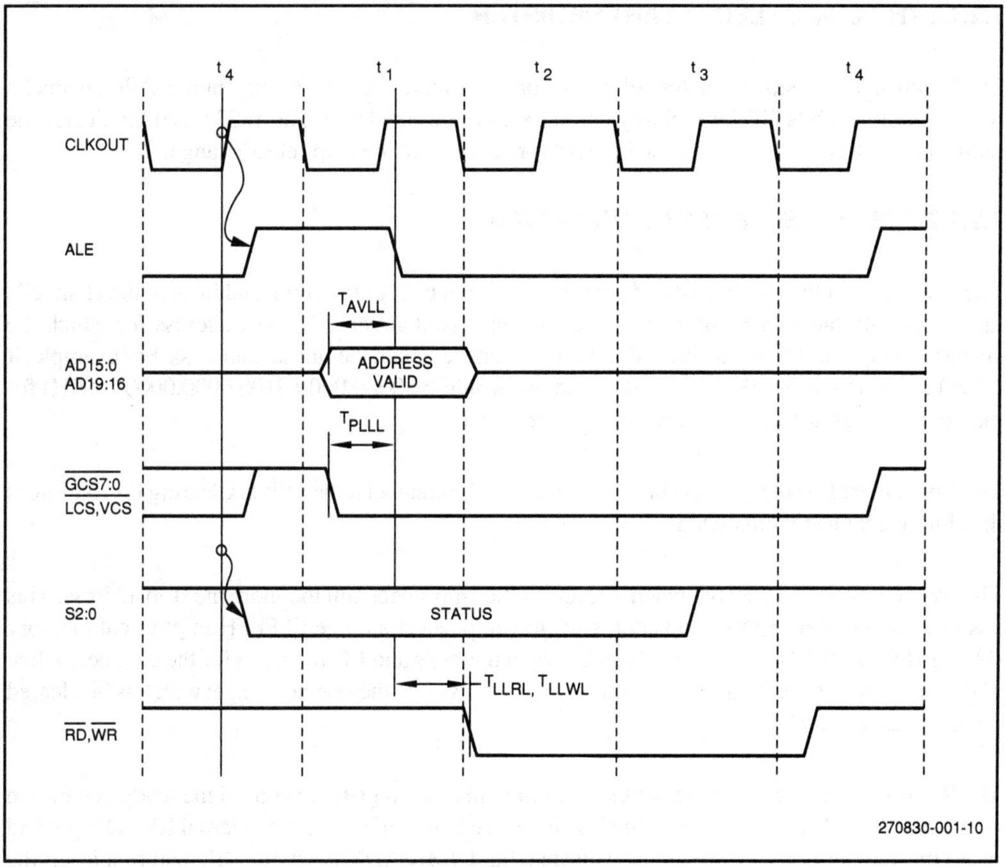

Figure 7.8. CSU Relative Timings

7.2 PROGRAMMING THE CSU

7.2.1 THE CHIP SELECT REGISTERS

Two PCB registers are used to program each channel. The chip select start registers (GCS0ST to GCS7ST, UCSST, and LCSST) define both the starting address for a chip select and the desired number of wait states. The chip select stop registers (GCS0SP to GCS7SP, UCSSP, LCSSP) define the ending address for a chip select's range as well as selecting the READY, ignore stop address, memory/peripheral, and enable options (Figure 7.2).

7.2.1.1 THE CHIP SELECT START REGISTER

The CS9:0 bits of the **start register** define the upper ten address bits for the beginning of the channel's range. The lower bits (10 for memory and 6 for I/O) are fixed at 0. The WS3:0 field indicates the number of wait states (0 to 15) to be inserted for accesses in the chip select's range.

7.2.1.2 THE CHIP SELECT STOP REGISTER

The CS9:0 bits of the **stop register** define the upper ten bits for the ending address of the channel's range. As with the start register, the lower bits are fixed at zero. The last address for which the channel's chip select line is active will actually be one less than the full stop address. For example, if CS9:0 contained 0000.0000.01 the stop address would be 0000.0000.0100.0000.0000 (400H) for memory. The last active address would then be 3FFH.

The Chip Select ENable (CSEN) bit must be set for the channel to be active. Clearing this bit forces the chip select line to remain high.

The Ignore STOP (ISTOP) bit, when set, forces the chip select unit to ignore the stop address. This has the effect of making the stop address of the chip select's range FFFFFH in physical memory (0FFFFH for I/O). The MEM bit selects between memory and I/O mapping for the channel. When MEM is set the channel will be active for memory accesses in the selected range; with this bit cleared it will be active for I/O.

The READY bit is used with the wait state field in the start register to control the ready generation circuitry. When READY is cleared the Bus Interface Unit will ignore the external READY pin and insert the number of wait states in the wait state field. If READY is set, the BIU will first insert the programmed number of wait states then transfer control to the READY pin. The bus cycle is extended until READY is asserted.

7.3 INITIAL CONDITIONS (RESET)

Following a RESET only $\overline{\text{UCS}}$ is enabled. The active range for $\overline{\text{UCS}}$ after reset is from FFC00H to FFFFFH in memory. This allows for the fetching of the initialization code at FFFF0H. Fifteen wait states are inserted and external READY control is enabled. Systems using external READY should be sure this line is valid during RESET. Systems not using READY should tie this pin high.

The Port 1 multiplexer selects the CSU as the source of data following a RESET.

Figure 7.2 shows the initial values for all of the CSU registers.

7.4 APPLICATIONS EXAMPLES

The following sections illustrate two potential applications of the CSU. The first is a small system with 3 separate memory selects and 2 I/O selects. The second example shows how bank switching can be used to access 2 megabytes of DRAM through a 512K byte window.

The following sections are provided as examples of CSU programming. As such the examples do not go into detailed timing analysis or hardware design issues.

7.4.1 EXAMPLE 1: SIMPLE CSU APPLICATION

The system shown in Figure 7.1 is a typical small 80C186EB system utilizing ROM, 2 separate banks of RAM, a Floppy Disk controller, and a DMA controller. The schematic has been simplified showing only the connections necessary for memory and I/O access. Detailed information on memory and I/O device connection can be found in the bus interface unit section.

The ROM occupies 128K bytes (64K words) from E0000H to FFFFFH (3 wait states, no external READY). The low RAM is 32K bytes and is located from 0H to 7FFFH (0 wait states, no external READY). The middle RAM is 64K bytes located at 10000H (1 wait state, no READY). At 0H in I/O space is the DMA controller with 16 total locations (2 wait states, no READY). The Floppy Disk controller is at 40H using 1 location. The Floppy Disk controller requires external READY. A memory map is shown in Figure 7.9.

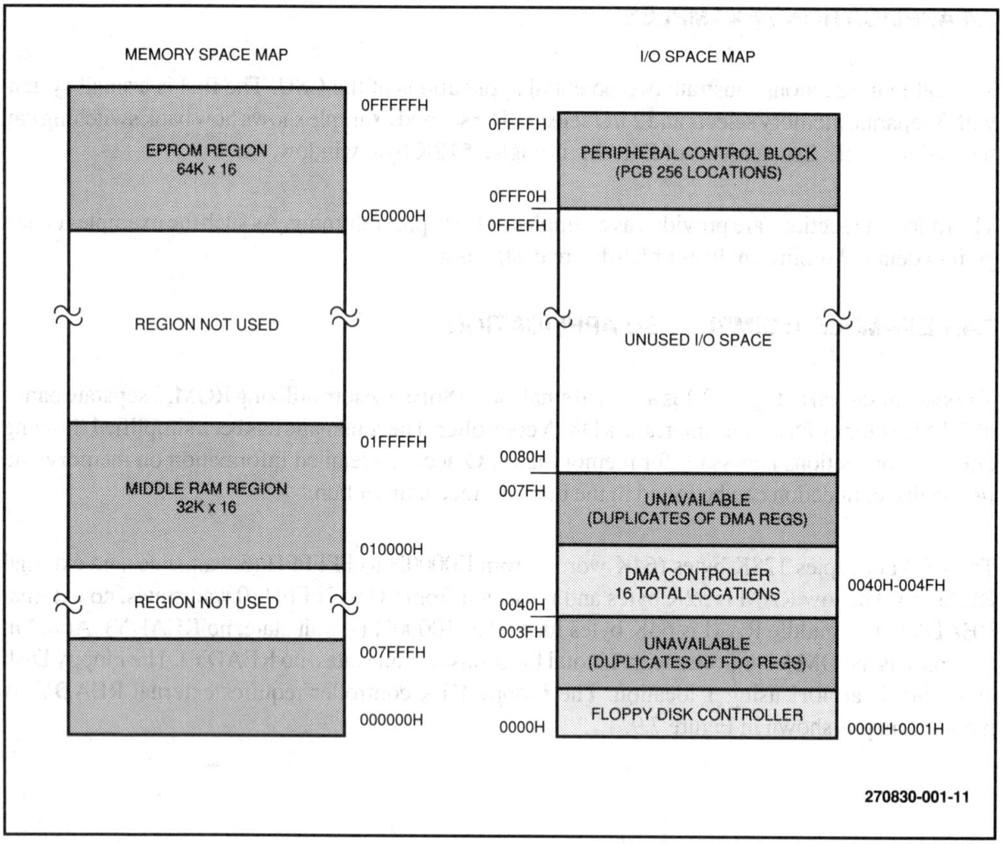

MEMORY SPACE MAP

0FFFFFH
EPROM REGION 64K x 16
0E0000H
REGION NOT USED
01FFFFH
MIDDLE RAM REGION 32K x 16
010000H
REGION NOT USED
007FFFH
000000H

I/O SPACE MAP

0FFFFH
PERIPHERAL CONTROL BLOCK (PCB 256 LOCATIONS)
0FFF0H
0FFEFH
UNUSED I/O SPACE
0080H
007FH
UNAVAILABLE (DUPLICATES OF DMA REGS)
DMA CONTROLLER 16 TOTAL LOCATIONS 0040H-004FH
0040H
003FH
UNAVAILABLE (DUPLICATES OF FDC REGS)
FLOPPY DISK CONTROLLER 0000H-0001H
0000H

270830-001-11

Figure 7.9. Memory Map for Example 1

The first step in setting up the CSU is assigning chip select channels to the individual memory and I/O blocks. The selection is arbitrary with the exception of $\overline{UCS}$. Since $\overline{UCS}$ is the only channel enabled at reset, it must select the ROM in which the boot code resides. The remainder of the devices are assigned as follows: low RAM is selected by $\overline{LCS}$, middle RAM is selected by $\overline{GCS1}$, the DMA controller is selected by $\overline{GCS0}$, and the disk controller is selected by $\overline{GCS2}$.

Example 1

```
$mod186
name csu_initialization_example

;
; This file contains an example of initialization code for
; the Chip Select Unit on the 80C186EB.
;

reset  segment at 0FFFFh            ; The 80C186EB resets to
                                    ; 0FFFF0H.

       jmp          far ptr initialize
reset  ends

; A new segment is located at FFF0:0H. The UCS channel is active
; down to FFC0:0 after reset. We do not need to jump this far for
; the setup. By jumping to FFF0:0 we stay within the active region
; of UCS. By not jumping all the way down to FFC0:0 we keep from
; fragmenting the ROM. We have 240 bytes from FFF0:0 to FFFF:0 in
; which to perform our initialization.

UCSST    EQU        0FFA4H          ; UCS START ADDRESS REG
UCSSP    EQU        0FFA6H          ; UCS STOP ADDRESS REG
LCSST    EQU        0FFA0H          ; LCS START ADDRESS REG
LCSSP    EQU        0FFA2H          ; LCS STOP ADDRESS REG
GCS0ST   EQU        0FF80H          ; GCS0 START
GCS0SP   EQU        0FF82H          ; GCS0 STOP
GCS1ST   EQU        0FF84H          ; GCS1 START
GCS1SP   EQU        0FF86H          ; GCS1 STOP
GCS2ST   EQU        0FF88H          ; GCS2 START
GCS2SP   EQU        0FF8AH          ; GCS2 STOP
GCS3ST   EQU        0FF8CH          ; GCS3 START
GCS3SP   EQU        0FF8EH          ; GCS3 STOP
P1CON    EQU        0FF54H          ; Port 1 mux control

init_seg    segment           at 0FFF0H
            assume cs:init_seg

initialize proc  far
    mov         dx, UCSST
    mov         ax, 0E003H          ; UCS begins at E000:0
    out         dx, ax              ; and requires 3 wait states
    mov         dx, UCSSP
    mov         ax, 0FFFEH          ; disable external ready
    out         dx, ax              ; control. Top of range
                                    ; is set at FFFF:F. Chip
                                    ; select is enabled. ISTOP=1.


    mov         dx, LCSST
    mov         ax, 00H             ; LCS starts at 0H
    out         dx, ax              ; and requires no wait states
    mov         dx, LCSSP           ; or external ready.
    mov         ax, 080AH           ; LCS ends at 07FFFH.
    out         dx, ax
```

Example 1 (Continued)

```
        mov         dx, GCS1ST
        mov         ax, 0101H             ; GCS1 starts at 10000H
        out         dx, ax                ; with 1 wait state.
        mov         dx, GCS1SP            ; GCS1 stops at 1FFFFH
        mov         ax, 020AH             ; ENabled for memory.

; All of the memory chip selects have now been set up. The next thing
; to do is set up the I/O chip selects.

        mov         dx, GCS0ST            ; This CS selects the DMA chip.
        mov         ax, 0042H             ; Starts at 40H; 2 wait states.
        out         dx, ax
        mov         dx, GCS0SP            ; Stop at 7FH, I/O mapped.
        mov         ax, 0088H             ; ENabled, no external READY.

        mov         dx, GCS2ST            ; This CS is for FDC system.
        mov         ax, 000FH             ; Starts at 0H; 15 wait states.
        out         dx, ax
        mov         dx, GCS2SP            ; Stops at 3FH, I/O mapped.
        mov         ax, 0049H             ; ENabled, use READY.

; The I/O chip selects have now been set up and enabled.

        jmp         far ptr program_code      ; jump to program code

initialize endp

init_seg    ends

code_seg    segment         at 0E000H
    assume cs:code_seg

program_code:       NOP

; program continues here........

code_seg    ends
end
```

Figure 7.10 contains the ASM186 code to properly initialize the CSU for this application. The 80C186EB begins fetching instructions at FFFF:0H immediately after reset. The $\overline{\text{UCS}}$ channel is active after reset with a range of FFC00H to FFFFFH in memory. The $\overline{\text{UCS}}$ is also programmed for 15 wait states **with external READY**. READY must be asserted for the boot code to be fetched. In this system the boot ROM requires 3 wait states with no external READY. For an in depth discussion of READY usage please refer to the Bus Interface Unit section.

The first instruction executed following reset is a JMP to location FFE00H (still within the $\overline{\text{UCS}}$ range). FFC00H was not jumped to in order to save contiguous memory space. The PCB is not being relocated for this example so it resides at FF00H in I/O space. The UCSST register has start field of 1110.0000.00 (E0000H start address) and a wait state field of 2 (2 wait states). The UCSSP register has the stop field programmed to 0 but the ISTOP bit is set making the stop address FFFFFH. In addition the MEM bit is set (memory chip select) and the READY bit is cleared (no external READY). Finally the CSEN bit is set to keep the $\overline{\text{UCS}}$ enabled. The $\overline{\text{LCS}}$ register is set up similarly in the following instructions.

Next, the middle RAM is set up. The same procedure is used as for $\overline{\text{UCS}}$ and $\overline{\text{LCS}}$. The setup for the peripherals follows; the only difference being in the programming of the MEM bit and the READY bit for the floppy disk controller.

The CSU initialization sequence is now completed. The program jumps to location E0000H to continue execution.

7.4.2 EXAMPLE 2: TWO MEGABYTE SOFTWARE PAGED RAM

Example 2 illustrates how the CSU can be used to extend the 80C186EB addressing capability beyond 1 megabyte through the use of software paging.

The paged memory array is shown in Figure 7.11. Each page is 512K bytes arranged as 256K x 16. The actual implementation of the memory is not pertinent to this example. Each page is enabled by a separate $\overline{\text{GCS}}$ line, $\overline{\text{GCS0}}$ through $\overline{\text{GCS3}}$. The four pages all occupy the same 512K space, or **window**, in physical memory from 10000H to 7FFFFH.

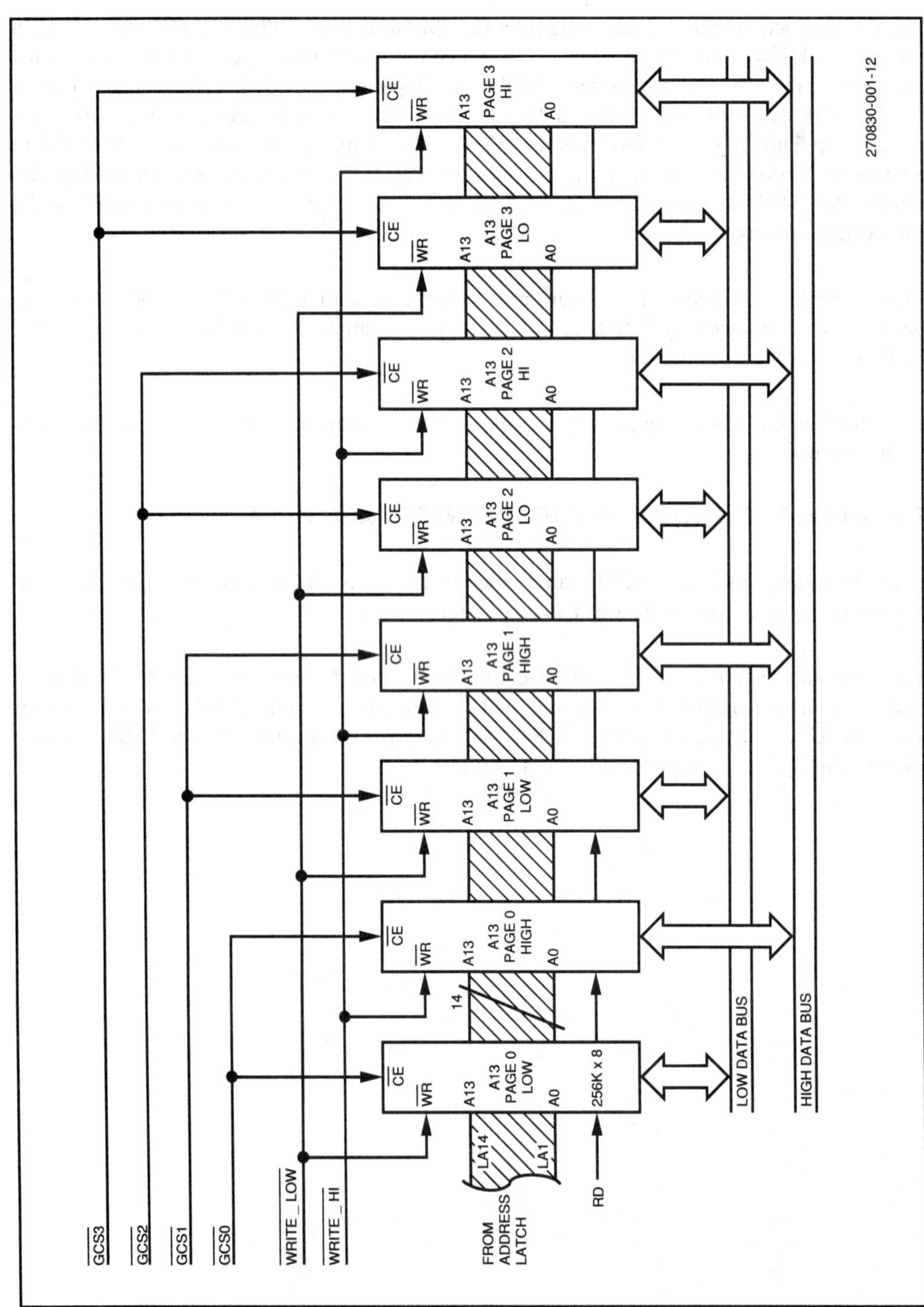

Figure 7.11. Paged memory Block Diagram

Two procedures are used in the paging implementation (Figure 7.12). The first procedure, SET_UP_PAGES, initializes the $\overline{GCS0}$ through $\overline{GCS3}$ channels. All four channels occupy the same memory space with zero wait states. The channels are all disabled when the procedure is exited.

The second procedure, SELECT_PAGE, enables the individual pages. The page to be enabled is passed on the stack by the calling program. Only one page is enabled at a time; enabling multiple pages would result in bus contention. If a page other than 0 through 3 is selected all pages will be disabled.

Example 2

```
$mod186
name csu_paged_memory_example
;
; This file contains an example of a paged memory implementation
; with the Chip Select Unit on the 80C186EB.
;

    UCSST       EQU     0FFA4H      ; UCS START ADDRESS REG
    UCSSP       EQU     0FFA6H      ; UCS STOP ADDRESS REG
    LCSST       EQU     0FFA0H      ; LCS START ADDRESS REG
    LCSSP       EQU     0FFA2H      ; LCS STOP ADDRESS REG
    GCS0ST      EQU     0FF80H      ; GCS0 START
    GCS0SP      EQU     0FF82H      ; GCS0 STOP
    GCS1ST      EQU     0FF84H      ; GCS1 START
    GCS1SP      EQU     0FF86H      ; GCS1 STOP
    GCS2ST      EQU     0FF88H      ; GCS2 START
    GCS2SP      EQU     0FF8AH      ; GCS2 STOP
    GCS3ST      EQU     0FF8CH      ; GCS3 START
    GCS3S       EQU     0FF8EH      ; GCS3 STOP
    P1CON       EQU     0FF54H      ; Port 1 mux control

; This example uses 2 procedures: SET_UP_PAGES and SELECT_PAGE.
; It is assumed that proper initialization of the other chip selects
; has already been accomplished.

; This code also assumes that the PCB is still located in I/O space
; at 0FF00H.

code_seg    segment
            assume cs: code_seg

;*****************************************
;**  PROC:   SET_UP_PAGES              **
;**                                    **
;**  PARAMETERS:  NONE                 **
;**                                    **
;**  FUNCTION:  Sets up 4 overlap-     **
;**  pages in memory from 10000H       **
;**  to 8FFFFH.  Leaves all of         **
;**  disabled.                         **
;*****************************************

SET_UP_PAGES        proc    far

    mov     ax, 0100H           ; The pages start at 10000H.
                                ; No wait states.
    mov     dx, GCS0ST          ; Set all pages the same.
    out     dx, ax
    mov     dx, GCS1ST
    out     dx, ax
    mov     dx, GCS2ST
```

Example 2 (Continued)

```
        out       dx, ax
        mov       dx, GCS3ST
        out       dx, ax
        mov       ax, 9002H                      ; Pages stop at 90000H.
                                                 ; They are DISABLED (CSEN=0).
                                                 ; Memory mapped without
                                                 ; external READY.
        mov       dx, GCS0SP                     ; Set up all pages the same.
        out       dx, ax
        mov       dx, GCS1SP
        out       dx, ax
        mov       dx, GCS2SP
        out       dx, ax
        mov       dx, GCS3SP
        out       dx, ax

;  The next step is programming the Port 1 Control to allow GCS0-3 to
;  appear at the package pins.  We must perform a READ-MODIFY-WRITE
;  so that any previous setups for the other GCS pins are not
;  affected.

        mov         dx, P1CON
        in          ax, dx                       ; read the previous setup
        or          ax, 00001111B                ; Set the lower 4 bits
                                                 ; to select GCS lines
                                                 ; at the package pins.
        out         dx, ax

; At this point the 4 Chip selects share the overlapping region
; 10000H to 8FFFFH, a total of 512K bytes.  They are all disabled.

        ret

SET_UP_PAGES        ENDP

;***********************************
;**  PROC:   SELECT_PAGE         **
;**                              **
;**  PARAMETERS:  Passes page    **
;**  number on the stack.        **
;**  FUNCTION:  Accepts page     **
;**  number then enables the     **
;**  selected page.  If page     **
;**  does not exists (>3) all    **
;**  pages will be disabled.     **
;***********************************

SELECT_PAGE proc  far
                                                 ; first, disable
                                                 ; all pages to prevent
                                                 ; connection.

        mov         dx, GCS0SP                   ; Read current setup.
        in          ax, dx
        and         ax, 0FFF7H                   ; Turn off CSEN bit.
        out         dx, ax                       ; Repeat for other 3
        mov         dx, GCS1SP                   ; channels.
        out         dx, ax
        mov         dx, GCS2SP
        out         dx, ax
        mov         dx, GCS3SP
        out         dx, ax
        mov         bp, sp
```

Example 2 (Continued)

```
    mov        ax, [bp+4]           ; [bp+4] points to page number
                                    ; stored on the stack above
                                    ; CS:IP.

    cmp        ax, 3
    jg         invalid page         ; If the page is not between
                                    ; 0 and 3 THEN shut them all
                                    ; off.

; Since the stop registers we will be modifying are sequential the
; following alogorithm may be used to calculate the I/O address:
;  Page stop register address = GCS0SP address + page * 2

    imul       ax, 2                 ; Calculate offset into PCB.
    add        ax, GCS0SP
    mov        dx, ax

; Now we enable the selected page.  A READ-MODIFY-WRITE is used to
; set just the enable bit without affecting any others.

    in         ax, dx
    or         ax, 0008H             ; set CSEN bit
    out        dx, ax

invalid_page:

    ret        2                     ; return and clean up
                                     ; stack

SELECT_PAGE endp

code_seg    ends
end
```

Serial Communications Unit 8

CHAPTER 8
SERIAL COMMUNICATIONS UNIT

The Serial Communications Unit of the 80C186EB contains two independent channels. The Serial Communications Unit (SCU) can implement several different serial communications protocols: Synchronous mode is used to expand the I/O capability of the 80C186EB by communicating with serial I/O peripherals, the asynchronous modes all implement the standard "start bit-data-stop bit" protocol. The asynchronous data frame size is programmable between seven and nine bits. Parity generation/checking and break detection/transmission are additional features available in the asynchronous modes. The synchronous and asynchronous modes both have the "Clear-To-Send" feature. Clear-To-Send control allows external devices to selectively enable the transmitter.

The serial ports on the 80C186EB can be readily interfaced with those found on a wide variety of embedded controller (e.g. MCS-51, MCS-96) and data communications devices. Several different processors and systems can be connected to a common serial bus using a multiprocessor protocol (see 8.1.1.3.2). Such serial networks are attractive in systems where full parallel bus connectivity is either impossible or impractical.

A block diagram of the Serial Communications Unit is shown in Figure 8.1. The two serial channels are identical in operation although only channel 0 is supported by the integrated interrupt controller. The interrupt request signal from channel 1 can be routed to an output pin through the port 2 multiplexer. Each channel generates an interrupt request when either a reception or a transmission is completed. Both channels have independent baud rate generators that can use either the CPU clock or an external clock as their time base.

Communication between the Serial Communications Unit and the CPU takes place through several Peripheral Control Block (PCB) registers. The PCB map and a summary of register operation is shown in Figure 8.2.

8.1 FUNCTIONAL OVERVIEW

The operation of the Serial Communications unit is logically divided between the synchronous and asynchronous modes. The following discussions apply to both channels. Programming of the SCU is described in Section 8.2.

8.1.1 ASYNCHRONOUS COMMUNICATION

The asynchronous serial communication modes (Modes 1 through 4) of the 80C186EB follow the industry standard "start bit-data-stop bit" protocol. Data is transmitted and received in serial **frames**. A frame is a sequence of bits shifted serially on to (or off of) the communication line. The **baud rate** of a channel is the number of bits per second shifted on to the line. The amount of time that each bit is valid is called the "bit-time" (equal to 1/baudrate).

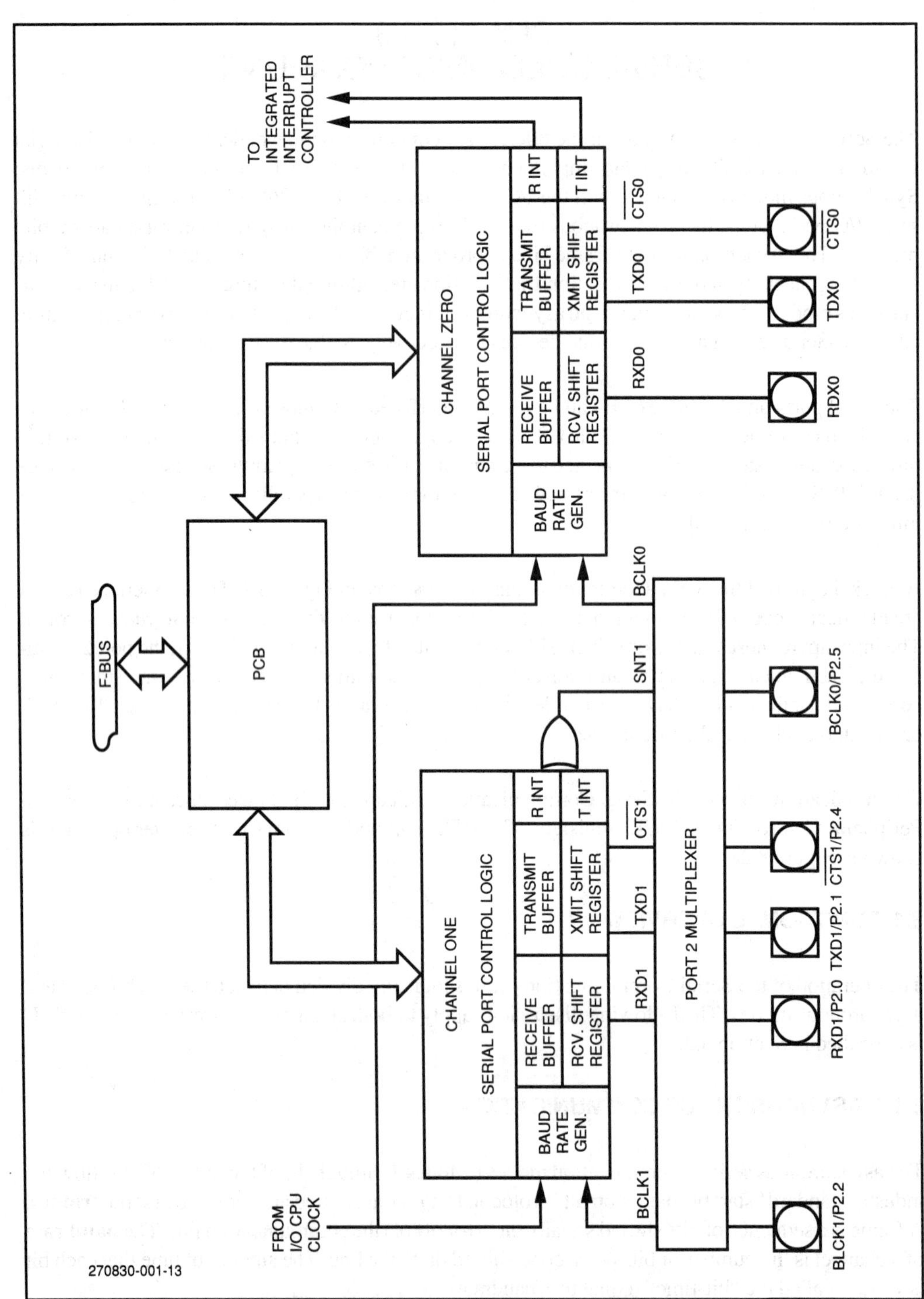

Figure 8.1. SCU Block Diagram

REGISTER NAME	OFFSET
B0CMP	60H
B0CNT	62H
S0CON	64H
S0STS	66H
S0RBUF	68H
S0TBUF	6AH
RESERVED	6CH
RESERVED	6EH
B1CMP	70H
B1CNT	72H
S1CON	74H
S1STS	76H
S1RBUF	78H
S1TBUF	7AH

Figure 8.2(a)

BAUD RATE COMPARE REGISTERS: (B0CMP, B1CMP)

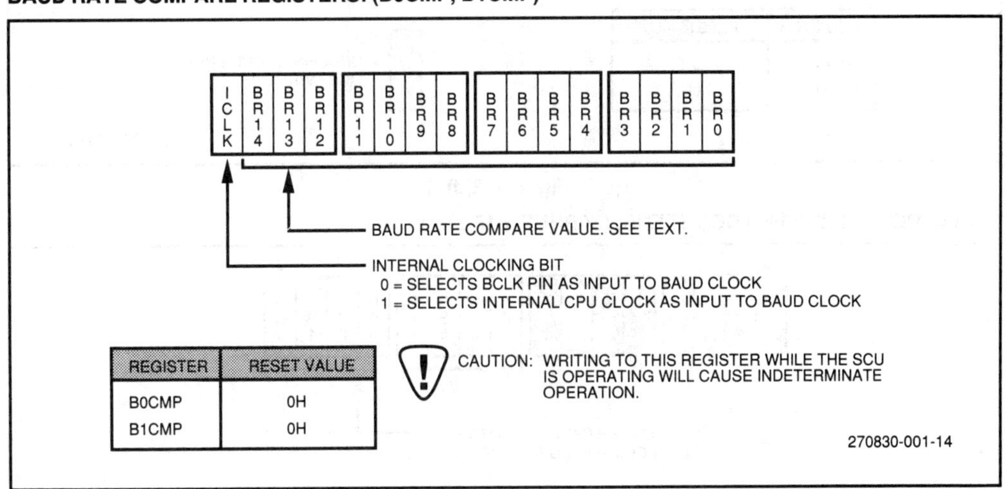

REGISTER	RESET VALUE
B0CMP	0H
B1CMP	0H

Figure 8.2(b).

BAUD RATE COUNTER REGISTERS: (B0CNT, B1CNT)

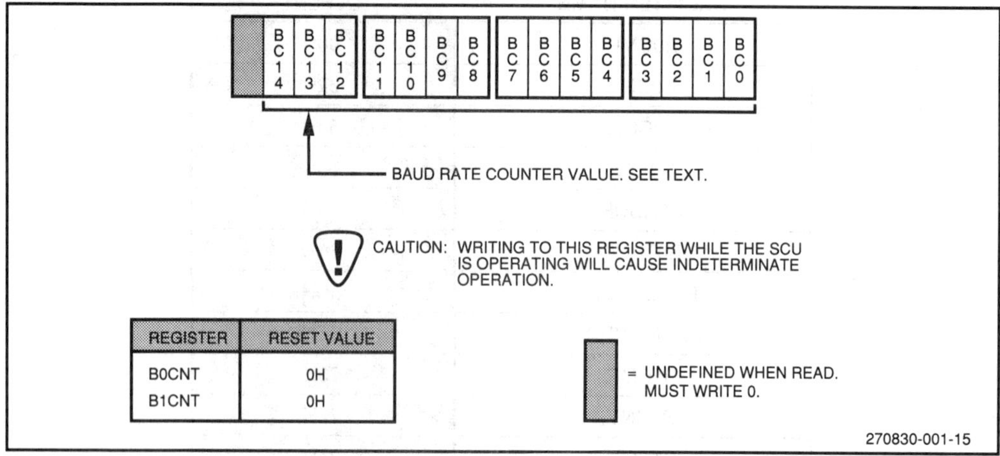

Figure 8.2(c).

SERIAL TRANSMIT BUFFER REGISTERS: (S0TBUF, S1TBUF)

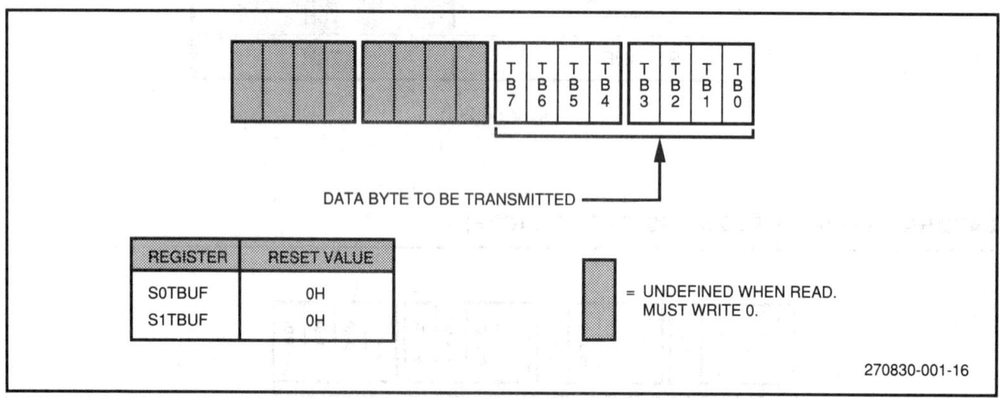

Figure 8.2(d).

SERIAL RECEIVE BUFFER REGISTERS: (S0RBUF, S1RBUF)

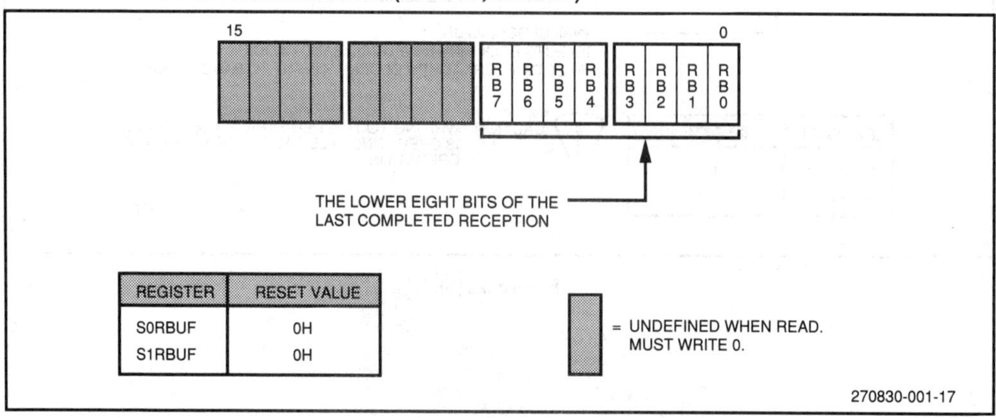

Figure 8.2(e).

SERIAL STATUS REGISTERS: (S0STS, S1STS)

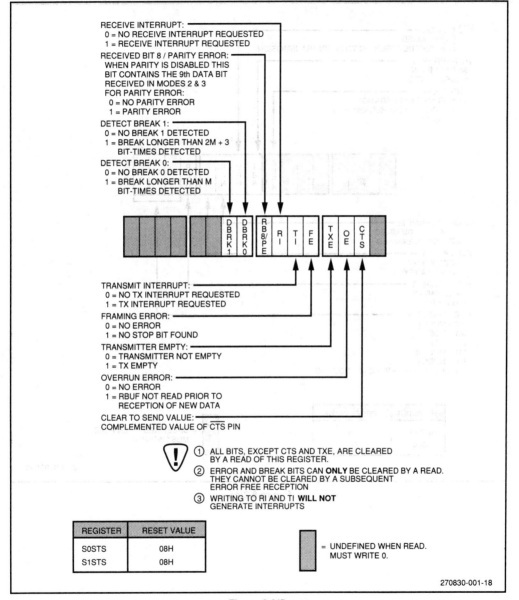

① ALL BITS, EXCEPT CTS AND TXE, ARE CLEARED BY A READ OF THIS REGISTER.

② ERROR AND BREAK BITS CAN **ONLY** BE CLEARED BY A READ. THEY CANNOT BE CLEARED BY A SUBSEQUENT ERROR FREE RECEPTION

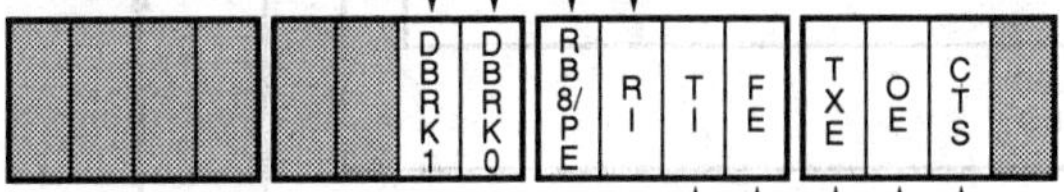

③ WRITING TO RI AND TI **WILL NOT** GENERATE INTERRUPTS

REGISTER	RESET VALUE
S0STS	08H
S1STS	08H

▒ = UNDEFINED WHEN READ. MUST WRITE 0.

270830-001-18

Figure 8.2(f).

SERIAL CONTROL REGISTERS: (S0CON, S1CON)

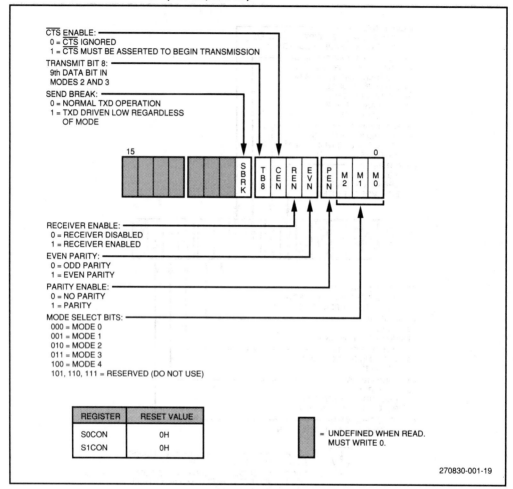

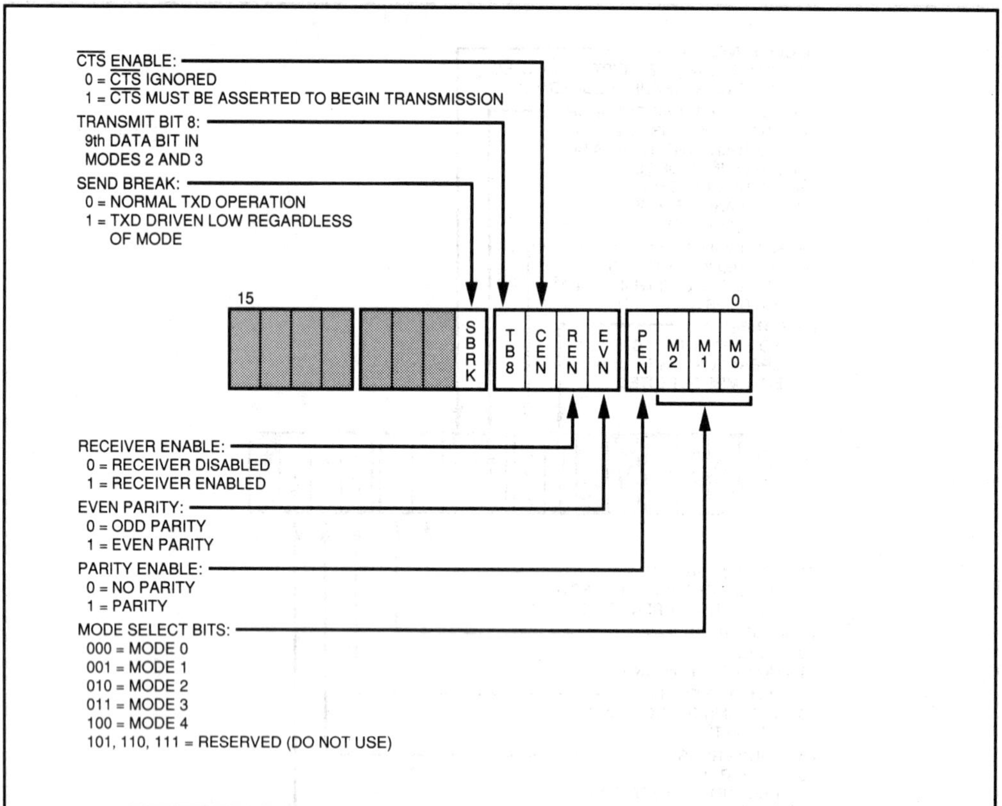

REGISTER	RESET VALUE
S0CON	0H
S1CON	0H

Figure 8.2(g).

Each frame consists of a start bit (a logic 0) followed by the data bits (7,8, or 9 for the 80C186EB) and a terminating stop bit (a logic one). The last data bit may replaced by a parity bit in situations where error detection is needed. Figure 8.3 shows a typical ten bit frame (8 bits data plus stop and start bits).

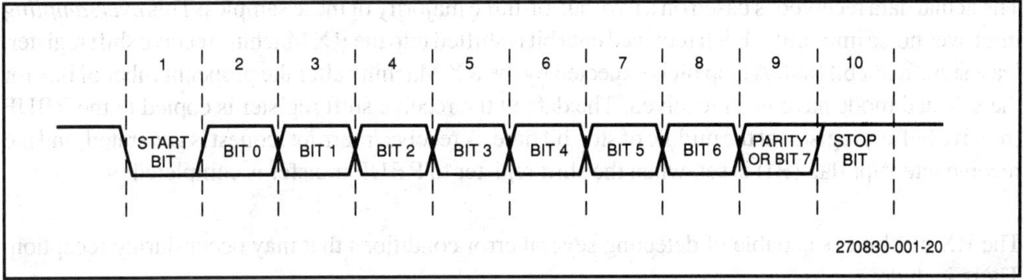

Figure 8.3. Typical 10-bit Asynchronous Data Frame.

A special "break character" may be used in some systems. The term "break character" is a misnomer as the break condition is really a **signal** that extends longer than a serial frame. The break condition is indicated on a serial channel by the presence of a logic low value for a preset amount of time equal to or longer than an entire frame. This signal is used for several purposes. Popular applications for break signalling include modem handshaking and catastrophic condition indication.

The serial communications unit on the 80C186EB recognizes only CMOS logic levels. Some serial communications systems may require the use of alternate levels. RS232-C, for example, requires a logic 1 be between -5V and -25V and a logic 0 be between +5V and +25V. Another common standard, the 20ma current loop, requires the presence and absence of current to indicate logic states. Interface circuitry for such systems is readily available from several manufacturers.

Each serial communications channel is divided into separate reception and transmission modules. These are referred to as the "RX Machine" and the "TX Machine" respectively. These modules are autonomous allowing transmission and reception to occur simultaneously (full duplex). Both the RX and TX machines operate at the baud rate supplied by the baud rate generator for that channel. The following sections describe the operation of the RX and TX machines in the asynchronous modes.

8.1.1.1 RX MACHINE

The RX machine must be enabled (through the REN bit) before reception in **any** mode can occur. Once enabled, the RX machine begins sampling the RXD pin in search of a falling edge signifying a start bit. Each data bit following the start bit is sampled three times near the center of the bit time. The actual data received is based on a two-out-of-three majority of these samples. This *oversampling* improves noise immunity. Each received data bit is shifted into the RX Machine receive shift register, least significant bit first. A stop bit is expected by the RX Machine after the proper number of bits for the selected mode have been received. The data in the receive shift register is copied to the RBUF (receive buffer) register at the middle of stop bit time. A receive interrupt request is generated, and the receive interrupt flag (RI) is set, when the shift register to RBUF transfer is completed.

The RX machine is capable of detecting several error conditions that may occur during reception. These include:

1) Parity Errors: If the parity feature has been enabled and the parity of the received data is incorrect, the Parity Error (PE) bit will be set.
2) Framing Errors: Failure to receive a valid stop bit during the bit time in which it is expected will result in the Framing Error (FE) bit being set.
3) Overrun Errors: If the RBUF register (containing the data from a previous reception) has not been read before the current reception completes, the Overrun Error bit (OE) will be set. This bit indicates that data from an earlier reception has been lost. The data in RBUF will **always** be the last byte received.

In addition, the RX Machine can recognize two different break signals. The DBRK0 bit indicates the detection of a break condition on the RXD pin of longer than M bit times, where M is equal to the total number of bits (start+data+stop) in a frame. The DBRK1 bit signifies that a longer break condition, greater than 2*M+3 bit times, has been received. It's important to note that the break condition will result in the RX Machine receiving at least one null (all zeros) character with the framing error bit set. Other error bits may also be set depending on the length of the break signal and the mode of operation of the channel.

The receiver can tolerate incoming baud rates that differ from the internal baud rate by 2.5% overspeed and 5.5% underspeed. These values exceed the CCITT extended signalling rate specifications.

A block diagram of the RX Machine is shown in Figure 8.4.

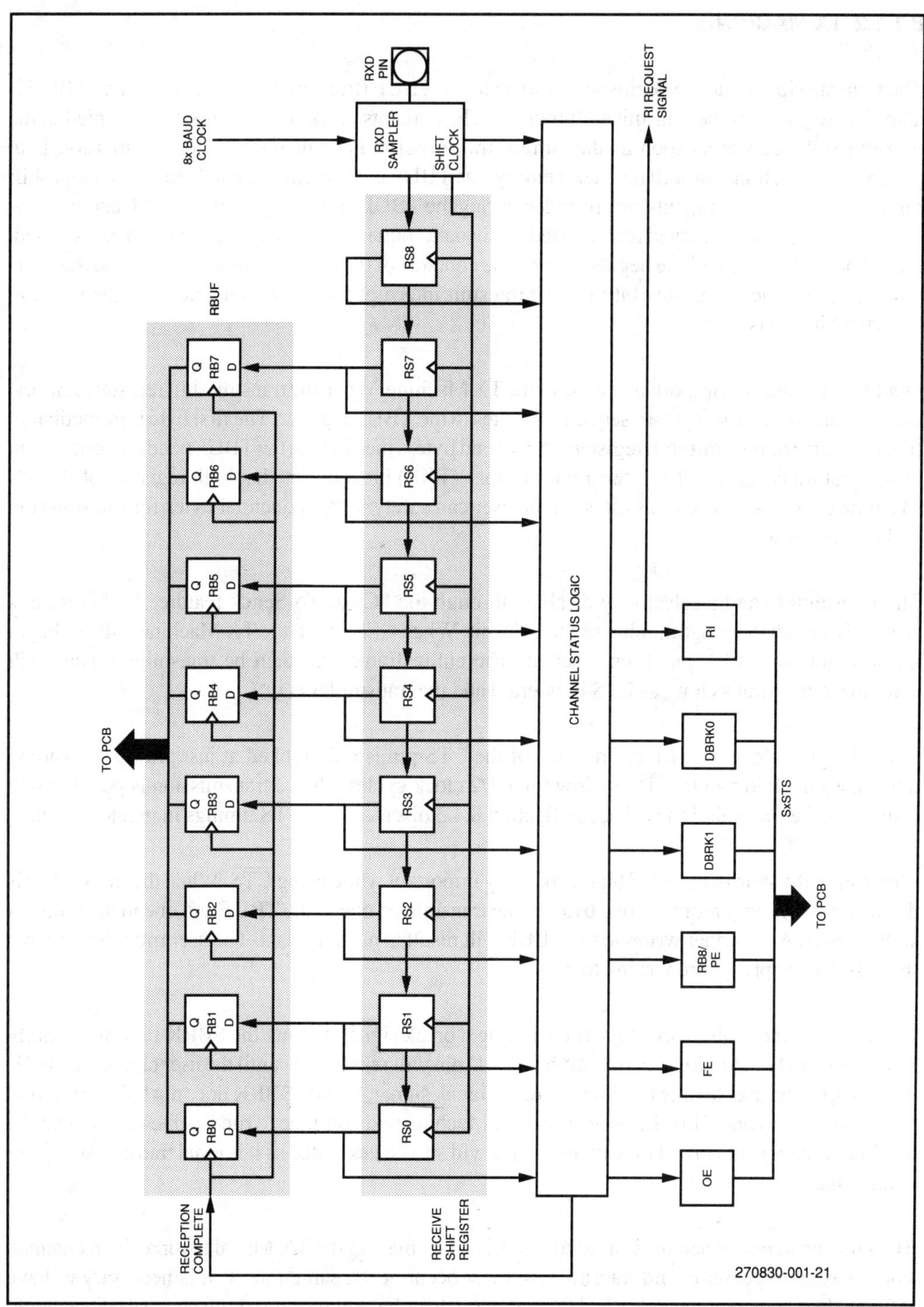

Figure 8.4 RX Machine Block Diagram

8.1.1.2 TX MACHINE

The transmission sequence begins with a write to the TBUF (transmit buffer) register. The TBUF is a holding register for the transmit shift register. The contents of the TBUF register are copied to the transmit shift register as soon as the current transmission is completed. If no transmission is in progress (i.e. the transmit shift register is empty) the TBUF is copied immediately to the transmit shift register. The start and stop bits are appended during the TBUF to shift register transfer. Concurrently, the parity bit is also generated and inserted in the data frame, if the parity feature has been selected. At this point the TX Machine begins shifting the contents of the transmit shift register on to the TXD pin. At the middle of the stop bit time the transmit interrupt request is generated and the transmit interrupt bit (TI) is set.

Double buffering is an important feature of the TX Machine. When the transmit shift register is empty, the TX Machine can accept **two** sequential writes to the TBUF register. The first byte is immediately transferred to the transmit shift register. The second byte is then held in the TBUF pending completion of the first transmission. The Transmitter Empty (TXE) bit signifies that both registers of the TX Machine are empty. When this bit is set the user can safely write sequential bytes for transmission without loss of data.

The transmitter can be selectively disabled through the "Clear-To-Send" feature. This feature is selected through the programming of the CEN bit. When CEN is set, the TX Machine will not begin transmission until $\overline{CTS}$ has been asserted. The entire frame will then be transmitted. Data will continue to transmit as long as $\overline{CTS}$ is asserted and the transmitter is full.

The $\overline{CTS}$ pin is **level sensitive**. The state of the $\overline{CTS}$ pin is only looked at just prior to a pending transmission. Holding the $\overline{CTS}$ pin low for 1 1/2 clock cycles when a transmission is pending will insure that the transmission will occur. Section 8.4.3 discusses the $\overline{CTS}$ timings in greater detail.

Monitoring the state of the TXE bit is especially important while using $\overline{CTS}$. When the transmitter is disabled there is only room for two bytes in the transmitter; one in the TBUF and one in the transmit shift register. Any further writes to the TBUF will result in a loss of data. The user **must** be sure that the TBUF is empty before writing to it.

The TX Machine is also capable of transmitting a break signal. Setting the SBRK bit **immediately** forces the TXD pin to a logic zero state. The TXD pin will remain low until the user clears the SBRK bit. It is up to the user to time the duration of the break signal. Setting SBRK does not halt the internal transmission sequence. In other words, the TX Machine will continue to run despite the fact that the TXD pin is being held low. Transmit interrupts will still be generated as if normal transmission were taking place.

The same baud rate generator is used for the RX Machine and the TX Machine for a given channel. For this reason reception and transmission must occur at the same rate. If it is necessary to have different baud rates for reception and transmission then the user must use both channels. One would be dedicated to reception, the other to transmission.

A block diagram of the TX Machine is shown in Figure 8.5.

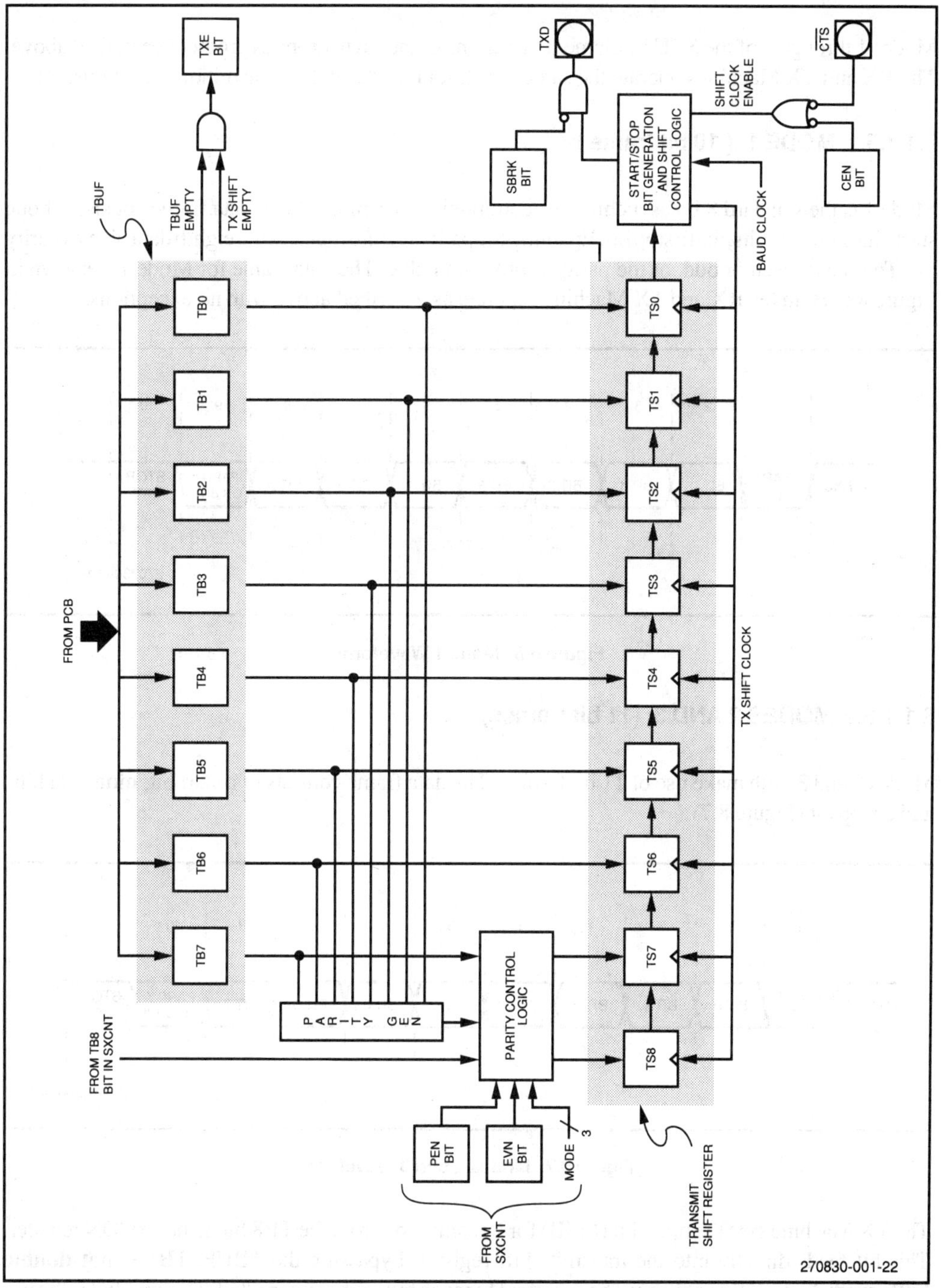

270830-001-22

Figure 8.5. TX Machine

8.1.1.3 THE ASYNCHRONOUS MODES

Modes 1 through 4 of the SCU implement variations of the asynchronous protocol described above. The RX and TX Machines operate the same for all four modes with some minor exceptions.

8.1.1.3.1 MODE 1: (10 bit frame)

Mode 1 is the standard 8 bit asynchronous communications mode. Each data frame consists of one start bit, eight data bits, and a stop bit. Enabling the parity feature replaces the eighth data bit by a parity bit. The sense, even or odd, of the parity is programmable. The data frame for Mode 1 is shown in Figure 8.6. Both the RX and TX Machines operate as described above with no exceptions.

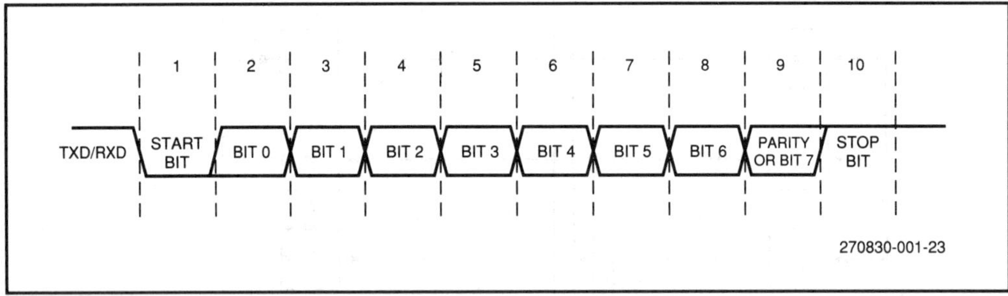

Figure 8.6. Mode 1 Waveform

8.1.1.3.2 MODES 2 AND 3: (11 bit frames)

Modes 2 and 3 both make use of 11 bit frames. The data frame consists of a start bit, **nine** data bits, and a stop bit (Figure 8.7).

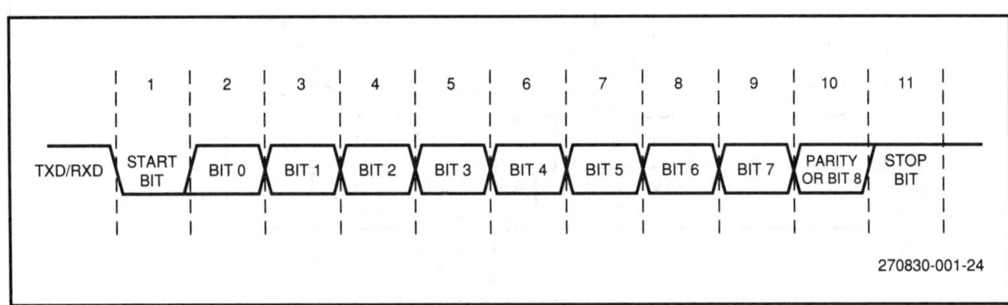

Figure 8.7. Modes 2 and 3 Waveform

The TX Machine gets the ninth bit (MSB) for transmission from the TB8 bit in the SxCON register. This bit feeds directly into the transmit shift register, bypassing the TBUF. TB8 **is not double bufferred**. A new TB8 value must be specified for each byte to be transmitted. This precludes the use of the double buffering feature when the user needs to explicitly program the ninth bit value.

There are two situations where TB8 can be generated by the TX Machine. The TB8 bit is cleared after every transmission. If TB8 is cleared before transmission starts, and never set thereafter, every transmission will have the ninth bit low. If the parity feature has been selected, bit 9 will be replaced with the parity bit. This is a convenient method of generating an 8 bits plus parity data frame. In both cases double buffering may once again be used since TB8 is automatically generated.

The RX Machine places the ninth received data bit in the RB8/PE (Receive Bit 8 / Parity Error) bit in the SxSTS register. If the parity feature is enabled, the RB8/PE bit will instead contain the parity error flag (set to indicate an error). All other error detection capabilities and interrupt requests function as described above.

The RX Machine has an important functional difference between Modes 2 and 3. Mode 2 is commonly referred to as the "ninth bit recognition mode". **Reception in Mode 2 will not complete unless bit 9 of the data frame is a logic one.** Any data received with bit 9 cleared will be **completely ignored.** No flags will be set, no interrupts will be generated, and no data will be transferred to RBUF. Reception in Mode 3, however, will complete regardless of the state of bit 9.

Modes 2 and 3 are commonly combined to implement multiprocessor communications. One possible application is called the "master/slave network" (Figure 8.8). All slaves connected to the network have their RXD pins directly connected to the "master transmit" line (TXD pin of the master). The slaves' TXD pins are all tied to the "master receive" line (RXD pin of the master) through a 3-state buffer. The buffer is necessary to avoid contention as the TXD line cannot be floated.

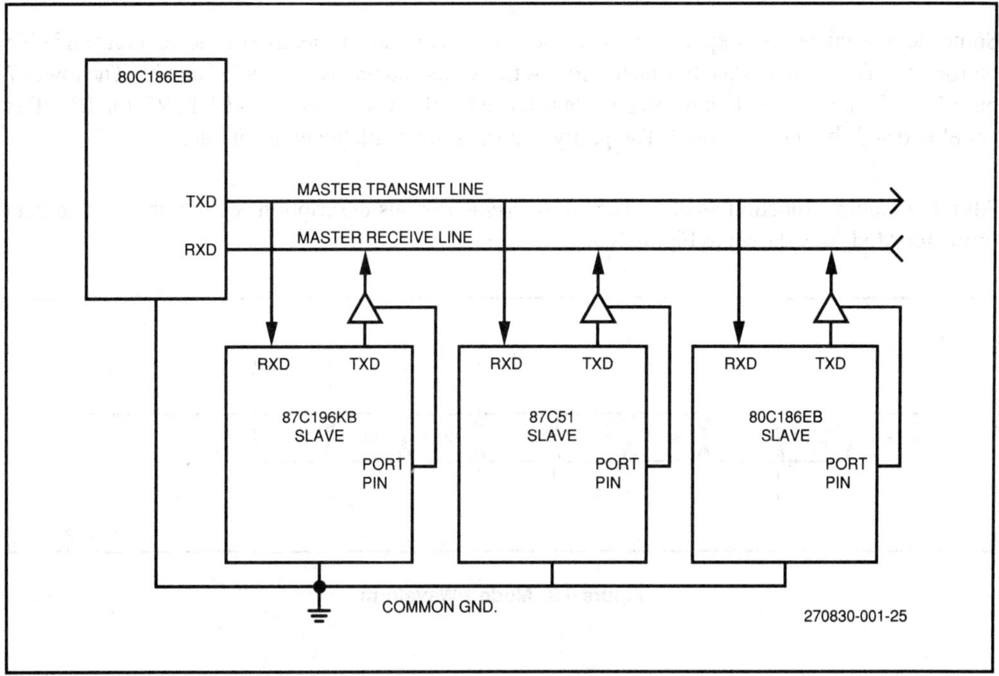

Figure 8.8. Multiprocessor Network

Initially all slaves are receiving in Mode 2 with their transmitters disconnected from the master receive line. The master is set permanently in Mode 3. There are two types of transactions that can occur in this system: a global slave command and a local master/slave data transfer.

When the master wishes to broadcast a command to all slaves, it transmits the eight bit command with bit 9 set high. Every slave in the network is interrupted upon reception of the global command byte. An example of a global command is "initiate system reset routine" to force all slaves to a known state. Such global commands are unidirectional and require no response from the slaves.

If the master wishes to communicate bidirectionally with a particular slave it would issue a special global "address" command (again with bit 9 high). Each slave would check its address against the received address. The addressed slave would then gate its TXD line onto the master receive bus and switch to Mode 3. Once in Mode 3 the slave could freely communicate with the master. During a master/slave data transfer bit 9 would be kept low to prevent interrupting the other slave processors on the network. Once the transaction was completed, the slave would detach itself from the master receive bus and return to Mode 2.

It is not recommended that the parity feature be used in Mode 2, as bit 9 is intended to be a control bit. If parity were used in Mode 2 only those data frames whose parity resulted in setting bit 9 would be received.

8.1.1.3.3 MODE 4 (9 bit frame)

Some older serial devices require the use of a seven bit data frame instead of the newer eight and nine bit formats. To accommodate this need Mode 4 transmits and receives only 7 data bits. The lower 7 bits of TBUF are transmitted; received data is placed in the lower 7 bits of RBUF. RB7 in RBUF is undefined and should be ignored. The parity feature is not available in this mode.

All other features function as described in the asynchronous description section above. The data frame for Mode 4 is shown in Figure 8.9.

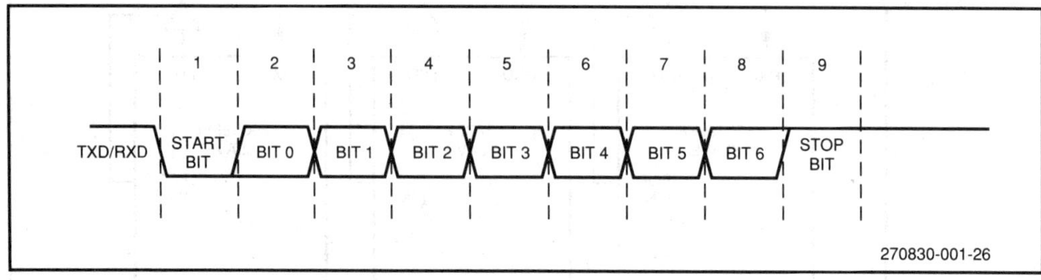

Figure 8.9. Mode 4 Waveform

8.1.2 SYNCHRONOUS COMMUNICATION

The synchronous mode (Mode 0) of the SCU is intended for use primarily with shift register based peripheral devices. In this mode the TXD pin provides the synchronizing transmission/reception clock while the RXD pin sends or receives data in eight bit frames (Figure 8.10). Communication in Mode 0 is half-duplex; the RXD pin cannot receive and transmit data simultaneously.

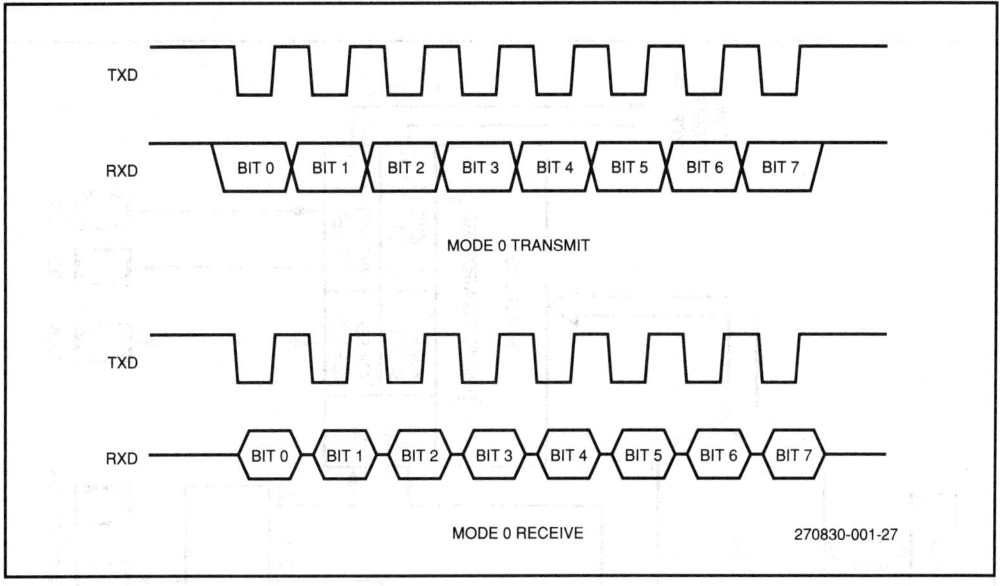

Figure 8.10. Mode 0 Waveforms

Transmission in Mode 0 begins with a write to the TBUF register. TBUF will be copied into the transmit shift register as soon as that register is empty (i.e. when any previous transmission is completed). The data in the transmit shift register is then shifted out of the **RXD** pin (vs. the TXD pin for the asynchronous modes) while the synchronizing clock is provided on the **TXD** pin. The receiving circuit must sample the transmitted data on the rising edge of TXD. **The 80C186EB always provides the synchronizing clock signal; it can never receive a synchronous clock signal on TXD.** The TI request bit is set in the middle of the 8th bit time; when transmission is complete. The RXD pin floats prior to and following a transmission. The TXD pin never floats; when it is inactive between transmissions it remains at a high logic state.

Transmissions are double bufferred in Mode 0 just as they are in the asynchronous modes described above.

Reception in Mode 0 is initiated only when the receiver enable (REN) bit is set and the receiver interrupt request (RI) bit is clear. As soon as these conditions are met the SCU begins shifting in the data on the RXD pin. The TXD pin provides the synchronizing clock as in the case of transmission.

Received data is sampled by the SCU just prior to the rising edge of TXD. The device driving the RXD pin must adhere to the setup and hold times (with respect to TXD) outlined in the 80C186EB datasheet. Reception of the eighth bit sets the receive interrupt request (RI) bit. Simultaneously, the contents of the receive shift register are copied into the RBUF.

Reception of another data byte will not begin until the RI bit is cleared. The receiver can be disabled during a reception although this will result in a loss of data.

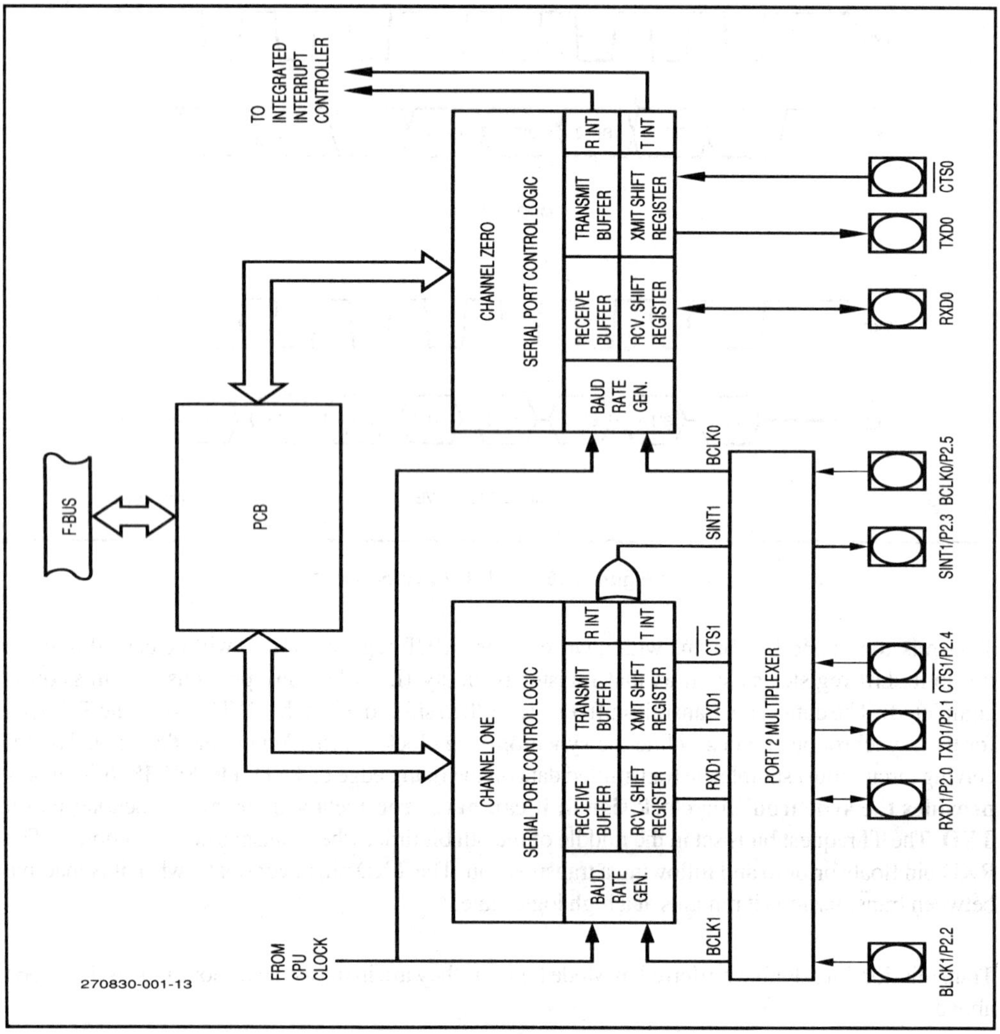

270830-001-13

Figure 8.11. Mode 0 Port Expansion

A typical application for Mode 0 is shown in Figure 8.11. The 74HC165 is a parallel in / serial out shift register. The eight configuration byte dip switches control the logic level applied to the parallel input pins of the 74HC165. To read the configuration byte the port 1.7 pin is pulsed low to latch the parallel data. Then the receiver would be enabled in Mode 0. This would immediately shift the eight bits in the 74HC165 in to the serial receive buffer. A similar design could be used to construct an output port.

8.2 PROGRAMMING THE SERIAL COMMUNICATIONS UNIT

Six Peripheral Control Block registers are used to program each channel of the SCU. The receive and transmit buffers, RBUF and TBUF, have already been described. The Baud Rate Compare (BxCMP) and Baud Rate Count (BxCNT) Registers are used by the Baud Rate Generator as described in the Baud Rate section below. The Serial Control (SxCON) Register is used to set the mode of operation and select the feature set for a channel. Each channel reports its current operational state through the use of the Serial Status (SxSTS) Register. This section will highlight the function of these two registers.

8.2.1 THE SERIAL CONTROL REGISTER (S0CON, S1CON)

The SxCON registers consists of the following seven fields:

Mode Field: These three bits, M2 to M0, control the operational mode of the channel. They are defined as follows:

M2	M1	M0	
0	0	0	Mode 0
0	0	1	Mode 1
0	1	0	Mode 2
0	1	1	Mode 3
1	0	0	Mode 4
1	0	1	Reserved for future use
1	1	0	Reserved for future use
1	1	1	Reserved for future use

PEN Bit: The Parity Enable Bit. When this bit is set the parity feature will be enabled. Every transmission (except in modes 0 and 4) will have the MSB replaced by a parity bit. All receptions will be parity checked and error conditions will be reported in the PE bit. The sense of the parity is controlled by the EVN bit.

EVN Bit: EVEN/ODD Parity Sense Select. Setting this bit selects even parity; clearing it selects odd.

REN Bit: Receiver enable bit. Setting this bit enables reception in all Modes.

CEN Bit: Clear-To-Send enable. Setting this bit invokes the Clear-To-Send transmission control feature. With this option selected transmission will not begin until $\overline{\text{CTS}}$ is asserted.

TB8 Bit: The eighth bit for data transmission in Modes 2 and 3. This bit is cleared after every transmission. This bit is not double buffered.

SBRK Bit: Send Break Bit. When this bit is set the TXD is immediately driven low regardless of the current mode. TXD will remain low until this bit is cleared. Timing for break signal duration is the users responsibility.

All of the remaining bits in the SxCON register are reserved for future use. These are all undefined when read.

The SxCON is a read/write register. Reading the SxCON register will not affect its contents.

8.2.2 THE SERIAL STATUS REGISTER (S0STS, S1STS)

The Serial Status Register is used to monitor the current state of a channel. It is important to note that **the entire SxSTS register** (with the exception of the CTS bit) **is cleared every time it is accessed** (either read or written). If it is necessary to preserve the contents of the SxSTS register, it must be saved in memory.

The Serial Status Register has nine bit fields:

CTS bit: Clear to Send status. This bit is the complement of the value on $\overline{\text{CTS}}$ pin. This bit is the only one in the SxSTS that is not cleared by a read.

OE bit: Overrun error flag. This bit is set by the RX Machine to indicate a receive overrun error has occurred. An overrun error occurs when the data in the RBUF register is not read before the data in the receive shift register has overwritten it.

TXE bit: Transmitter Empty Flag. This bit will be set when both the TBUF and the transmit shift register are empty. This indicates that the TX Machine can accept 2 sequential bytes for transmission.

FE bit: Framing Error Flag. Set to indicate a framing error (valid stop bit not detected) has occurred.

TI bit: Transmit Interrupt Request Flag. Set to indicate a transmission has completed and a transmit interrupt request has been issued. Writing this bit will **not** generate an interrupt for channel 0.

RI bit: Receive Interrupt Request Flag. Set to indicate a reception has completed and a receive interrupt has been issued. Clearing this bit when REN is set in Mode 0 initiates a reception. Writing this bit will **not** generate an interrupt for channel 0.

RB8/PE bit: Received Bit 8 / Parity Error Flag. In Modes 2 and 3 this will be the value of the ninth received bit if parity is not enabled. If parity is enabled (in Modes 1, 2, and 3) this bit will be set to indicate a parity error was detected for the byte currently in RBUF (the last received byte).

DBRK0 bit: Break Detect 0 flag. Set to indicate the detection of a break condition of longer than M bit times (M = total bits in frame).

DBRK1 bit: Break Detect 1 flag. Set to indicate the detection of a break condition of longer than 2M+3 bit times (M = total bits in frame).

All of the error bits (OE, PE, and FE) and the break detect bits (DBRK1 and DBRK0) are **only** cleared by reading the SxSTS register. For example, if a frame is received with a parity error (setting the PE bit) then a subsequent error-free frame is received, **and the SxSTS has not been read between the two receptions**, the PE bit will remain **set**. This allows the SxSTS register to be checked only at the end of a long block of receptions.

8.3 OPERATION AND PROGRAMMING OF BAUD RATE GENERATOR

The Baud Rate Generator uses two PCB registers: the Baud Rate Counter (BxCNT) and the Baud Rate Compare (BxCMP) Register. The Baud Rate Counter is a free running fifteen bit counter that increments every cycle of the baud timebase clock. The baud timebase clock can either be the CPU clock (1/2 the CLKIN frequency) or an external clocking signal applied to the BCLKx pin. If an external timebase is selected, it is limited to 1/2 the frequency of the CPU clock. This limitation stems from synchronization requirements.

The Baud Rate Compare Register contains two fields. The most significant bit is the **ICLK** select bit. Setting this bit selects the internal CPU clock for the baud timebase; clearing it selects the BCLKx pin. The lower 15 bits make up the baud rate comparison value. The Baud Rate Counter is compared against the Baud Rate Compare value after every cycle of the baud timebase clock. If the two match, the baud rate generator outputs a pulse and resets the BxCNT register. This repetitive process generates a pulse train that is equal to the baud rate in Mode 0. Modes 1 through 4, due to their asynchronous nature, require repetitive sampling of the input waveform to insure reliable reception. Eight baud rate generator cycles are required to perform this operation. For this reason, the baud rate in Modes 1 through 4 is 1/8 the frequency of the baud rate pulse train.

The following equations may be used to calculate the proper value of the BxCMP for a specific desired baud rate (FCPU=CPU operating frequency, 1/2 CLKIN frequency):

Mode 0:

Baud Rate Compare value= [FCPU/(BAUDRATE)]-1

Mode 1:

Baud Rate Compare value= [FCPU/(8*BAUDRATE)]-1

For an external clock source with a frequency Fbclk, use the following:

Mode 0:

Baud Rate Compare value= [FBCLK/(BAUDRATE)]-1

Mode 1:

Baud Rate Compare value= [FBLCK/(8*BAUDRATE)]-1

Note that a baud rate compare value of 0 is illegal and will result in unpredictable operation. Common baud rates based on the crystal frequency are shown in Table 8.1.

Table 8.1 Common Baud Rates in Asynchronous Modes

CPU FREQUENCY	BAUD RATE	BxCMP Value	% ERROR
16 MHz	19,200	8067H	0.16
16 MHz	9,600	80CFH	0.16
16 MHz	4,800	81A0H	-0.08
16 MHz	2,400	8340H	0.04
16 MHz	1,200	8682H	-0.02
16 MHz	600	8D04H	0.01
16 MHz	300	9A0AH	0
13 MHz	19,200	8054H	-0.43
13 MHz	9,600	80A8H	0.16
13 MHz	4,800	8152H	-0.14
13 MHz	2,400	82A4H	0.01
13 MHz	1,200	8549H	0.01
13 MHz	600	8A93H	0.01
13 MHz	300	9528H	-0.01
8 MHz	19,200	8033H	0.16
8 MHz	9,600	8067H	0.16
8 MHz	4,800	80CFH	0.16
8 MHz	2,400	81A0H	-0.08
8 MHz	1,200	8340H	0.04
8 MHz	600	8682H	-0.02
8 MHz	300	8D04H	0.01

8.4 TIMINGS

8.4.1 ASYNCHRONOUS (MODES 1-4)

For the asynchronous Modes (1 through 4) each bit of a data frame is valid for what is called a "bit-time" (Figure 8.12). A bit-time is equal to 1/(baud rate). As an example, if the baud rate is set at 9600 each bit is valid for 104uS. Since it takes 10 bits (in Mode 1) to transmit one ASCII character the **data rate** is 960 characters per second. The RX Machine expects the incoming data to have a baud rate within a +2.5% to -5.5% range from internal (transmit) baud rate.

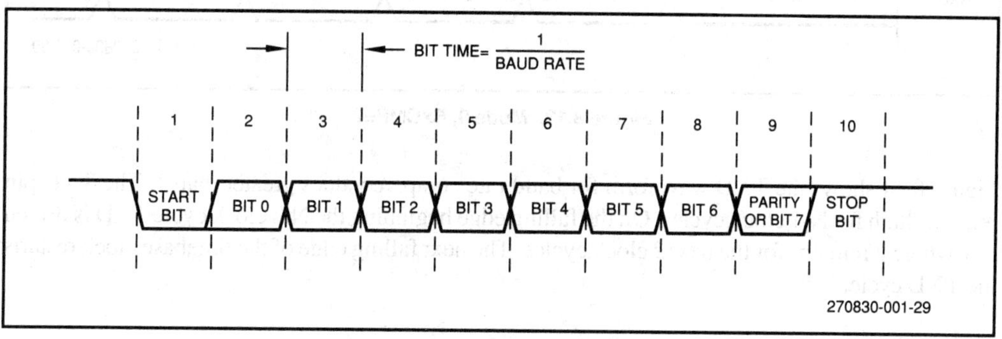

Figure 8.12. Asynchronous Timings

8.4.2 SYNCHRONOUS (MODE 0)

In Mode 0 all timings are relative to the baud timebase clock (either CLKOUT or BCLK). Two cases govern the behavior of the transmit/receive clock (on the TXD pin).

The first case is unique and occurs when the Baud Rate Compare Value is equal to 1 (see Figure 8.13). In this situation the TXD pin toggles every cycle of the baud timebase clock resulting in a 50% duty cycle waveform at 1/2 the baud timebase frequency. Transitions on TXD occur on the falling edge of the timebase clock.

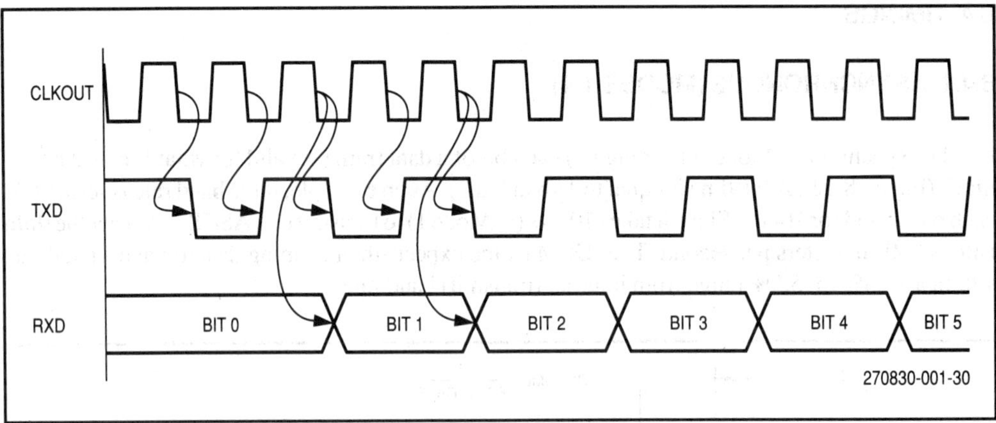

Figure 8.13. Mode 0, BxCMP=2

Figure 8.14 shows the TXD waveform for baud rate compare values greater than 1. The TXD pin remains high for N-1 clock cycles. On the falling edge beginning the Nth clock cycle TXD is driven low where it remains for the next 2 clock cycles. The next falling edge of the timebase clock restarts the TXD cycle.

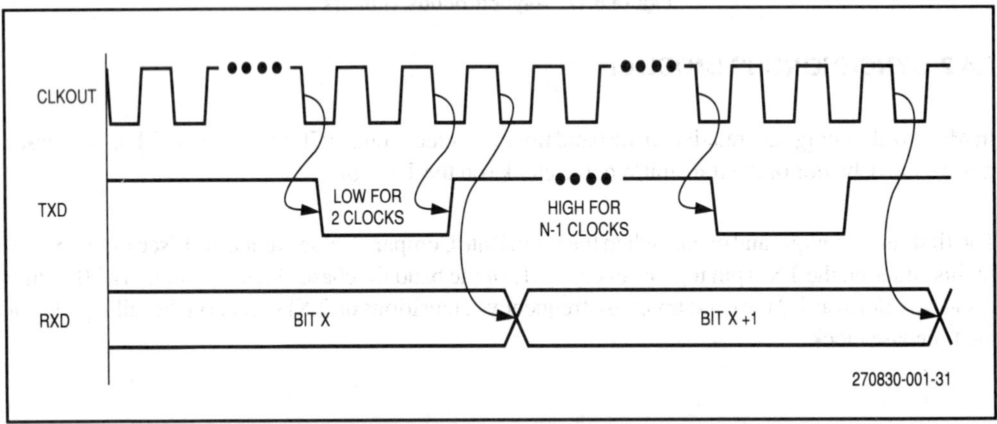

Figure 8.14. Mode 0, BxCMP>2

During a transmission the state of the RXD pin changes state on the first falling edge of CLKOUT following the rising edge of TXD. This is true for both of the above cases. For reception incoming data on RXD must meet setup and hold timings with respect to the rising edge of TXD (Figure 15). These timings can be found in the data sheet.

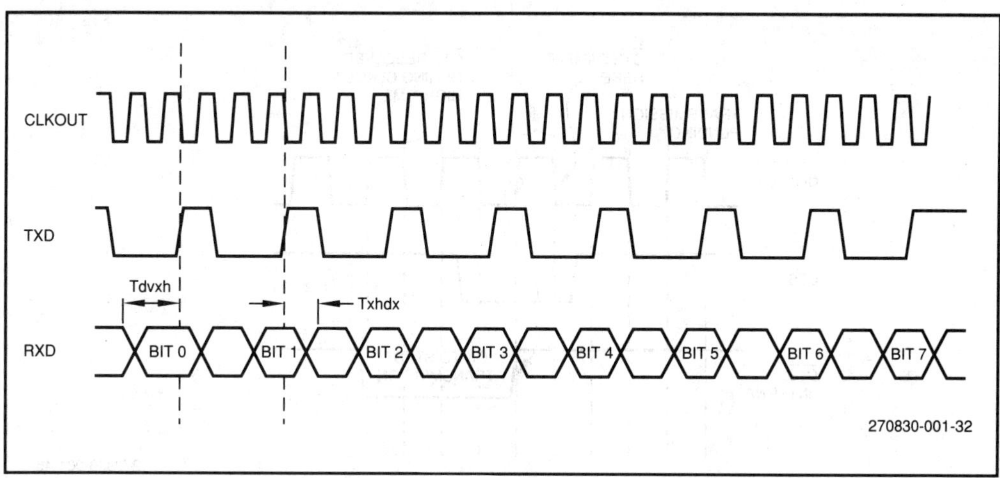

Figure 8.15. Mode 0, Receive Timings

8.4.3 $\overline{\text{CTS}}$ PIN TIMINGS

When the clear-to-send feature is enabled (CEN bit is set) transmission will not begin in any mode until the $\overline{\text{CTS}}$ signal is asserted **while a transmission is pending**. Figure 8.16 shows the sequence of events involved in the recognition of a valid $\overline{\text{CTS}}$ signal.

The $\overline{\text{CTS}}$ pin is sampled by the rising edge of CLKOUT (not BCLKx). The high time of the clock cycle is used to resolve (synchronize) the $\overline{\text{CTS}}$ signal. On the falling edge of CLKOUT the synchronized $\overline{\text{CTS}}$ signal is presented to the SCU. If it is necessary to have a very narrow pulse on $\overline{\text{CTS}}$, the set up and hold times in Figure 8.17 **must be met**. It is recommded that $\overline{\text{CTS}}$ have a valid pulse width of at least 1 1/2 clock periods. This will guarantee recognition.

The state of $\overline{\text{CTS}}$ is not latched. If it is asserted **before** a transmission is initiated (i.e., a write to TBUF occurs) the subsequent transmission **will not begin**. One can think of a write to the TBUF as "arming" the $\overline{\text{CTS}}$ sense circuitry.

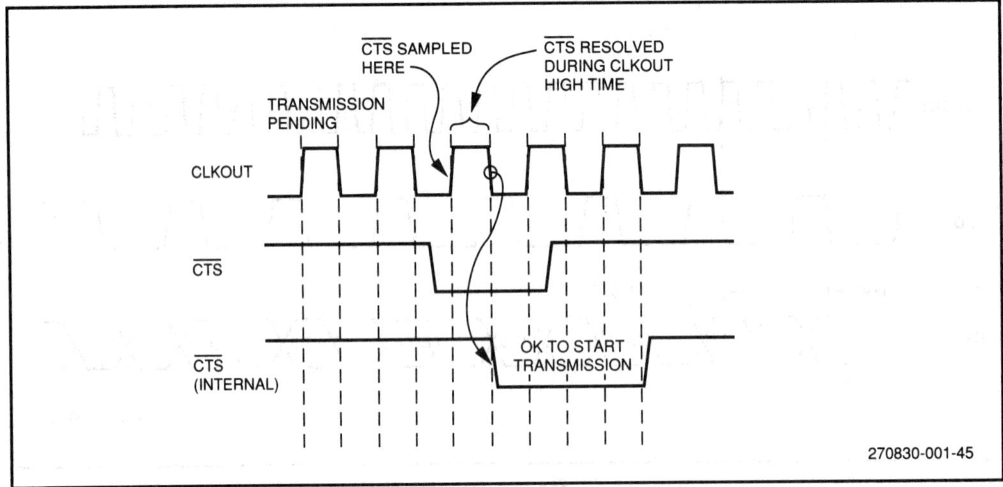

Figure 8.16. $\overline{CTS}$ Recognition Sequence

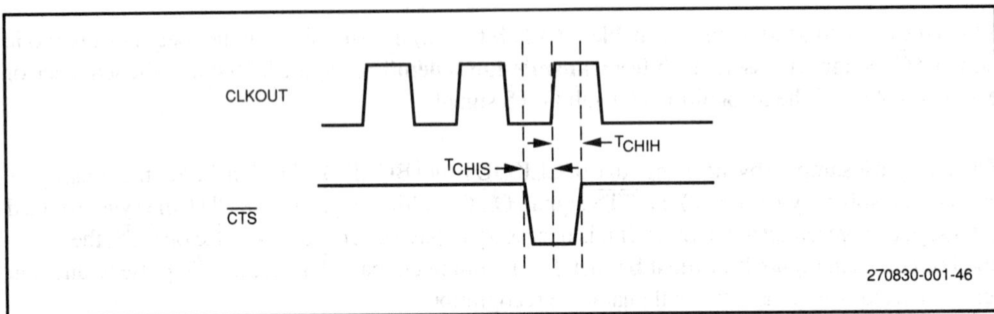

Figure 8.17. $\overline{CTS}$ Setup and Hold

8.5 SERIAL CONTROL UNIT INTERRUPTS

A serial interrupt request will be generated when either channel completes a serial transaction (transmission or reception). For the asynchronous modes, a reception or transmission is completed at the middle of the stop bit. During synchronous communication the transaction is completed in the middle of the eighth bit. The RI and TI bits (in the SxSTS register) indicate that either a receive or transmit interrupt request has been generated.

The interrupt request circuitry differs between channel 0 and channel 1. The difference between the two is best understood by following the interrupt request signals for each channel.

8.5.1 CHANNEL 0 INTERRUPTS

When a reception completes in channel 0, an internal receive-interrupt-request signal is generated. This signal is routed to the S0STS register and the internal interrupt controller (Figure 8.18). The RI bit of the S0STS signal is set by the receive-interrupt-request signal. Note that the RI bit **does not generate or affect the internal interrupt request**. RI is merely an indicator that says: "Channel 0 has posted a receive-interrupt-request with the integrated interrupt unit." The transmit-interrupt-request signal and TI behave the same for the case of transmission.

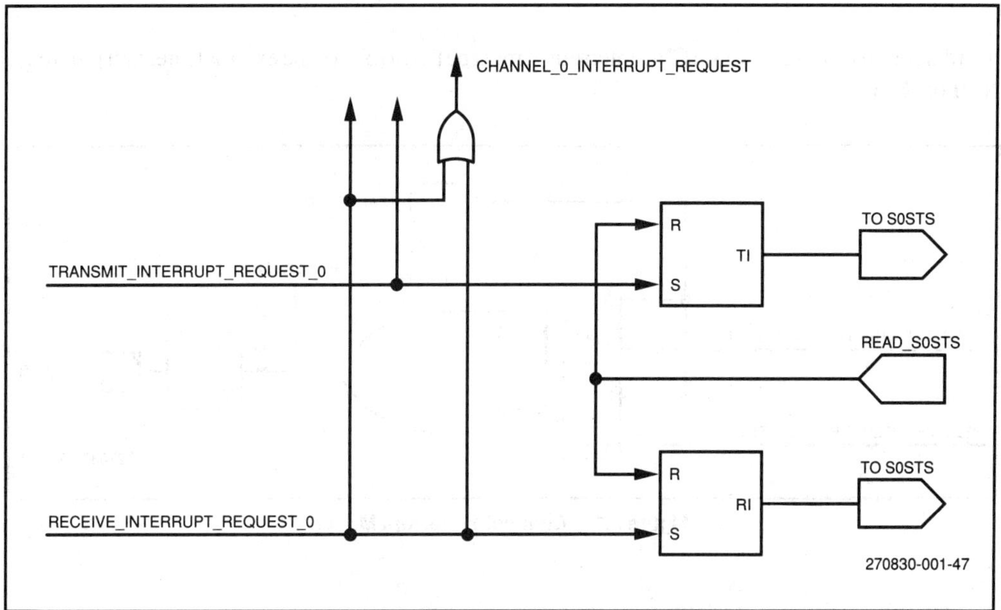

Figure 8.18. Channel 0 Interrupt Model

At the interrupt unit the receive interrupt request is ORed with the transmit interrupt request from channel 0 to generate a single "serial channel 0 interrupt request." The interrupt controller, however, maintains separate vectors for receive and transmit interrupts. The receive and transmit interrupt requests cannot be independently masked.

It is not necessary to clear the RI and TI bits for channel 0 to prevent further interrupts from occurring. They are an indication that a request **has** occurred; they are not the **source** of the request. Setting these bits by writing S0STS will not generate an interrupt.

Receive interrupts take priority over transmit interrupts. They cannot nest, however, since they share one interrupt request.

8.5.2 CHANNEL 1 INTERRUPTS

Channel 1 is not directly supported by the integrated interrupt controller. When a receive or transmit interrupt request is generated by channel 1 the appropriate bit, RI or TI, is set in the S1STS. The serial channel 1 interrupt request signal (SINT1) is a direct ORing of these register bits (see Figure 8.19). **This is different from channel 0.** For channel 1, setting the RI and TI bits by writing to S1STS will cause the SINT1 line to go active. The only way to deassert SINT1 is by clearing the RI and TI bits (by reading S1STS). SINT1 is routed to a package pin through the Port 2 multiplexer.

In order for SINT1 to generate a CPU interrupt, it must be tied to one of the external interrupt pins (e.g., NMI or INT0).

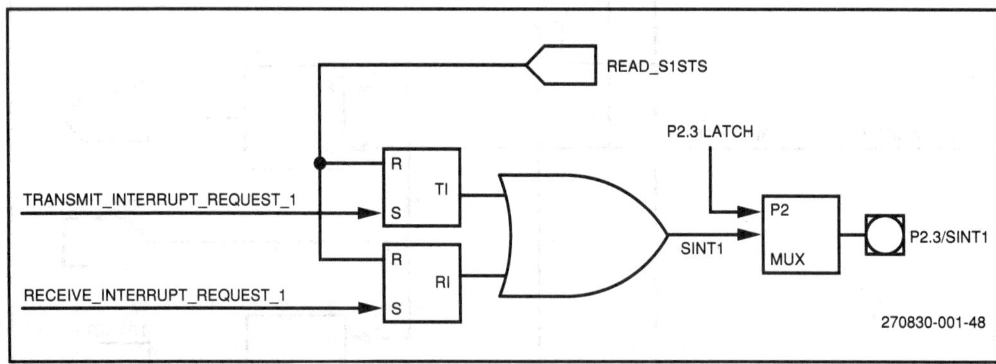

Figure 8.19. Channel 1 Interrupt Model

8.6 PORT 2 MULTIPLEXER

All of the pins for channel 1, and the BCLK0 pin for channel 0, are multiplexed with output port 2. The I/O port section of this manual describes programming of the multiplexer.

8.7 APPLICATION EXAMPLES

The following sections show the proper programming of the SCU for two different applications. The first application configures channel 0 as a standard 9600 baud full duplex asynchronous port. The second application uses channel 1 to read the configuration dip switch example shown in Figure 8.11.

8.7.1 Example 1: 9600 Baud, Full-Duplex Asynchronous Channel

The ASM186 code for example 1 consists of 3 procedures. Procedure ASYNC_CHANNEL_SETUP configures channel 0 for 9600 baud, 7 bits plus even parity, with CTS control enabled. ASYNC_CHANNEL_SETUP also initializes the interrupt vectors for the two interrupt procedures ASYNC_REC_INT_PROC and ASYNC_XMIT_INT_PROC.

The body of the two interrupt handler procedures has been left empty. The code inserted in these procedures is application dependent. Typically the receive procedure would check for error conditions then store the received byte in a buffer. The transmit routine would get the next byte for transmission out of a buffer and write it to the TBUF.

8.7.2 Example 2: Synchronous Port Expansion

Section 8.1.2 detailed how the SCU could be used in synchronous mode to expand the I/O capability of the 80C186EB. This example shows the ASM186 code necessary to read the configuration byte information for the circuit in Figure 8.11.

The code consists of one procedure: READ_CONFIG_BYTE. First, the procedure sets up channel 1 as a synchronous (mode 0) channel. A baud rate of 1 Mbaud is chosen. Next, the RXD1 and TXD1 signals are routed to the package pins by programming the Port 1 multiplexer.

To read the expansion port, pin P1.7 is pulsed low to load the 74HC165 register with the dip switch values. The REN (Receiver ENable) bit is then set and the data is shifted in to the RBUF. Since the SINT line is not being used the RI bit must be polled. When a "1" is found in the RI flag the reception is completed. The configuration data is returned in the AL register.

Example 1

```
$mod186
name                        scu_async_example

;
; This file contains an example of initialization code for the
; Serial Communications Unit on the 80C186EB.
;
;
; This example has 3 procedures:
;
; ASYNC_CHANNEL_SETUP: Sets up channel 0 as 9600 baud,
;                      full duplex, 7 data bits-plus-partiy,
;                      with CTS# control.
; ASYNC_REC_INT_PROC:  Interrupt handler for a reception.
;                      This procedure is nearly empty since
;                      the code to perform error checking and
;                      receive buffer handling is application
;                      dependent.
; ASYNC_XMIT_INT_PROC: Interrupt handler for a transmission.
;                      As with the above procedure this is
;                      nearly devoid of code. A typical appli-
;                      cation would test the TXE bit and then
;                      copy data from the transmit buffer in
;                      memory to the TBUF.

; We assume PCB has NOT BEEN RELOCATED!


B0CMP       EQU     0FF60H      ; Channel 0 Baud Rate Compare
S0CON       EQU     0FF64H      ; Channel 0 Control
S0STS       EQU     0FF66H      ; Channel 0 Status
S0RBUF      EQU     0FF68H      ; Channel 0 Receive Buffer
S0TBUF      EQU     0FF6AH      ; Channel 0 Transmit Buffer
RI_TYPE     EQU     20          ; Receive is type 20 interrupt
TI_TYPE     EQU     21          ; Xmit is type 21 interrupt
EOI         EQU     0FF02H      ; End-Of-Interrupt Register
SCUCON      EQU     0FF14H      ; SCU interrupt control reg

code_seg    segment public
            assume cs:code_seg

ASYNC_CHANNEL_SETUP proc near
; First, set up the Interrupt handler vectors....

    xor     ax, ax
    mov     ds, ax                      ; Need DS to point to
                                        ; int vector table at 0H

    mov     bx, RI_TYPE*4
    mov     ax, offset ASYNC_REC_INT_PROC
    mov     [bx], ax
    mov     ax, seg ASYNC_REC_INT_PROC
    mov     [bx+2], ax
```

Example 1 (Continued)

```
        mov     bx, TI_TYPE*4
        mov     ax, offset ASYNC_XMIT_INT_PROC
        mov     [bx], ax
        mov     ax, seg ASYNC_XMIT_INT_PROC
        mov     [bx+2], ax

; Now set up channel 0 options......

        mov     ax, 80CFH               ; for 9600 baud from 16MHz
        mov     dx, B0CMP               ; CPU clock.
        out     dx, ax                  ; Set baud rate.

        mov     ax, 0059H               ; CEN=1 (CTS enabled)
                                        ; REN=0 (receiver not enabled yet)
                                        ; EVN=1 (even parity)
                                        ; PEN=1 (parity turned ON)
                                        ; MODE=1 (10 bit frame)
        mov     dx, S0CON
        out     dx, ax                  ; write to Serial Control Reg.

; Clear any old pending RI or TI, just for safety's sake.

        mov     dx, S0STS
        in      ax, dx                  ; clear any old RI or TI

; Clear interrupt mask bit in interrupt unit to allow SCU
  interrupts.

        mov     dx, SCUCON              ; SCU interrupt control
        in      ax, dx
        and     ax, 0007H               ; Clear mask bit to enable

; Turn on the receiver

        mov     dx, S0CON
        in      ax, dx                  ; Read S0CON

        or      ax, 0020                ; Set REN bit
        out     dx, ax                  ; Write S0CON

; Now receiver is enabled and sampling of the RXD line begins.

; Any write to the TBUF will initiate a transmission.

        ret

ASYNC_CHANNEL_SETUP endp

; The next procedure is executed every time a reception is
  completed.

ASYNC_REC_INT_PROC proc near

     mov        dx, S0STS
     in         ax, dx                  ; Get status info

     test       al, 10000000B           ; Test for parity error
     jnz        parity_error

     test       al, 00010000B           ; Test for framing error
     jnz        framing_error

     test       al, 00000100B           ; Test for overrun error
     jnz        overrun_error
```

Example 1 (Continued)

```
; At this point we know the received data is OK.

     mov     dx, SORBUF
     in      ax, dx                  ; Read received data

     and     ax, 07FH                ; Strip off parity bit

; Code to store the data in a receive buffer would go here.
; It has been ommitted since this is heavily application dependent.

     jmp     eoi_rcv_int

parity_error:

; Code for parity error handling goes here.

     jmp     eoi_rcv_int

framing_error:

; Code for framing error handling goes here.

     jmp     eoi_rcv_int

overrun_error:

; Code for overrun error handling goes here.

     jmp     eoi_rcv_int

; Must now issue END-OF-INTERRUPT command to interrupt unit....

eoi_rcv_int: mov     dx, EOI
             mov     ax, 8000H       ; issue non-specific EOI
             out     dx, ax

     iret

ASYNC_REC_INT_PROC endp

ASYNC_XMIT_INT_PROC proc near

; This procedure is entered whenever a transmission completes.
; Typical code would be inserted here to transmit the next byte
; from a transmit buffer set up in memory. Since the configuration
; of such a buffer is application dependent this section wil be
; left blank.

; Must now issue END-OF-INTERRUPT command to interrupt unit....

eoi_xmit_int:   mov dx, EOI
                mov ax, 8000H        ; issue non-specific EOI
                out dx, ax

     iret

ASYNC_XMIT_INT_PROC endp



code_seg    ends
end
```

Example 2

```
$mod186
name                    scu_sync_port_example

;
; This file contains an example of initialization code for the
; Serial Communications Unit on the 80C186EB.
;
;
; This example has 1 procedure:
;
; READ_CONFIG_BYTE:    Sets up channel 1 as 1 M baud,
;                      synchronous with no CTS# control.
;                      It then reads in the configuration
;                      byte from the shift register connected
;                      as in Figure 8.11.
;

; We assume PCB has NOT BEEN RELOCATED!


B1CMP    EQU     0FF70H        ; Channel 1 Baud Rate Compare
S1CON    EQU     0FF74H        ; Channel 1 Control
S1STS    EQU     0FF76H        ; Channel 1 Status
S1RBUF   EQU     0FF78H        ; Channel 1 Receive Buffer
P1CON    EQU     0FF54H        ; Port 1 Multiplex control
P1LTCH   EQU     0FF56H        ; Port 1 data latch
P2CON    EQU     0FF5CH        ; Port 2 Multiplex control

code_seg    segment public
            assume cs:code_seg

READ_CONFIG_BYTE   proc   near

        mov     ax, 8007H      ; Mode 0 baud rate of
        mov     dx, B1CMP      ; 1 megabaud
        out     dx, ax


        mov     ax, 0FFH       ; Set Port 2.1 for TXD
        mov     dx, P2CON
        out     dx, ax

; The next piece of code pulses P1.7 low to load the 74HC165.

        mov     dx, P1CON      ; Get state of P1 controls
        in      ax, dx
        or      ax, 7FH        ; Make sure P1.7 is port
        out     dx, ax

        mov     dx, P1LTCH
        in      ax, dx         ; get state of P1 Latch
        or      ax, 0080H      ; set P1.7 to  1
        out     dx, ax
        and     ax, 0FF7FH     ; Clear P1.7
        out     dx, ax
        or      ax, 0080H      ; Set P1.7
        out     dx, ax
```

Example 2 (Continued)

```
; Now set up the receiver in mode 0 and turn it on.

        mov         ax, 0020H       ; Mode 0, No CTS
        mov         dx, S1CON       ; Receiver ON
        out         dx, ax
        mov         dx, S1STS
check_4_RI:         in ax, dx
                    test ax, 0040H ; look for SET RI bit
        jz          check_4_RI      ; loop until RI set.

; RI bit set. Reception is completed.

        mov         dx, S1RBUF
        in          ax, dx

        ret

READ_CONFIG_BYTE endp


code_seg            ends
end
```

Interrupts 9

CHAPTER 9
INTERRUPTS

80C186EB family interrupts can be software- or hardware-initiated. Software interrupts originate from three sources:

- Execution of INT instructions.
- A direct result of program execution, that is, execution of a breakpointed instruction.
- An indirect result of program logic, for example, attempted division by zero.

Hardware interrupts originate from either the integrated peripherals or external logic. In the 80C186EB family, an integrated Interrupt Control Unit performs the tasks which would otherwise be left to an external 82C59 Interrupt Controller. Hardware interrupts are classified as either non-maskable or maskable.

All interrupts, whether software- or hardware-initiated, result in the transfer of control to a new program location. A 256-entry vector table (see Figure 9.1), which contains address pointers to the interrupt routines, resides in memory locations 0 through 3FFH. Each entry in this table consists of two 16-bit address values (four bytes) that are loaded into the code segment (CS) and the instruction pointer (IP) registers when an interrupt is accepted.

All interrupts save the machine status by pushing the current contents of the flags onto the stack. The 80C186EB family CPU then clears the interrupt-enable and trap bits in the flags register to prevent subsequent maskable and single step interrupts. Next, the CPU establishes the routine return linkage by pushing the current CS and IP register contents onto the stack before loading the new CS and IP register values from the vector table.

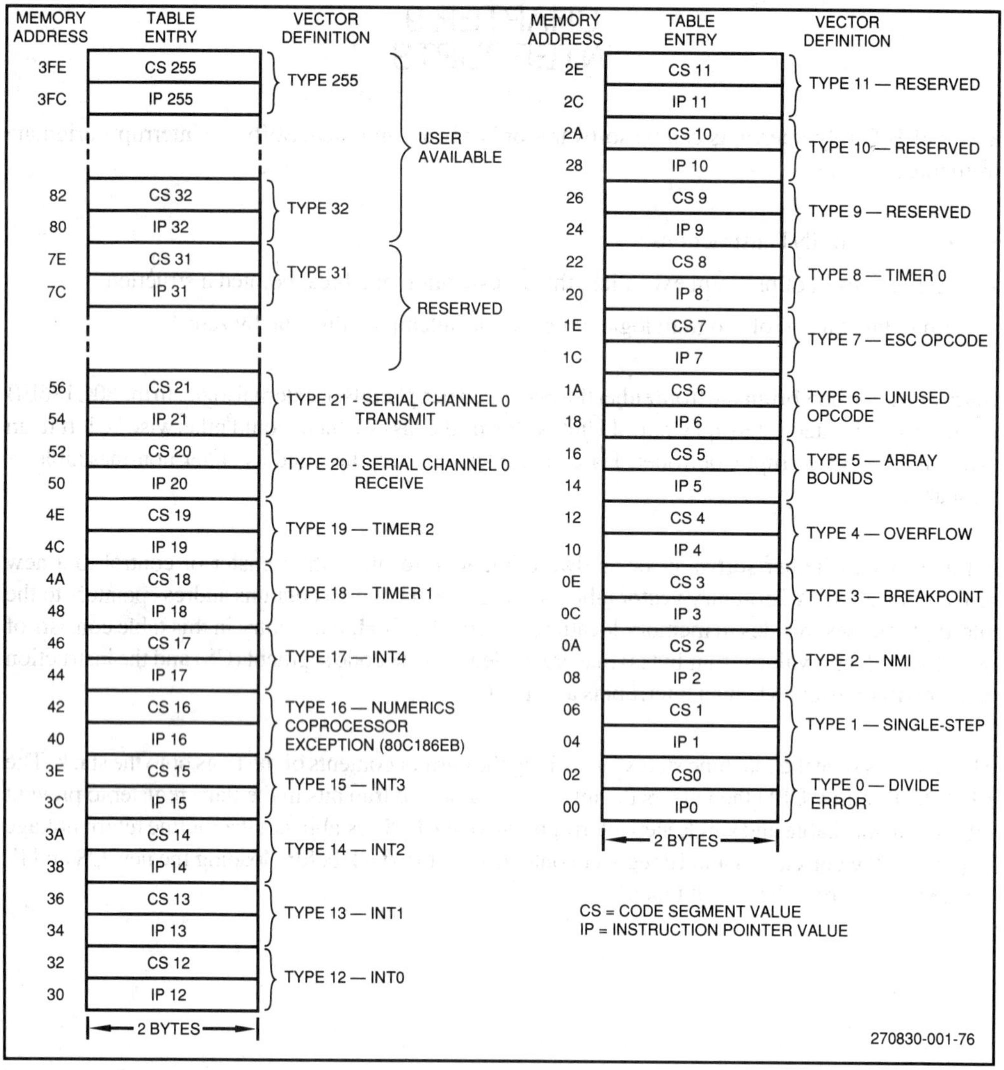

MEMORY ADDRESS	TABLE ENTRY	VECTOR DEFINITION	
3FE	CS 255	TYPE 255	USER AVAILABLE
3FC	IP 255		
⋮	⋮		
82	CS 32	TYPE 32	
80	IP 32		
7E	CS 31	TYPE 31	RESERVED
7C	IP 31		
⋮	⋮		
56	CS 21	TYPE 21 - SERIAL CHANNEL 0 TRANSMIT	
54	IP 21		
52	CS 20	TYPE 20 - SERIAL CHANNEL 0 RECEIVE	
50	IP 20		
4E	CS 19	TYPE 19 — TIMER 2	
4C	IP 19		
4A	CS 18	TYPE 18 — TIMER 1	
48	IP 18		
46	CS 17	TYPE 17 — INT4	
44	IP 17		
42	CS 16	TYPE 16 — NUMERICS COPROCESSOR EXCEPTION (80C186EB)	
40	IP 16		
3E	CS 15	TYPE 15 — INT3	
3C	IP 15		
3A	CS 14	TYPE 14 — INT2	
38	IP 14		
36	CS 13	TYPE 13 — INT1	
34	IP 13		
32	CS 12	TYPE 12 — INT0	
30	IP 12		
	←2 BYTES→		

MEMORY ADDRESS	TABLE ENTRY	VECTOR DEFINITION
2E	CS 11	TYPE 11 — RESERVED
2C	IP 11	
2A	CS 10	TYPE 10 — RESERVED
28	IP 10	
26	CS 9	TYPE 9 — RESERVED
24	IP 9	
22	CS 8	TYPE 8 — TIMER 0
20	IP 8	
1E	CS 7	TYPE 7 — ESC OPCODE
1C	IP 7	
1A	CS 6	TYPE 6 — UNUSED OPCODE
18	IP 6	
16	CS 5	TYPE 5 — ARRAY BOUNDS
14	IP 5	
12	CS 4	TYPE 4 — OVERFLOW
10	IP 4	
0E	CS 3	TYPE 3 — BREAKPOINT
0C	IP 3	
0A	CS 2	TYPE 2 — NMI
08	IP 2	
06	CS 1	TYPE 1 — SINGLE-STEP
04	IP 1	
02	CS0	TYPE 0 — DIVIDE ERROR
00	IP0	
	←2 BYTES→	

CS = CODE SEGMENT VALUE
IP = INSTRUCTION POINTER VALUE

270830-001-76

Figure 9.1. Interrupt Vector Table

9.1 INTERRUPT CONTROL MODEL

80C186EB family software interrupts are presented directly to the CPU, while hardware interrupts are managed through the integrated Interrupt Controller.

The tasks performed by the integrated Interrupt Controller include synchronization of interrupt requests, prioritization of interrupt requests, and management of interrupt acknowledge sequences. Nesting is provided so interrupt service routines for lower priority interrupts may themselves be interrupted by higher priority interrupts. The integrated Interrupt Controller can be a master to two external 8259A or 82C59A Interrupt Controllers.

The integrated Interrupt Controller block diagram is shown in Figure 9.2. It contains registers and a control element. Five inputs are provided for external interfacing to the Interrupt Controller. Their functions change according to the mode of the Interrupt Controller. Like the other 80C186EB family integrated peripheral registers, the Interrupt Controller registers are available for CPU reading or writing at any time.

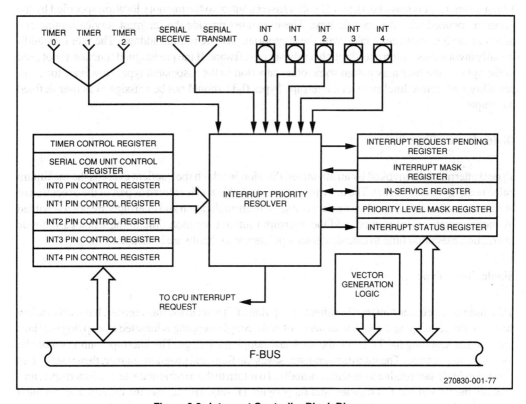

Figure 9.2. Interrupt Controller Block Diagram

9.2 INTERRUPT CHARACTERISTICS RELATED TO INTERRUPT TYPE

The interrupts handled directly by the CPU are varied and specific, while the interrupts handled by the integrated Interrupt Controller are processed like each other.

9.2.1 INTERRUPTS HANDLED DIRECTLY BY THE CPU

The integrated Interrupt Controller does not intervene in interrupt processing related to INT instructions, instruction traps and exceptions, and the Non-Maskable Interrupt.

9.2.1.1 INSTRUCTION-GENERATED TRAPS AND EXCEPTIONS

Software interrupts have higher priority than hardware interrupts, with the exception of NMI. There are eight dedicated software interrupts associated with instruction execution or attempted instruction execution, leaving room in the vector table from Type numbers 32 through 255 for user-defined interrupts.

The predefined software interrupts in the 80C186EB family are listed below with brief descriptions. When an interrupt is invoked, the CPU will transfer control to the memory location specified by the vector associated with the specific type. The user must provide the interrupt service routine and initialize the interrupt vector table with the appropriate service routine address. The user may additionally invoke these interrupts through hardware or software. If the preassigned function is not used in the system, the user may assign some other function to the associated type. However, for compatibility with future Intel products, interrupt Types 0-31 should not be reassigned as user defined interrupts.

Divide Error - Type 0:

Type 0 interrupts are invoked by an attempted division in which the quotient exceeds the maximum value (e.g., division by zero). The interrupt is non-maskable and is entered as part of the execution of the divide instruction. If divide errors are common in an application and interrupts are not re-enabled by the interrupt service routine, add the interrupt routine execution time to the worst case divide instruction execution time to calculate interrupt latency for hardware interrupts.

Single Step - Type 1:

This interrupt occurs one instruction after the trap flag (TF) is set in the flag register. It is used to allow software single stepping through a sequence of code. Single stepping is initiated by copying the flags onto the stack, setting the TF bit on the stack and popping the flags. The interrupt routine should be the single step routine. The interrupt sequence saves the flags and program counter, then resets TF to allow the single step routine to execute normally. To return to the routine under test, an interrupt return restores the IP register, CS register, and flags (with TF set). This allows the execution of the next instruction in the program under test before trapping back to the single step routine.

Breakpoint Interrupt - Type 3:

This is a special version of the INT instruction. Since it requires only a single byte of code space, the breakpoint interrupt can map into the smallest instruction for absolute breakpoint resolution. This interrupt is not maskable.

Interrupt on Overflow - Type 4:

This non-maskable interrupt occurs if the overflow flag (OF) is set in the flag register and the INTO instruction is executed. This instruction allows trapping to an overflow error service routine.

Array Bounds Exception - Type 5:

If an array index is outside the array bounds during the BOUND instruction, a Type 5 interrupt results. The array bounds are located in memory at a location indicated by one of the instruction operands. The other operand indicates the value of the index to be checked.

Unused Opcode Exception - Type 6:

Attempted execution of undefined opcodes generates this interrupt. This interrupt is non-maskable.

ESCape Opcode Exception - Type 7:

This exception is the result of attempted ESCape opcode (D8H-DFH) execution. On the 80C186EB, the ESC trap is enabled by setting a bit in the relocation register. On the 80C188EB, ESC instructions always generate this trap. The return address of this exception will point to the ESC instruction causing the exception. If a segment override prefix preceded the ESC instruction, the return address will point to the segment override prefix.

Numerics Coprocessor Exception (80C186EB Only) - Type 16:

When the execution of numerics (ESCape) instruction causes an unmasked exception in the 80C187 Numerics Processor Extension, the result is an interrupt Type 16. Although this is classified as a software interrupt, signaling is performed in hardware from the 80C187 to the 80C186EB on the ERROR pin. In general, this exception is detected by the 80C186EB upon execution of the instruction subsequent to the one causing the error condition.

9.2.1.2 NON-MASKABLE INTERRUPT (NMI)

The Non-Maskable Interrupt (NMI), a hardware interrupt, is interrupt Type 2. It has the highest priority among hardware interrupts and is typically reserved for catastrophic events such as impending power failure or timeout of a system watchdog timer. NMI cannot be prevented by programming and multiple NMI inputs will lead to nesting of NMI interrupt service routines. Noise on the NMI pin can cause unnecessary system upsets.

NMI must be asserted for one CLKOUT period in order to be internally synchronized. The signal is edge-triggered and level-latched. The vectoring sequence for NMI starts at the next available instruction edge after NMI is latched. The interrupt response time for NMI is 42 processor clocks.

The processor will start recognizing the NMI input pin at the same clock edge on which the $\overline{RES}$ input goes inactive. If NMI is asserted within 10 clocks after RESET goes inactive, the processor will vector to the NMI service routine before it executes the first instruction. This procedure is useful when it is desired to begin execution somewhere other than the default starting address of 0FFFF0H.

9.2.1.3 USER-DEFINED SOFTWARE INTERRUPTS

The user can generate an interrupt through the software with a two byte interrupt instruction INT nn. The first byte is the INT opcode while the second byte (nn) contains the type number of the interrupt to be performed. The INT instruction is not maskable by the interrupt-enable flag. This instruction can be used to transfer control to routines that are dynamically relocatable and whose location in memory is not known by the calling program. This technique also saves the flags of the calling program on the stack prior to transferring control. The called procedure must return control with an interrupt return (IRET) instruction to remove the flags from the stack and fully restore the state of the calling program.

All interrupts invoked through software (all interrupts discussed thus far with the exception of NMI) are not maskable with IF and initiate the transfer of control at the end of the instruction in which they occur. They do not initiate interrupt acknowledge bus cycles and will disable subsequent maskable interrupts by resetting the flags IF and TF. The vectors for these interrupts are implied in the instruction.

9.2.2 INTERRUPTS HANDLED BY THE INTEGRATED INTERRUPT CONTROLLER

The 80C186EB family integrated Interrupt Controller receives and prioritizes hardware interrupts from five external pins and five integrated peripheral sources. The Interrupt Controller was designed to allow these interrupts to be flexibly managed. For example, it is possible to mask one or more interrupt sources and handle them by polling while allowing vectored interrupts for all the other sources to proceed.

Requests on interrupt pins INT0-4 **are not latched**. If a normally LOW INT input is pulsed HIGH briefly while that interrupt is disabled or another interrupt is in service, that request will not be saved, even if the corresponding bit gets temporarily set in the interrupt request register. It is necessary to hold the INT input active until the processor starts the vectoring sequence, either by running interrupt acknowledge cycles or reading the new CS and IP values from the interrupt vector table. The 80C186EB processor family does not employ a default vector as does the 8259A or 82C59A.

All interrupt requests from the integrated peripherals **are latched** in the integrated Interrupt Controller for presentation to the CPU.

9.3 OTHER INTERRUPT CHARACTERISTICS

To understand how interrupts participate in the overall microprocessor system, it is necessary to understand latency, masking and priority.

9.3.1 INTERRUPT LATENCY

Interrupt latency is the time it takes the 80C186EB family processor to begin to respond to an interrupt. This is different from interrupt response time, the time from reception of the interrupt until it actually executes the first instruction of the interrupt service routine.

Two factors affecting interrupt latency are the instruction being executed and the state of the interrupt-enable flip-flop. The interrupt-enable flip-flop must be explicitly set by issuing the STI instruction. Since interrupt vectoring automatically clears the flip-flop, it is necessary to set the flip-flop within the interrupt service routine if nested interrupts are desired.

In general, an interrupt can be acknowledged only when the CPU finishes executing an instruction, i.e., interrupts are acknowledged at the first available instruction boundary. For the purpose of determining instruction boundaries, prefixes (LOCK, REP, and segment override) are considered to be part of the following instruction. Thus, interrupt latency time can be as long as 69 CPU clocks, the amount of time it takes the processor to execute an integer divide instruction with a segment override prefix. There are a number of exceptions to these rules.

MOVs and POPs to a segment register cause interrupt processing to be delayed until after the next instruction. This delay allows a 32-bit pointer to be loaded to the SS and SP stack registers without the danger of an interrupt occurring between the two loads.

The WAIT instruction causes the CPU to suspend processing while checking the $\overline{\text{TEST}}$ pin for a logic LOW condition. If an interrupt is detected, the processor will vector to the interrupt service routine with the return pointer aimed back to the WAIT instruction. The 80C186EB does not check the $\overline{\text{ERROR}}$ pin for 80C187 exceptions during the WAIT instruction.

When the repeat prefix (REP) is used in front of a string operation, the processor does allow interrupt vectoring between repetitions, including those which are LOCKed. If multiple prefixes precede a repeated string operation and the instruction is interrupted, only the prefix immediately preceding the string primitive is restored.

With the 80C186EB/80C187 processor combination, interrupts on the external interrupt pins INT0-4 can be serviced after the 80C186 starts a numerics instruction. However, once communication is completely established with the 80C187 (i.e., the 80C187 is not busy), interrupts are blocked until the end of the instruction.

Interrupt latency is also affected by activity of the integrated peripheral set. Interrupt latency is increased if the processor does not have control of the bus due to the HOLD/HLDA protocol.

Finally, the 80C186EB/80C188EB will not accept interrupts during DRAM refresh bus cycles.

9.3.2 INTERRUPT MASKS AND NESTING

To provide a high degree of flexibility in designing complex interrupt structures, the 80C186EB family has an elaborate mechanism to control the enabling and disenabling of individual interrupts. The programmer must understand this structure to utilize the processor most efficiently in a heavily interrupt-driven system. The rules of masking are as follows:

- The non-maskable interrupt (NMI), cannot be prevented by programming, as its name implies.
- Software interrupts, both user-defined and execution exception, cannot be masked.
- All other hardware interrupts are subject to the condition of the interrupt-enable flag which is set by the STI instruction and cleared by the CLI instruction. Since every interrupt vectoring sequence clears the flag, programmer intervention is required to enable interrupt nesting. The flag is automatically restored upon execution of the IRET instruction.
- The integrated Interrupt Controller has a priority mask register which disables interrupts below a programmable priority limit.
- The integrated Interrupt Controller has a mask register with programmable bits for each possible interrupt source, including the Serial Communications Unit, timers, and the external interrupt pins. (Timers share a mask bit. The receive and transmit interrupt requests share a bit.)
- The integrated Interrupt Controller has a control register for each interrupt source. (Timers share a control register.) Each control register addresses the same mask bit as does the mask register.

Interrupts under control of the integrated Interrupt Controller are nestable subject to the states of their in-service bits. Additionally, INT0 and INT1 have a provision called Special Fully Nested Mode (SFNM), which allows successive interrupts on those pins to ignore the state of their in-service bits.

9.3.3 INTERRUPT PRIORITY

When considering the precedence of interrupts for multiple simultaneous interrupts, apply the following guidelines:

1. Of the non-maskable interrupts (NMI, instruction trap, and user-defined software), single step has the highest priority (will be serviced first), followed by NMI, followed by all other software interrupts.
2. The interrupts controlled by the 80C186EB family integrated Interrupt Controller are all maskable hardware interrupts. Their priorities levels are lower than the non-maskable interrupts.

A simultaneous NMI and single step trap will cause the NMI service routine to follow single step. A simultaneous software trap and single step trap will cause the software interrupt service routine to follow single step. Finally, and simultaneous NMI and software trap will cause the NMI service routine to be executed followed by the software interrupt service routine. An exception to this priority structure occurs if all three interrupts are pending. For this case, transfer of control to the software interrupt service routine followed by the NMI trap will cause both the NMI and software interrupt service routines to be executed without single stepping. Single stepping resumes upon execution of the instruction following the instruction causing the software interrupt (the next instruction in the routine being single stepped).

If the user does not wish to single step before hardware interrupt service routines, the single step routine need only disable interrupts during execution of the program being single stepped and re-enable interrupts on entry to the single step routine. Disabling the interrupts within the program under test prevents entry into the interrupt service routine while single step (TF = 1) is active. To prevent single stepping before NMI service routines, the single step routine must check the return address and return control to that routine without single step enabled. As examples, consider Figures 9.3 and 9.4. In Figure 9.3 single step and NMI occur simultaneously. In Figure 9.4, NMI, a timer interrupt and a divide error all occur while single stepping a divide instruction.

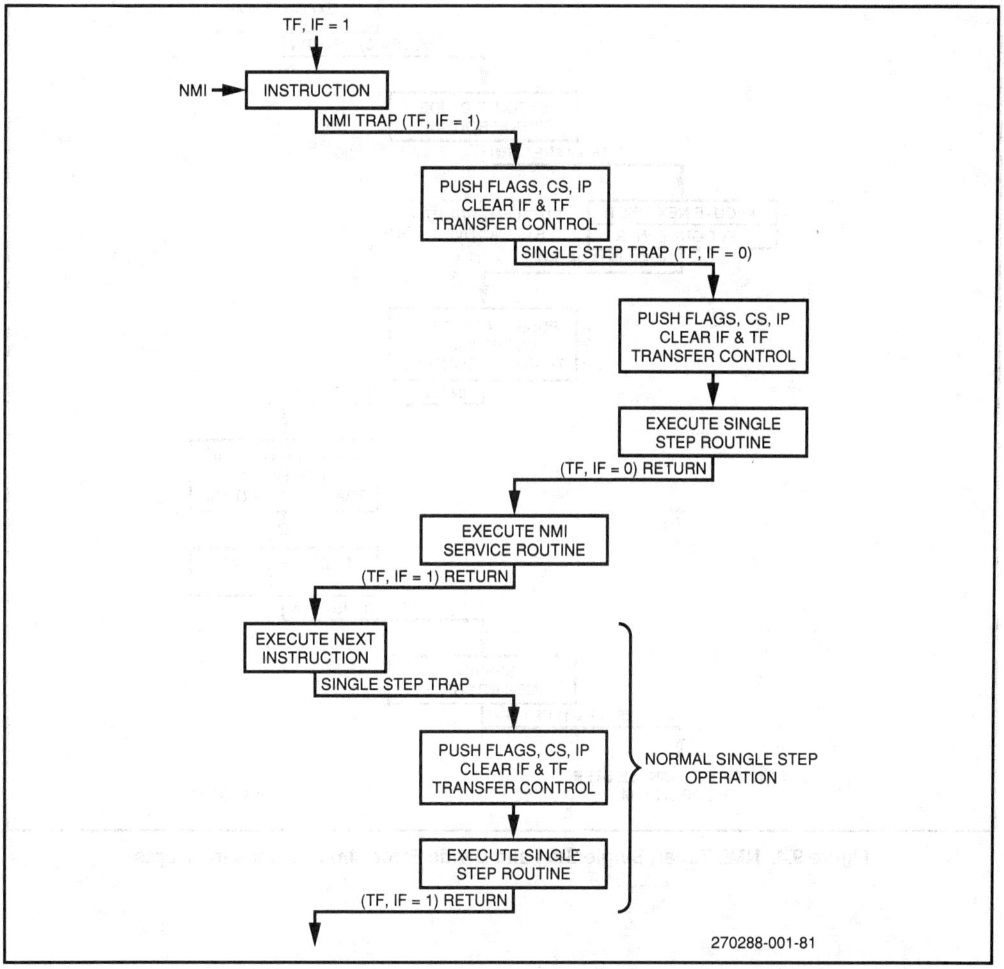

Figure 9.3. NMI During Single Stepping and Normal Single Step Operation

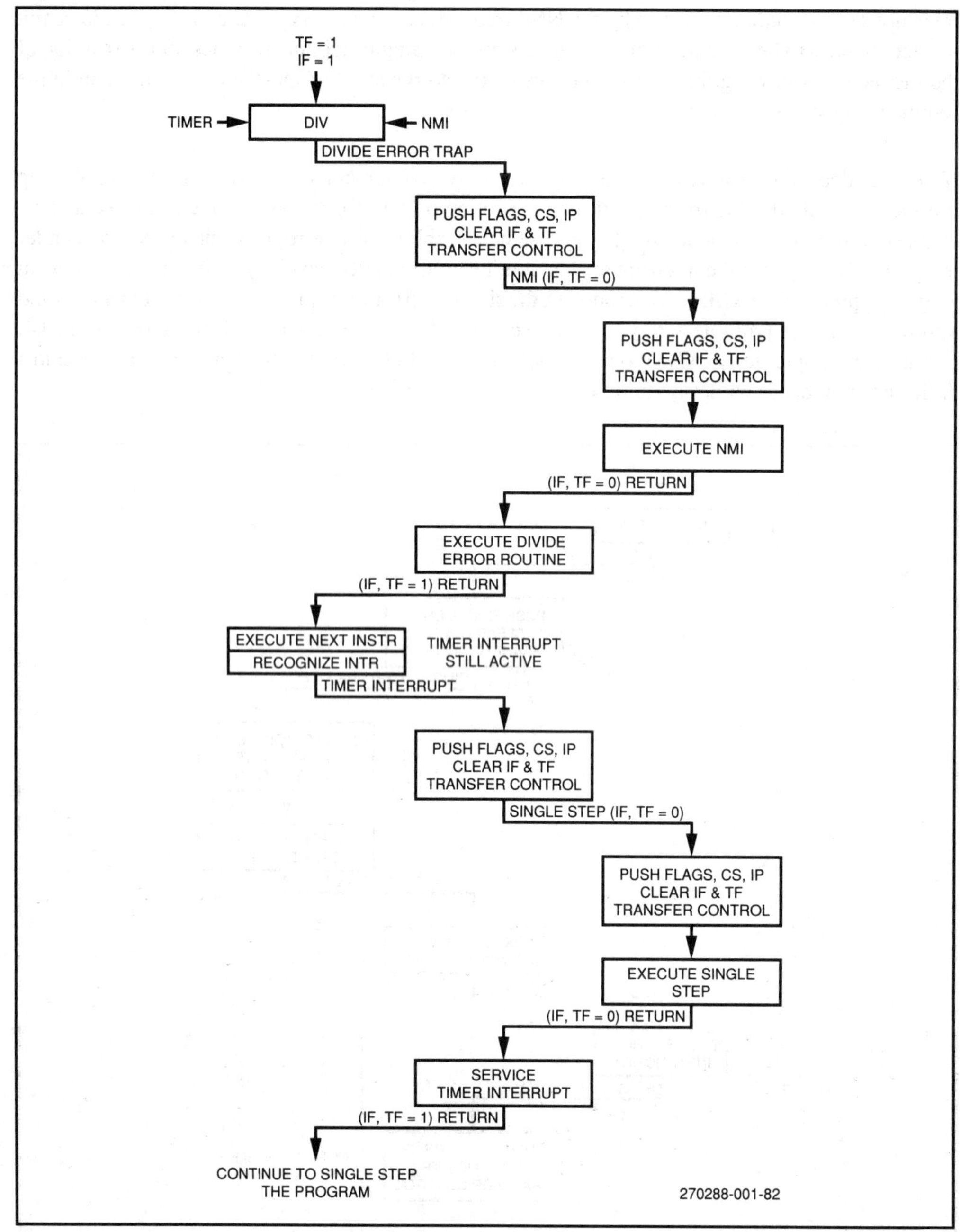

Figure 9.4. NMI, Timer, Single Step and Divide Error Simultaneous Interrupts

9.4 INTERRUPT CONTROL UNIT OPERATION

The Interrupt Control Unit acts as the master interrupt controller for the system, receiving and arbitrating hardware interrupts generated both internally and externally. The Interrupt Controller presents interrupts directly to the CPU of the 80C186EB family processor. As many as two 8259A (or 82C59A) Interrupt Controllers may act as slaves to the master processor.

User's familiar with the 80186 and 80C186 may remember that the interrupt controller on those products has two modes: Master and Slave. The 80C186EB has only one mode which is functionally equivalent to master mode. Slave mode was rarely used on the 80186 and 80C186 and was deleted from the 80C186EB.

9.4.1 EXTERNAL CONNECTIONS

The INT0 through INT3 external interrupt pins are configurable according to two options, direct and cascade. INT4 can only be configured as a direct input. With the pins configured in Direct Input Mode the integrated Interrupt Controller provides interrupt vectors. With the pins configured in Cascade Mode, interrupt types are furnished by an external Interrupt Controller. Mixed mode operation (two pins as direct inputs and two pins as an INT/$\overline{\text{INTA}}$ pair) is also possible.

9.4.1.1 DIRECT INPUT MODE

When the Cascade Mode bits are cleared, the interrupt input pins are configured as direct interrupt pins (see Figure 9.5). Whenever an interrupt is received on the input line, the integrated controller will do nothing unless the interrupt is enabled, and it is the highest priority pending interrupt. At this time, the Interrupt Controller will present the interrupt to the CPU and wait for an interrupt acknowledge. When the acknowledge occurs, it will present the interrupt vector address to the CPU. In Direct Input Mode, the CPU will not run any external interrupt acknowledge (INTA) cycles.

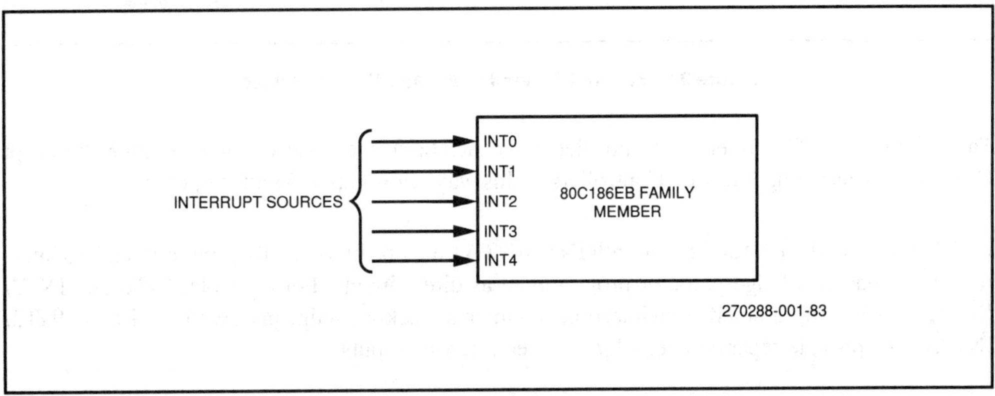

Figure 9.5. Direct Input Mode Interrupt Connections

9.4.1.2 CASCADE MODE

The INT2/$\overline{\text{INTA0}}$ and INT3/$\overline{\text{INTA1}}$ lines are dual purpose; they can function as direct input lines, or they can function as interrupt acknowledge outputs. When the Cascade Mode bit is set, the interrupt input lines are configured in Cascade Mode. In this mode, the interrupt input line is paired with an interrupt acknowledge line. $\overline{\text{INTA0}}$ provides the interrupt acknowledge for an INT0 input, and $\overline{\text{INTA1}}$ provides the interrupt acknowledge for an INT1 input. Figure 9.6 shows this connection.

The $\overline{\text{INTA0}}$ and $\overline{\text{INTA1}}$ are configured as inputs until cascade mode is selected. The pullup resisters in Figure 9.6 insure that the INTA lines never float (and thus issue a spurious interrupt acknowledge to the 8259). The value of the resisters is not critical. The value must be high enough to prevent excessive loading on the $\overline{\text{INTA0}}$ and $\overline{\text{INTA1}}$ pins.

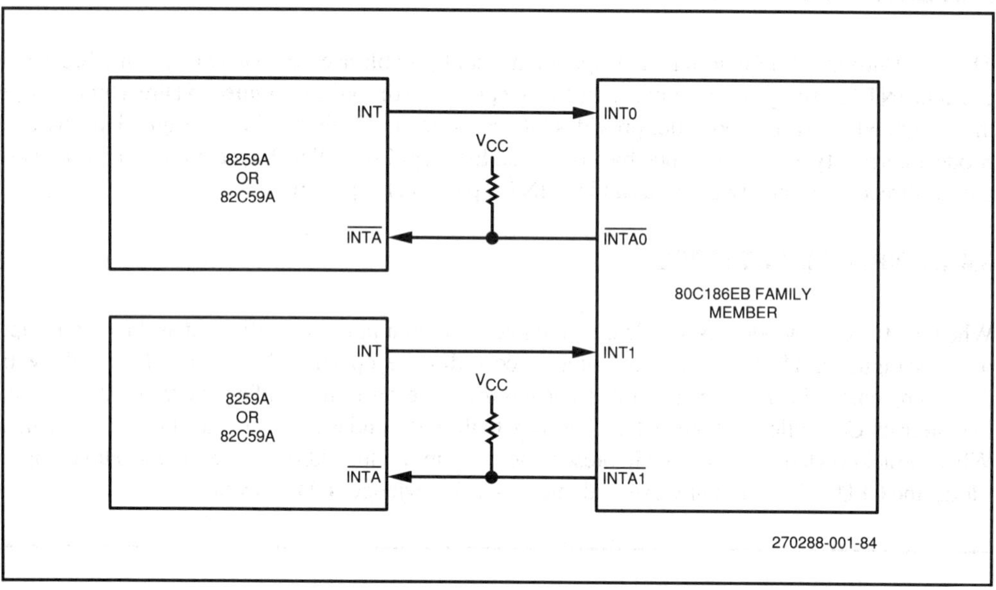

Figure 9.6. 80C186EB Family Cascade Mode Interface

The 8259A or 82C59A Interrupt Controllers may each be further cascaded to eight more Interrupt Controllers. Cascading Interrupt Controllers in this way allows up to 64 interrupt levels.

INTO with INT2/$\overline{\text{INTA0}}$ and INT1 with INT3/$\overline{\text{INTA1}}$ may be individually programmed into interrupt request/acknowledge pairs, or programmed as direct inputs. For example, INT0 and INT2/$\overline{\text{INTA0}}$ may be programmed as an interrupt and interrupt acknowledge pair, while INT1 and INT3/$\overline{\text{INTA1}}$ each provide separate internally vectored interrupt inputs.

9.4.2 INTERRUPT UNIT PROGRAMMING

The Interrupt Controller registers are defined according to Figure 9.7.

REGISTER NAME	OFFSET
EOI	02H
POLL	04H
POLL STS	06H
IMASK	08H
PRIMSK	0AH
INSERV	0CH
REQST	0EH
INTSTS	10H
TCUCON	12H
SCUCON	14H
I4CON	16H
I0CON	18H
I1CON	1AH
I2CON	ICH
I3CON	IEH

Figure 9.7. Peripheral Control Block Map

9.4.2.1 THE CONTROL REGISTERS

Each interrupt source to an 80C186EB family processor has a control register in the internal controller. These registers contain three bits which select one of eight interrupt priority levels for the device (0 is highest priority, 7 is lowest priority), and a mask bit to enable the interrupt (see Figure 9.8). When the mask bit is zero, the interrupt is enabled; when it is one, the interrupt is masked. All interrupt sources have default priority levels.

INTERRUPT CONTROL REGISTER (Internal Sources):
(SCUCON, TCUCON)

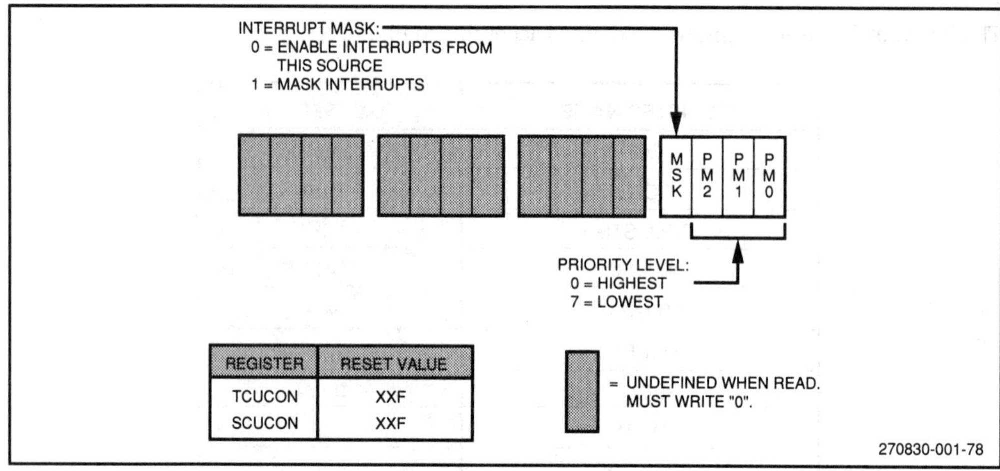

INTERRUPT MASK:
0 = ENABLE INTERRUPTS FROM THIS SOURCE
1 = MASK INTERRUPTS
MSK
PM2
PM1
PM0
PRIORITY LEVEL:
0 = HIGHEST
7 = LOWEST

REGISTER	RESET VALUE
TCUCON	XXF
SCUCON	XXF

= UNDEFINED WHEN READ. MUST WRITE "0".

270830-001-78

Figure 9.8(a).

INTERRUPT CONTROL REGISTER (Cascadable Pins):
(I0CON, I1CON)

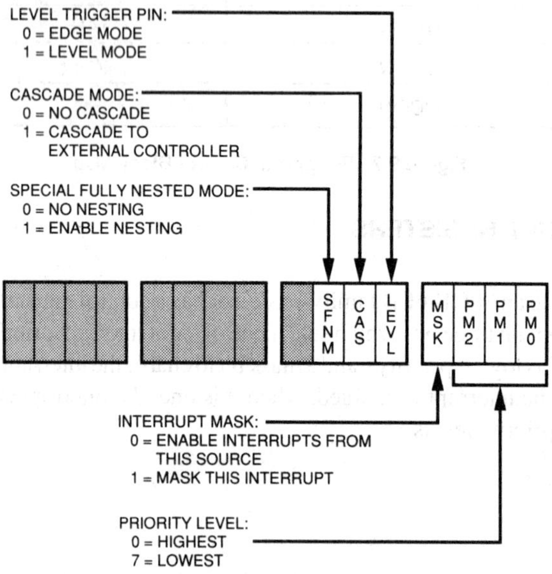

LEVEL TRIGGER PIN:
0 = EDGE MODE
1 = LEVEL MODE
CASCADE MODE:
0 = NO CASCADE
1 = CASCADE TO EXTERNAL CONTROLLER
SPECIAL FULLY NESTED MODE:
0 = NO NESTING
1 = ENABLE NESTING
SFNM
CAS
LEVL
MSK
PM2
PM1
PM0
INTERRUPT MASK:
0 = ENABLE INTERRUPTS FROM THIS SOURCE
1 = MASK THIS INTERRUPT
PRIORITY LEVEL:
0 = HIGHEST
7 = LOWEST

REGISTER	RESET VALUE
I0CON	XX0F
I1CON	XX0F

= UNDEFINED WHEN READ. MUST WRITE "0".

270830-001-79

Figure 9.8(b).

INTERRUPT CONTROL REGISTER (External Pins): (I2CON, I3CON, I4CON)

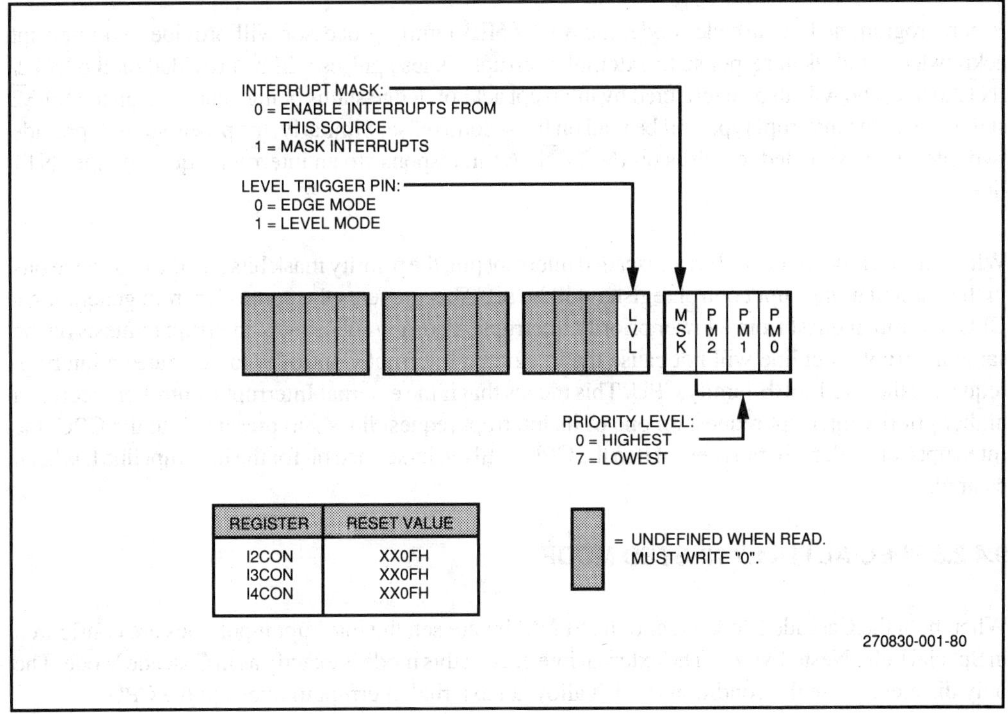

Figure 9.8(c).

There are seven control registers in the integrated Interrupt Controller: five of these serve the external interrupt inputs, one for serial channel zero, and one for the collective timer interrupts.

The control registers for the external interrupt pins contain special bits not present for other interrupt sources. Setting the LTM bit in these registers selects level-triggered operation as opposed to edge-triggered operation. The INT0 and INT1 control registers contain C and SFNM bits to select Cascade and Special Fully Nested Modes, respectively.

Setting the LTM bit in these registers selects level-triggered operation over edge-triggered operation. With edge-triggered operation, a LOW-to-HIGH transition must occur before the interrupt will be recognized. The interrupt input must also be LOW for one clock before the active-going edge. With level-triggered operation, only a HIGH level is required to generate an interrupt. **In both types of operation, the interrupt input must remain active until acknowledged.**

With level-triggered operation only, an interrupt request input left active until after the end-of-interrupt causes another interrupt request.

Level triggering must be used when an 8259 (or 82C59) is cascaded to the Interrupt Control Unit.

9.4.2.2 CASCADE MODE

When programmed in cascade mode, the 80C186EB family processor will provide two interrupt acknowledge pulses in response to external interrupts. These pulses will be provided on the INT2/$\overline{\text{INTA0}}$ line, and will also be reflected by interrupt acknowledge status being generated on the $\overline{\text{S0}}$-$\overline{\text{S2}}$ status lines. The interrupt type will be read on the second pulse. Similarly, the processor will provide two interrupt acknowledge pulses on INT3/$\overline{\text{INTA1}}$ in response to an interrupt request on the INT1 line.

When an interrupt is received on a cascaded interrupt pin, the priority mask bits and the in-service bits in the particular interrupt control register will be set. This prevents the controller from generating a CPU interrupt request from a lower priority interrupt. Also, any subsequent interrupt requests on the same interrupt input line will not cause the integrated Interrupt Controller to generate an interrupt request to the 80C186EB family CPU. This means that if the external Interrupt Controller receives a higher priority interrupt request on one of its interrupt request lines and presents it to the CPU, the Interrupt Controller will not present it to the CPU until the in-service bit for the interrupt line has been cleared.

9.4.2.3 SPECIAL FULLY NESTED MODE

When both the Cascade Mode bit and the SFNM bit are set, the interrupt input lines are configured in Special Fully Nested Mode. The external interface in this mode is exactly as in Cascade Mode. The only difference is in the conditions which allow an external interrupt to interrupt the CPU.

When an interrupt is received from a Special Fully Nested Mode interrupt line, it will interrupt the CPU if it is the highest priority pending interrupt regardless of the state of the in-service bit for the source in the Interrupt Controller. When the processor acknowledges an interrupt from a Special Fully Nested Mode interrupt line, it sets corresponding bits in the priority mask and in-service registers. This prevents the Interrupt Controller from accepting a lower priority interrupt. However, the Interrupt Controller will allow additional requests generated by the same external source to interrupt the CPU. This means that if the external (cascaded) Interrupt Controller receives higher priority interrupts on its interrupt request lines and presents them to the integrated controller's request line, these interrupts will be nested.

If the SFNM bit is set and the Cascade Mode bit is not set, the controller will provide internal interrupt vectoring. It will also ignore the state of the in-service bit in determining whether to present an interrupt request to the CPU. In other words, it will use the SFNM conditions of interrupt generation with an internally vectored interrupt response, i.e., if the interrupt pending is the highest priority type pending, it will cause a CPU interrupt regardless of the state of the in-service bit for the interrupt. This operation is only applicable to INT0 and INT1, which have SFNM bits in their control registers.

9.4.2.4 THE REQUEST REGISTER

The Interrupt Controller includes an interrupt request register (see Figure 9.9). This register contains seven active bits, one for every interrupt source with an interrupt control register. Whenever an interrupt request is made, the bit in the interrupt request register is set regardless of whether the interrupt is enabled. Interrupt request bits are automatically cleared when the interrupt is acknowledged by starting the interrupt vectoring sequence.

INTERRUPT REQUEST REGISTER:
(REQST)

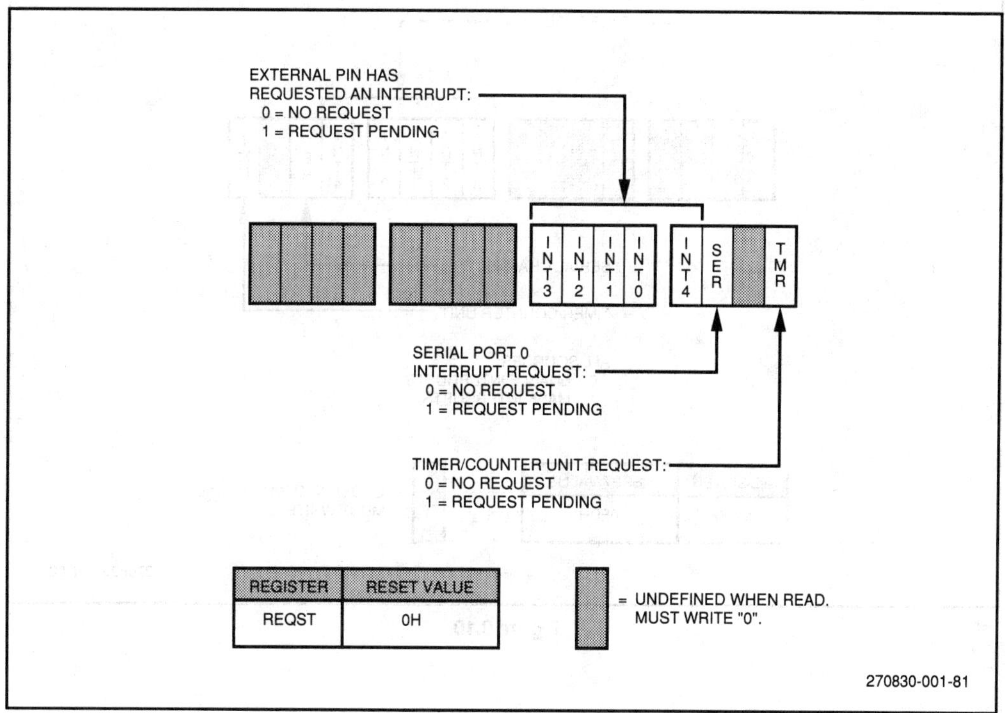

Figure 9.9.

9.4.2.5 THE MASK REGISTER

The Interrupt Controller mask register (see Figure 9.10) contains a mask bit for each interrupt source associated with an interrupt control register. The bit for an interrupt source in the mask register is the same bit as provided in the interrupt control register; modifying a mask bit in the control register will also modify it in the mask register, and vice versa.

INTERRUPT MASK REGISTER:
(IMASK)

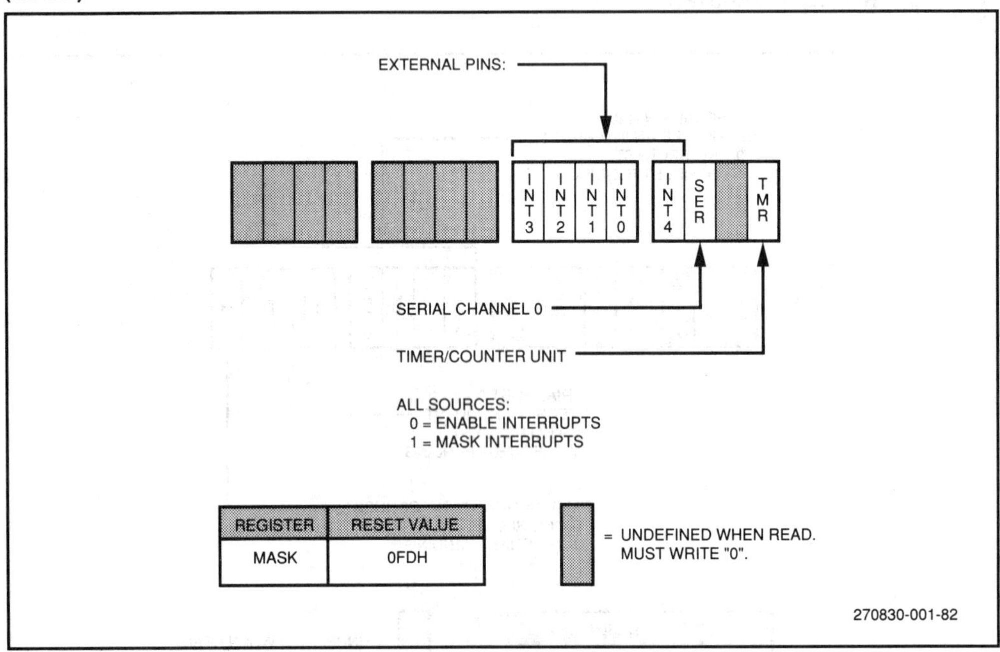

Figure 9.10.

9.4.2.6 THE PRIORITY MASK REGISTER

The interrupt priority mask register (see Figure 9.11) contains three bits which indicate the lowest priority an interrupt must have to cause an interrupt request to be serviced. Interrupts which have a lower priority will be masked. Upon RESET, the register is set to the lowest priority of 7 to enable interrupts of any priority. This register may be read or written.

INTERRUPT PRIORITY MASK REGISTER:
(PRIMASK)

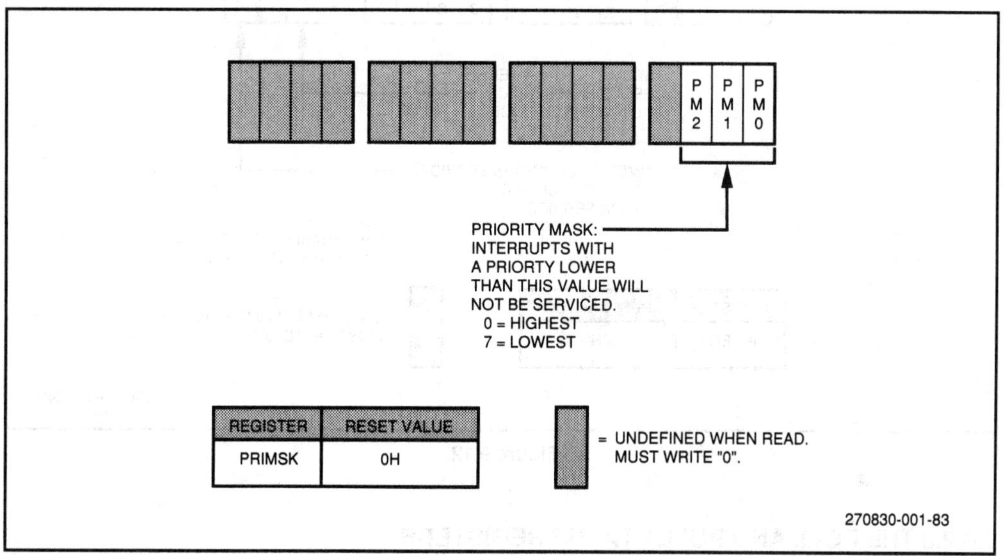

Figure 9.11.

9.4.2.7 THE IN-SERVICE REGISTER

The Interrupt Controller contains an in-service register (see Figure 9.12). A bit in the in-service register is associated with each interrupt control register so that when an interrupt request by the device associated with the control register is acknowledged by the processor (either by interrupt acknowledge cycles or by reading the poll register) the bit is set. The bit is reset when the CPU issues an End Of Interrupt to the Interrupt Controller. This register may be both read and written, i.e., the CPU may set in-service bits without an interrupt ever occurring, or may reset them without using the EOI function of the Interrupt Controller.

INTERRUPT IN-SERVICE REGISTER:
(INSERV)

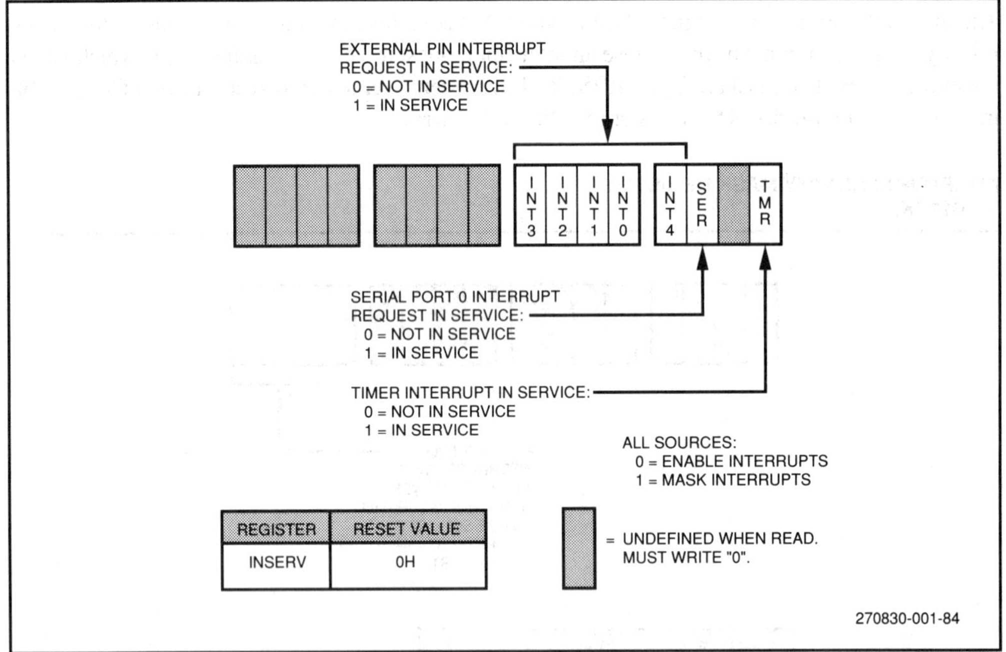

Figure 9.12.

9.4.2.8 THE POLL AND POLL STATUS REGISTERS

The Interrupt Controller contains both a poll register and a poll status register (see Figure 9.13). These registers contain the same information. They have a single bit to indicate an interrupt is pending and five bits to indicate the type of the pending interrupt. The request bit is set if an interrupt of sufficient priority has been received. It is automatically cleared when the interrupt is acknowledged. If an interrupt is pending, the remaining bits contain information about the highest priority pending interrupt. These registers are read-only.

Reading the poll register will acknowledge the pending interrupt to the Interrupt Controller just as if the processor had started the interrupt vectoring sequence. The processor will not actually run any interrupt acknowledge cycles, and will not vector through a location in the interrupt vector table. The contents of the interrupt request, in-service, poll, and poll status registers will change appropriately.

Reading the poll status register will merely transmit the status of the polling bits without modifying any of the other Interrupt Controller registers.

POLL AND POLL STATUS REGISTERS:
(POLL, POLLSTS) READ ONLY

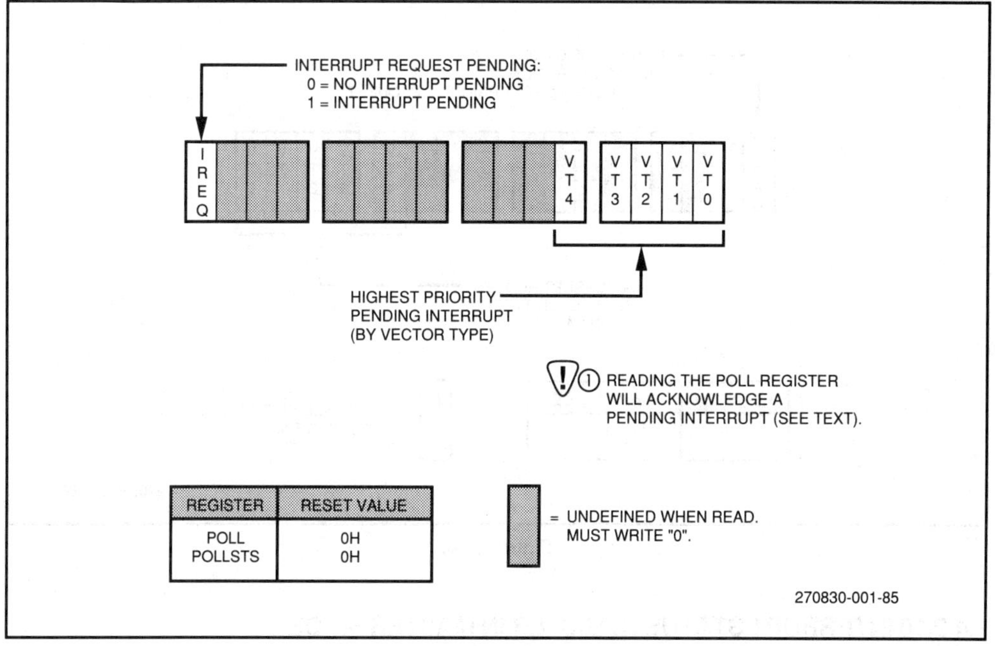

Figure 9.13.

9.4.2.9 THE END OF INTERRUPT REGISTER

The Interrupt Controller contains an End Of Interrupt register (see Figure 9.14). The programmer issues an End Of Interrupt (EOI) to the controller by writing to this register. After receiving the EOI, the Interrupt Controller automatically resets the in-service bit for the interrupt. The value of the word written to this register determines whether the EOI is specific or non-specific. A non-specific EOI is requested by setting the non-specific bit in the word written to the EOI register. In a non-specific EOI, the in-service bit of the highest priority interrupt set is automatically cleared, while a specific EOI allows the in-service bit cleared to be explicitly specified. If the highest priority interrupt is reset, the poll and poll status registers change to reflect the next lowest priority interrupt to be serviced. If a less than highest priority interrupt in-service bit is reset, the poll and poll status registers will not be modified (because the highest priority interrupt to be serviced has not changed). This register is write-only.

To issue a specific EOI for any timer interrupt the value 8 must be written to the EOI register. Similarly, for both receive and transmit SCU interrupts the EOI register must be written with a 20 (decimal) for a specific EOI.

To issue a non-specific end-of-interrupt a value of 8000H is written to the EOI register. To issue a specific end-of-interrupt the interrupt vector type of the interrupt to clear is written to the EOI register.

END OF INTERRUPT REGISTER:
(EOI) WRITE ONLY

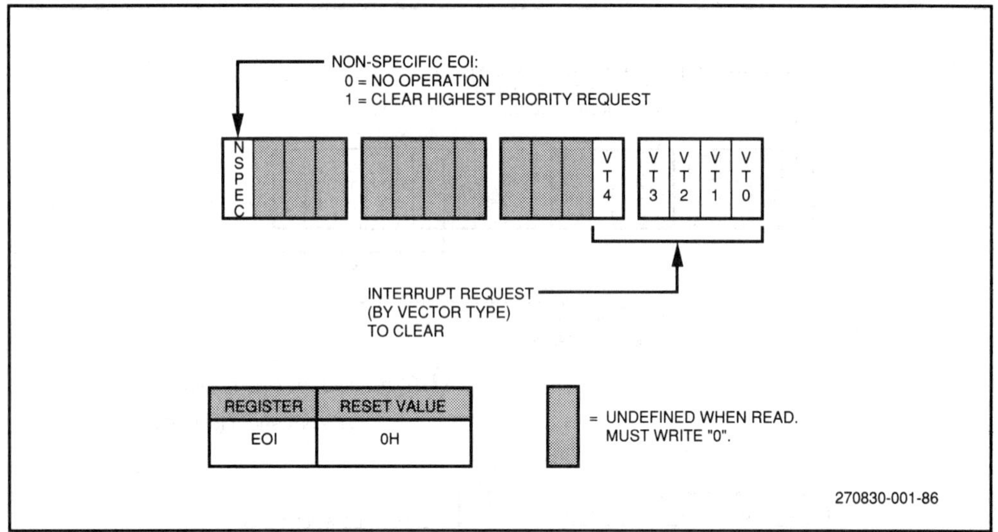

Figure 9.14.

9.4.2.10 INTERRUPT STATUS REGISTER IN MASTER MODE

The Interrupt Controller also contains an interrupt status register (see Figure 9.15). This register contains five bits. Three bits show which timer is causing an interrupt. This is required because the timers share a single interrupt control register. A bit in this register is set to indicate which timer generated an interrupt. The bit associated with a timer is automatically cleared after the interrupt request for the timer is acknowledged. More than one of these bits may be set at a time.

The transmit and receive interrupt requests from serial channel 0 also share on interrupt request. The SRX and STX bits are provided to distinguish between these interrupts.

INTERRUPT STATUS REGISTER:
(INTSTS)

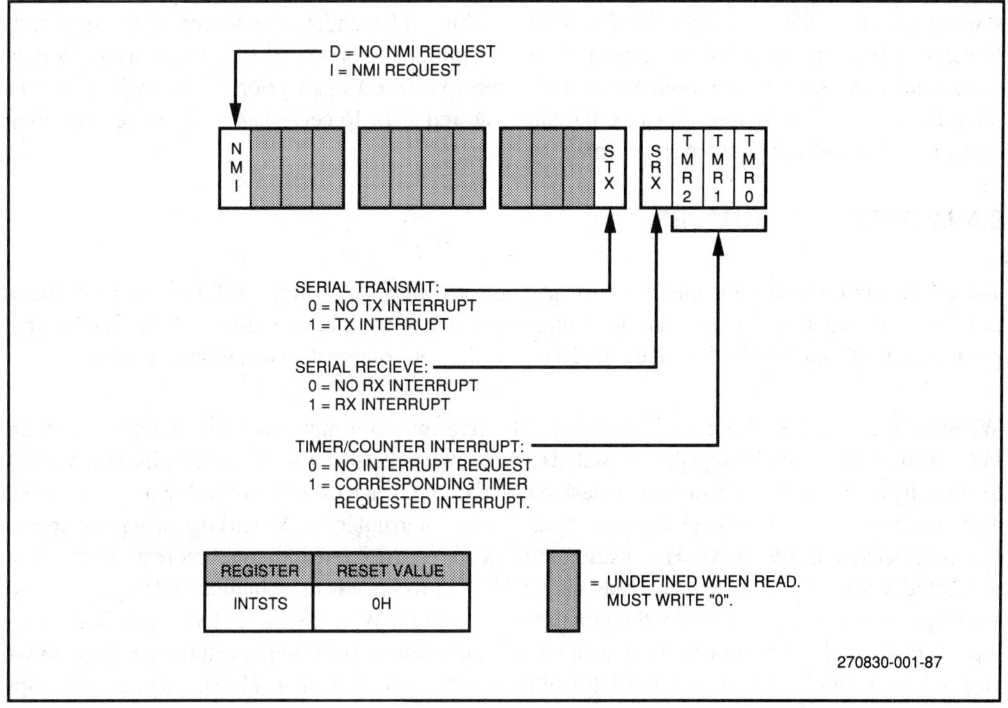

Figure 9.15.

9.4.3 INTERRUPT SOURCES

The 80C186EB family Interrupt Controller receives requests and arbitrates among many different interrupt sources, both internal and external. Each interrupt source may be programmed to be a different priority level.

9.4.3.1 INTERNAL SOURCES

The internal interrupt sources are the three timers and serial channel 0. An interrupt from any of these interrupt sources is latched in the Interrupt Controller. The state of the pending interrupt can be obtained by reading the interrupt request register. Note that all timers share a common bit in the interrupt request register. The Interrupt Controller status register may be read to determine which timer is actually causing the interrupt request. Each timer has a unique interrupt vector (see Section 9.0). Thus, polling is not required to determine which timer has caused the interrupt in the interrupt service routine. Also, because the timers share a common interrupt control register, they are placed at a common priority level relative to other interrupt sources. Among themselves they have a fixed priority, with Timer 0 as the highest priority timer and Timer 2 as the lowest priority timer.

Serial channel 0 generates an interrupt request whenever a reception or transmission is completed. Like the timers, there is only one bit in the request register for the two serial interrupts. The interrupt status register contains two bits, SRX and STX, which differentiate the source of the interrupt. Receive and transmit interrupts have seperate vectors; polling is not necessary to determine the source of the interrupt. The serial communications unit interrupts have a single priority with respect to other internal and external sources (because they are one request). Receive has a higher priority than transmit when both occur at the same time.

9.4.3.2 EXTERNAL SOURCES

The external pins associated with the Interrupt Controller may serve either as direct interrupt inputs, or as cascaded interrupt inputs from other Interrupt Controllers. These options are selected by programming the C and SFNM bits in the INT0 and INT1 control registers (see Figure 9.8(b)).

When programmed as direct interrupt inputs, the five interrupt inputs are each controlled by an individual interrupt control register. As stated earlier, each of these registers contain bits which select the priority level for the interrupt and a mask bit. In addition, each of these control registers contains a bit which selects edge- or level-triggered mode for the interrupt input. When edge-triggered operation is selected, a LOW-to-HIGH transition must occur on the interrupt input before an interrupt is generated, while in level-triggered mode, only a HIGH level needs to be maintained to generate an interrupt. In edge-triggered mode, the input must remain LOW at least one clock cycle before the input is rearmed. In both modes, the interrupt level must remain HIGH until the interrupt is acknowledged, i.e., the interrupt request **is not latched** in the Interrupt Controller. The status of the interrupt input can be shown by reading the interrupt request register. Since interrupt requests on these inputs **are not latched** by the Interrupt Controller, if an input goes inactive, the interrupt request (and its request bit) will also go inactive.

If the C (Cascade) bit of either the INT0 or INT1 control register is set, the interrupt input is cascaded to an external Interrupt Controller. In this mode, whenever the interrupt presented on the INT0 or INT1 line is acknowledged, the integrated Interrupt Controller will not provide the interrupt type for the interrupt. Instead, two INTA bus cycles will be run, with $\overline{\text{INTA0}}$ or $\overline{\text{INTA1}}$ lines providing the interrupt acknowledge pulses for the INT0 and INT1 interrupt requests, respectively. This allows up to 128 (plus INT4) individually vectored interrupt sources if two banks of 8 external Interrupt Controllers each are used.

9.4.4 INTERRUPT RESPONSE

The 80C186EB family processor can respond to an interrupt in two different ways. The first response will occur if the internal controller is providing the interrupt vector information with the controller. The second response will occur if the CPU reads interrupt type information from an external Interrupt Controller. In both instances the interrupt vector information driven by the integrated Interrupt Controller is not available outside the microprocessor.

When the integrated Interrupt Controller receives an interrupt, it will automatically set the in-service bit and reset the interrupt request bit. In addition, unless the interrupt control register for the interrupt is set in Special Fully Nested Mode, the Interrupt Controller will prevent any interrupts from occurring from the same interrupt line until the in-service bit for that line has been cleared.

9.4.4.1 INTERNAL VECTORING

The interrupt types associated with all the interrupt sources are fixed and unalterable. These types are given in Table 9.1. In response to an internal CPU interrupt acknowledge the Interrupt Controller will generate the vector address rather than the interrupt type. On 80C186EB family microprocessors the interrupt vector address is the interrupt type multiplied by four.

Table 9.1. 80C186EB Internal Vectoring Default Priority

Interrupt Name	Vector Type	Relative Priority
Timer 0	8	0 (a)
Timer 1	18	0 (b)
Timer 2	19	0 (c)
Serial Channel 0: Receive	20	1 (a)
Serial Channel 0: Transmit	21	1 (b)
INT4	17	2
INT0	12	3
INT1	13	4
INT2	14	5
INT3	15	6

No external Interrupt Controller need know when the integrated controller is providing an interrupt vector, nor when the interrupt acknowledge is taking place. As a result, no interrupt acknowledge bus cycles will be generated. The first external indication that an interrupt has been acknowledged will be the processor reading the interrupt vector from the interrupt vector table in memory.

Interrupt response to an internally vectored interrupt is 42 clock cycles because the processor does not run interrupt acknowledge cycles. This is faster than the interrupt response when external vectoring is required.

If two interrupts of the same programmed priority occur, the default priority scheme (shown in Table 9.1) is used.

9.4.4.2 EXTERNAL VECTORING

External interrupt vectoring occurs whenever the Interrupt Controller is placed in Cascade Mode. With external vectoring, the 80C186EB family processor generates two interrupt acknowledge cycles, reading the interrupt type off the lower 8 bits of the address/data bus on the second interrupt acknowledge cycle (see Figure 9.16). In the 8259A or 82C59A, the upper five bits are user-programmable and the lower three bits are determined by a defined interrupt request level. Interrupt acknowledge bus cycles have the following characteristics:

- The two interrupt acknowledge cycles are LOCKed.
- Two idle T-states are always inserted between the two interrupt acknowledge cycles.
- Wait states will be inserted in an interrupt acknowledge cycle if READY is not returned to the processor.

Also notice that the processor provides two interrupt acknowledge signals, one for interrupts signaled by the INT0 line, and one for interrupts signaled by the INT1 line (on the INT2/$\overline{\text{INTA0}}$ and INT3/$\overline{\text{INTA1}}$ lines, respectively). These two interrupt acknowledge signals are mutually exclusive. Interrupt acknowledge status will be driven on the status lines ($\overline{\text{S0}}$-$\overline{\text{S2}}$) when either INT2/$\overline{\text{INTA0}}$ or INT3/$\overline{\text{INTA1}}$ signal an interrupt acknowledge. The interrupt type generated on the second INTA cycle is read by the CPU and then multiplied by four. The resultant value is used as a pointer into the interrupt vector table.

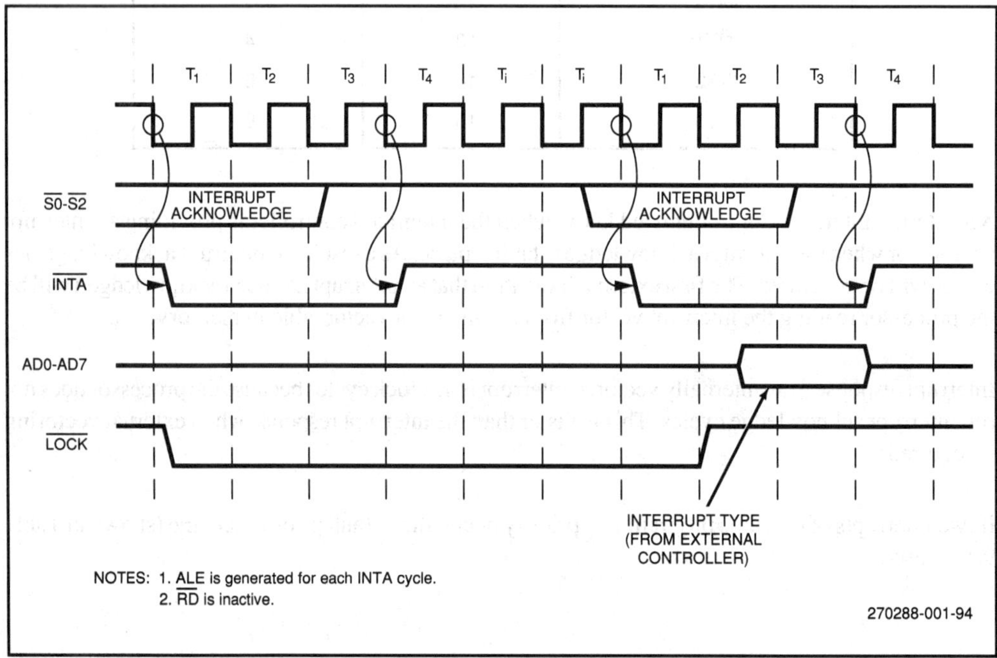

Figure 9.16. Cascaded Interrupt Acknowledge Timing

9.4.4.3 INTERRUPT RESPONSE TIME

The interrupt response time for the 80C186EB family is 42-55 CPU clocks. Figure 9.17 shows how the total is obtained. The clock count changes when the processor replaces the indicated idle states with bus cycles for other tasks such as refresh cycles. The processor does not necessarily flush the queue until the very last moment, so prefetching may continue for a while during the vectoring sequence. Also, the clock count must be adjusted for wait states or for the 80C188EB. For the 80C188EB, double the number of clocks given for each bus cycle accessing the stack or memory.

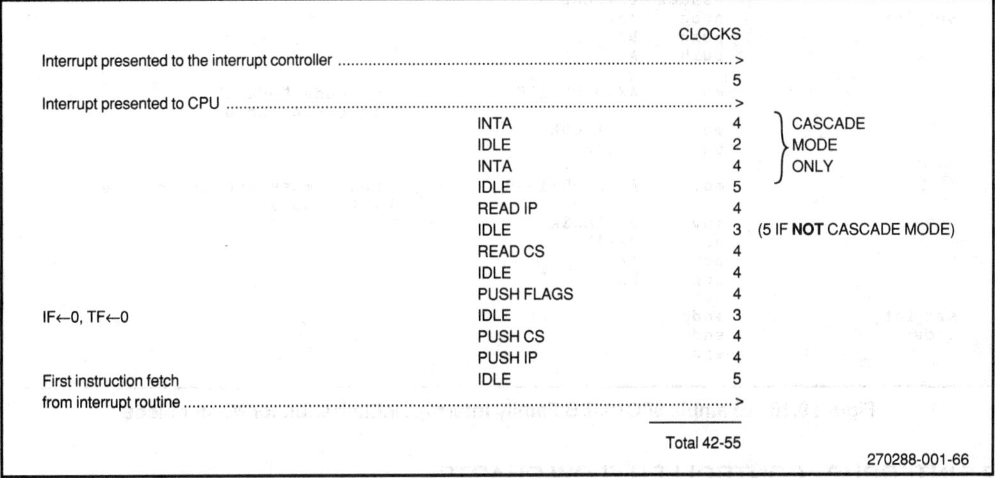

Figure 9.17. 80C186EB Family Master Mode Interrupt Response Time

These clock counts are also applicable to software interrupts and NMI (notice there are no INTA cycles).

9.4.5 INITIALIZATION EXAMPLE

The code to initialize the Interrupt Control Unit for a combination of direct inputs and Cascade Mode inputs is given in Figure 9.18. Refer to Figures 9.5 and 9.6 for the corresponding hardware configurations. Notice that a READY signal must be returned to the processor to prevent the generation of wait states in response to the interrupt acknowledge cycles. This configuration provides 10 external input lines: two provided by the Interrupt Controller itself (pins INT1 and INT3), and eight from the external 8259A (cascaded at pins INT0 and $\overline{\text{INTA0}}$). The 80C186EB integrated Interrupt Control Unit is the master system Interrupt Controller. The 8259A will only receive interrupt acknowledge pulses in response to interrupts it has generated. The 8259A may be cascaded again as a master to as many as eight additional 8259A Interrupt Controllers (configured as slaves).

```
$mod186
name                    example_80186_family_interrupt_code
;
;  This routine configures the interrupt controller to provide two cascaded
;        interrupt inputs (through an  external 8259A internal controller on
;        pins INT0 and INT2/INTA0) and two direct interrupt inputs (on pins INT1
and
;        INT3). The default priority levels are used. Because of this, the
;        priority level programmed into the control register is set to 111, the
;        level all interrupts assume at reset.
;
IOCON                   equ     0FF18H
IMASK                   equ     0FF08H
;
code                    segment                 ; public 'code'
                        assume  CS:code
set_int_                proc    near
                        push    DX
                        push    AX

                        mov     AX,0100111B     ; Cascade Mode
                                                ; interrupt unmasked
                        mov     DX,IOCON
                        out     DX,AX

                        mov     AX,01001101B    ; now unmask the other external
                                                ; interrupts
                        mov     DX,IMASK
                        out     DX,AX
                        pop     AX
                        pop     DX
                        ret
set_int_                endp
code                    ends
                        end
```

Figure 9.18. Example 80C186EB Family Interrupt Initialization for Master Mode

9.5 INTERRUPT CONTROLLER FLOW CHARTS

Figure 9.19 shows an interrupt request generation flow chart and Figure 9.20 shows an interrupt acknowledge sequence flow chart. Each interrupt source processed by an 80C186EB family integrated Interrupt Controller follows each flow chart independently.

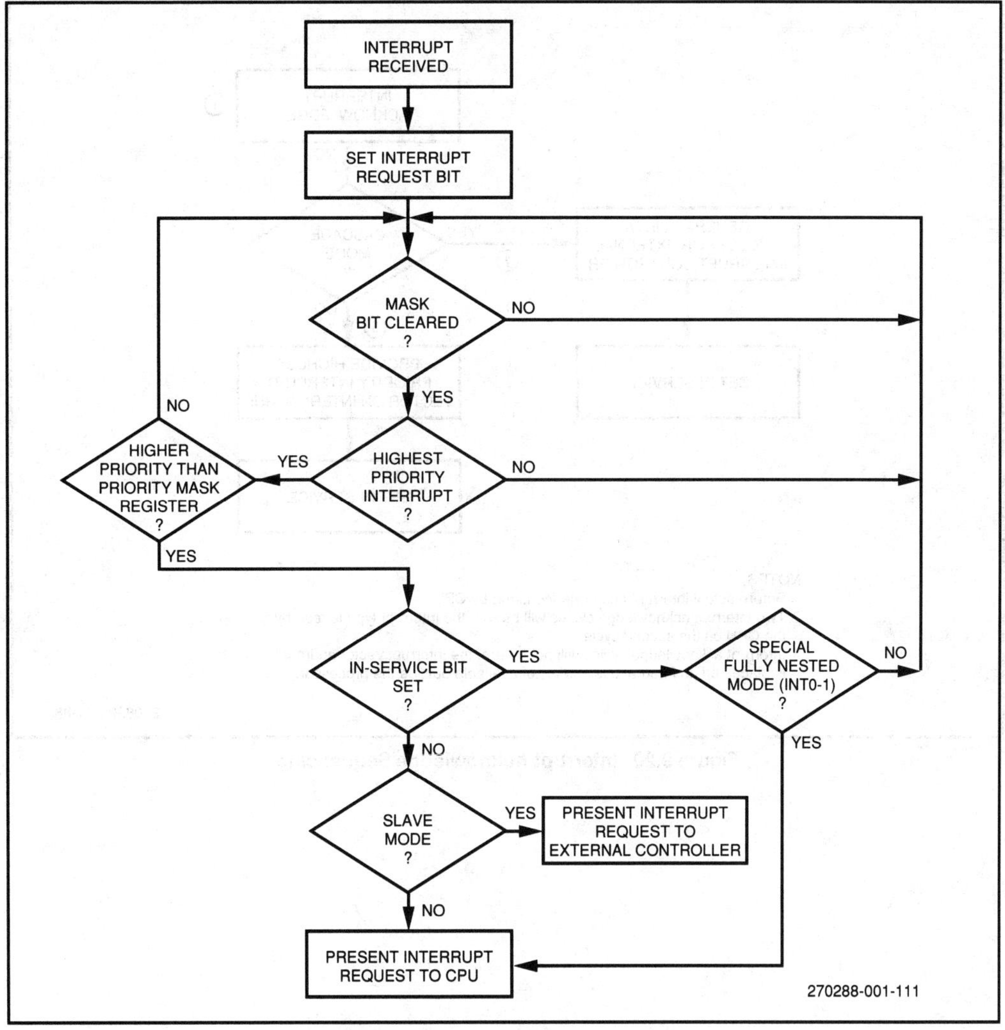

Figure 9.19. Interrupt Request Sequencing

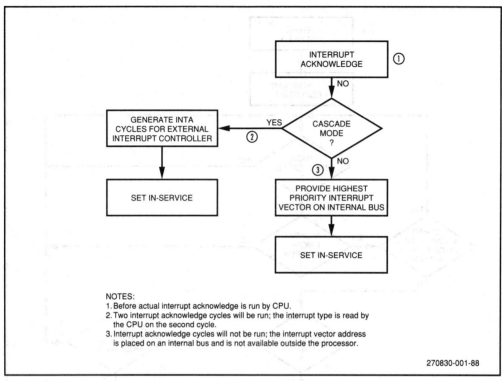

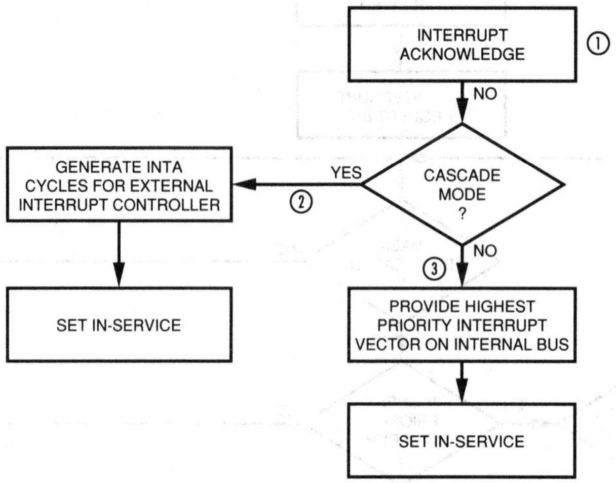

NOTES:
1. Before actual interrupt acknowledge is run by CPU.
2. Two interrupt acknowledge cycles will be run; the interrupt type is read by the CPU on the second cycle.
3. Interrupt acknowledge cycles will not be run; the interrupt vector address is placed on an internal bus and is not available outside the processor.

270830-001-88

Figure 9.20. Interrupt Acknowledge Sequencing

Refresh Control Unit 10

CHAPTER 10
REFRESH CONTROL UNIT

To simplify the design of a dynamic memory controller, the 80C186EB family incorporates integrated address and clock counters into a Refresh Control Unit (RCU). Its relationship to the BIU is shown in Figure 10.1. To the memory interface a refresh request looks exactly like a memory read bus cycle. Integration of the RCU into the 80C186EB family means that chip selects, wait state logic, and status lines may be used by an external DRAM controller. The external DRAM controller generates the $\overline{RAS}$, $\overline{CAS}$, and enable signals actually needed by the DRAMs.

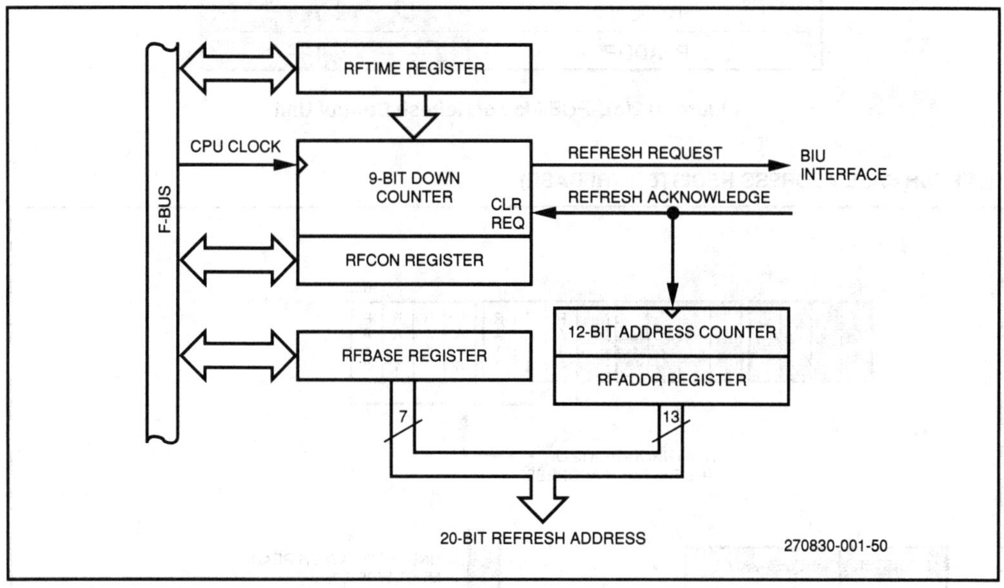

Figure 10.1 Refresh Control Unit Block Diagram

The 12-bit address counter is used in the formation of refresh addresses. Thus, any dynamic memory whose refresh address requirements (rows of memory cells) do not exceed twelve bits can be directly supported by the 80C186EB. The 12-bit address counter, a 7-bit base register, and one fixed bit define a full 20-bit refresh address. The 9-bit refresh clock counter decrements every clock cycle and generates a refresh request to the BIU whenever it reaches 1. When the bus is free, the BIU will run the refresh (dummy read) bus cycle. Refresh requests have a higher priority than any other bus request (i.e., CPU, HOLD).

10.1 REFRESH CONTROL UNIT PROGRAMMING

There are three registers in the Peripheral Control Block that control the RCU. The three control registers are RFBASE, RFTIME, and RFCON (see Figure 10.2). These registers define the operating characteristics of the RCU.

REGISTER NAME	OFFSET
RFBASE	B0H
RFTIME	B2H
RFCON	B4H
RFADDR	B6H

Figure 10.2(a). PCB Map of Refresh Control Unit

REFRESH BASE ADDRESS REGISTER: (RFBASE)

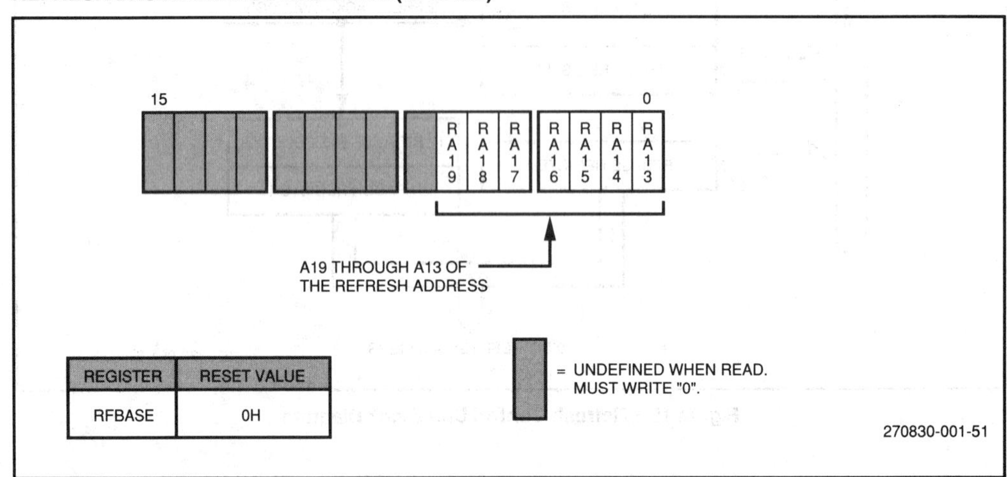

Figure 10.2(b).

The RFBASE register programs the base address (upper 7 bits) of the refresh address. This allows the refresh address to be mapped to any 4 kilobyte boundary within the one megabyte address space. The RFBASE register is not altered whenever the refresh address bits (RA1 through RA12 in Figure 10.3) roll over. In other words, the refresh address does not act like a linear counter found in a typical DMA controller.

REFRESH CLOCK RELOAD VALUE: (RFTIME)

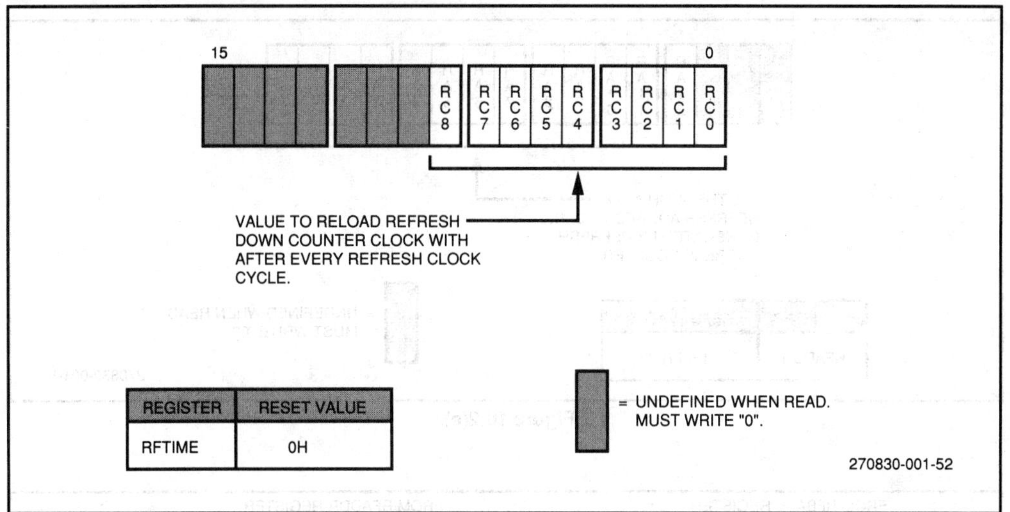

REGISTER	RESET VALUE
RFTIME	0H

Figure 10.2(c).

REFRESH CONTROL REGISTER: (RFCON)

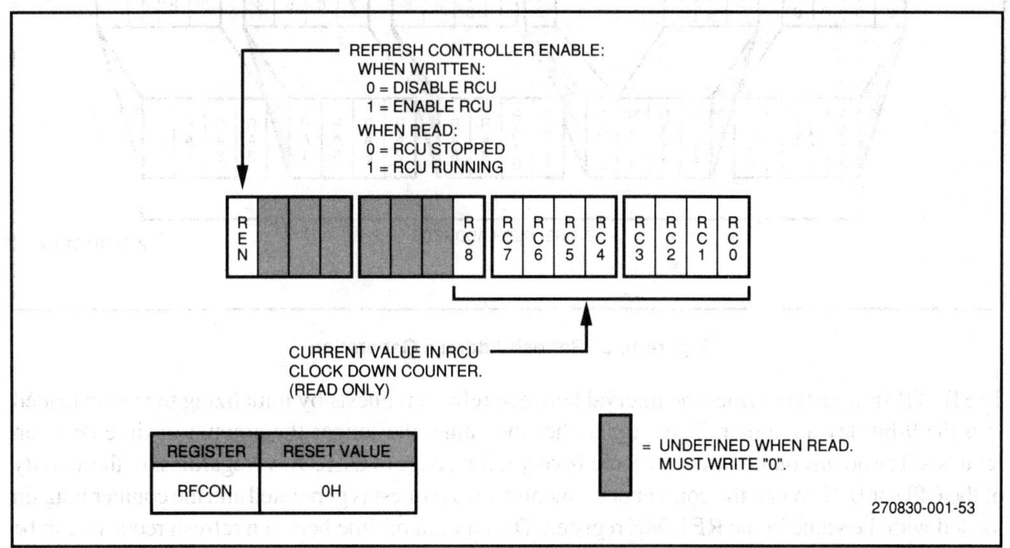

REGISTER	RESET VALUE
RFCON	0H

Figure 10.2(d).

REFRESH ADDRESS REGISTER: (RFADDR)

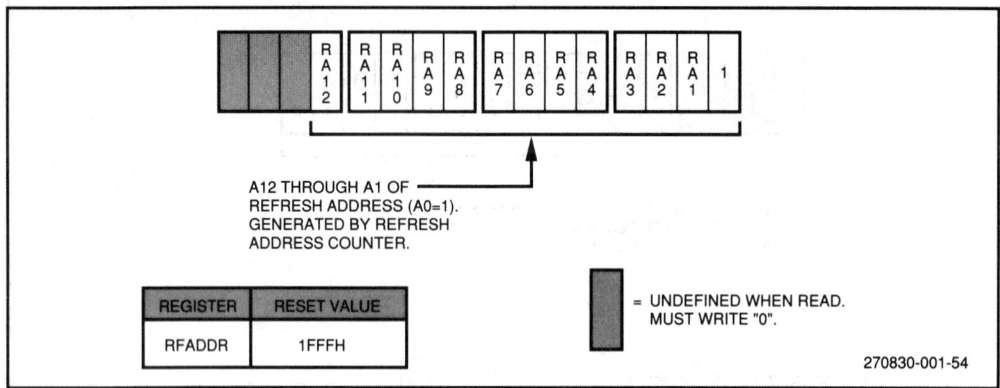

Figure 10.2(e).

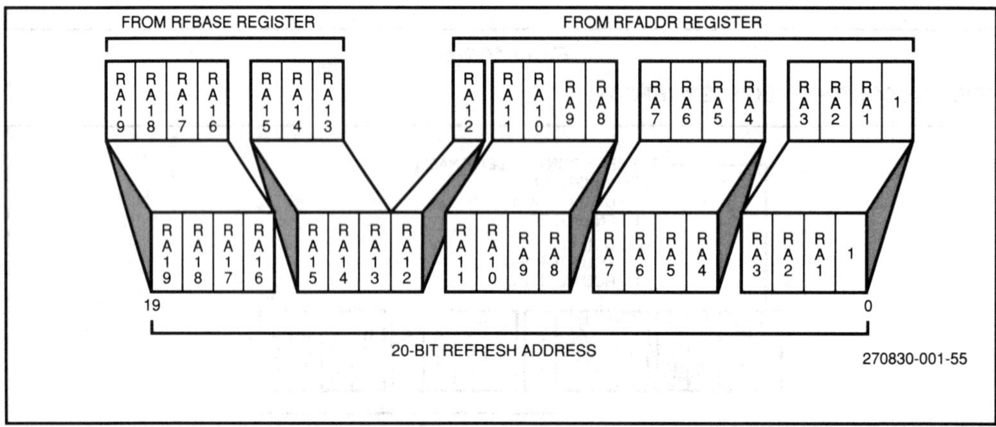

Figure 10.3. Refresh Address Generation

The RFTIME register defines the interval between refresh requests by initializing the value loaded into the 9-bit down counter. Thus, the higher the value, the longer the amount of time between requests. The down counter is decremented every falling edge of CLKOUT, regardless of the activity of the CPU or BIU. When the counter decrements to 1, a request is generated and the counter is again loaded with the value in the RFTIME register. The amount of time between refresh requests can be calculated using the equation shown in Figure 10.4.

$$\frac{R_{PERIOD}(\mu s) \times f(MHz)}{\#\ \text{Refresh Rows} + \#\ (\text{Refresh Rows} \times \%\ \text{Overhead})} = \text{RFTIME Register Value}$$

R_{PERIOD} = Maximum refresh period specified by DRAM manufacturer (microseconds).

f = Operating frequency of 80C186/C188EB in MHz.

Refresh Rows = Total number of rows to be refreshed.

% Overhead = Derating factor to compensate for missed refresh requests (typically 1-5%).

270830-001-56

Figure10.4. Equation to Calculate Refresh Interval

The minimum value that can be programmed into the RFTIME register is 18 (12H) regardless of operating frequency. This minimum count ensures that the BIU has enough time to execute the refresh bus cycle. The BIU cannot queue DRAM refresh requests. If another request is generated before the current request is executed, the current request is lost. However, the address associated with the request is not lost; the refresh address changes only after the BIU runs a refresh bus cycle. Thus it is possible to miss refresh requests, but not refresh addresses.

The RFCON register has two functions, depending on whether it is being written or read. During writes to the RFCON register, only the Enable bit is active. Setting the Enable bit turns on the RCU while clearing the Enable bit deactivates the RCU. When the RCU is enabled, the contents of the RFCON register are loaded into the 9-bit down counter and refresh requests are generated when the counter reaches 1. Disabling the RCU stops and clears the counter. A read of the RFCON register will return the current value of the Enable bit as well as the current value of the 9-bit down counter (zero if the RCU is not enabled). **Writing to the RFCON register when the RCU is running does not modify the count value in the 10-bit counter.**

10.2 REFRESH CONTROL UNIT OPERATION

Figure 10.5 illustrates the two major functions of the Refresh Control Unit that are responsible for initiating and controlling the refresh bus cycles.

The RFCON down counter is loaded on the falling edge of CLKOUT, when either the Enable bit is set or the counter decrements to 1. Once loaded, the RFCON down counter will decrement every falling edge of CLKOUT (as long as the Enable bit remains set).

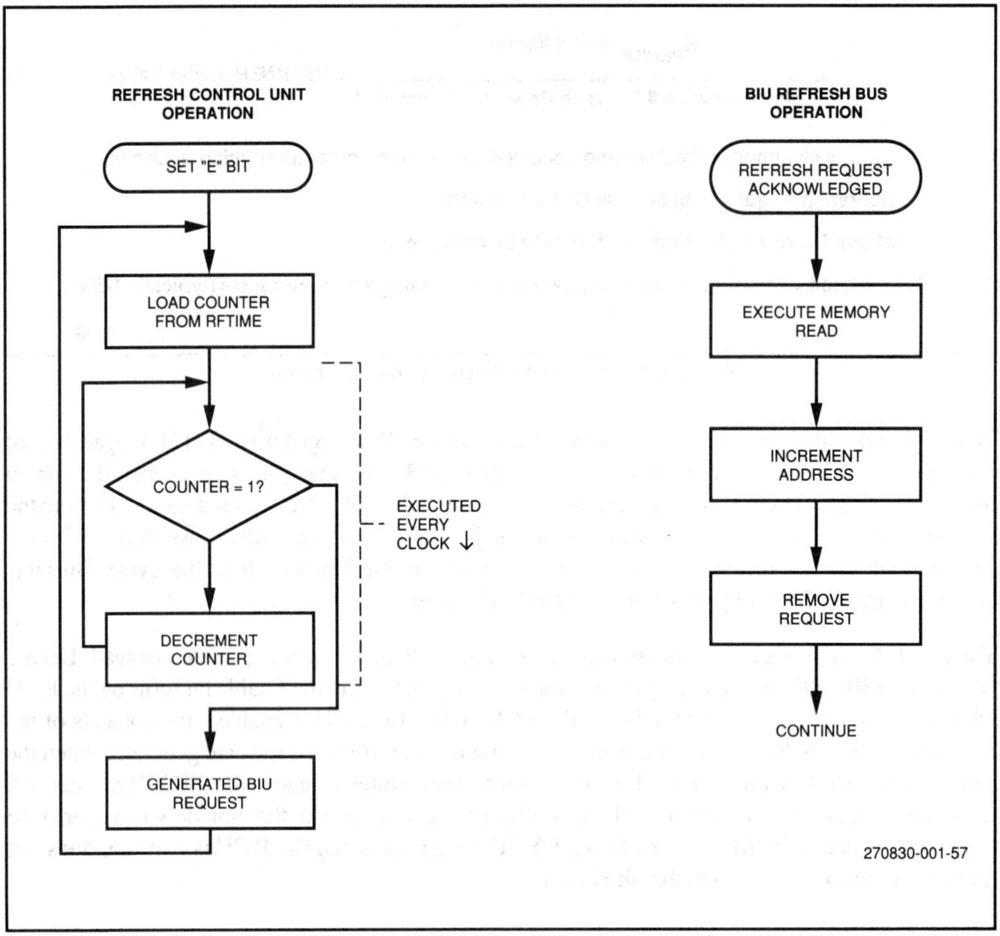

Figure 10.5. Flowchart of RCU Operation

When the counter decrements to 1, two things happen. First, a request is generated to the BIU to run a refresh bus cycle. The request remains active until the bus cycle is run or the RCU is disabled. Second, the down counter is reloaded with the value contained in the RFTIME register. At this time, the down counter will again begin counting down every clock cycle. It does not wait until the request has been serviced. This is done to ensure that each refresh request occurs at the correct interval. Otherwise, the time between refresh requests would also be a function of varying bus activities. When the BIU services the refresh request, it will clear the request and increment the refresh address.

Refresh bus cycles are specially encoded to distinguish them from ordinary read cycles according to Table 10.1.

Table 10.1. Identification of 80C186EB/80C188EB DRAM Refresh Cycles

	$\overline{\text{BHE}}$/$\overline{\text{RFSH}}$	A0
80C186EB	1	1
80C188EB	0	1

NOTE:
$\overline{\text{BHE}}$ applies to be 80C186EB and
$\overline{\text{RFSH}}$ applies to the 80C188EB.

10.3 REFRESH ADDRESSES

The physical address that is generated during a refresh bus cycle is shown in Figure 10.3, and applies to both the 80C186EB and 80C188EB. The refresh address bits RA1 through RA12 are generated using a linear-feedback shift counter which does not increment the addresses linearly from 0 through FFFH (although they do follow a predicable algorithm). Further, note that for the 80C188EB, address bit A0 does not toggle during refresh operation, which means that it cannot be used as part of the refresh (row) address applied to the dynamic memory device. Typically, A0 is used as part of memory decoding in 80C188EB applications, unlike 80C186EB applications which use A0 along with $\overline{\text{BHE}}$ to select an upper or lower bank.

10.4 REFRESH OPERATION AND BUS HOLD

When another bus master has control of the bus, the HLDA signal is kept active as long as the HOLD input remains active. If a refresh request is generated while HOLD is active, the 80C186EB/C188EB will drive the HLDA signal inactive to indicate to the current bus master that the CPU wishes to regain control of the bus (see Figure 10.6). Only when the HOLD input is removed will the BIU begin the refresh bus cycle.

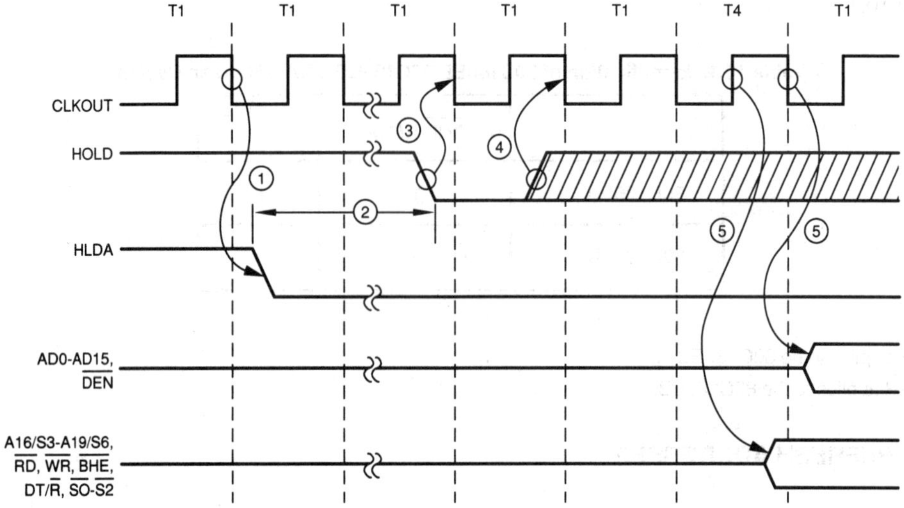

NOTES:

1. HLDA deasserted, signaling need to run DRAM refresh cycles less than T_{CLOV}
2. External bus master terminates use of the bus.
3. HOLD deasserted; greater than T_{CLIS}
4. HOLD may be reasserted after one clock.
5. Lines come out of float in order to run DRAM refresh cycle.

270830-001-58

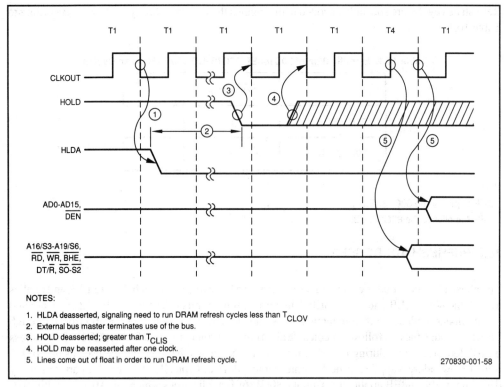

Figure 10.6. Release of 80C186/80C188 HOLD to Run Refresh Cycle.

Therefore, it is the responsibility of the system designer to ensure that the 80C186EB/C188EB can regain the bus if a refresh request is signalled. The sequence of HLDA going inactive while HOLD is active can be used to signal a pending refresh. If HOLD is again asserted, the CPU core will give up the bus after the refresh bus cycle has been run (provided another refresh request is not generated during that time).

10.5 DECODING REFRESH BUS CYCLES

The BIU distinguishes between refresh cycles and other bus cycle types. The 80C186EB and 80C188EB differ in their methods of signalling a refresh in progress.

On the 80C186EB, a refresh cycle is indicated when both $\overline{\text{BHE}}$ and A0 are high. These two signals may be ANDed together to signal a refresh in progress.

The 80C188EB does not use the $\overline{\text{BHE}}$ pin. The $\overline{\text{BHE}}$ signal has been replaced by the $\overline{\text{RFSH}}$ signal which is LOW whenever a refresh cycle is in progress. The $\overline{\text{RFSH}}$ signal has the same timings as the $\overline{\text{BHE}}$ signal on the 80C186EB.

10.6 EXAMPLE RCU INITIALIZATION CODE

Sample code to initialize the 80C186EB/80C188EB DRAM Refresh Control Unit is included in Example 1.

Example 1.

```
$mod186
name rcu_initialization_example
;
; This file contains an example of initialization code for the
; Refresh Control Unit on the 80C186EB.
;
; For the purposes of our example we will assume the system has
; 512K of DRAM at 40000H. We choose 256K x 4 DRAMS with 2 chips in
; the low byte and 2 chips in the high byte. The data sheet specs
; 256 refresh cycles are required every 4 milliseconds. This
; information also tells us that the array is organized as 256 rows
; by 1024 columns. To calculate the maximum number of clocks
; between refresh cycles, we multiply the totalrefresh period by
; the CLKOUT frequency and divide by the total number of rows. For
; an 80C186EB at 16MHz, the refresh rate is:
; 4E-03 * 16E+06 / 256 = 250 clocks.
; We will assume the chip selects have been set up to select the
; DRAM array correctly.

RFBASE      EQU         0FFB0H
RFTIME      EQU         0FFB2H
RFCON       EQU         0FFB4H

code        segment     public
            assume cs:code

init_rcu          proc  near

      mov         dx, RFBASE
      mov         ax, 4000H          ; Set upper 7 address bits for
      out         dx, ax             ; starting address of 40000H.

      mov         dx, RFTIME
      mov         ax, 250            ; Set up down counter start value.
      out         dx, ax             ; RCU request every 250 clocks.

      mov         dx, RFCON
      mov         ax, 8000H          ; Set ENable bit to start RCU.
      out         dx, ax

; The RCU is now initialized and running.

      ret

      init_rcu    endp

      code        ends
                  end
```

Input/Output Port Unit 11

CHAPTER 11
INPUT/OUTPUT PORT UNIT

Two general purpose I/O ports are available on the 80C186EB. Port 1 is an 8 bit output only port. Port 2 is an 8 bit port consisting of 4 pure input, 2 pure output, and 2 open drain bidirectional signals.

Both ports are multiplexed with other integrated peripherals. Port 1 shares its pins with the general purpose chip select ($\overline{GCS}$) lines of the chip select unit. The pure input and output lines of Port 2 are multiplexed with some serial communications unit signals. The open drain I/O pins of Port 2 are not multiplexed. A block diagram of the I/O Port unit is shown in Figure 11.1.

Each I/O port is controlled by 4 Peripheral Control Block registers. The PCB map and a summary of register operation can be found in Figure 11.2.

REGISTER NAME	OFFSET
P1DIR	50H
P1PIN	52H
P1CON	54H
P1LTCH	56H
P2DIR	58H
P2PIN	5AH
P2CON	5CH
P2LTCH	5EH

Figure 11.2(a). PCB Map of I/O Port Unit

11.1 FUNCTIONAL OVERVIEW

All three port pin types are derived from a common logic module (Figure 11.3). Every port pin, be it an input or an output, was derived from the common bi-directional module. This modular design approach results in some normally unused circuitry. For example, the Port Direction Control register bit exists for output only ports although it is not used.

These normally unused features are not necessarily useless. In the following discussions the unimplemented functions are described along with potential secondary uses for them.

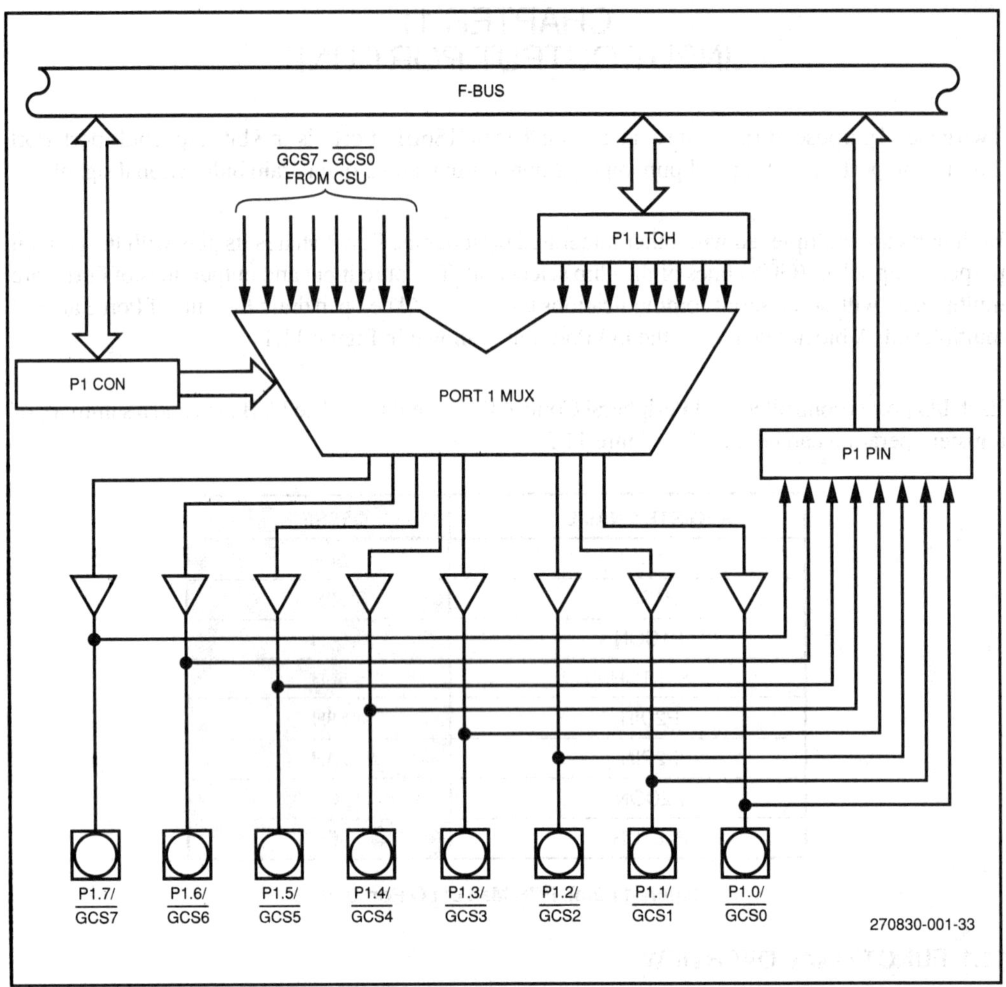

Figure 11.1(a). Port 1 Block Diagram

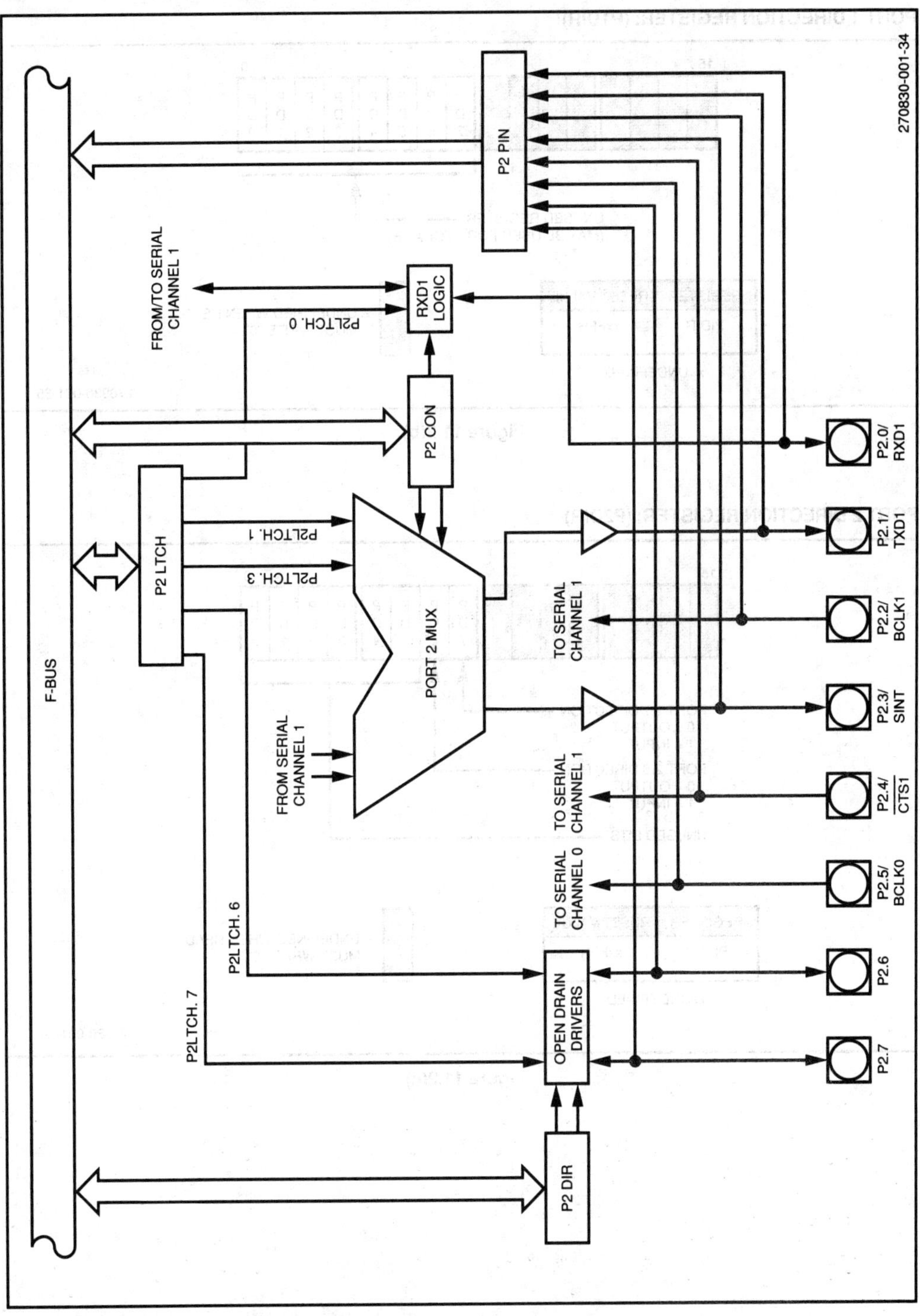

Figure 11.1(b). Port 2 Block Diagram

PORT 1 DIRECTION REGISTER: (P1DIR)

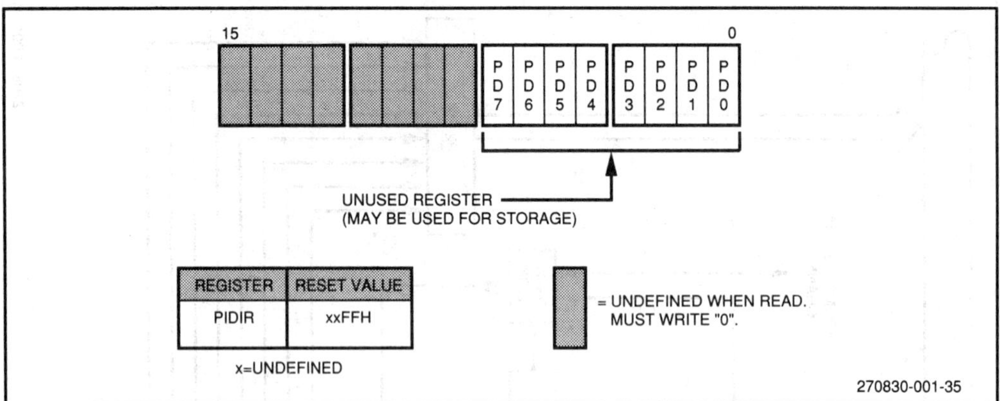

Figure 11.2(b).

PORT 2 DIRECTION REGISTER: (P2DIR)

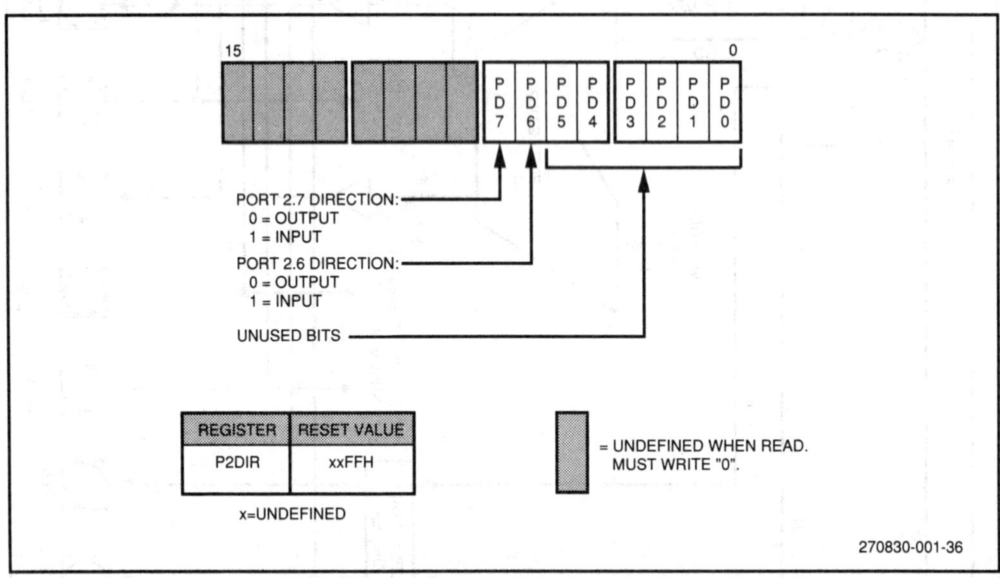

Figure 11.2(c).

PORT PIN REGISTERS: (P1PIN, P2PIN) READ ONLY

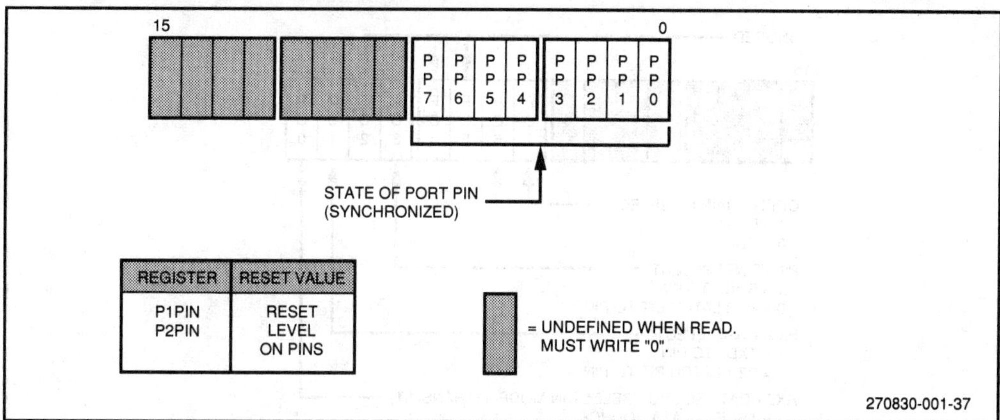

Figure 11.2(d).

PORT 1 MULTIPLEXER CONTROL REGISTER: (P1CON)

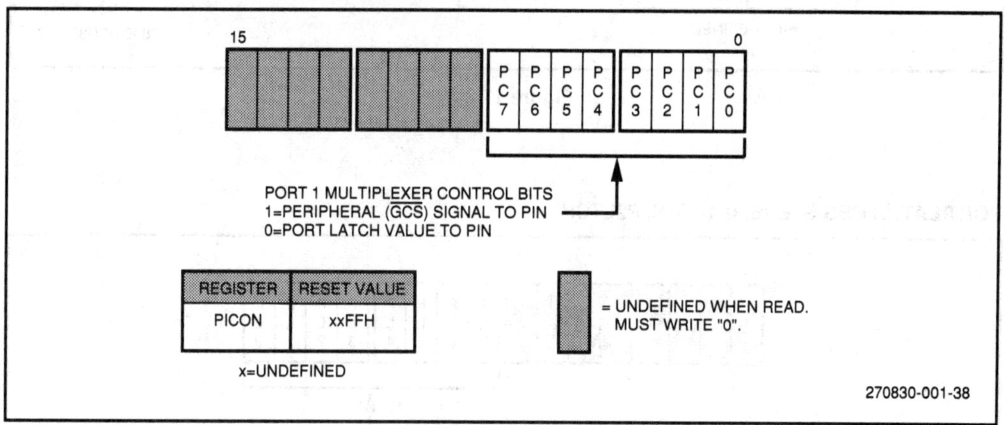

Figure 11.2(e).

PORT 2 MULTIPLEXER CONTROL REGISTER (P2CON)

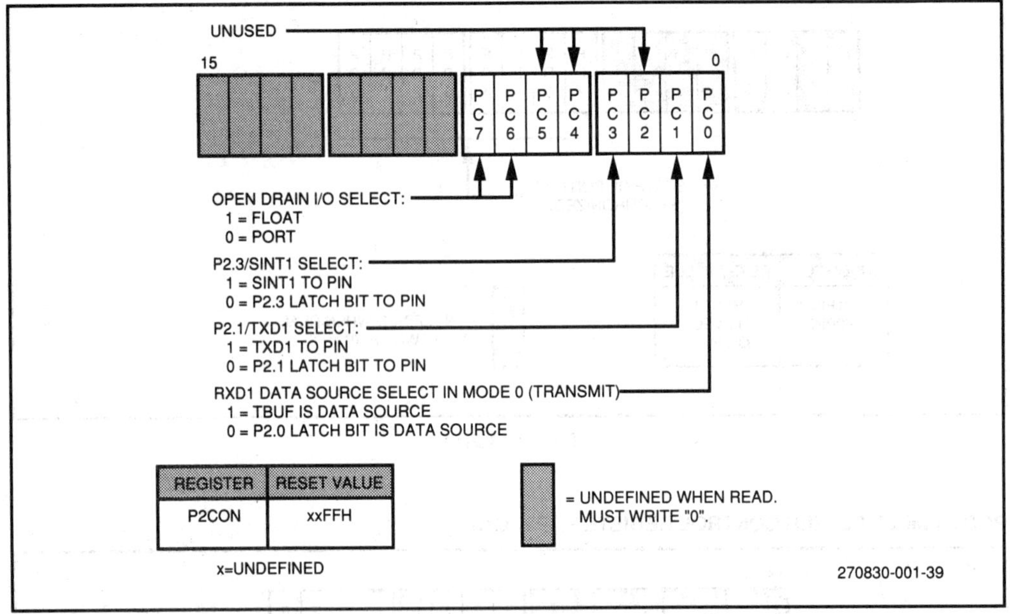

REGISTER	RESET VALUE
P2CON	xxFFH

x=UNDEFINED

Figure 11.2(f).

PORT LATCH REGISTERS: (P1LTCH, P2LTCH)

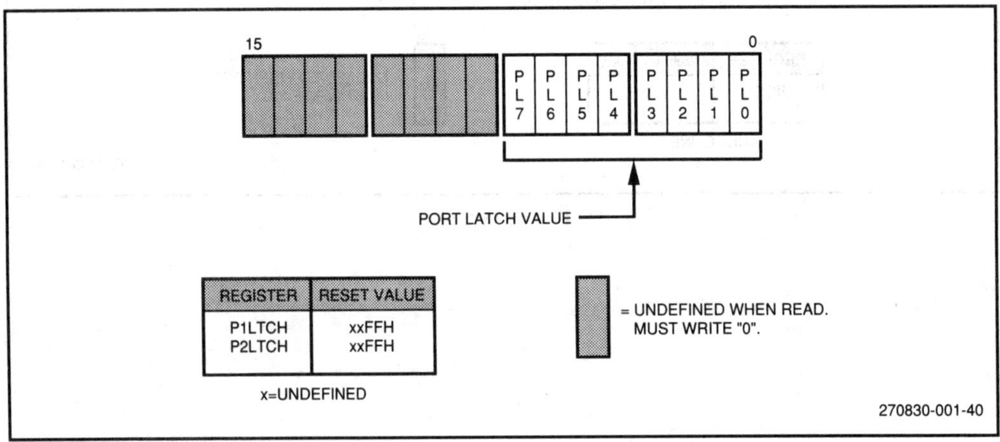

REGISTER	RESET VALUE
P1LTCH P2LTCH	xxFFH xxFFH

x=UNDEFINED

Figure 11.2(g).

11.1.1 OUTPUT PORTS

The internal construction of an output port pin is shown in Figure 11.4. An internal connection permanently enables the 3-state output driver. The source of the data driven on the pin is selected by the Port Control bit. This bit controls the multiplexing of data between the Port Latch bit and the integrated peripheral. If the Port Control bit is a logic one, the pin will be controlled by the integrated peripheral. A logic zero Port Control bit gates the data in the Port Latch to the pin.

The Port Latch bit value is set by writing to the corresponding Port Latch register in the PCB. The latched value can be read back from this register. Note that the value read from the Port Latch Register is the state of the latch, **not** the state of the pin.

The actual state of the output pin can be read from the Port Pin register.

All of Port 1 and pins P2.1 and P2.3 of Port 2 are pure output.

11.1.2 INPUT PORTS

The internal control logic for an input port pin is shown in Figure 11.5. The 3-state output driver has been internally disabled making the pin input only. The current state of the input pin is read from the Port Pin register. The state of the port pin is synchronized to the CPU clock.

The Serial Communications Unit shares the input pins of Port 2. There is no need to configure these pins as either peripheral or port as the input signals route to both units. Users can still read the state of these pins even when they are being used for Serial Control Unit functions.

The Port Latch circuitry functions the same as it does for the output port described above. Since the output is disabled, however, the value cannot affect the port pin. This vestigial latch can be used as bit storage.

Port pins P2.2, P2.4, and P2.5 are pure input pins.

Input port P2.0 is a special case. P2.0 is shared with the RXD1 function of serial communications channel 1. The RXD1 pin becomes an output during a synchronous transmission (Mode 0) regardless of the state of the P2.0 Direction Bit. The data that appears at the P2.0/RXD1 pin during synchronous transmission depends on the P2.0 Control bit. If the P2.0 Control bit is a 1 (peripheral function selected) the proper data from the TBUF will appear at the P2.0/RXD1 pin. If the control bit is a 0, the data contained in the Port 2.0 Latch bit will appear at the P2.0/RXD1 pin. In both cases when the transmission is completed the P2.0/RXD1 will float.

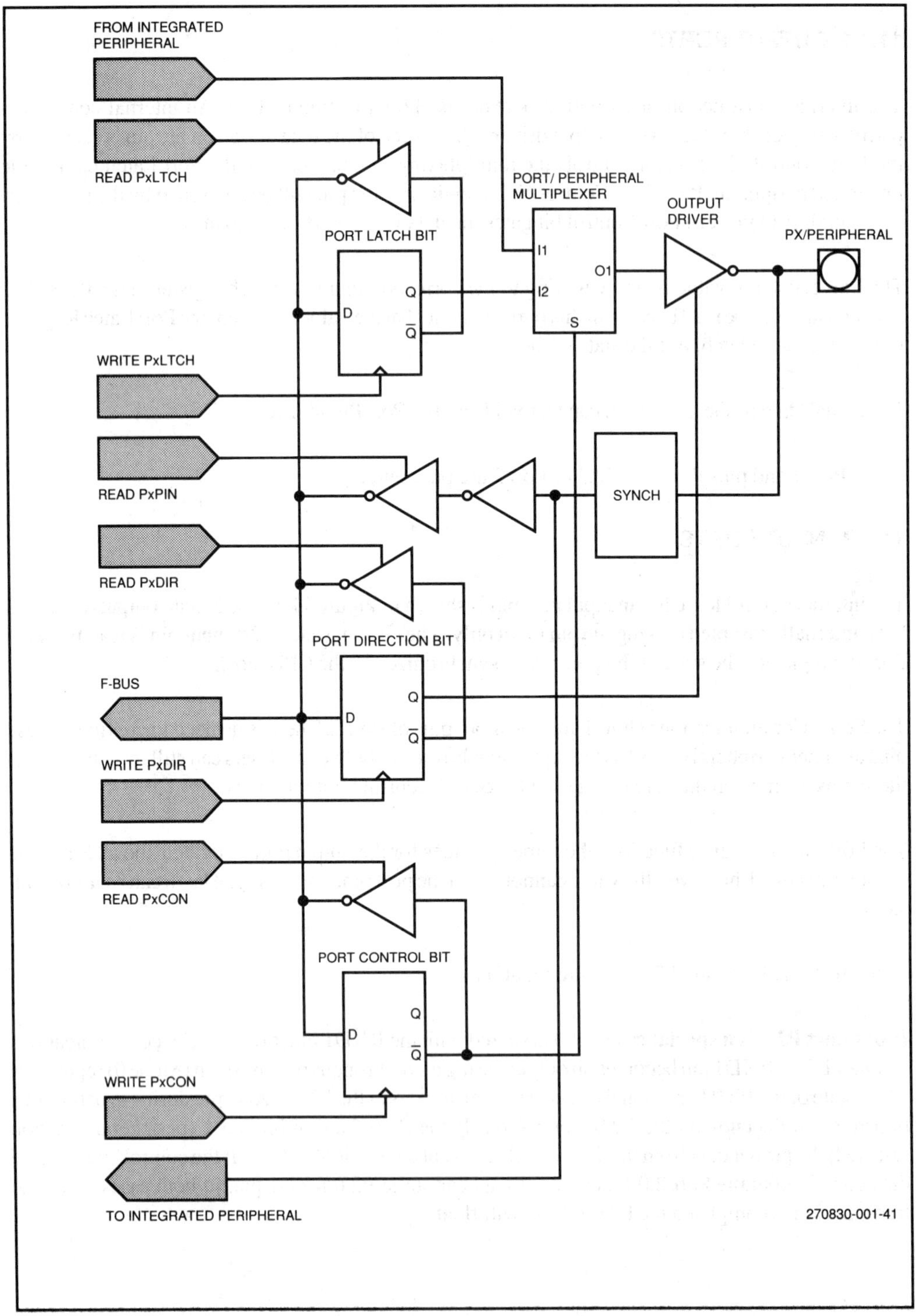

FROM INTEGRATED PERIPHERAL
READ PxLTCH
PORT/ PERIPHERAL MULTIPLEXER
OUTPUT DRIVER
PX/PERIPHERAL
PORT LATCH BIT
I1
I2
O1
S
Q
D
$\overline{Q}$
WRITE PxLTCH
READ PxPIN
SYNCH
READ PxDIR
PORT DIRECTION BIT
F-BUS
WRITE PxDIR
READ PxCON
PORT CONTROL BIT
WRITE PxCON
TO INTEGRATED PERIPHERAL
270830-001-41

Figure 11.3. Common I/O Module Block Diagram

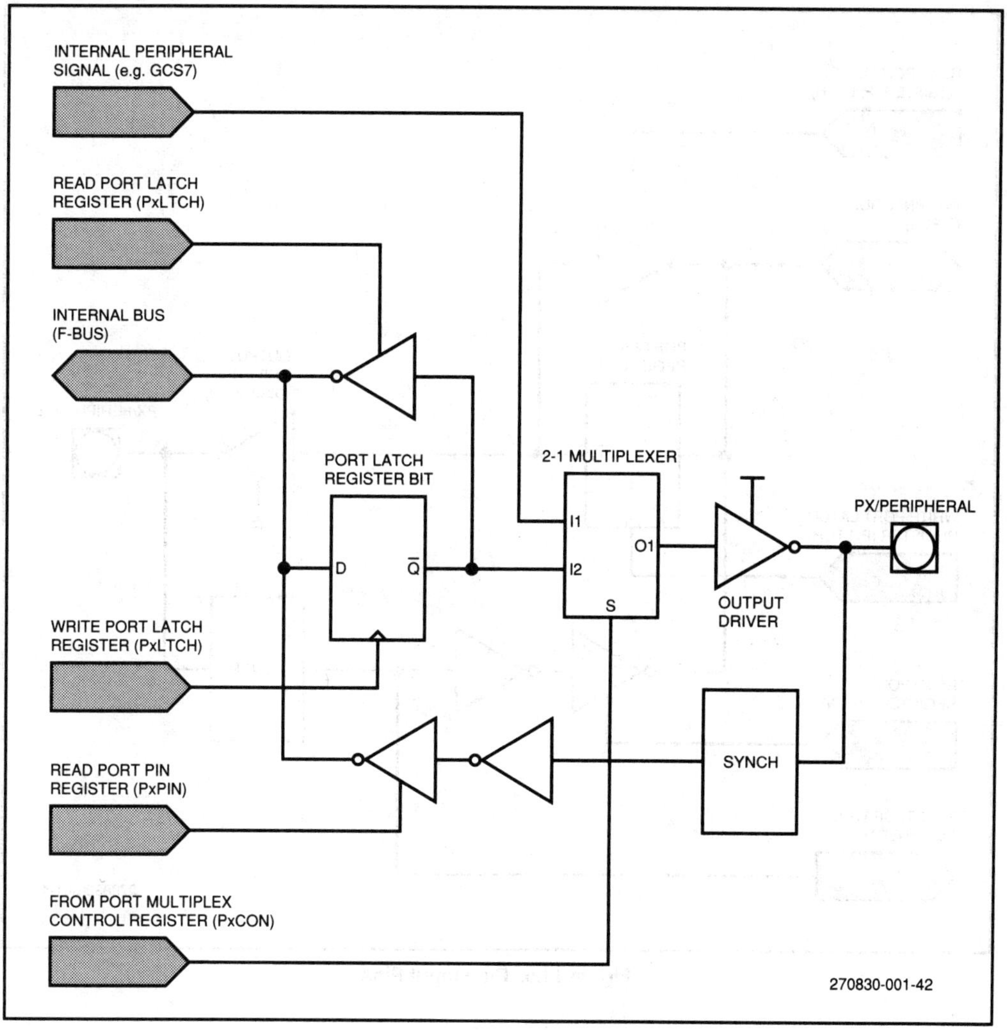

INTERNAL PERIPHERAL SIGNAL (e.g. GCS7)

READ PORT LATCH REGISTER (PxLTCH)

INTERNAL BUS (F-BUS)

PORT LATCH REGISTER BIT

D

$\overline{Q}$

2-1 MULTIPLEXER

I1

I2

O1

S

OUTPUT DRIVER

PX/PERIPHERAL

WRITE PORT LATCH REGISTER (PxLTCH)

SYNCH

READ PORT PIN REGISTER (PxPIN)

FROM PORT MULTIPLEX CONTROL REGISTER (PxCON)

270830-001-42

Figure 11.4. Pure Output Pins

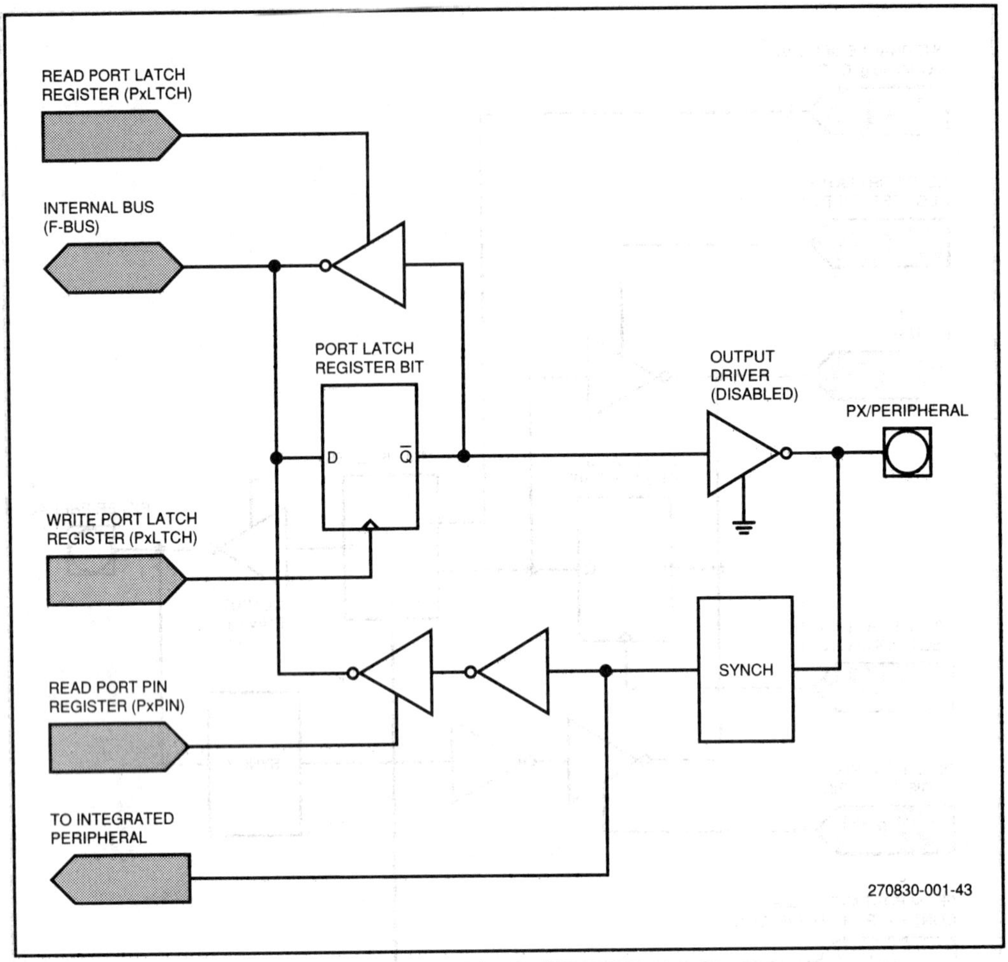

READ PORT LATCH
REGISTER (PxLTCH)
INTERNAL BUS
(F-BUS)
PORT LATCH
REGISTER BIT
D
$\overline{Q}$
OUTPUT
DRIVER
(DISABLED)
PX/PERIPHERAL
WRITE PORT LATCH
REGISTER (PxLTCH)
SYNCH
READ PORT PIN
REGISTER (PxPIN)
TO INTEGRATED
PERIPHERAL
270830-001-43

Figure 11.5. Pure Input Pins

11.1.3 OPEN DRAIN BI-DIRECTIONAL PORTS

Port pins P2.6 and P2.7 are open drain bi-directional (Figure 11.4). With a low logic level on the Port Direction signal the state of the PX Pin is controlled by the $\overline{Q}$ signal from the Port Latch. Writing a zero to the Port Latch turns on the N-channel driver resulting in a "hard zero" being present at the PX Pin. A one value in the Port Latch shuts off the driver resulting in a high impedance (input) state at the Px Pin.

The PX Pin can be floated directly by setting its Port Direction bit to a 1. The state of the PX Pin can be read from the Port Pin register.

The port/peripheral multiplexer exists for P2.6 and P2.7 even though the pins are not shared with 2 peripheral functions. The peripheral function input multiplexer is internally strapped to always float the open drain pin if it is selected.

11.2 PROGRAMMING THE I/O PORT UNIT

11.2.1 PORT DIRECTION REGISTER

The **Port Direction Register** (P1DIR, P2DIR) controls the direction (input or output) for each bit in the port. The direction control feature is not enabled for Port 1 and pins P2.0 through P2.5 of Port 2. These unused direction control bits may be used for bit storage.

Only the direction bits for the open drain pins (P2.6 and 2.7) are used by the IPU. Setting the direction bits for these pins puts the P2.6 and P2.7 pins in a high impedance state. Clearing these bits allows the state of the open drain pins to be controlled by the Port 2 Latch Register.

The Port Direction Register is read/write. When read each register will return the value written to it previously. Pins with their direction fixed will return the value in this register, not a value indicating their direction.

11.2.2 PORT PIN REGISTER

The **Port Pin Register** (P1PIN, P2PIN) is a read only register that is used to determine the state of a port pin. When read, the current state of the port pins (either an input or output) will be gated to the internal data bus.

11.2.3 PORT CONTROL REGISTER

The **Port Control Register** (P1CON, P2CON) selects the source of data driven on each output port pin. Setting a bit in this register selects an integrated peripheral as the source; clearing it selects the corresponding Port Latch bit. Tables 11.1 and 11.2 show the multiplexing options available for Port 1 and Port 2 respectively.

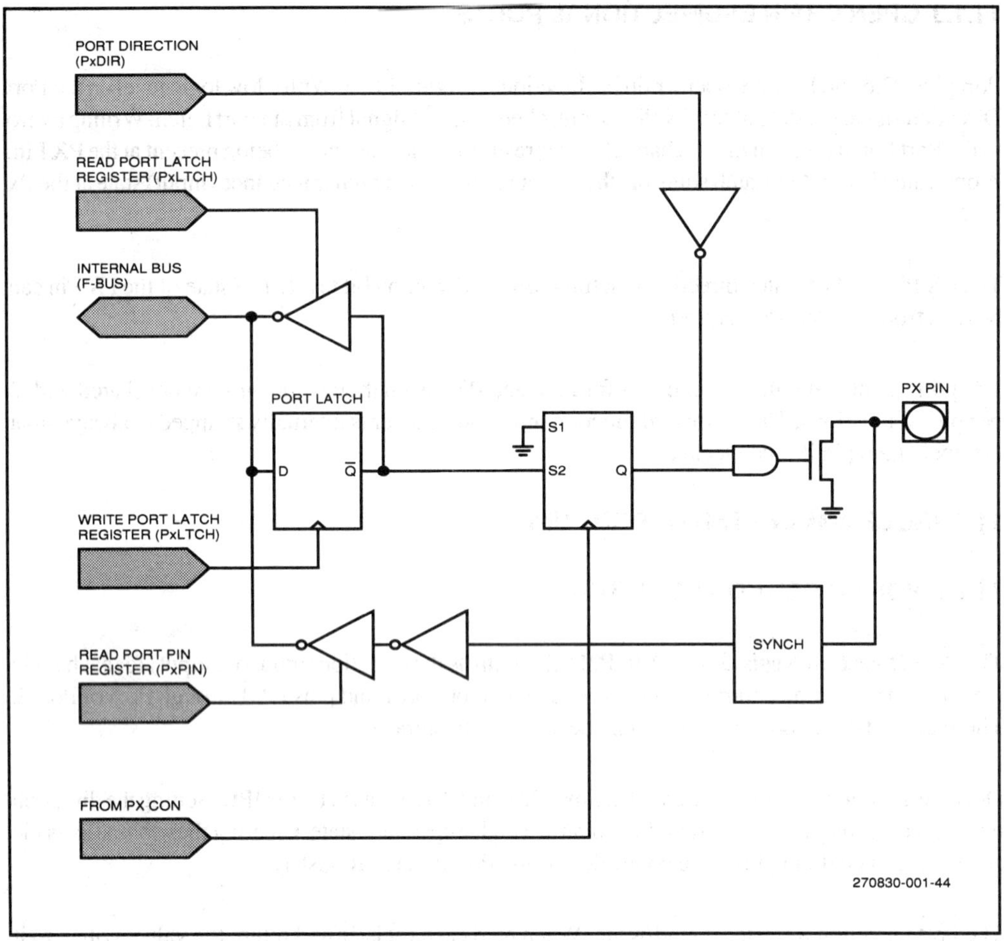

Figure 11.6. Open Drain Pins (P2.6, P2.7)

Table 11.1. P1CON Port 1 Multiplex Control

P1CON BIT	PIN FUNCTION
P1CON.7 = 1	$\overline{\text{GCS7}}$
= 0	PORT1.7
P1CON.6 = 1	$\overline{\text{GCS6}}$
= 0	PORT1.6
P1CON.5 = 1	$\overline{\text{GCS5}}$
= 0	PORT1.5
P1CON.4 = 1	$\overline{\text{GCS4}}$
= 0	PORT1.4
P1CON.3 = 1	$\overline{\text{GCS3}}$
= 0	PORT1.3
P1CON.2 = 1	$\overline{\text{GCS2}}$
= 0	PORT1.2
P1CON.1 = 1	$\overline{\text{GCS1}}$
= 0	PORT1.1
P1CON.0 = 1	$\overline{\text{GCS0}}$
= 0	PORT1.0

Table 11.2. P2CON Port 2 Multiplex Control

P2CON BIT FUNCTION	PIN FUNCTION
P2CON.7 = 1	FLOAT
= 0	P2.7
P2CON.6 = 1	FLOAT
= 0	P2.6
P2CON.5	NOT USED
P2CON.4	NOT USED
P2CON.3 = 1	SINT1.
= 0	P2.3
P2CON.1 = 1	TXD1
= 0	P2.1
P2CON.0 = 1	RXD1*
= 0	PS.0

* NOTE: P2CON.0 only has an effect during a synchronous transmission in Mode 0 by SCU channel 1. See text.

The Port Control Register exists for input only pins although it has no affect on their operation (except P2.0/RXD1, see 11.2.1). These unused bits may be used as storage.

11.2.4 PORT LATCH REGISTER

The **Port Latch Register** (P1LTCH, P2LTCH) holds the value to be driven on an output pin. This value will only appear at an output pin if the corresponding bit in the Port Control Register is cleared.

The Port Latch Register bits corresponding to input only pins exist but are not used by the IPU. These vestigial latches may be used as storage.

The Port Latch Register is read/write. Reading a Port Latch Register returns the value of the latch itself and **not** the associated port pin.

11.3 INITIAL CONDITIONS (RESET)

At reset the Port 1 multiplexer is configured with the Generic Chip Selects as the source of the output data.

The Port 2 multiplexer resets with serial channel 1 as the source of data for all output pins. The P2.6 and P2.7 open drain ports reset to a high impedance state (their corresponding PxDIR bits are = 1).

The reset values for all of the IPU registers is shown in Figure 11.2.

11.4 PROGRAMMING EXAMPLE

The example in Figure 11.7 shows a typical ASM186 routine to configure the IPU. $\overline{GCS7}$ through $\overline{GCS4}$ are routed to the pins while P1.0 throught P1.4 are used as output ports. The binary value 0101 is written to P1.0 through P1.3. The state of pins P2.6 and P2.7 is read and stored in the AL register.

```
$mod186
name io_port_unit_example

;
; This file contains an example of programming code for
; the I/O Port Unit on the 80C186EB.
;

; We assume PCB has NOT BEEN RELOCATED!

P1DIR       EQU       0FF50H
P1PIN       EQU       0FF52H
P1CON       EQU       0FF54H
P1LTCH      EQU       0FF56H
P2DIR       EQU       0FF58H
P2PIN       EQU       0FF5AH
P2CON       EQU       0FF5CH
P2LTCH      EQU       0FF5EH


code_seg          segment public
                  assume cs:code_seg

IO_UNIT_EXMPL     proc  near

; first, select GCS7# through GCS4# to output pins.

  mov             dx, P1CON
  mov             ax, 0F0H
  out             dx, ax

; write 0101B to pins P1.3 through P1.0

  mov             dx, P1LTCH
  mov             ax, 0101B
  out             dx, ax

; Read P2.6, P2.7. We assume they have not been changed to output
; pins since reset.

  mov             dx, P2PIN
  in              ax, dx
  and             ax, 3H             ; strip unused and undefined bits

; AL now holds the state of the P2.6 and P2.7 pins

IO_UNIT_EXMPL     endp

code_seg          ends
end
```

Figure 11.7. IPU Programming Example

Power Management Unit 12

CHAPTER 12
POWER MANAGEMENT UNIT

The majority of VLSI devices on the market today make use of dynamic circuitry. A dynamic circuit is one that makes use of a capacitance (usually parasitic gate or diffusion capacitance) to store information. The charge stored on the capacitance will decay through time due to leakage currents in the silicon. If the information stored on a dynamic node is not used before it decays, the state of the entire machine may be lost. Dynamic RAMs, for example, must be refreshed periodically to insure data retention. A dynamic microprocessor is one for which the minimum clock frequency is greater than zero. When the clock on a dynamic microprocessor is frozen, the dynamic nodes within it will begin to discharge. With a long enough delay it is likely that, when the clock is restarted, the microprocessor will begin to execute in an unknown state. Normal operation can only be reinstated through a reset.

The 80C186EB is a **fully static device**. The clock signal to both the CPU core and the peripherals may be stopped without the loss of any internal information (provided Vcc is maintained). When the clock is restarted the 80C186EB will begin to execute in the same state as when the clock was stopped. This feature, coupled with the fact that CMOS devices consume virtually no current when quiescent, allows tremendous power savings in applications where the 80C186EB will be idle for long periods.

The Power Management Unit of the 80C186EB is provided to control the current consumption of the device. Three modes are available: Active, Idle, and Powerdown.

In Active Mode the clock signal is gated to the CPU core and all of the integrated peripherals. This is the default operating mode that the 80C186EB enters on reset. Current consumption is at its maximum.

During Idle Mode operation the clock signal is routed only to the integrated peripheral devices. The clock to the CPU core (Execution and Bus Interface Units) is frozen. All peripherals operate normally. Any unmasked interrupt, NMI, or a processor reset will return the 80C186EB to Active mode. A DRAM refresh or HOLD request will awaken the core temporarily in order to respond. Current consumption in Idle Mode is reduced to just the amount necessary to maintain the peripherals.

Entering Powerdown Mode freezes the clock to the entire device (CPU and peripherals) and disables the crystal oscillator. All internal devices (registers, state machines, etc.) maintain their state as long as Vcc is applied. DRAM refresh and HOLD requests will not be acknowledged in Powerdown mode. An NMI or a processor reset will cause the 80C186EB to return to Active Mode. A timing pin is provided to allow the crystal oscillator to stabilize before restarting the internal clocks. Current consumption in Powerdown Mode is reduced to just transistor junction leakage (typically in the microamp range).

The Power Management Unit is programmed through the use of the Power Control Register at offset B8H in the Peripheral Control Block (Figure 12.1).

**POWER MANAGEMENT CONTROL REGISTER:
(PWRCON):**

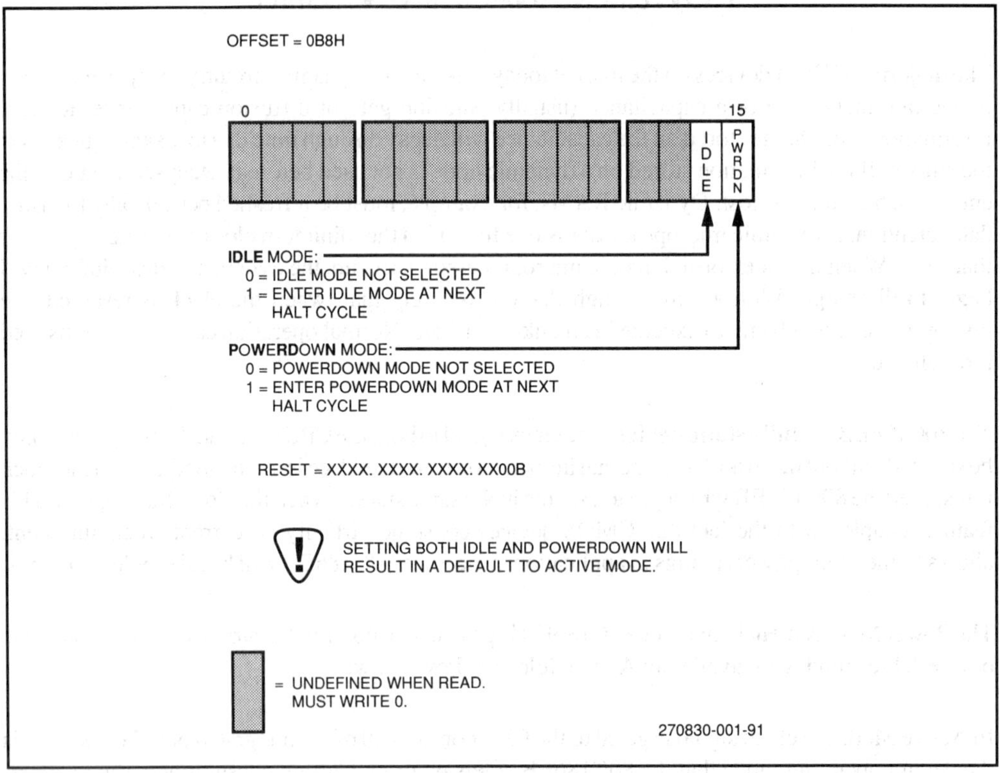

Figure 12.1.

12.1 FUNCTIONAL OVERVIEW

The two low-power modes are armed by setting the appropriate bit in the Power Control Register. The chosen mode is entered when a HLT instruction is executed. If both modes are selected (or no mode is selected) the device will HaLT and remain in Active Mode. Section 3.4.4.2 describes the HALT cycle in detail.

12.1.1 IDLE MODE

At the completion of the HALT execution, with the IDLE bit set, the clock signals routed to the CPU core (Execution and Bus Unit) will be frozen in a logic low state. The clock signals to the integrated peripherals continue to toggle as does CLKOUT. Current consumption will be cut by nearly half, although this is dependent on the level of activity in the peripheral units.

Figure 12.2 shows the internal and external waveforms during entry into Idle Mode.

The core clocks can be restarted by several means. A DRAM refresh will turn on the core clock temporarily in order to run the dummy read cycle. A HOLD request will turn on the core clock as long as HOLD is asserted. Any unmasked interrupt or NMI will return the 80C186EB family device to Active mode. A RESET will also return the device to Active Mode (although the state of the device when the HALT was executed is lost). The following sections describe, in detail, each of these situations.

12.1.1.1 REFRESH DURING IDLE MODE

Figure 12.3 shows the sequence of events for a refresh cycle while the CPU is in Idle Mode. The refresh counter decrements on the falling edge of CLKOUT. The internal core clock begins to toggle on the falling edge of CLKOUT after the down-counter reaches zero. After one idle T-state the refresh request is run (the T_i-T_1-T_2-T_3-T_4 sequence in Figure 12.3). There is one idle T-state after T_4 before the internal core clock shuts off again.

The READY, wait state generation, and chip select circuitry are all active for refresh cycles during Idle Mode.

12.1.1.2 HOLD/HLDA DURING IDLE MODE

The core in Idle Mode will also respond to bus HOLD requests (Figure 12.4). The core clock restarts one CLKOUT cycle after HOLD has been asserted (see Section 3.6 for requirements on HOLD timing). HLDA is driven high one cycle after the core clock starts. The core clock turns off and HLDA is deasserted one cycle after HOLD is dropped.

Refresh requests will force the BIU to drop HLDA during a HOLD request. Section 10.4 contains more information on refresh cycles during HOLD.

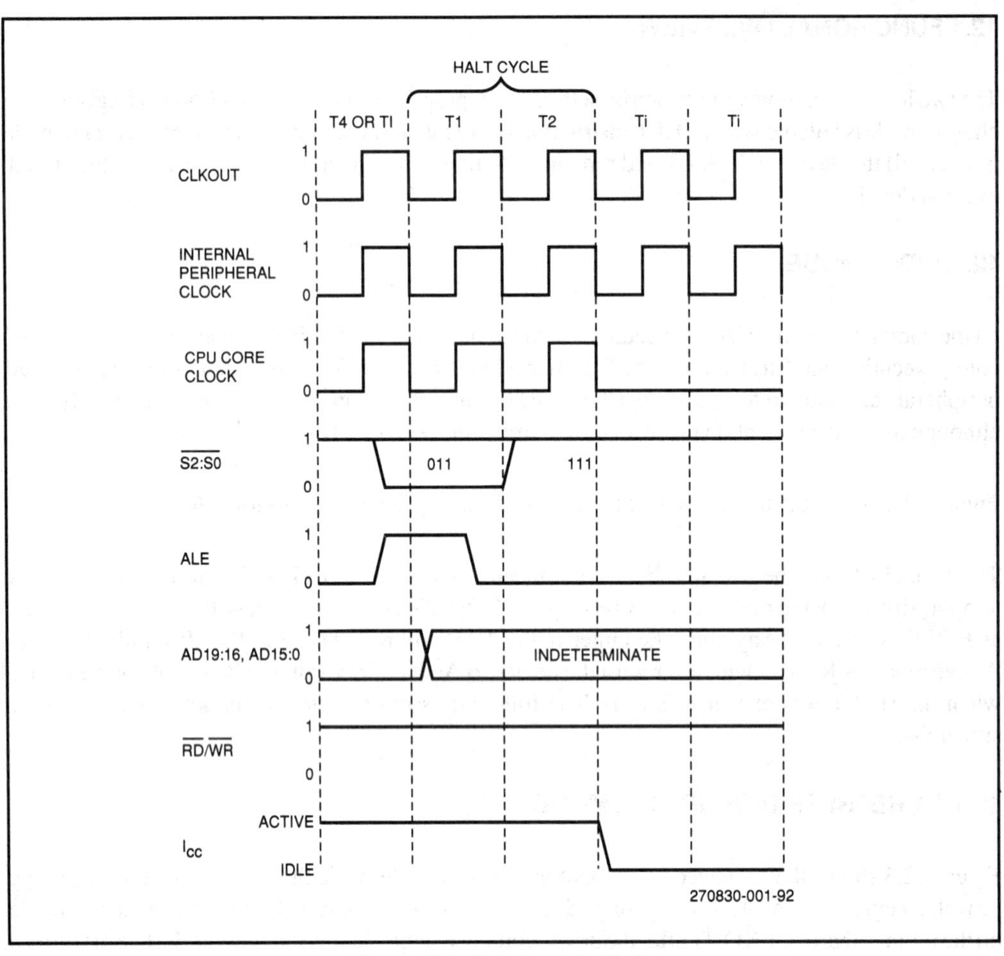

Figure 12.2. Entering Idle Mode

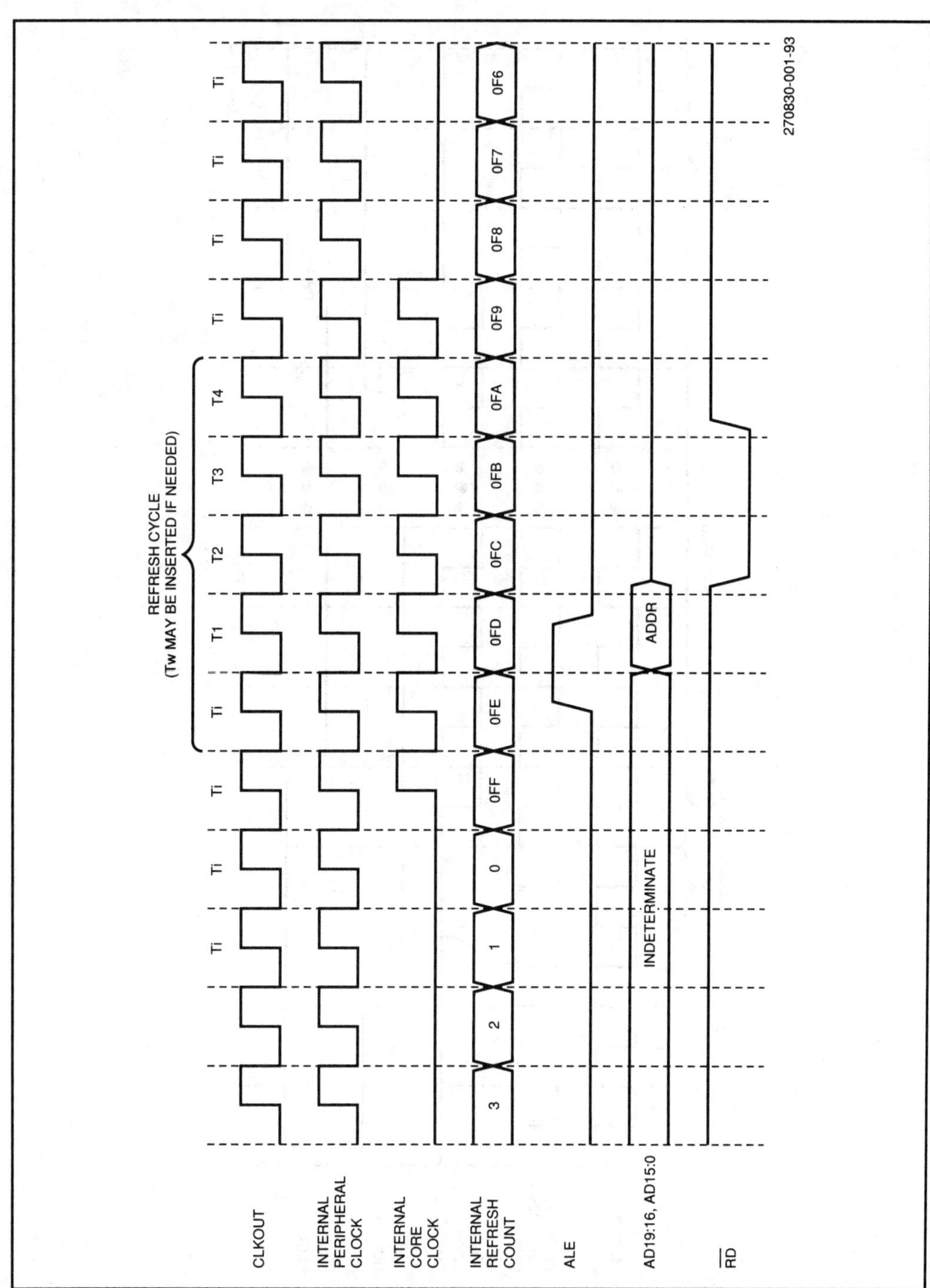

Figure 12.3. Refresh Cycle during Idle Mode (0 wait states)

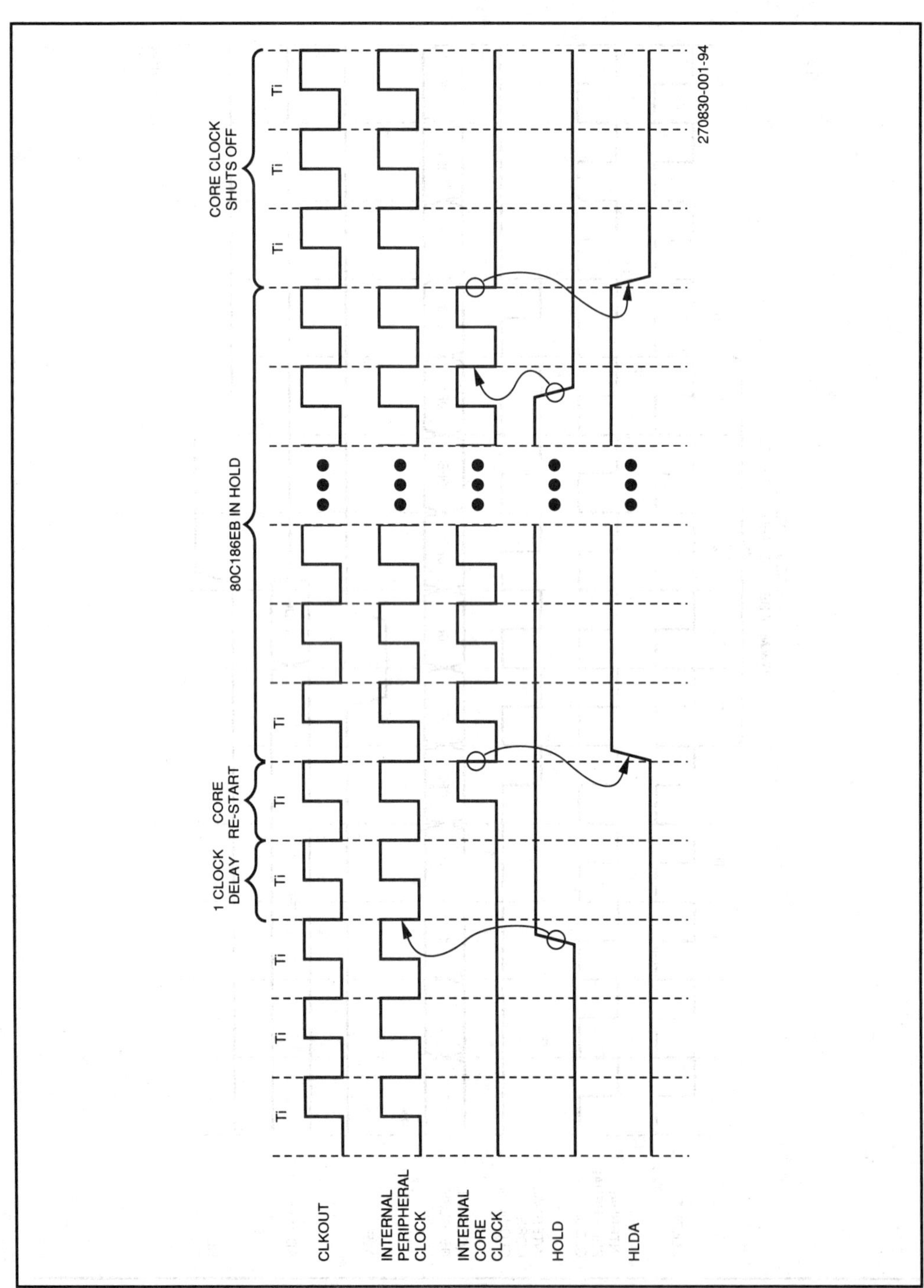

Figure 12.4. HOLD/HLDA during Idle Mode

12.1.1.3 EXITING IDLE MODE VIA AN UNMASKED INTERRUPT

Any **unmasked** interrupt received by the core will return the 80C186EB to Active Mode. Unlike the HOLD and refresh situations, another HALT must be executed for the core to return to Idle Mode.

For the example shown in Figure 12.5, the Interrupt Unit has been programmed for cascade mode on pin INT0. The core clock begins toggling seven clocks after INT0 (which is unmasked) goes high. These seven clocks are required to perform mask and priority level checking. It takes another 6 CLKOUT cycles for the core to begin to respond to the interrupt request (in this case begin the interrupt acknowledge cycle).

After the execution of the IRET (interrupt return) instruction in the interrupt service routine, the CS:IP will be pointing to the instruction following the HALT. **The PWRCON register is not modified by interrupt execution**. If the PWRCON register is not modified after exiting Idle Mode then the 80C186EB family device will re-enter IDLE at the next HALT instruction.

12.1.1.4 EXITING IDLE MODE VIA A NON-MASKABLE INTERRUPT (NMI)

Like an unmasked interrupt, a non-maskable interrupt will return the core to Active mode from Idle mode (Figure 12.6). It takes only 2 CLKOUT cycles to restart the core clock after an NMI is received. The NMI signal does not have to go through the mask and priority checks that a maskable interrupt does. This results in the 5 clock cycle difference in clock restart time between an NMI and an unmasked interrupt.

The core begins the interrupt response 6 cycles after the core clock re-starts when it fetches the NMI vector from location 00008. The PWRCON register is not affected by an NMI.

12.1.1.5 EXITING IDLE MODE VIA A RESET

Resetting the 80C186EB family processor will return the device to Active Mode. Unlike the case of the interrupts, however, the PWRCON register will be cleared. Execution begins as it would following a warm reset (see Section 4.4).

12.1.2 POWERDOWN MODE

Powerdown Mode is entered by the execution of a HLT instruction after the PWRDN bit in the Power Control Register has been set. Following a normal software HLT cycle both the core and peripheral clocks will be shut off and the crystal oscillator will be disabled. While in Powerdown Mode the device will not respond to HOLD requests, nor will it run DRAM refresh cycles (as the clock to the DRAM Refresh Unit is turned off).

Active Mode is re-entered after the reception of an NMI or a reset. A delay must be provided after the NMI request to allow the crystal oscillator to stabilize before it is connected to the internal phase

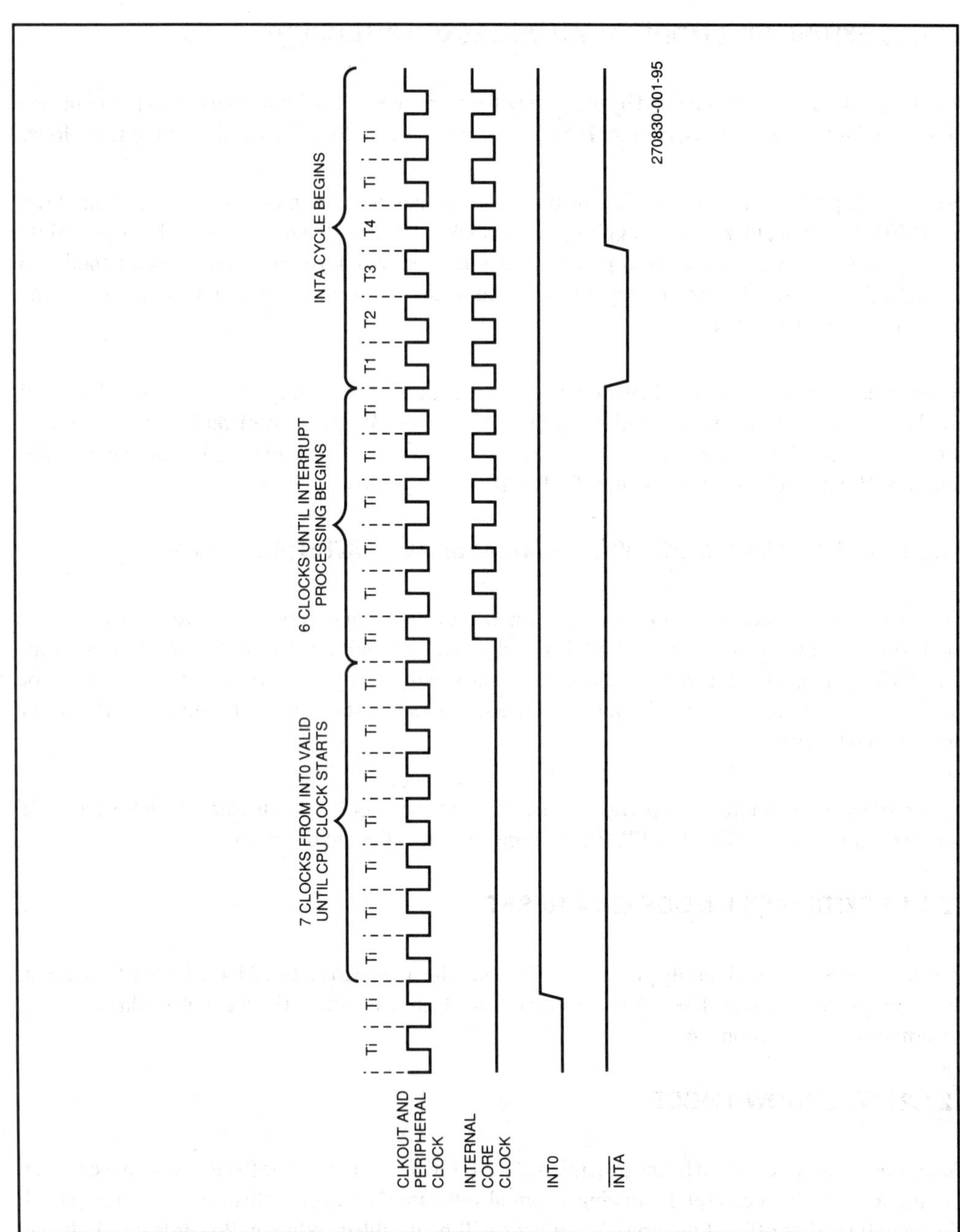

Figure 12.5. Exiting from Idle Mode via an Unmasked Interrupt

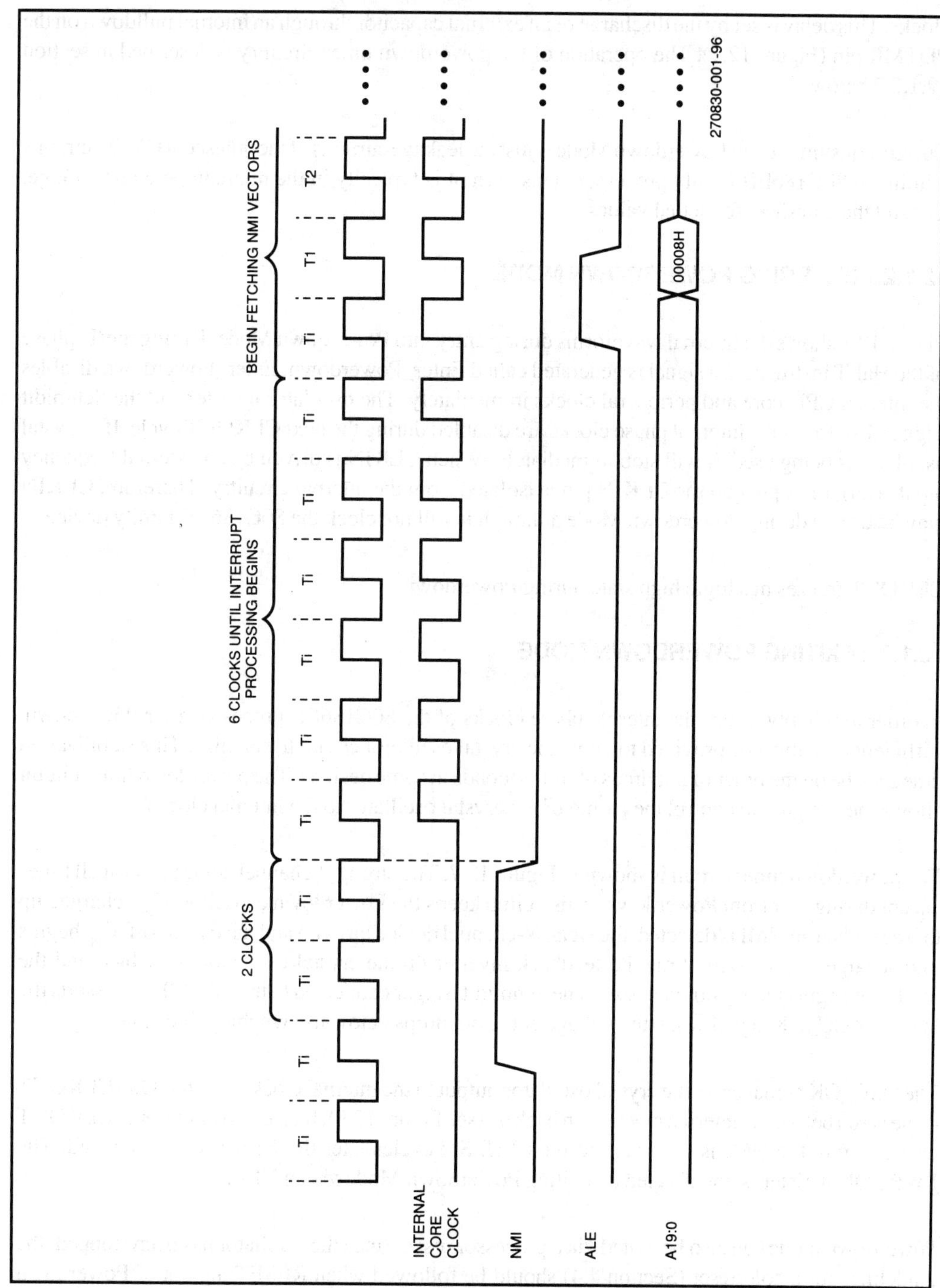

Figure 12.6. Exiting from Idle Mode via an NMI

clocks. This delay is set by the discharge of an external capacitor through an internal pulldown on the PDTMR pin (Figure 12.7). The operation of the powerdown timer circuitry is described in section 12.1.2.2 below.

Current consumption in Powerdown Mode is just the leakage currents of the quiescent CMOS circuits within the 80C186EB family processor. This current is typically in the microampere (10^{-6}) range. Consult the datasheet for actual values.

12.1.2.1 ENTERING POWERDOWN MODE

Figure 12.8 shows the internal waveforms during entry into Powerdown Mode. During the T_2 phase of the HaLT instruction, a signal is generated called Enter_Powerdown. Enter_Powerdown disables the internal CPU core and peripheral clocks immediately. The oscillator inverter and the Schmidtt trigger that drives the internal phase clocks are disabled during the next CLKOUT cycle. If a crystal oscillator is being used, it will stop immediately. When CLKIN is driven by an external frequency input (EFI), the signal on the CLKIN pin is isolated from the internal circuitry. Therefore, CLKIN may be driven during Powerdown Mode although it will not clock the 80C186EB family device.

CLKOUT freezes in a logic high state during Powerdown.

12.1.2.2 EXITING POWERDOWN MODE

In order to reliably restart the internal phase clocks of the 80C186EB processor after Powerdown, sufficient time must be provided to allow the crystal oscillator circuit to stabilize. This stabilization time may be on the order of hundreds of milliseconds in some designs. The powerdown timer circuit allows the designer to control the gating of the crystal oscillator to the internal clocks.

The powerdown timer circuit is shown in Figure 12.7. The strong P-channel device is on at all times except during exit from Powerdown. This pullup keeps the Powerdown capacitor (C_{PD}) charged up to Vcc. When an NMI is detected, the weak N-channel device turns on and the P turns off. C_{PD} begins to discharge. At the same time the feedback inverter on the crystal oscillator is enabled and the oscillator begins its startup processes. The Schmidtt trigger connected to the PDTMR pin asserts the internal OSC_OK signal when the voltage at the pin drops below its switching threshold.

The OSC_OK signal gates the crystal oscillator output to the internal clock circuitry. One CLKOUT cycle is run before the internal clocks turn back on (see Figure 12.9). It takes two additional CLKOUT cycles before the NMI is presented to the CPU. Six cycles later the NMI vector is fetched. The PWRCON register is not affected by exiting Powerdown Mode via an NMI.

Powerdown mode can also be exited via a processor reset. Since the oscillator has been stopped, the guidelines for a cold reset (Section 4.4) should be followed when RESETting out of Powerdown Mode.

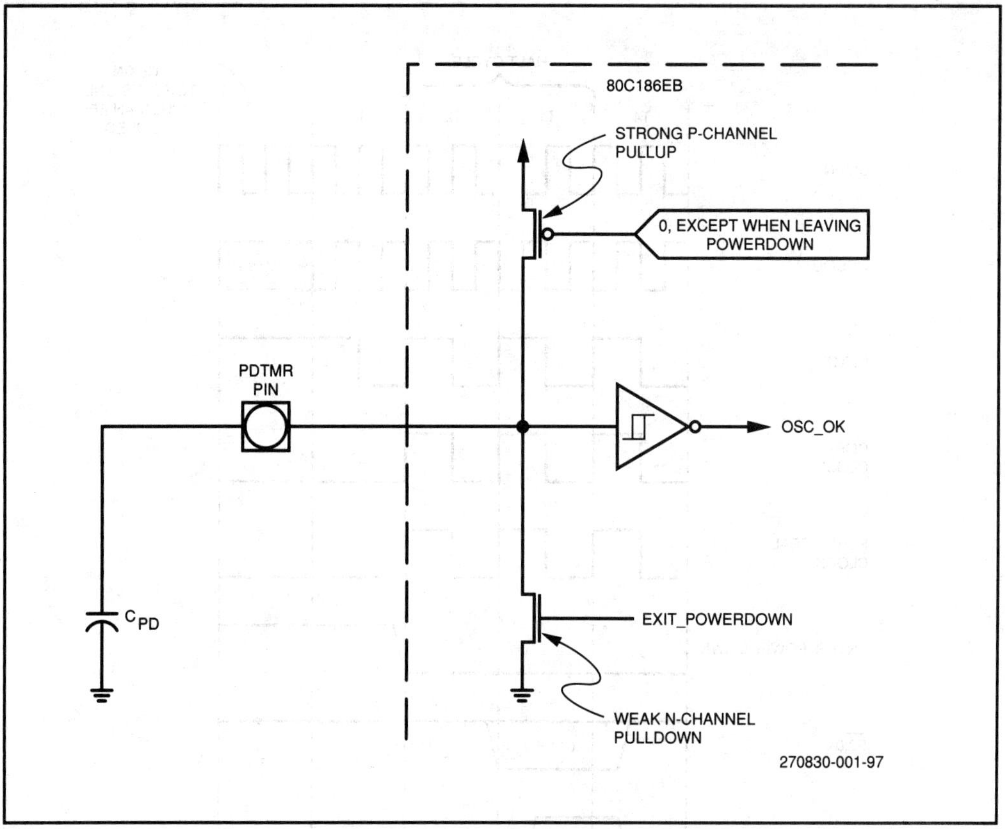

Figure 12.7. Powerdown Timer Circuit

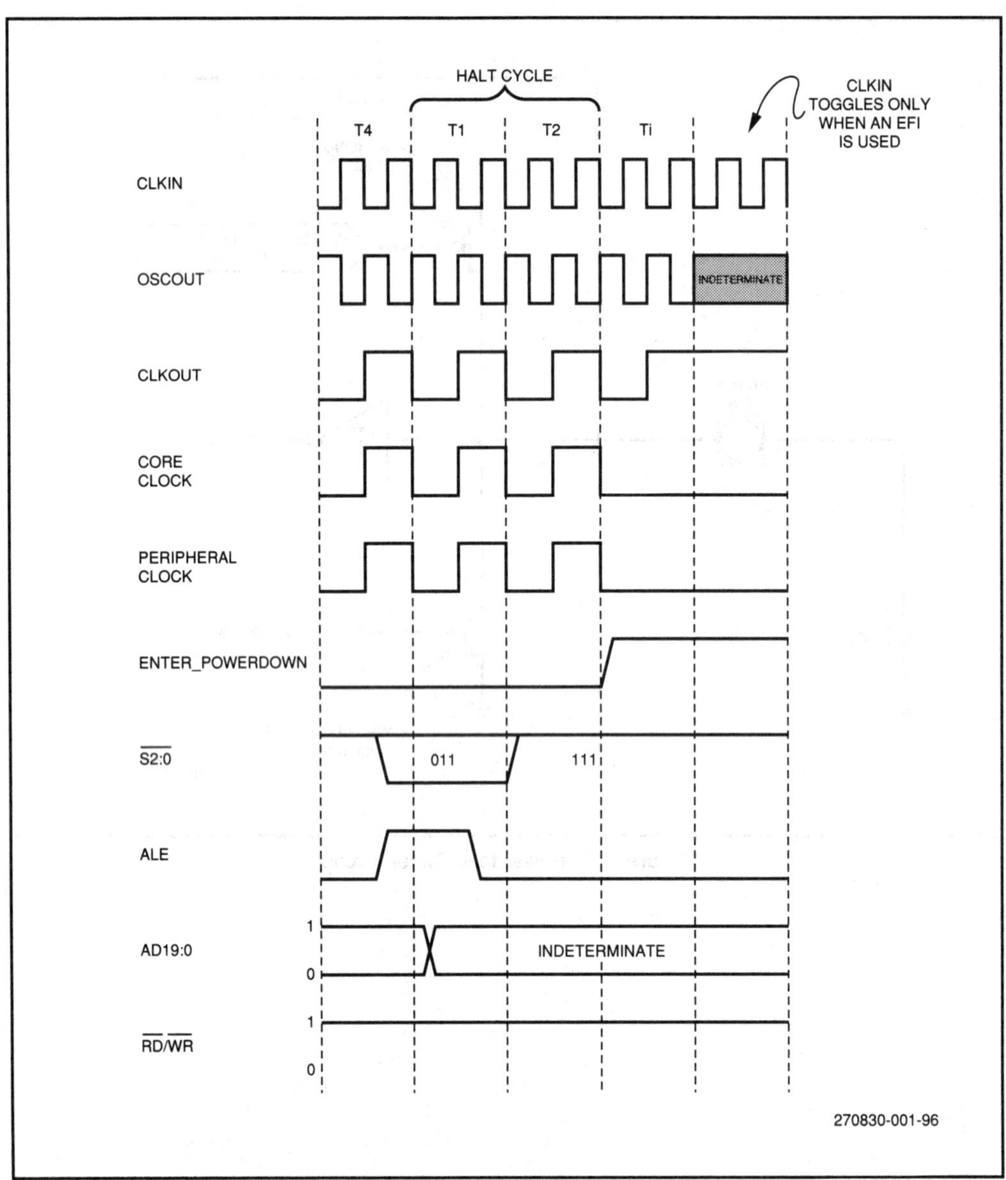

Figure 12.8. Entering Powerdown Mode

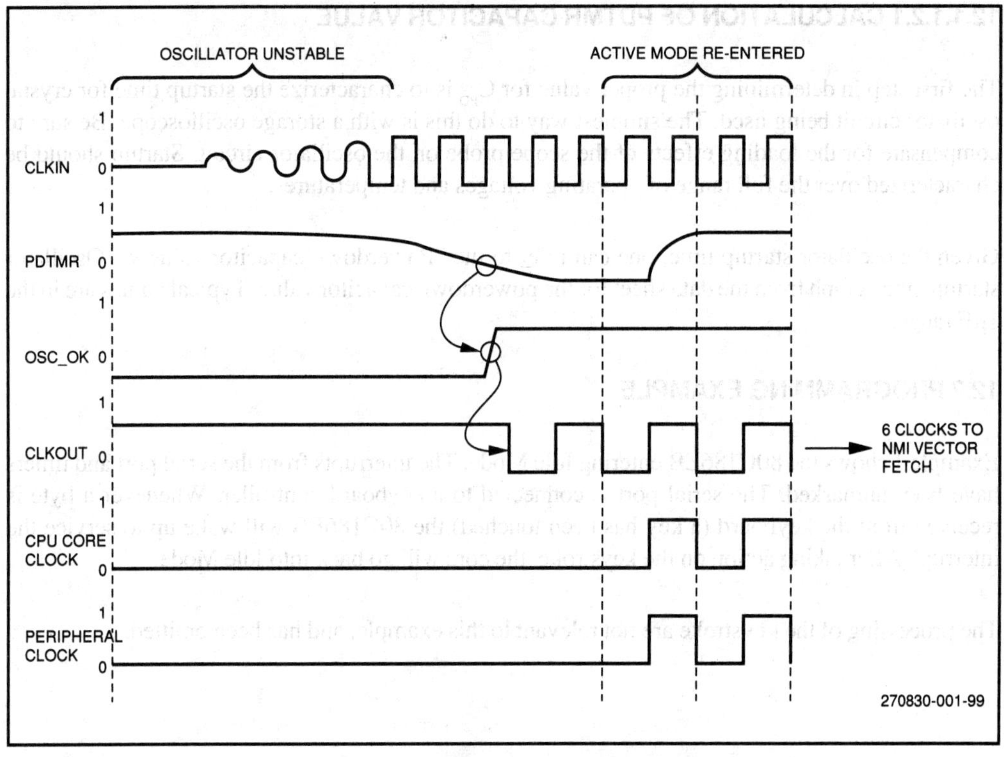

Figure 12.9. Leaving Powerdown after NMI

12.1.1.2.1 CALCULATION OF PDTMR CAPACITOR VALUE

The first step in determining the proper value for C_{PD} is to characterize the startup time for crystal oscillator circuit being used. The simplest way to do this is with a storage oscilloscope. Be sure to compensate for the loading effects of the scope probe on the oscillator circuit. Startup should be characterized over the full range of operating voltages and temperatures.

Given the oscillator startup time, one can refer to the "Powerdown capacitor value vs. Oscillator startup time" graph from the data sheet for the powerdown capacitor value. Typical values are in the 1μF range.

12.2 PROGRAMMING EXAMPLE

Example 1 shows the 80C186EB entering Idle Mode. The interrupts from the serial port and timers have been unmasked. The serial port is connected to a keyboard controller. Whenever a byte is received from the keyboard (a key has been touched) the 80C186EB will wake up to service the interrupt. After taking action on the keystroke, the core will go back into Idle Mode.

The processing of the keystroke are not relevant to this example, and has been omitted.

Example 1.

```
$mod186
name pmu_initialization_example
;
; This file contains an example of initialization code for the
; Power Management Unit on the 80C186EB.
;
; For this example, the CPU core is placed in IDLE Mode while
; waiting for serial input from an keyboard controller.
; Timer interrupts will also be recognized.
; After interrupt processing the core will return to IDLE Mode.

; It is assumed that all interrupt vectors and procedures have
; been previously set up.

; The PCB is at FF00H in I/O space.

IMASK        EQU    0FF08H
PWRCON       EQU    0FFB8H


code         segment       public
             assume cs:code

idle proc   near

   mov              dx, IMASK
   mov              ax, 0005H          ; Enable Timer and SCU interrupts
   out              dx, ax

   mov              dx, PWRCON
   mov              ax, 02H            ; Arm IDLE Mode
   out              dx, ax

   cli                                 ; Clear global interrupt mask.

 in_idle:           hlt                ; Enter IDLE Mode

   jmp              in_idle            ; After INT return to IDLE

idle                endp

code                ends
   end
```

Hardware Provisions for Floating Point Math 13

CHAPTER 13
HARDWARE PROVISIONS FOR FLOATING POINT MATH

The 80C186EB microprocessor family was designed for general-purpose microprocessing. In most data controller applications, the actual arithmetic performed on data values is fairly simple, while fast, efficient data movement and control instructions are very important. However, some applications require more powerful arithmetic instructions and more complex data types than provided by a general purpose data processor. Characteristics of such applications include the following:

- Numeric data vary over a wide range of values or include non-integral values.
- Algorithms produce very large or very small intermediate results.
- Computations must be very precise, i.e., a large number of significant digits must be retained.
- Computations must be extremely reliable without undue dependence on programmed algorithms.
- Overall math performance exceeds the power provided by a general-purpose processor and software alone.

The 80C186EB family supports these needs by providing the necessary hardware interface to the 80C187, Figure 13.2 and a numerics coprocessor extension. The 80C188EB does not support numerics coprocessing.

13.1 80C187 INSTRUCTION SET

80C187 instructions are divided into six functional groups: data transfer, arithmetic, comparison, transcendental, constant, and processor control. Typical 80C187 instructions accept one or two operands and produce a single result. Operands are most often located in memory or the 80C187 stack. The operands of some instructions are predefined; for example, FSQRT always takes the square root of the number in the top stack element. Others allow, or require, the programmer to explicitly code the operand(s) along with the instruction mnemonic. Still others accept one explicit operand and one implicit operand, usually the top stack element.

As with the basic 80C186EB family instruction set, there are two types of operands, source and destination. Source operands are not altered by the instruction. Even when an instruction converts the source operand from one format to another (e.g., real to integer), the conversion is actually performed in an internal work area to avoid altering the source operand. A destination operand is distinguished from a source operand because its contents may be altered when it receives the result of the operation; that is, the destination is replaced by the result.

13.1.1 DATA TRANSFER INSTRUCTIONS

These instructions move operands among elements of the 80C187 register stack, and between stack top and memory. Any of the seven data types can be converted to temporary real and loaded onto the stack in a single operation; they can be stored to memory in the same manner. Data transfer instruction are summarized in Table 13.1.

13.1.2 ARITHMETIC INSTRUCTIONS

The 80C187's arithmetic instruction set (Table 13.2) provides a wealth of variations on the basic add, subtract, multiply, and divide operations, and a number of other useful functions. These range from a simple absolute value to a square root instruction that executes faster than ordinary division. Other arithmetic instructions perform exact modulo division, round real numbers to integers, and scale values by powers of two.

Table 13.2 summarizes the available operation and operand forms provided for basic arithmetic. In addition to the four normal operations, two "reversed" instructions make subtraction and division "symmetrical" like addition and multiplication. The variety of instruction and operand forms give the programmer unusual flexibility:

- Operands may be located in registers or memory.
- Results may be deposited in a choice of registers.
- Operands may be a variety of data types, including temporary real, long real, short real, short integer, or word integer, with automatic type conversion to temporary real performed by the 80C187.

13.1.3 COMPARISON INSTRUCTIONS

Each of these instructions (Table 13.3) analyzes the stack top element, often in relationship to another operand, and reports the result in the status word condition code. The basic operations are compare, test (compare with zero), and examine (report tag, sign, and normalization).

13.1.4 TRANSCENDENTAL INSTRUCTIONS

The instructions in this category perform the time-consuming core calculations for common trigonometric, hyperbolic, inverse hyperbolic, logarithmic, and exponential functions. Prologue and epilogue software may be used to reduce arguments to the range accepted by the instructions and to adjust the result to correspond to the original arguments if necessary. The transcendentals operate on the top one or two stack elements and they return their results to the stack. Table 13.4 lists the transcendental instructions.

Table 13.1. Data Transfer Instructions

REAL TRANSFERS	
FLD	Load real
FST	Store real
FSTP	Store real and pop
FXCH	Exchange registers
INTEGER TRANSFERS	
FILD	Integer load
FIST	Integer store
FISTP	Integer store and pop
PACKED DECIMAL TRANSFERS	
FBLD	Packed decimal (BCD) load
FBSTP	Packed decimal (BCD) store and pop

Table 13.2. Arithmetic Instructions

ADDITION	
FADD	Add real
FADDP	Add real and pop
FIADD	Integer add
SUBTRACTION	
FSUB	Subtract real
FSUBP	Subtract real and pop
FISUB	Integer subtract
FSUBR	Subtract real reversed
FSUBRP	Subtract real reversed and pop
FISUBR	Integer subtract reversed
MULTIPLICATION	
FMUL	Multiply real
FMULP	Multiply real and pop
FIMUL	Integer multiply
DIVISION	
FDIV	Divide real
FDIVP	Divide real and pop
FIDIV	Integer divide
FDIVR	Divide real reversed
FDIVRP	Divide real reversed and pop
FIDIVR	Integer divide reversed
OTHER OPERATIONS	
FSQRT	Square root
FSCALE	Scale
FPREM	Partial remainder
FRNDINT	Round to integer
FXTRACT	Extract exponent and significand
FABS	Absolute value
FCHS	Change sign
FPREMI	Partial reminder (IEEE)

Table 13.3. Comparison Instructions

FCOM	Compare real
FCOMP	Compare real and pop
FCOMPP	Compare real and pop twice
FICOM	Integer compare
FICOMP	Integer compare and pop
FTST	Test
FXAM	Examine
FUCOM	Unordered compare
FUCOMP	Unordered compare and pop
FUCOMPP	Unordered compare and pop twice

Table 13.4. Transcendental Instructions

FPTAN	Partial tangent
FPATAN	Partial arctangent
F2XM1	2^X-1
FYL2X	$Y \cdot \log_2 X$
FYL2XP1	$Y \cdot \log_2(X+1)$
FCOS	Cosine
FSIN	Sine
FSINCOS	Sine and cosine

Table 13.5. Constant Instructions

FLDZ	Load +0.1
FLD1	Load +1.0
FLDPI	Load π
FLDL2T	Load $\log_2 10$
FLDL2E	Load $\log_2 e$
FLDLG2	Load $\log_{10} 2$
FLDLN2	Load $\log_e 2$

13.1.5 CONSTANT INSTRUCTIONS

Each of these instructions (Table 13.5) loads a commonly used constant onto the stack. The values have full temporary real precision (80 bits) and are accurate to approximately 19 decimal digits. Since a temporary real constant occupies 10 memory bytes, the constant instructions, only two bytes long, save memory space. These instructions simplify programming as well.

13.1.6 PROCESSOR CONTROL INSTRUCTIONS

Most of these instructions (Table 13.6) are not used in computations; they are provided principally for system-level activities. These include initialization, exception handling and task switching.

Table 13.6. Processor Control Instructions

FINIT/FNINIT	Initialize processor
FDISI/FNDISI	Disable interrupts
FENI/FNENI	Enable interrupts
FLDCW	Load control word
FSTCW/FNSTCW	Store control word
FSTSW/FNSTCW	Store status word
FCLEX/FNCLEX	Clear exceptions
FSTENV/FNSTENV	Store environment
FLDENV	Load environment
FSAVE/FNSAVE	Save state
FRSTOR	Restore state
FINCSTP	Increment stack pointer
FDECSTP	Decrement stack pointer
FFREE	Free register
FNOP	No operation
FWAIT	CPU wait

13.2 80C187 DATA TYPES

An 80C186EB/80C187 system supports the following seven data types:

- Word Integer - A signed binary numeric value contained in a 16-bit word. All operations assume a 2's complement representation.
- Short Integer - A signed binary numeric value contained in a 32-bit double word. All operations assume a 2's complement representation.
- Long Integer - A signed binary numeric value contained in a 64-bit quad word. All operations assume a 2's complement representation.
- Packed Decimal - A signed numeric value contained in an 80-bit BCD format.
- Short Real - A signed, floating point numeric value contained in a 32-bit format.

- Long Real - A signed, floating point numeric value contained in a 64-bit format.
- Temporary Real - A signed, floating point numeric value contained in an 80-bit format. Temporary real is the native 80C187 format.

Figure 13.1 graphically represents these data types.

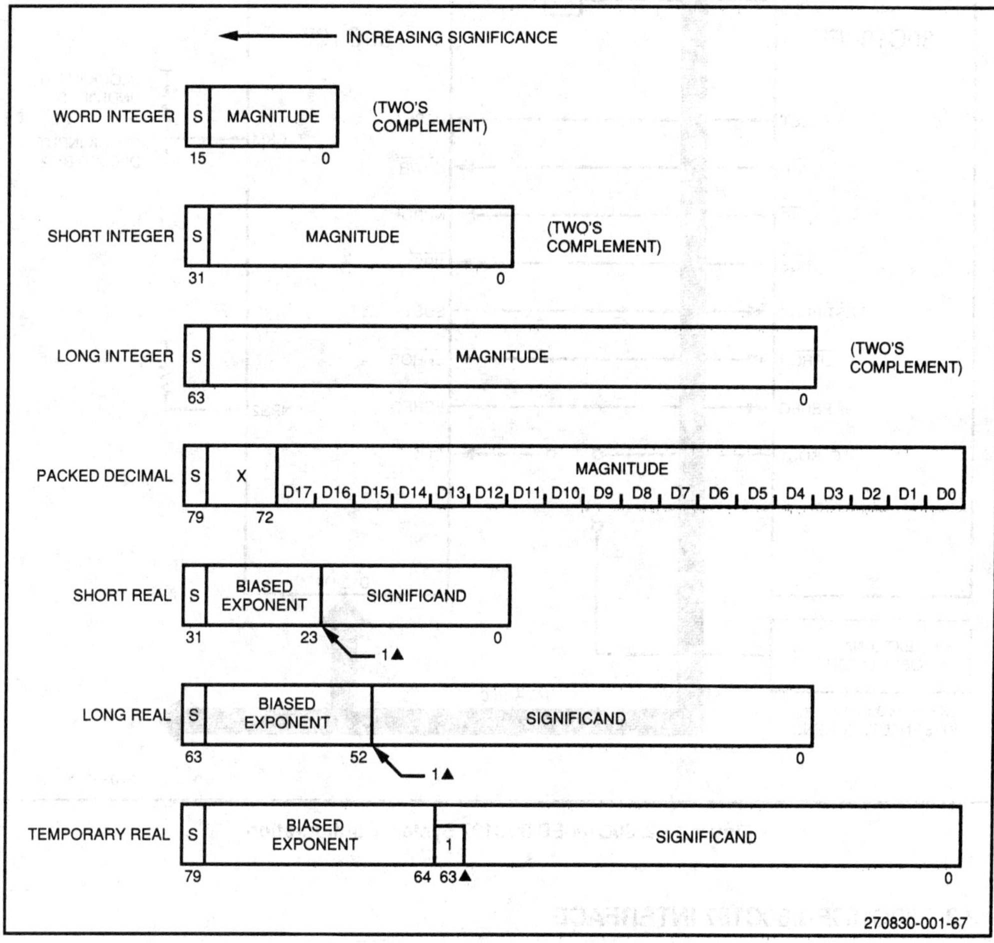

INCREASING SIGNIFICANCE

WORD INTEGER: S (15) | MAGNITUDE (0) — (TWO'S COMPLEMENT)

SHORT INTEGER: S (31) | MAGNITUDE (0) — (TWO'S COMPLEMENT)

LONG INTEGER: S (63) | MAGNITUDE (0) — (TWO'S COMPLEMENT)

PACKED DECIMAL: S (79) | X (72) | MAGNITUDE: D17 D16 D15 D14 D13 D12 D11 D10 D9 D8 D7 D6 D5 D4 D3 D2 D1 D0

SHORT REAL: S (31) | BIASED EXPONENT (23) | SIGNIFICAND (0) — 1▲

LONG REAL: S (63) | BIASED EXPONENT (52) | SIGNIFICAND (0) — 1▲

TEMPORARY REAL: S (79) | BIASED EXPONENT (64) | 1 (63▲) | SIGNIFICAND (0)

270830-001-67

Figure 13.1. 80C187 Supported Data Types

13.3 USING THE 80C186EB WITH THE 80C187 NUMERICS PROCESSOR EXTENSION

The 80C186EB supports floating point calculations by providing the necessary hardware interface to the 80C187 numerics processor extension.

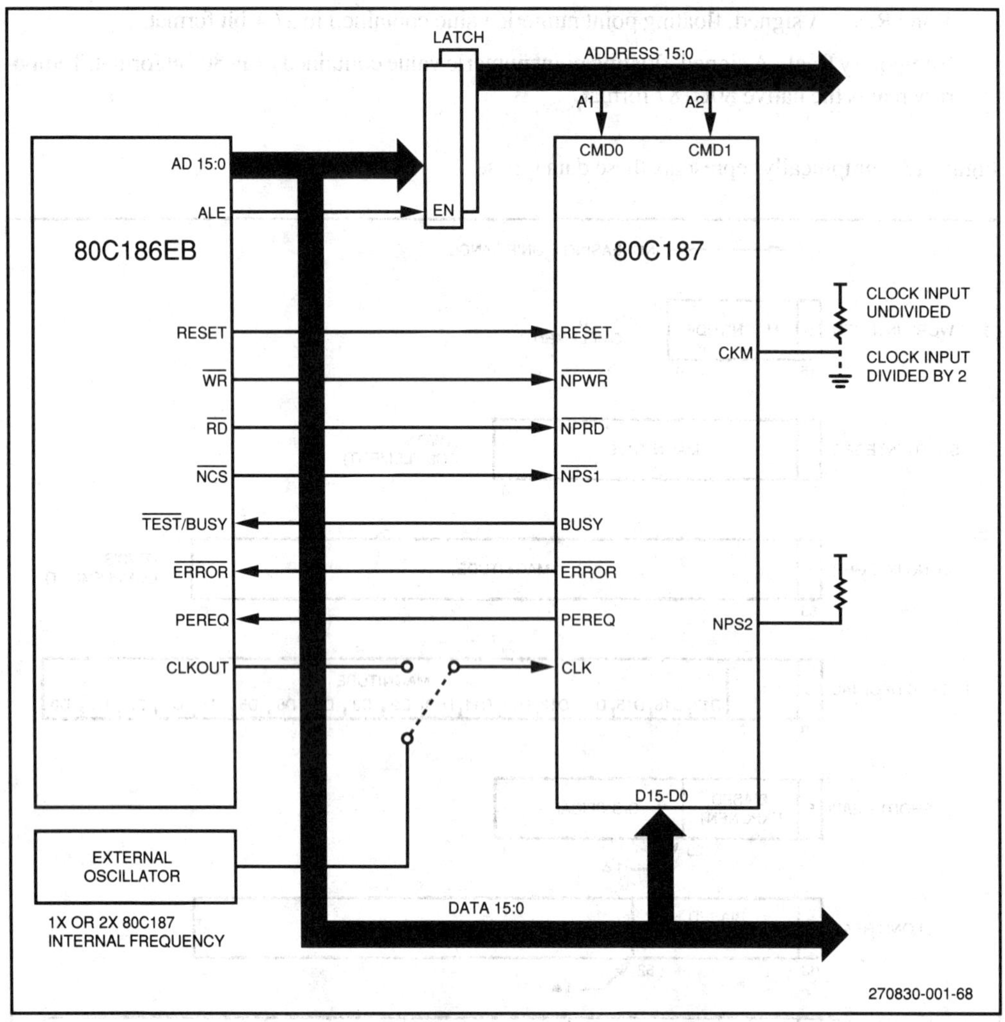

Figure 13.2. 80C186EB/80C187 System Configuration

13.3.1 80C186EB/80C187 INTERFACE

The 80C186EB interfaces directly to the 80C187 (see Figure 13.2). The 80C186EB and 80C187 operate asynchronously, each up to its maximum rated clock speed. CLKOUT from the 80C186EB may be used as the 80C187 clock input up to 12.5 MHz. The 80C188EB cannot be used because the flow of opcodes, instruction pointers, and data passes through 16-bit I/O ports.

The 80C187 is referred to as a numerics processor extension because it operates as a slave device to the host 80C186EB. All communication between the 80C186EB and 80C187 occurs through the dedicated I/O ports shown in Table 13.7. When the 80C186EB encounters a numerics opcode, it writes the opcode to the 80C187, which decodes the instruction and passes elementary instruction information (Opcode Status) back to the 80C186EB. Since the 80C187 is a slave processor, all loads and stores to memory are performed by the 80C186EB.

Please note that the 80C186EB cannot process any numerics (ESC) opcodes alone. If the 80C186EB encounters a numerics instruction (including the FINIT/FNINIT initialization instruction) and the 80C187 is not present, the operation of the 80C186EB is indeterminate. In those applications where the 80C187 is offered as an option, problems can be prevented in three ways:

- Remove all numerics (ESC) instructions, including any code which checks for the presence of the NPX.
- Use a jumper or switch setting to indicate the presence of the 80C187, and have the software branch away from numerics instructions when the 80C187 socket is empty.
- Add pull-up and pull-down resistors to various data and control lines to force the 80C186EB into predictable operation when the 80C187 socket is empty.

Table 13.7. Numerics Coprocessor I/O Port Assignments

I/O Address	Read Definition	Write Definition
00F8H	Status/Control	Opcode
00FAH	Data	Data
00FCH	reserved	CS:IP, DS:EA
00FEH	Opcode Status	reserved

13.3.2 80C186EB BUS CYCLES WITH THE 80C187 NUMERICS PROCESSOR EXTENSION

The 80C186EB performs bus cycles to the 80C187 numerics processor extension (NPX) exactly like other I/O bus cycles. This fact has important implications:

- Operations to the 80C187 require external READY to be provided.
- If a chip select address range is programmed to cover the NPX port addresses, chip select line goes active during each read or write from the 80C186EB to the 80C187. However, ordinary reads and writes to those addresses do not activate $\overline{\text{NCS}}$ on the 80C186EB. Overlapping chip select ranges and the NPX port addresses is not recommended due to the hardware conflicts that could result.
- DT/$\overline{\text{R}}$ and $\overline{\text{DEN}}$ function normally during NPX transfers. In a buffered system with the 80C187 residing on the local bus, use $\overline{\text{NCS}}$ to qualify $\overline{\text{DEN}}$ to the bus transceivers. Otherwise, contention between the NPX and the transceivers occurs on read cycles.
- The 80C186EB local bus is available to the integrated peripherals during execution of numerics instructions when it is not needed by the CPU. This means that DRAM refresh cycles may be interspersed with accesses to the 80C187.

- The 80C186EB local bus is available to alternate bus masters during execution of numerics instructions when it is not needed by the CPU. This means that bus cycles originating from alternate masters (via the HOLD/HLDA protocol) can suspend numerics bus cycles for an indefinite period.
- The $\overline{\text{LOCK}}$ pin functions normally during numerics operations. This means that LOCKed numerics instructions can monopolize the bus for a very long time.

ONCE™ Mode 14

CHAPTER 14
ONCE™ MODE

ONCE™ mode (*ON Circuit Emulation*) provides the ability to 3-state all pins (except VCC and VSS) of the 80C186EB for either emulation or testing purposes. An emulator or test probe can be placed over an existing 80C186EB in ONCE™ mode and emulation or testing can be performed without conflicts.

14.1 ENTERING ONCE™ MODE

ONCE™ mode (pronounced: *ahnce*) is entered by driving A19 low while $\overline{\text{RESIN}}$ is asserted. All pins immediately float. As soon as $\overline{\text{RESIN}}$ transitions from low to high, the ONCE™ request is latched and the state of A19 is ignored. The 80C186EB has been effectively removed from the circuit.

14.2 LEAVING ONCE™ MODE

ONCE™ mode is terminated by a normal reset of the device **without** A19 being driven (it is left floating).

Appendix A

Differences Between the 80C186 Family and the 8086/8088

APPENDIX A
DIFFERENCES BETWEEN THE 80C186 MODULAR CORE FAMILY AND THE 8086/8088

A.1 CPU PERFORMANCE

Because of 80C186 Modular Core family hardware enhancements in both the Bus Interface Unit and the Execution Unit, most instructions require fewer clock cycles to execute than on the 8086/8088. Execution speed is gained by performing the effective address calculations (base + displacement + index) with a dedicated hardware adder, which takes only four clock cycles in the 80C186 Modular Core family Bus Interface Unit, rather than with a microcode routine. These calculations are three to six times faster than the 8086/8088 at the same frequency.

In addition, the execution speed of specific instructions was improved. All multiple-bit shift and rotate instructions execute 1.5 to 2.5 times faster than the (same speed) 8086/8088. Multiply and divide instructions execute three times faster. String move instructions run at bus bandwidth, about twice the speed of the 8086/8088. Overall, the 80C186 Modular Core family processors run benchmark programs 1.2 - 2.6 times the performance level of the (same speed) 8086/8088.

A.2 CLOCKING

The 80C186 Modular Core family employs an integrated clock generator which provides a 50 percent duty cycle CPU clock. This is different from the 8086 which utilizes an external clock generator to provide a 33 percent (1/3 HIGH, 2/3 LOW) duty cycle CPU clock. The following points relate to 80186 clock generation:

- The 80C186 Modular Core family uses a crystal or external frequency input that is twice the desired processor clock frequency.
- An 80C186 Modular Core family processor does not provide a clock output at reduced frequency. However, a timer output may be easily programmed for this purpose.

A.3 LOCAL BUS CONTROLLER AND CONTROL SIGNALS

In general, the output drivers on 80C186 Modular Core family products are much larger than those of the 8086. This leads to larger systems without as much need for bus buffering. It also means that the designer should be more careful to provide adequate grounding and bypassing, since large drivers are more apt to cause current transients.

A.4 HOLD/HLDA VS. $\overline{\text{REQUEST}}/\overline{\text{GRANT}}$

The 80C186 Modular Core family uses a HOLD/HLDA protocol for bus arbitration rather than the $\overline{\text{REQUEST}}/\overline{\text{GRANT}}$ protocol used by the 8086 in max mode. This allows compatibility with newer generation Intel bus master peripheral devices.

A.5 STATUS INFORMATION

Three status signals are available on the 8086 but not on the 80C186 Modular Core family. They are S3, S4, and S5. Taken together, S3 and S4 indicate the segment register from which the current physical address has been derived. S5 indicates the state of the interrupt flip-flop. On 80C186 Modular Core family processors, these signals will always be LOW.

An 80C186 Modular Core family processor simultaneously provides both local bus control outputs and status outputs for use with external Bus Controllers. This is different from the 8086 where the local bus control outputs are sacrificed if status outputs are desired. These differences will manifest themselves in 8086 systems and 80C186 Modular Core family systems as follows:

- Many systems supporting both a system bus and a local bus will not require two separate external bus controllers. The bus control signals may be used to control the local bus while the status signals are concurrently connected to the 82C88 Bus Controller to drive the control signals of the system bus.
- The ALE signal goes active a clock phase earlier on the 80C186 Modular Core family than on the 8086 or 82C88. This minimizes address propagation time through the address latches, since typically the delay time through these latches from valid inputs is less than the propagation delay from the strobe input active.

A.6 BUS UTILIZATION

A typical instruction mix will require greater bus utilization on the 80C186 Modular Core family than on the 8086. The 80C186 Modular Core family executes most instructions in fewer clock cycles, requiring instructions from the queue at a faster rate. This also means that the effect of wait states is more pronounced in an 80C186 Modular Core family microprocessor system than in an 8086 system.

A.7 INSTRUCTION EXECUTION

The following paragraphs explain the instruction execution differences between the 8086 and the 80186.

ADDED INSTRUCTIONS:

The 80C186 Modular Core family executes PUSHA, POPA, INS, OUTS, BOUND, ENTER, and LEAVE.

IMPROVED INSTRUCTIONS:

PUSH, IMUL, and SHIFTS/ROTATES may use immediate operands on the 80C186 Modular Core family.

UNDEFINED OPCODES:

When the opcodes 63H, 64H, 65H, 66H, 67H, F1H, FEH XX111XXXB and FFH XX111XXXB are executed, the 80C186 Modular Core family executes an illegal instruction exception, interrupt Type 6. The 8086 will ignore the opcode.

0FH OPCODE:

When the opcode 0FH is encountered, the 8086 will execute a POP CS, while the 80C186 Modular Core family will execute an illegal instruction exception, interrupt Type 6.

WORD WRITE AT OFFSET FFFFH:

When a word write is performed at offset FFFFH in a segment, the 8086 will write one byte at offset FFFFH, and the other at offset 0, while an 80C186 Modular Core family processor will write one byte at offset FFFFH, and the other at offset 10000H (one byte beyond the end of the segment). One byte segment underflow will also occur if a stack PUSH is executed and the stack pointer contains the value 1.

SHIFT/ROTATE BY VALUE GREATER THAN 31:

Before the 80C186 Modular Core family performs a shift or rotate by a value (either in the CL register, or an immediate value) it ANDs the value with 1FH, limiting the number of bits rotated to less than 32. The 8086 does not limit the rotation count.

LOCK PREFIX:

The 8086 activates its $\overline{\text{LOCK}}$ signal immediately upon executing the LOCK prefix. An 80C186 Modular Core family processor does not activate the $\overline{\text{LOCK}}$ signal until the processor is ready to begin the data cycles associated with the LOCKed instruction.

INTERRUPTED STRING MOVE INSTRUCTIONS:

If an 8086 is interrupted during the execution of a repeated string move instruction, the return value it will push on the stack will point to the last prefix instruction before the string move instruction. If the instruction has more than one prefix (e.g., a segment override prefix in addition to the repeat prefix), the other prefixes will not be reexecuted upon returning from the interrupt. An 80C186 Modular Core family processor will push an IP value pointing to the first prefix of the repeated instruction (as long as prefixes are not repeated), allowing the string instruction to properly resume.

CONDITIONS CAUSING DIVIDE ERROR WITH AN INTEGER DIVIDE:

The 8086 will cause a divide error whenever the absolute value of the quotient is greater than 7FFFH (for word operations) or if the absolute value of the quotient is greater than 7FH (for byte operations). The 80C186 Modular Core family expanded the range of negative numbers allowed as a quotient by 1 to include 8000H and 80H. These numbers represent the most negative numbers representable using 2's complement arithmetic (equaling -32768 and -128 in decimal, respectively).

ESC OPCODES:

An 80C186 Modular Core family microprocessor has a bit (the ET bit) in the relocation register which can be programmed to cause a Type 7 interrupt upon attempted execution of a coprocessor (ESCape) instruction. The 8086 has no such provision.

Execution of numerics opcodes proceeds differently in the 80C186EB than in the 8086/8088 or 80186/80188. See Chapter 12 for details. The 80C188EB cannot utilize a numerics processor extension at all. When migrating from the 8086/8088 or 80186/80188 to the 80C186/80C188, the user should be aware of these differences. In particular, it may be necessary to check software for unexpected numerics (ESCape) opcodes.

Appendix B

Differences Between all 80186/80C186/80C186EB Family Members

APPENDIX B
SUMMARY OF DIFFERENCES BETWEEN THE 80186, 80C186, AND 80C186EB FAMILIES

The 80C186EB is the third member in a line of 80186 code compatible, high integration, embedded microprocessors. There are differences between all members of the product line. The description of these differences is handled in this Appendix on a functional block basis. The family matrix in figure B-1 summarizes the family differences.

The original NMOS 80186 has only one major mode of operation. The 80C186, to remain pin and software compatible with the 80186, has two. In *Compatible Mode* the 80C186 is a pin for pin replacement of the 80186 (with the exception of numerics co-processing capability). In *Enhanced Mode* the user has access to two additional peripherals: the Refresh Control Unit, and the Power Save Unit. Enhanced mode maps three of the chip select pins into numerics processor communications functions. Mode selection is made only at reset.

The 80C186EB has only one mode. The on-board peripherals of the 80C186EB are different from the 80186 (and 80C186) and therefore a "compatible mode" is not necessary.

B.1 CPU DIFFERENCES

FEATURE	80186	80C186		80C186EB
		COMPATIBLE	ENHANCED	
ENHANCED 8086 INSTRUCTION SET				
NMOS TECHNOLOGY				
CHMOS III				
CHMOS IV (1MICRON)				
DYNAMIC NON-MODULAR CORE				
LOW-POWER STATIC MODULAR CORE				
POWER SAVE (CLOCK DIVIDE) MODE				
POWERDOWN AND IDLE MODES				
QUEUE STATUS MODE				
MULTIPLEXED 80C187 INTERFACE				
DIRECT 80C187 INTERFACE				
ONCE TEST MODE				
INTERRUPT CONTROL UNIT				NO SLAVE MODE
TIMER/CONTER UNIT				
CHIP SELECT UNIT				
DMA UNIT				
SERIAL COMMUNICATIONS UNIT				
REFRESH CONTROL UNIT				
INPUT/OUTPUT PORT UNIT				

COMPATIBLE WITH ORIGINAL 80186 — IMPROVED VERSION

Figure B-1: Family Feature Matrix

B.1.1 INSTRUCTION SET

All three devices execute the same instruction set. There have been no additions or deletions to this set since the original 80186. Any code written for an 80186/80C186/80C186EB will be fully portable amongst family members. **Peripheral register locations have been moved, however, on the 80C186EB (see below).**

All family members are upward compatible with the 8086/8088 instruction set.

B.1.2 SEMICONDUCTOR TECHNOLOGY DIFFERENCES

The 80186 is implemented in NMOS technology. As such, it dissipates more power and runs slower than the more recent CMOS implementations. The 80186/188 is *dynamic,* which means the clock must always be applied for the device to operate normally.

The 80C186 is implemented in CHMOS III, a high performance CMOS technology. Like the 80186, the 80C186 is dynamic. The 80C186 can run at up to twice the clock rate of the 80186.

The 80C186EB is implemented in CHMOS IV, a 1 micron CMOS technology. The 80C186EB is a **fully static device**. The clock can be shut off without a loss of state (provided Vcc is maintained). The new modular core was also designed to consume less power than an 80C186 operating at the same frequency. These two features allow significant power savings over earlier 80186 family products. The 80C186EB's execution speed is equal to that of the 80C186.

B.1.3 QUEUE STATUS MODE

The 80186 and 80C186 families have an optional "queue status mode." This mode is entered during reset by tying $\overline{RD}$ low. In queue status mode, the ALE and $\overline{WR}$ pins changed functionality to indicate the internal queue status.

Queue status mode was deleted from the 80C186EB.

B.1.4 NUMERICS INTERFACE

The 80186 does not directly support a numerics interface. The 80186 can be connected to an 8087 through an 82188.

The 80C186/80C188 in compatible mode does not support any numerics operations. The ET (Escape Trap) bit in the relocation register has no effect in Compatible Mode; encountering an ESCape opcode causes a type 7 interrupt to be executed.

The 80C186 in enhanced mode directly supports the 80C187 Numerics Processor Extension. The $\overline{MCS0}$, $\overline{MCS1}$, and $\overline{MCS3}$ chip select lines become the PEREQ, $\overline{ERROR}$, and $\overline{NPS}$ pins respectively. The ET bit controls whether numerics instructions are dispatched to the 80C187 or trapped for emulation.

The 80C186EB directly supports the 80C187 with 3 dedicated pins, no pin multiplexing is used. The ET bit on the 80C186EB functions the same as the ET bit on the 80C186 in enhanced mode. Some packaging options for the 80C186EB delete the numerics pins.

B.1.5 TRANSCEIVER INTERFACE (DEN AND DT/R)

The timings for the transceiver interface pins (DEN and DT/$\overline{R}$) on the 80C186EB family have been improved to prevent bus contention.

B.1.6 READY INTERFACE

The 80186 and 80C186 family devices have two ready input pins: SRDY and ARDY. SRDY has to be synchronized externally while ARDY is partially synchronized internally. The 80C186EB has only one ready input, READY, which is functionally equivalent to ARDY.

B.2 CLOCK OSCILLATOR CIRCUITRY AND EXTERNAL FREQUENCY INPUT

The external frequency input (EFI) requirements differ somewhat between the NMOS 80186/80188 and the CMOS devices. On the NMOS device, it is possible to drive either X1 (with X2 unconnected) or X2 (with X1 grounded). This is possible because of the nature of NMOS inverter pullups.

The only acceptable EFI configuration for the CMOS devices is to drive X1 and leave X2 unconnected. These pins were renamed CLKIN and OSCOUT on the 80C186EB to reinforce this point. Driving X2 (OSCOUT) will overdrive the CMOS oscillator inverter and will, in time, render the clock circuitry inoperable.

B.3 POWER CONSUMPTION MANAGEMENT MODES

The 80186 family and the 80C186 in compatible mode have no power management features.

The 80C186 in enhanced mode has a power save unit. This unit allows the user to conserve power by dividing the internal CPU frequency by a programmable prescalar between 1 and 16. The minimum internal CPU frequency is 500 KHz in any mode. Power save mode is entered by programming the power-save register. Execution continues at the slowed clock rate.

The 80C186EB has two power management modes that make use of its static design: idle and powerdown. Idle mode shuts off the CPU while leaving the peripheral set running. Any unmasked interrupt, NMI, or reset will re-awaken the core. Refresh requests and HOLD requests will temporarily re-awaken the core for servicing. Powerdown mode shuts off all clocks and the external oscillator. Power consumption is reduced to transistor leakage (typically in the microamp range). Powerdown can only be exited via an NMI or reset. Both modes are entered by setting the corresponding bit in the power control register and executing a HALT instruction.

B.4 INTERRUPT CONTROLLER

The 80186 and 80C186 family devices have a slave mode (formally RMX mode) which allows the internal interrupt unit to become a slave to an external 8259. The 80C186EB does not have this mode.

The 80C186EB provides one extra external interrupt pin, INT4.

B.5 TIMER COUNTER UNIT

The timer counter unit operates identically in all members of the 80186/80C186/80C186EB family.

B.6 DMA UNIT

The 80186 and 80C186 families include a DMA unit. This unit is not available on the 80C186EB.

B.7 SERIAL COMMUNICATIONS UNIT

The 80C186EB includes a 2 channel serial communications unit. This peripheral is not on the 80186 or the 80C186 family.

B.8 CHIP SELECT UNIT

The 80186 and 80C186 family devices include a chip select unit capable of accessing up to 768K of memory and up to 7 peripheral devices. A maximum of 3 wait states can be inserted in bus cycles automatically. Chip select areas cannot overlap and they cannot be disabled by software.

The 80C186EB includes an enhanced chip select unit that is not compatible with the 80186 chip select unit. The enhanced chip select unit has a total of 10 channels that can be configured for any size region of either memory or peripheral space. The channels can overlap and can be software enabled and disabled. Up to 10 megabytes of physical memory can be accessed through software paging. Up to fifteen wait states can be internally generated.

B.9 REFRESH CONTROL UNIT

The 80186 and 80C186 in compatible mode do not have a refresh control unit.

The 80C186/80C188 in enhanced mode has a refresh control unit capable of refreshing dynamic RAMs with a row address of 9 bits or less.

The 80C186EB refresh control unit can refresh dynamic RAMs with row addresses of 12 bits or less.

B.10 PERIPHERAL CONTROL BLOCK

The 80186 and 80C186 peripheral control blocks are completely compatible. The register locations of some peripherals (i.e. the timers) have been moved on the 80C186EB family to allow functional groups of registers to remain together. The change of register locations must be kept in mind when porting code among family members.

Appendix C

Differences Between 80C186EB and 80C188EB

APPENDIX C
SUMMARY OF DIFFERENCES BETWEEN THE 80C186EB AND THE 80C188EB

The 80C186EB and the 80C188EB have the same execution unit. The Bus Interface Unit, however, differs between the two devices. The 80C188EB uses an 8-bit data bus to communicate with external memories and peripherals, where the 80C186EB uses a 16-bit bus. The following list summarizes the effects of the bus width difference:

- The 80C188EB has a four byte prefetch queue, rather than the six byte prefetch queue present on the 80C186EB. The reason is that the 80C188EB fetches opcodes one byte at a time, requiring more bus cycles to fill the queue. A smaller queue is required to prevent an inordinate number of bus cycles being wasted by prefetching opcodes to be discarded during a jump.
- AD8-AD15 on the 80C186EB are transformed to A8-A15 on the 80C188EB. Valid address information is present on these lines throughout the bus cycle of the 80C188EB. Valid address information is not guaranteed on these lines during idle T-states.
- $\overline{BHE}$ on the 80C186EB is replaced by $\overline{RFSH}$ (refresh cycle running) on the 80C188EB. The 80C188EB has no high byte on the data bus.
- Execution times for most data transfer instructions increases because the BIU funnels the accesses through a narrower data bus. The narrower bus also means that the prefetch queue will run empty more often, causing the Execution Unit itself to be bus-limited. The execution time within the processor, however, is not changed between the 80C186EB and 80C188EB.

Another important point is that the 80C188EB is internally a 16-bit machine. This means that access to the integrated peripheral registers of the 80C188EB will be done in 16-bit words, not in 8-bit bytes. When a word access is made to the internal registers, the BIU will run two bus cycles externally.

Access to the control block may also be done with byte operations. Internally the full 16 bits of the AX register will be written, while only one bus cycle will be executed externally.

Synchronization Appendix D

APPENDIX D
SYNCHRONIZATION OF EXTERNAL INPUTS

Many input signals to an 80C186EB family processor are asynchronous, that is, a specified set up or hold time is not required to ensure proper functioning of the device. Associated with each of these inputs is a synchronizer which samples this external asynchronous signal, and synchronizes it to the internal clock.

D.1 WHY SYNCHRONIZERS ARE REQUIRED

Every data latch requires a certain set up and hold time in order to operate properly. At a certain window within the specified set up and hold time, the part will actually try to latch the data. If the input makes a transition within this window, the output will not attain a stable state within the given output delay time. The actual size of this sampling window is typically much smaller than the window specified by the data sheet; however, part to part variation could move the actual window around within the specified window.

Even if the input to a data latch makes a transition while a data latch is attempting to latch this input, the output of the latch will attain a stable state after a certain amount of time, typically much longer than the normal strobe to output delay time. Figure D-1 shows a normal input to output strobed transition and one in which the input signal makes a transition during the latch's sample window. To synchronize an asynchronous signal, all one needs to do is to sample the signal into one data latch long enough for the output to stabilize, then latch it into a second data latch. The time between the first latch strobe and the second latch strobe allows the first latch to attain a steady state. With the asynchronous signal resolved in this way, the input signal at the second latch satisfies its setup and hold requirements.

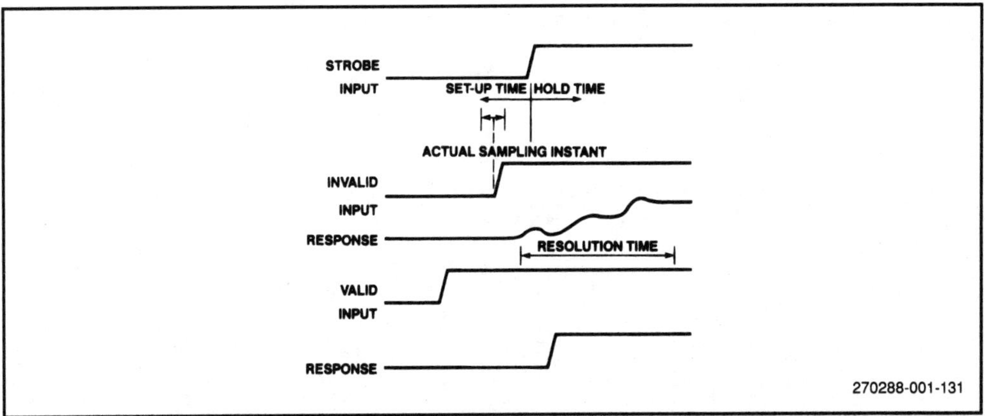

Figure D-1. Valid and Invalid Latch Input Transitions and Response

Thus, the output of this second latch is a synchronous signal with respect to its strobe input.

A synchronization failure can occur if the synchronizer fails to resolve the asynchronous transition within the time between the strobes of the two latches. The rate of failure is determined by the actual size of the sampling window of the data latch, and by the amount of time between the strobe signals of the two latches. Obviously, as the sampling window gets smaller, the number of times an asynchronous transition will occur during the sampling window will drop. In addition, however, a smaller sampling window is also indicative of a faster resolution time for an input transition which manages to fall within the sampling window.

D.2 80C186EB FAMILY SYNCHRONIZERS

The 80C186EB family uses the two stage synchronization technique on T1IN, T2IN, P2.x, P1.x, NMI, INT0-4, and HOLD input lines. READY uses a slight modification (see Section 3.6).

Appendix E

Instruction Summary

Appendix E. Instruction Set Summary

FUNCTION	FORMAT				Clock Cycles	Comments
DATA TRANSFER						
MOV = MOVE:						
Register to Register/Memory	1 0 0 0 1 0 0 w	mod reg r/m			2/12	
Register/memory to register	1 0 0 0 1 0 1 w	mod reg r/m			2/9	
Immediate to register memory	1 1 0 0 0 1 1 w	mod 0 0 0 r/m	data	data if w = 1	12-13	8/16-bit
Immediate to register	1 0 1 1 w reg	data	data if w = 1		3-4	8/16-bit
Memory to accumulator	1 0 1 0 0 0 0 w	addr-low	addr-high		9	
Accumulator to memory	1 0 1 0 0 0 1 w	addr-low	addr-high		8	
Register/memory to segment register	1 0 0 0 1 1 1 0	mod 0 reg r/m			2/9	
Segment register to register/memory	1 0 0 0 1 1 0 0	mod 0 reg r/m			2/11	
PUSH = Push:						
Memory	1 1 1 1 1 1 1 1	mod 1 1 0 r/m			16	
Register	0 1 0 1 0 reg				10	
Segment register	0 0 0 reg 1 1 0				9	
Immediate	0 1 1 0 1 0 s 0	data	data if s = 0		10	
PUSHA = Push All	0 1 1 0 0 0 0 0				36	
POP = Pop:						
Memory	1 0 0 0 1 1 1 1	mod 0 0 0 r/m			20	
Register	0 1 0 1 1 reg				10	
Segment register	0 0 0 reg 1 1 1	(reg≠01)			8	
POPA = Pop All	0 1 1 0 0 0 0 1				51	
XCHG = Exchange:						
Register/memory with register	1 0 0 0 0 1 1 w	mod reg r/m			4/17	
Register with accumulator	1 0 0 1 0 reg				3	
IN = Input from:						
Fixed port	1 1 1 0 0 1 0 w	port			10	
Variable port	1 1 1 0 1 1 0 w				8	
OUT = Output to:						
Fixed port	1 1 1 0 0 1 1 w	port			9	
Variable port	1 1 1 0 1 1 1 w				7	
XLAT = Translate byte to AL	1 1 0 1 0 1 1 1				11	
LEA = Load EA to register	1 0 0 0 1 1 0 1	mod reg r/m			6	
LDS = Load pointer to DS	1 1 0 0 0 1 0 1	mod reg r/m	(mod≠11)		18	
LES = Load pointer to ES	1 1 0 0 0 1 0 0	mod reg r/m	(mod≠11)		18	
LAHF = Load AH with flags	1 0 0 1 1 1 1 1				2	
SAHF = Store AH into flags	1 0 0 1 1 1 1 0				3	
PUSHF = Push flags	1 0 0 1 1 1 0 0				9	
POPF=Pop flags	1 0 0 1 1 1 0 1				8	
SEGMENT = Segment Override:						
CS	0 0 1 0 1.1 1 0				2	
SS	0 0 1 1 0 1 1 0				2	
DS	0 0 1 1 1 1 1 0				2	
ES	0 0 1 0 0 1 1 0				2	

Shaded areas indicate instructions not available in iAPX 86, 88 microsystems.

Appendix E. Instruction Set Summary (continued)

FUNCTION	FORMAT				Clock Cycles	Comments
ARITHMETIC						
ADD = Add:						
Reg/memory with register to either	0 0 0 0 0 0 d w	mod reg r/m			3/10	
Immediate to register/memory	1 0 0 0 0 0 s w	mod 0 0 0 r/m	data	data if s w = 01	4/16	
Immediate to accumulator	0 0 0 0 0 1 0 w	data	data if w=1		3/4	8/16-bit
ADC = Add with carry:						
Reg/memory with register to either	0 0 0 1 0 0 d w	mod reg r/m			3/10	
Immediate to register/memory	1 0 0 0 0 0 s w	mod 0 1 0 r/m	data	data if s w=01	4/16	
Immediate to accumulator	0 0 0 1 0 1 0 w	data	data if w=1		3/4	8/16-bit
INC = Increment:						
Register/memory	1 1 1 1 1 1 1 w	mod 0 0 0 r/m			3/15	
Register	0 1 0 0 0 reg				3	
SUB = Subtract:						
Reg/memory and register to either	0 0 1 0 1 0 d w	mod reg r/m			3/10	
Immediate from register/memory	1 0 0 0 0 0 s w	mod 1 0 1 r/m	data	data if s w=01	4/16	
Immediate from accumulator	0 0 1 0 1 1 0 w	data	data if w = 1		3/4	8/16-bit
SBB = Subtract with borrow:						
Reg/memory and register to either	0 0 0 1 1 0 d w	mod reg r/m			3/10	
Immediate from register/memory	1 0 0 0 0 0 s w	mod 0 1 1 r/m	data	data if s w=01	4/16	
Immediate from accumulator	0 0 0 1 1 1 0 w	data	data if w=1		3/4	8/16-bit
DEC=Decrement:						
Register/memory	1 1 1 1 1 1 1 w	mod 0 0 1 r/m			3/15	
Register	0 1 0 0 1 reg				3	
CMP=Compare:						
Register/memory with register	0 0 1 1 1 0 1 w	mod reg r/m			3/10	
Register with register/memory	0 0 1 1 1 0 0 w	mod reg r/m			3/10	
Immediate with register/memory	1 0 0 0 0 0 s w	mod 1 1 1 r/m	data	data if s w = 01	3/10	
Immediate with accumulator	0 0 1 1 1 1 0 w	data	data if w=1		3/4	8/16-bit
NEG=Change sign	1 1 1 1 0 1 1 w	mod 0 1 1 r/m			3	
AAA=ASCII adjust for add	0 0 1 1 0 1 1 1				8	
DAA = Decimal adjust for add	0 0 1 0 0 1 1 1				4	
AAS=ASCII adjust for subtract	0 0 1 1 1 1 1 1				7	
DAS=Decimal adjust for subtract	0 0 1 0 1 1 1 1				4	
MUL=Multiply (unsigned):	1 1 1 1 0 1 1 w	mod 1 0 0 r/m				
Register-Byte					26-28	
Register-Word					35-37	
Memory-Byte					32-34	
Memory-Word					41-43	
IMUL=Integer multiply (signed):	1 1 1 1 0 1 1 w	mod 1 0 1 r/m				
Register-Byte					25-28	
Register-Word					34-37	
Memory-Byte					31-34	
Memory-Word					40-43	
IMUL=Integer Immediate multiply (signed)	0 1 1 0 1 0 s 1	mod reg r/m	data	data if s = 0	22-25/29-32	

Shaded areas indicate instructions not available in iAPX 86,88 microsystems.

Appendix E. Instruction Set Summary (continued)

FUNCTION	FORMAT				Clock Cycles	Comments
ARITHMETIC (Continued):						
DIV=Divide (unsigned):	1 1 1 1 0 1 1 w	mod 1 1 0 r/m				
Register-Byte					29	
Register-Word					38	
Memory-Byte					35	
Memory-Word					44	
IDIV=Integer divide (signed):	1 1 1 1 0 1 1 w	mod 1 1 1 r/m				
Register-Byte					44-52	
Register-Word					53-61	
Memory-Byte					50-58	
Memory-Word					59-67	
AAM=ASCII adjust for multiply	1 1 0 1 0 1 0 0	0 0 0 0 1 0 1 0			19	
AAD=ASCII adjust for divide	1 1 0 1 0 1 0 1	0 0 0 0 1 0 1 0			15	
CBW=Convert byte to word	1 0 0 1 1 0 0 0				2	
CWD=Convert word to double word	1 0 0 1 1 0 0 1				4	
LOGIC						
Shift/Rotate Instructions:						
Register/Memory by 1	1 1 0 1 0 0 0 w	mod TTT r/m			2/15	
Register/Memory by CL	1 1 0 1 0 0 1 w	mod TTT r/m			5+n/17+n	
Register/Memory by Count	1 1 0 0 0 0 0 w	mod TTT r/m	count		5+n/17+n	
AND = And:						
Reg/memory and register to either	0 0 1 0 0 0 d w	mod reg r/m			3/10	
Immediate to register/memory	1 0 0 0 0 0 0 w	mod 1 0 0 r/m	data	data if w = 1	4/16	
Immediate to accumulator	0 0 1 0 0 1 0 w	data	data if w=1		3/4	8/16-bit
TEST=And function to flags, no result:						
Register/memory and register	1 0 0 0 0 1 0 w	mod reg r/m			3/10	
Immediate data and register/memory	1 1 1 1 0 1 1 w	mod 0 0 0 r/m	data	data if w=1	4/10	
Immediate data and accumulator	1 0 1 0 1 0 0 w	data	data if w=1		3/4	8/16-bit
OR=Or:						
Reg/memory and register to either	0 0 0 0 1 0 d w	mod reg r/m			3/10	
Immediate to register/memory	1 0 0 0 0 0 0 w	mod 0 0 1 r/m	data	data if w=1	4/16	
Immediate to accumulator	0 0 0 0 1 1 0 w	data	data if w=1		3/4	8/16-bit
XOR=Exclusive or:						
Reg/memory and register to either	0 0 1 1 0 0 d w	mod reg r/m			3/10	
Immediate to register/memory	1 0 0 0 0 0 0 w	mod 1 1 0 r/m	data	data if w=1	4/16	
Immediate to accumulator	0 0 1 1 0 1 0 w	data	data if w=1		3/4	8/16-bit
NOT=Invert register/memory	1 1 1 1 0 1 1 w	mod 0 1 0 r/m			3	
STRING MANIPULATION:						
MOVS=Move byte/word	1 0 1 0 0 1 0 w				14	
CMPS=Compare byte/word	1 0 1 0 0 1 1 w				22	
SCAS=Scan byte/word	1 0 1 0 1 1 1 w				15	

TTT	Instruction
0 0 0	ROL
0 0 1	ROR
0 1 0	RCL
0 1 1	RCR
1 0 0	SHL/SAL
1 0 1	SHR
1 1 1	SAR

Shaded areas indicate instructions not available in iAPX 86,88 microsystems.

Appendix E. Instruction Set Summary (continued)

FUNCTION	FORMAT				Clock Cycles	Comments
LODS=Load byte/wd to AL/AX	1 0 1 0 1 1 0 w				12	
STOS=Stor byte/wd from AL/A	1 0 1 0 1 0 1 w				10	
INS=Input byte/wd from DX port	0 1 1 0 1 1 0 w				14	
OUTS=Output byte/wd to DX port	0 1 1 0 1 1 1 w				14	
STRING MANIPULATION (Continued):						
Repeated by count in CX						
MOVS - Move string	1 1 1 1 0 0 1 0	1 0 1 0 0 1 0 w			8+8n	
CMPS - Compare string	1 1 1 1 0 0 1 z	1 0 1 0 0 1 1 w			5+22n	
SCAS - Scan string	1 1 1 1 0 0 1 z	1 0 1 0 1 1 1 w			5+15n	
LODS - Load string	1 1 1 1 0 0 1 0	1 0 1 0 1 1 0 w			6+11n	
STOS - Store string	1 1 1 1 0 1 0 0	0 1 0 1 0 0 1 w			6+9n	
INS - Input string	1 1 1 1 0 0 1 0	0 1 1 0 1 1 0 w			8+8n	
OUTS - Output string	1 1 1 1 0 0 1 0	0 1 1 0 1 1 1 w			8+8n	
CONTROL TRANSFER						
CALL = Call:						
Direct within segment	1 1 1 0 1 0 0 0	disp-low	disp-hour		15	
Register memory indirect within segment	1 1 1 1 1 1 1 1	mod 0 1 0 r/m			13/19	
Direct intersegment	1 0 0 1 1 0 1 0	segment offset			23	
		segment selector				
Indirect intersegment	1 1 1 1 1 1 1 1	mod 0 1 1 r/m		(mod≠11)	38	
JMP=Unconditional jump:						
Short/long	1 1 1 0 1 0 1 1	disp-low			14	
Direct within segment	1 1 1 0 1 0 0 1	disp-low	disp-high		14	
Register/memory indirect with segment	1 1 1 1 1 1 1 1	mod 1 0 0 r/m			26	
Direct intersegment	1 1 1 0 1 0 1 0	segment offset			14	
		segment selector				
Indirect intersegment	1 1 1 1 1 1 1 1	mod 1 0 1 r/m		(mod ≠ 11)	11/17	
RET = Return from CALL:						
Within segment	1 1 0 0 0 0 1 1				16	
With seg adding immed to SP	1 1 0 0 0 0 1 0	data-low	data-high		18	
Intersegment	1 1 0 0 1 0 1 1				22	
Intersegment adding immediate to SP	1 1 0 0 1 0 1 0	data-low	data-high		25	

Shaded areas indicate instructions not available in iAPX 86,88 microsystems.

Appendix E. Instruction Set Summary (continued)

FUNCTION	FORMAT				Clock Cycles	Comments
CONTROL TRANSFER (Continued):						
JE/JZ = Jump on equal zero	0 1 1 1 0 1 0 0	disp			4/13	13 if JMP taken 4 if JMP not taken
JL/JNGE = Jump on less/not greater or equal	0 1 1 1 1 1 0 0	disp			4/13	
JLE/JNG = Jump on less or equal/not greater	0 1 1 1 1 1 1 0	disp			4/13	
JB/JNAE = Jump on below/not above or equal	0 1 1 1 0 0 1 0	disp			4/13	
JBE/JNA = Jump on below or equal/not above	0 1 1 1 0 1 1 0	disp			4/13	
JP/JPE = Jump on parity/parity even	0 1 1 1 1 0 1 0	disp			4/13	
JO = Jump on overflow	0 1 1 1 0 0 0 0	disp			4/13	
JS = Jump on sign	0 1 1 1 1 0 0 0	disp			4/13	
JNE/JNZ = Jump on not equal/not zero	0 1 1 1 0 1 0 1	disp			4/13	
JNL/JGE = Jump on not less/greater or equal	0 1 1 1 1 1 0 1	disp			4/13	
JNLE/JG = Jump on not less or equal/greater	0 1 1 1 1 1 1 1	disp			4/13	
JNB/JAE = Jump on not below/above or equal	0 1 1 1 0 0 1 1	disp			4/13	
JNBE/JA = Jump on not below or equal/above	0 1 1 1 0 1 1 1	disp			4/13	
JNP/JPO = Jump on not par/par odd	0 1 1 1 1 0 1 1	disp			4/13	
JNO = Jump on not overflow	0 1 1 1 0 0 0 1	disp			4/13	
JNS = Jump on not sign	0 1 1 1 1 0 0 1	disp			5/15	
JCXZ = Jump on CX zero	1 1 1 0 0 0 1 1	disp			6/16	
LOOP = Loop CX times	1 1 1 0 0 0 1 0	disp			6/16	
LOOPZ/LOOPE = Loop while zero/equal	1 1 1 0 0 0 0 1	disp			16	JMP taken/
LOOPNZ/LOOPNE = Loop while not zero/equal	1 1 1 0 0 0 0 0	disp			5	JMP not taken
ENTER = Enter Procedure	1 1 0 0 1 0 0 0	data-low	data-high	L		
L = 0					15	
L = 1					25	
L>1					22+16(n-1)	
Leave = Leave Procedure	1 1 0 0 1 0 0 1				8	
INT = Interrupt:						
Type specified	1 1 0 0 1 1 0 1	type			47	if INT. taken/
Type 3	1 1 0 0 1 1 0 0				45	if INT. not taken
INTO = Interrupt on overflow	1 1 0 0 1 1 1 0				48/4	
IRET = Interrupt return	1 1 0 0 1 1 1 1				28	
BOUND = Detect value out of range	0 1 1 0 0 0 1 0	mod reg r/m			33-35	

Shaded areas indicate instructions not available in iAPX 86,88 microsystems.

Appendix E. Instruction Set Summary (continued)

FUNCTION	FORMAT		Clock Cycles	Comments
PROCESSOR CONTROL				
CLC = Clear carry	1 1 1 1 1 0 0 0		2	
CMC = Complement carry	1 1 1 1 0 1 0 1		2	
STC = Set Carry	1 1 1 1 1 0 0 1		2	
CLD = Clear direction	1 1 1 1 1 1 0 0		2	
STD = Set direction	1 1 1 1 1 1 0 1		2	
CLI = Clear interrupt	1 1 1 1 1 0 1 0		2	
STI = Set interrupt	1 1 1 1 1 0 1 1		2	
HLT = Halt	1 1 1 1 0 1 0 0		2	
WAIT = Wait	1 0 0 1 1 0 1 1		6	if $\overline{\text{test}}$ = 0
LOCK = Bus lock prefix	1 1 1 1 0 0 0 0		2	
ESC = Processor Extension Escape	1 1 0 1 1 T T T	mod LLL r/m	6	
	(TTT LLL are opcode to processor extension)			

Shaded areas indicate instructions not available in iAPX 86,88 microsystems.

FOOT NOTES

The Effective Address (EA) of the memory operand is computed according to the mod and r/m fields:

if mod = 11 then r/m is treated as a REG field
if mod = 00 then DISP = 0*, disp-low and disp-high are absent
if mod = 01 then DISP = disp-low sign-extended to 16-bits, disp-high is absent
if mod = 10 then DISP = disp-high:disp-low

if r/m = 000 then EA = (BX) + (SI) + DISP
if r/m = 001 then EA = (BX) + (DI) + DISP
if r/m = 010 then EA = (BP) + (SI) + DISP
if r/m = 011 then EA = (BP) + (DI) + DISP
if r/m = 100 then EA = (SI) + DISP
if r/m = 101 then EA = (DI) + DISP
if r/m = 110 then EA = (BP) + DISP*
if r/m = 111 then EA = (BX) + DISP

DISP follows 2nd byte of insturction (before data if required)

*except if mod = 00 and r/m = 110 then EA = disp-high:disp-low.

SEGMENT OVERRIDE PREFIX

0 0 1 reg 1 1 0

reg is assigned according to the following:

reg	Segment Register
00	ES
01	CS
10	SS
11	DS

REG is assigned according to the following table:

16-Bit (w=1)	8-Bit (w=0)
000 AX	000 AL
001 CX	001 CL
010 DX	010 DL
011 BX	011 BL
100 SP	100 AH
101 BP	101 CH
110 SI	110 DH
111 DI	111 BH

The physical address of all operands addressed by the BP register are computed using the SS segment register. The physical addresses of the destination operands of the string primitive operation (those addressed by the DI register) are computed using the ES segment, which may not be overriden.

Instruction Summary 2

Appendix F

Appendix F. Machine Instruction Decoding Guide

1ST BYTE		2ND BYTE	BYTES 3,4,5,6	ASM-86 INSTRUCTION FORMAT
HEX	BINARY			
00	0000 0000	MOD REG R/M	(DISP-LO),(DISP-HI)	ADD REG8/MEM8,REG8
01	0000 0001	MOD REG R/M	(DISP-LO),(DISP-HI)	ADD REG16/MEM16,REG16
02	0000 0010	MOD REG R/M	(DISP-LO),(DISP-HI)	ADD REG8,REG8/MEM8
03	0000 0011	MOD REG R/M	(DISP-LO),(DISP-HI)	ADD REG16,REG16/MEM16
04	0000 0100	DATA-8		ADD AL,IMMED8
05	0000 0101	DATA-LO	DATA-HI	ADD AX,IMMED16
06	0000 0110			PUSH ES
07	0000 0111			POP ES
08	0000 0100	MOD REG R/M	(DISP-LO),(DISP-HI)	OR REG8/MEM8,REG8
09	0000 1001	MOD REG R/M	(DISP-LO),(DISP-HI)	OR REG16/MEM16,REG16
0A	0000 1010	MOD REG R/M	(DISP-LO),(DISP-HI)	OR REG8,REG8/MEM8
0B	0000 1011	MOD REG R/M	(DISP-LO),(DISP-HI)	OR REG16,REG16/MEM16
0C	0000 1100	DATA-8		OR AL,IMMED8
0D	0000 1101	DATA-LO	DATA-HI	OR AX,IMMED16
0E	0000 1110			PUSH CS
0F	0000 1111			(not used)
10	0001 0000	MOD REG R/M	(DISP-LO),(DISP-HI)	ADC REG8/MEM8,REG8
11	0001 0001	MOD REG R/M	(DISP-LO),(DISP-HI)	ADC REG16/MEM16,REG16
12	0001 0010	MOD REG R/M	(DISP-LO),(DISP-HI)	ADC REG8,REG8/MEM8
13	0001 0011	MOD REG R/M	(DISP-LO),(DISP-HI)	ADC REG16,REG16/MEM16
14	0001 0100	DATA-8		ADC AL,IMMED8
15	0001 0101	DATA-LO	DATA-HI	ADC AX,IMMED16
16	0001 0110			PUSH SS
17	0001 0111			POP SS
18	0001 1000	MOD REG R/M	(DISP-LO),(DISP-HI)	SBB REG8/MEM8,REG8
19	0001 1001	MOD REG R/M	(DISP-LO),(DISP-HI)	SBB REG16/MEM16,REG16
1A	0001 1010	MOD REG R/M	(DISP-LO),(DISP-HI)	SBB REG8,REG8/MEM8
1B	0001 1011	MOD REG R/M	(DISP-LO),(DISP-HI)	SBB REG16,REG16/MEM16
1C	0001 1100	DATA-8		SBB AL,IMMED8
1D	0001 1101	DATA-LO	DATA-HI	SBB AX,IMMED16
1E	0001 1110			PUSH DS
1F	0001 1111			POP DS
20	0010 0000	MOD REG R/M	(DISP-LO),(DISP-HI)	AND REG8/MEM8,REG8
21	0010 0001	MOD REG R/M	(DISP-LO),(DISP-HI)	AND REG16/MEM16,REG16
22	0010 0010	MOD REG R/M	(DISP-LO),(DISP-HI)	AND REG8,REG8/MEM8
23	0010 0011	MOD REG R/M	(DISP-LO),(DISP-HI)	AND REG16,REG16/MEM16
24	0010 0100	DATA-8		AND AL,IMMED8
25	0010 0101	DATA-LO	DATA-HI	AND AX,IMMED16
26	0010 0110			ES: (segment override prefix)
27	0010 0111			DAA
28	0010 1000	MOD REG R/M	(DISP-LO),(DISP-HI)	SUB REG8/MEM8,REG8
29	0010 1001	MOD REG R/M	(DISP-LO),(DISP-HI)	SUB REG16/MEM16, REG16
2A	0010 1010	MOD REG R/M	(DISP-LO),(DISP-HI)	SUB REG8,REG8/MEM8
2B	0010 1011	MOD REG R/M	(DISP-LO),(DISP-HI)	SUB REG16,REG16/MEM16
2C	0010 1100	DATA-8		SUB AL,IMMED8
2D	0010 1101	DATA-LO	DATA-HI	SUB AX,IMMED16
2E	0010 1110			CS: (segment override prefix)
2F	0010 1111			DAS
30	0011 0000	MOD REG R/M	(DISP-LO),(DISP-HI)	XOR REG8/MEM8,REG8
31	0011 0001	MOD REG R/M	(DISP-LO),(DISP-HI)	XOR REG16/MEM16,REG16

Appendix F. Machine Instruction Decoding Guide (continued)

1ST BYTE		2ND BYTE	BYTES 3,4,5,6	ASM-86 INSTRUCTION FORMAT
HEX	BINARY			
32	0011 0010	MOD REG R/M	(DISP-LO),(DISP-HI)	XOR REG8,REG8/MEM8
33	0011 0011	MOD REG R/M	(DISP-LO),(DISP-HI)	XOR REG16,REG16/MEM16
34	0011 0100	DATA-8		XOR AL,IMMED8
35	0011 0100	DATA-LO	DATA-HI	XOR AX,IMMED16
36	0011 0110			SS: (segment override prefix)
37	0011 0111			AAA
38	0011 1000	MOD REG R/M	(DISP-LO),(DISP-HI)	CMP REG8/MEM8,REG8
39	0011 1001	MOD REG R/M	(DISP-LO),(DISP-HI)	CMP REG16/MEM16,REG16
3A	0011 1010	MOD REG R/M	(DISP-LO),(DISP-HI)	CMP REG8,REG8/MEM8
3B	0011 1011	MOD REG R/M	(DISP-LO),(DISP-HI)	CMP REG16,REG16/MEM16
3C	0011 1100	DATA-8		CMP AL,IMMED8
3D	0011 1101	DATA-LO	DATA-HI	CMP AX,IMMED16
3E	0011 1110			DS: (segment override prefix)
3F	0011 1111			AAS
40	0100 0000			INC AX
41	0100 0001			INC CX
42	0100 0010			INC DX
43	0100 0011			INC BX
44	0100 0100			INC SP
45	0100 0101			INC BP
46	0100 0110			INC SI
47	0100 0111			INC DI
48	0100 1000			DEC AX
49	0100 1001			DEC CX
4A	0100 1010			DEC DX
4B	0100 1011			DEC BX
4C	0100 1100			DEC SP
4D	0100 1101			DEC BP
4E	0100 1110			DEC SI
4F	0100 1111			DEC DI
50	0101 0000			PUSH AX
51	0101 0001			PUSH CX
52	0101 0010			PUSH DX
53	0101 0011			PUSH BX
54	0101 0100			PUSH SP
55	0101 0101			PUSH BP
56	0101 0110			PUSH SI
57	0101 0111			PUSH DI
58	0101 1000			POP AX
59	0101 1001			POP CX
5A	0101 1010			POP DX
5B	0101 1011			POP BX
5C	0101 1100			POP SP
5D	0101 1101			POP BP
5E	0101 1110			POP SI
5F	0101 1111			POP DI
60	0110 0000			PUSHA (186/8 ONLY)
61	0110 0001			POPA (186/8 ONLY)
62	0110 0010	MOD REG R/M		BOUND REG16,MEM16(186/8 ONLY)
63	0110 0011			(not used)

Appendix F. Machine Instruction Decoding Guide (continued)

1ST BYTE		2ND BYTE	BYTES 3,4,5,6	ASM-86 INSTRUCTION FORMAT	
HEX	BINARY				
64	0110 0100			(not used)	
65	0110 0101			(not used)	
66	0110 0110			(not used)	
67	0110 0111			(not used)	
68	0110 1000	DATA-LO	DATA-HI	PUSH	IMMED16(186/8 ONLY)
69	0110 1001	MOD REG R/M	DATA-LO,DATA-HI	IMUL	IMMED16(186/8 ONLY)
6A	0110 1010	DATA-8		PUSH	IMMED8(186/8 ONLY)
6B	0110 1011	MOD REG R/M	DATA-8	IMUL	IMMED8(186/8 ONLY)
6C	0110 1100			INS	MEM8,DX(186/8 ONLY)
6D	0110 1101			INS	MEM16,DX(186/8 ONLY)
6E	0110 1110			OUTS	MEM8,DX(186/8 ONLY)
6F	0110 1111			OUTS	MEM16,DX(186/8 ONLY)
70	0111 0000	IP-INC8		JO	SHORT-LABEL
71	0111 0001	IP-INC8		JNO	SHORT-LABEL
72	0111 0010	IP-INC8		JB/JNAE/ JC	SHORT-LABEL
73	0111 0011	IP-INC8		JNB/JAE/ JNC	SHORT-LABEL
74	0111 0100	IP-INC8		JE/JZ	SHORT-LABEL
75	0111 0101	IP-INC8		JNE/JNZ	SHORT-LABEL
76	0111 0110	IP-INC8		JBE/JNA	SHORT-LABEL
77	0111 0111	IP-INC8		JNBE/JA	SHORT-LABEL
78	0111 1000	IP-INC8		JS	SHORT-LABEL
79	0111 1001	IP-INC8		JNS	SHORT-LABEL
7A	0111 1010	IP-INC8		JP/JPE	SHORT-LABEL
7B	0111 1011	IP-INC8		JNP/JPO	SHORT-LABEL
7C	0111 1100	IP-INC8		JL/JNGE	SHORT-LABEL
7D	0111 1101	IP-INC8		JNLJGE	SHORT-LABEL
7E	0111 1110	IP-INC8		JLE/JNG	SHORT-LABEL
7F	0111 1111	IP-INC8		JNLE/JG	SHORT-LABEL
80	1000 0000	MOD 000 R/M	(DISP LO),(DISP HI), DATA-8	ADD	REG8/MEM8,IMMED8
80	1000 0000	MOD 001 R/M	(DISP-LO),(DISP-HI), DATA-8	OR	REG8/MEM8,IMMED8
80	1000 0000	MOD 010 R/M	(DISP-LO),(DISP-HI), DATA-8	ADC	REG8/MEM8,IMMED8
80	1000 0000	MOD 011 R/M	(DISP-LO),(DISP-HI), DATA-8	SBB	REG8/MEM8,IMMED8
80	1000 0000	MOD 100 R/M	(DISP-LO),(DISP-HI), DATA-8	AND	REG8/MEM8,IMMED8
80	1000 0000	MOD 101 R/M	(DISP-LO),(DISP-HI), DATA-8	SUB	REG8/MEM8,IMMED8
80	1000 0000	MOD 110 R/M	(DISP-LO),(DISP-HI), DATA-8	XOR	REG8/MEM8,IMMED8
80	1000 0000	MOD 111 R/M	(DISP-LO),(DISP-HI), DATA-8	CMP	REG8/MEM8,IMMED8
81	1000 0001	MOD 000 R/M	(DISP-LO),(DISP-HI), DATA-LO,DATA-HI	ADD	REG16/MEM16,IMMED16
81	1000 0001	MOD 001 R/M	(DISP-LO),(DISP-HI) DATA-LO,DATA-HI	OR	REG 16/MEM16,IMMED16

Appendix F. Machine Instruction Decoding Guide (continued)

1ST BYTE		2ND BYTE	BYTES 3,4,5,6	ASM-86 INSTRUCTION FORMAT
HEX	BINARY			
81	1000 0001	MOD 010 R/M	(DISP-LO),(DISP-HI), DATA-LO,DATA-HI	ADC REG16/MEM16,IMMED16
81	1000 0001	MOD 011 R/M	(DISP-LO),(DISP-HI), DATA-LO,DATA-HI	SBB REG16/MEM16,IMMED16
81	1000 0001	MOD 100 R/M	(DISP-LO),(DISP-HI), DATA-LO,DATA-HI	AND REG16/MEM16,IMMED16
81	1000 0001	MOD 101 R/M	(DISP-LO),(DISP-HI), DATA-LO,DATA-HI	SUB REG16/MEM16,IMMED16
81	1000 0001	MOD 110 R/M	(DISP-LO),(DISP-HI), DATA-LO,DATA-HI	XOR REG16/MEM16,IMMED16
81	1000 0001	MOD 111 R/M	(DISP-LO),(DISP-HI), DATA-LO,DATA-HI	CMP REG16/MEM16,IMMED16
82	1000 0010	MOD 000 R/M	(DISP-LO),(DISP-HI), DATA-8	ADD REG8/MEM8,IMMED8
82	1000 0010	MOD 001 R/M		(not used)
82	1000 0010	MOD 010 R/M	(DISP-LO),(DISP-HI), DATA-8	ADC REG8/MEM8,IMMED8
82	1000 0010	MOD 011 R/M	(DISP-LO),(DISP-HI), DATA-8	SBB REG8/MEM8,IMMED8
82	1000 0010	MOD 100 R/M		(not used)
82	1000 0010	MOD 101 R/M	(DISP-LO),(DISP-HI), DATA-8	SUB REG8/MEM8,IMMED8
82	1000 0010	MOD 110 R/M		(not used)
82	1000 0010	MOD 111 R/M	(DISP-LO),(DISP-HI), DATA-8	CMP REG8/MEM8,IMMED8
83	1000 0011	MOD 000 R/M	(DISP-LO),(DISP-HI), DATA-SX	ADD REG16/MEM16,IMMED8
83	1000 0011	MOD 001 R/M		(not used)
83	1000 0011	MOD 010 R/M	(DISP-LO),(DISP-HI), DATA-SX	ADC REG16/MEM16,IMMED8
83	1000 0011	MOD 011 R/M	(DISP-LO),(DISP-HI), DATA-SX	SBB REG16/MEM16,IMMED8
83	1000 0011	MOD 100 R/M		(not used)
83	1000 0011	MOD 101 R/M	(DISP-LO),(DISP-HI), DATA-SX	SUB REG16/MEM16,IMMED8
83	1000 011	MOD 110 R/M		(not used)
83	1000 0011	MOD 111 R/M	(DISP-LO),(DISP-HI), DATA-SX	CMP REG16/MEM16,IMMED8
84	1000 0100	MOD REG R/M	(DISP-LO),(DISP-HI)	TEST REG8,MEM8,REG8
85	1000 0101	MOD REG R/M	(DISP-LO),(DISP-HI)	TEST REG16/MEM16,REG16
86	1000 0110	MOD REG R/M	(DISP-LO),(DISP-HI)	XCHG REG8,REG8/MEM8
87	1000 0111	MOD REG R/M	(DISP-LO),(DISP-HI)	XCHG REG16,REG16,MEM16
88	1000 1000	MOD REG R/M	(DISP-LO),(DISP-HI)	MOV REG8/MEM8,REG8
89	1000 1001	MOD REG R/M	(DISP-LO),(DISP-HI)	MOV REG16/MEM16/REG16
8A	1000 1010	MOD REG R/M	(DISP-LO),(DISP-HI)	MOV REG8,REG8/MEM8
8B	1000 1011	MOD REG R/M	(DISP-LO),(DISP-HI)	MOV REG16,REG16/MEM16
8C	1000 1100	MOD OSR R/M	(DISP-LO),(DISP-HI)	REG16/MEM16,SEGREG
8C	1000 1100	MOD 1 - R/M		(not used)
8D	1000 1101	MOD REG R/M	(DISP-LO),(DISP-HI)	LEA REG16,MEM16

Appendix F. Machine Instruction Decoding Guide (continued)

1ST BYTE		2ND BYTE	BYTES 3,4,5,6	ASM-86 INSTRUCTION FORMAT
HEX	BINARY			
8E	1000 1110	MOD 0SR R/M	(DISP-LO),(DISP-HI)	MOV SEGREG,REG16/MEM16
8E	1000 1110	MOD 1 - R/M		(not used)
8F	1000 1111	MOD 000 R/M	(DISP-LO),(DISP-HI)	POP REG16/MEM16
8F	1000 1111	MOD 001 R/M		(not used)
8F	1000 1111	MOD 010 R/M		(not used)
8F	1000 1111	MOD 011 R/M		(not used)
8F	1000 1111	MOD 100 R/M		(not used)
8F	1000 1111	MOD 101 R/M		(not used)
8F	1000 1111	MOD 110 R/M		(not used)
8F	1000 1111	MOD 111 R/M		(not used)
90	1001 0000			NOP (exchange AX,AX)
91	1001 0001			XCHG AX,CX
92	1001 0010			XCHG AX,DX
93	1001 0011			XCHG AX,BX
94	1001 0100			XCHG AX,SP
95	1001 0101			XCHG AX,BP
96	1001 0110			XCHG AX,SI
97	1001 0111			XCHG AX,DI
98	1001 1000			CBW
99	1001 1001			CWD
9A	1001 1010	DISP-LO	DISP-HI,SEG-LO, SEG-HI	CALL FAR _ PROC
9B	1001 1011			WAIT
9C	1001 1100			PUSHF
9D	1001 1101			POPF
9E	1001 1110			SAHF
9F	1001 1111			LAHF
A0	1010 0000	ADDR-LO	ADDR-HI	MOV AL,MEM8
A1	1010 0001	ADDR-LO	ADDR-HI	MOV AX,MEM16
A2	1010 0010	ADDR-LO	ADDR-HI	MOV MEM8,AL
A3	1010 0011	ADDR-LO	ADDR-HI	MOV MEM16,AL
A4	1010 0100			MOVS DEST-STR8,SRC-STR8
A5	1010 0101			MOVS DEST-STR 16, SRC-STR 16
A6	1010 0110			CMPS DEST-STR8,SR-STR8
A7	1010 0111			CMPS DEST-STR16,SRC-STR16
A8	1010 1000	DATA-8		TEST AL,IMMED8
A9	1010 1001	DATA-LO	DATA-HI	TEST AX,IMMED16
AA	1010 1010			STOS DEST-STR8
AB	1010 1011			STOS DEST-STR16
AC	1010 1100			LODS SRC-STR8
AD	1010 1101			LODS SRC-STR16
AE	1010 1110			SCAS DEST-STR8
AF	1010 1111			SCAS DEST-STR16
B0	1011 0000	DATA-8		MOV AL,IMMED8
B1	1011 0001	DATA-8		MOV CL,IMMED8
B2	1011 0010	DATA-8		MOV DL,IMMED8
B3	1011 0011	DATA-8		MOV BL,IMMED8
B4	1011 0100	DATA-8		MOV AH,IMMED8
B5	1011 0101	DATA-8		MOV CH,IMMED8
B6	1011 0110	DATA-8		MOV DH,IMMED8

Appendix F. Machine Instruction Decoding Guide (continued)

1ST BYTE		2ND BYTE	BYTES 3,4,5,6	ASM-86 INSTRUCTION FORMAT
HEX	BINARY			
B7	1011 0111	DATA-8		MOV BH,IMMED8
B8	1011 1000	DATA-LO	DATA-HI	MOV AX,IMMED16
B9	1011 1001	DATA-LO	DATA-HI	MOV CX,IMMED16
BA	1011 1010	DATA-LO	DATA-HI	MOV DX,IMMED16
BB	1011 1011	DATA-LO	DATA-HI	MOV BX,IMMED16
BC	1011 1100	DATA-LO	DATA-HI	MOV SP,IMMED16
BD	1011 1101	DATA-LO	DATA-HI	MOV BP,IMMED16
BE	1011 1110	DATA-LO	DATA-HI	MOV SI,IMMED16
BF	1011 1111	DATA-LO	DATA-HI	MOV DI,IMMED16
C0	1100 0000	MOD 000 R/M	DATA-8	ROL REG8/MEM8,IMMED8(186/8 ONLY)
C0	1100 0000	MOD 001 R/M	DATA-8	ROR REG8/MEM8,IMMED8(186/8 ONLY)
C0	1100 0000	MOD 010 R/M	DATA-8	RCL REG8/MEM8,IMMED8(186/8 ONLY)
C0	1100 0000	MOD 011 R/M	DATA-8	RCR REG8/MEM8,IMMED8(186/8 ONLY)
C0	1100 0000	MOD 100 R/M	DATA-8	SHL/SAL REG8/MEM8,IMMED8(186/8 ONLY)
C0	1100 0000	MOD 101 R/M	DATA-8	SHR REG8/MEM8,IMMED8(186/8 ONLY)
C0	1100 0000	MOD 111 RIM	DATA-8	SAR REG8/MEM8,IMMED8(186/8 ONLY)
C1	1100 0001	MOD 000 RIM	DATA-8	ROL REG16/MEM16,IMMED8(186/8 ONLY)
C1	1100 0001	MOD 001 R/M	DATA-8	ROR REG16/MEM16,IMMED8(186/8 ONLY)
C1	1100 0001	MOD 010 R/M	DATA-8	RCL REG16/MEM16,IMMED8(186/8 ONLY)
C1	1100 0001	MOD 011 R/M	DATA-8	RCR REG16/MEM16,IMMED8(186/8 ONLY)
C1	1100 0001	MOD 100 R/M	DATA-8	SHL/SAL REG16/MEM16,IMMED8(186/8 ONLY)
C1	1100 0001	MOD 101 R/M	DATA-8	SHR REG16/MEM16,IMMED8(186/8 ONLY)
C1	1100 0001	MOD 111 R/M	DATA-8	SAR REG16/MEM16,IMMED8(186/8 ONLY)
C2	1100 0010	DATA-LO	DATA-HI	RET IMMED16(intraseg)
C3	1100 0011			RET (intrasegment)
C4	1100 0100	MOD REG R/M	(DISP-LO),(DISP-H)	LES REG16,MEM16
C5	1100 0101	MOD REG R/M	(DISP-LO),(DISP-H)	LDS REG16,MEM16
C6	1100 0110	MOD 000 R/M	(DISP-LO),(DISP-HI) DATA-8	MOV MEM8,IMMED8
C6	1100 0110	MOD 001 R/M		(not used)
C6	1100 0110	MOD 010 R/M		(not used)
C6	1100 0110	MOD 011 R/M		(not used)
C6	1100 0110	MOD 100 R/M		(not used)
C6	1100 0110	MOD 101 R/M		(not used)
C6	1100 0110	MOD 110 R/M		(not used)
C6	1100 0110	MOD 111 R/M		(not used)
C7	1100 0111	MOD 000 R/M	(DISP-LO),(DISP-HI), DATA-LO,DATA-HI	MOV MEM16,IMMED16
C7	1100 0111	MOD 001 R/M		(not used)
C7	1100 0111	MOD 010 R/M		(not used)
C7	1100 0111	MOD 011 R/M		(not used)
C7	1100 0111	MOD 100 R/M		(not used)
C7	1100 0111	MOD 101 R/M		(not used)
C7	1100 0111	MOD 110 R/M		(not used)
C7	1100 0111	MOD 111 R/M		(not used)
C8	1100 1000	DATA-LO	DATA-HI,LEVEL	ENTER IMMED16,IMMED8(186/8 ONLY)
C9	1100 1001			LEAVE (186/8 ONLY)
CA	1100 1010	DATA-LO	DATA-HI	RET IMMED16 (intersegment)
CB	1100 1011			RET (intersegment)
CC	1100 1100			INT 3

Appendix F. Machine Instruction Decoding Guide (continued)

1ST BYTE		2ND BYTE	BYTES 3,4,5,6	ASM-86 INSTRUCTION FORMAT	
HEX	BINARY				
CD	1100 1101	DATA-8		INT	IMMED8
CE	1100 1110			INTO	
CF	1100 1111			IRET	
D0	1101 0000	MOD 000 R/M	(DISP-LO),(DISP-HI)	ROL	REG8/MEM8,1
D0	1101 0000	MOD 001 R/M	(DISP-LO),(DISP-HI)	ROR	REG8/MEM8,1
D0	1101 0000	MOD 010 R/M	(DISP-LO),(DISP-HI)	RCL	REG8/MEM8,1
D0	1101 0000	MOD 011 R/M	(DISP-LO),(DISP-HI)	RCR	REG8/MEM8,1
D0	1101 0000	MOD 100 R/M	(DISP-LO),(DISP-HI)	SAL/SHL	REG8/MEM8,1
D0	1101 0000	MOD 101 R/M	(DISP-LO),(DISP-HI)	SHR	REG8/MEM8,1
D0	1101 0000	MOD 110 R/M		(not used)	
D0	1101 0000	MOD 111 R/M	(DISP-LO),(DISP-HI)	SAR	REG8/MEM8,1
D1	1101 0001	MOD 000 R/M	(DISP-LO),(DISP-HI)	SAR	REG16/MEM16,1
D1	1101 0001	MOD 001 R/M	(DISP-LO),(DISP-HI)	ROR	REG16/MEM16,1
D1	1101 0001	MOD 010 R/M	(DISP-LO),(DISP-HI)	RCL	REG16/MEM16,1
D1	1101 0001	MOD 011 R/M	(DISP-LO),(DISP-HI)	RCR	REG16/MEM16,1
D1	1101 0001	MOD 100 R/M	(DISP-LO),(DISP-HI)	SAL/SHL	REG16/MEM16,1
D1	1101 0001	MOD 101 R/M	(DISP-LO),(DISP-HI)	SHR	REG16/MEM16,1
D1	1101 0001	MOD 110 R/M		(not used)	
D1	1101 0001	MOD 111 R/M	(DISP-LO),(DISP-HI)	SAR	REG16/MEM16,1
D2	1101 0010	MOD 000 R/M	(DISP-LO),(DISP-HI)	ROL	REG8/MEM8,CL
D2	1101 0010	MOD 001 R/M	(DISP-LO),(DISP-HI)	ROR	REG8/MEM8,CL
D2	1101 0010	MOD 010 R/M	(DISP-LO),(DISP-HI)	RCL	REG8/MEM8,CL
D2	1101 0010	MOD 011 R/M	(DISP-LO),(DISP-HI)	RCR	REG8/MEM8,CL
D2	1101 0010	MOD 100 R/M	(DISP-LO),(DISP-HI)	SAL/SHL	REG8/MEM8,CL
D2	1101 0010	MOD 101 R/M	(DISP-LO),(DISP-HI)	SHR	REG8/MEM8,CL
D2	1101 0010	MOD 110 R/M		(not used)	
D2	1101 0010	MOD 111 R/M	(DISP-LO),(DISP-HI)	SAR	REG8/MEM8,CL
D3	1101 0011	MOD 000 R/M	(DISP-LO),(DISP-HI)	ROL	REG16,MEM16,CL
D3	1101 0011	MOD 001 R/M	(DISP-LO),(DISP-HI)	ROR	REG16,MEM16,CL
D3	1101 0011	MOD 010 R/M	(DISP-LO),(DISP-HI)	RCL	REG16,MEM16,CL
D3	1101 0011	MOD 011 R/M	(DISP-LO),(DISP-HI)	RCR	REG16,MEM16,CL
D3	1101 0011	MOD 100 R/M	(DISP-LO),(DISP-HI)	SAL/SHL	REG16,MEM16,CL
D3	1101 0011	MOD 001 R/M	(DISP-LO),(DISP-HI)	SHR	REG16,MEM16,CL
D3	1101 0011	MOD 110 R/M		(not used)	
D3	1101 0011	MOD 111 R/M	(DISP-LO),(DISP-HI)	SAR	REG16,MEM16,CL
D4	1101 0100	00001010		AAM	
D5	1101 0101	00001010		AAD	
D6	1101 0110			(not used)	
D7	1101 0111			XLAT	SOURCE-TABLE
D8	1101 1000 1XXX	MOD 000 R/M MOD YYY R/M	(DISP-LO),(DISP-HI)	ESC	OPCODE,SOURCE
DF	1101 1111	MOD 111 R/M			
E0	1110 0000	IP-INC-8		LOOPNE/ LOOPNZ	SHORT-LABEL
E1	1110 0001	IP-INC-8		LOOPE/ LOOPZ	SHORT-LABEL
E2	1110 0010	IP-INC-8		LOOP	SHORT-LABEL
E3	1110 0011	IP-INC-8		JCXZ	SHORT-LABEL
E4	1110 0100	DATA-8		IN	AL,IMMED8
E5	1110 0101	DATA-8		IN	AX,IMMED8

Appendix F. Machine Instruction Decoding Guide (continued)

1ST BYTE		2ND BYTE	BYTES 3,4,5,6	ASM-86 INSTRUCTION FORMAT
HEX	BINARY			
E6	1110 0110	DATA-8		OUT AL,IMMED8
E7	1110 0111	DATA-8		OUT AX,IMMED8
E8	1110 1000	IP-INC-LO	IP-PINC-HI	CALL NEAR-PROC
E9	1110 1001	IP-INC-LO	IP-INC-HI	JMP NEAR-LABEL
EA	1110 1010	IP-LO	IP-HI,CS-LO,CS-HI	JMP FAR-LABEL
EB	1110 1011	IP-INC8		JMP SHORT-LABEL
EC	1110 1100			IN AL,DX
ED	1110 1101			IN AX,DX
EE	1110 1110			OUT AL,DX
EF	1110 1111			OUT AX,DX
F0	1111 0000			LOCK (prefix)
F1	1111 0001			(not used)
F2	1111 0010			REPNE/REPNZ
F3	1111 0011			REP/REPE/REPZ
F4	1111 0100			HLT
F5	1111 0101			CMC
F6	1111 0110	MOD 000 R/M	(DISP-LO),(DISP-HI), DATA-8	TEST REG8/MEM8,1MMED8
F6	1111 0110	MOD 001 R/M		(not used)
F6	1111 0110	MOD 010 R/M	(DISP-LO),(DISP-HI)	NOT REG8/MEM8
F6	1111 0110	MOD 011 R/M	(DISP-LO),(DISP-HI)	NEG REG8/MEM8
F6	1111 0110	MOD 100 R/M	(DISP-LO),(DISP-HI)	MUL REG8/MEM8
F6	1111 0110	MOD 101 R/M	(DISP-LO),(DISP-HI)	IMUL REG8/MEM8
F6	1111 0110	MOD 110 R/M	(DISP-LO),(DISP-HI)	DIV REG8/MEM8
F6	1111 0110	MOD 111 R/M	(DISPLO),(DISPHI)	IDIV REG8/MEM8
F7	1111 0111	MOD 000 R/M	(DISP-LO),(DISP-HI), DATA-LO,DATA-HI	TEST REG16/MEM16,IMMED16
F7	1111 0111	MOD 001 R/M		(not used)
F7	1111 0111	MOD 010 R/M	(DISP-LO),(DISP-HI)	NOT REG16/MEM16
F7	1111 0111	MOD 011 R/M	(DISP-LO),(DISP-HI)	NEG REG16/MEM16
F7	1111 0111	MOD 100 R/M	(DISP-LO),(DISP-HI)	MUL REG16/MEM16
F7	1111 0111	MOD 101 R/M	(DISP-LO),(DISP-HI)	IMUL REG16/MEM16
F7	1111 0111	MOD 110 R/M	(DISP-LO),(DISP-HI)	DIV REG16/MEM16
F7	1111 0111	MOD 111 R/M	(DISP-LO),(DISP-HI)	IDIV REG16/MEM16
F8	1111 0100			CLC
F9	1111 1001			STC
FA	1111 1010			CLI
FB	1111 1011			STI
FC	1111 1100			CLD
FD	1111 1101			STD
FE	1111 1110	MOD 000 R/M	(DISP-LO),(DISP-HI)	INC REG8/MEM8
FE	1111 1110	MOD 001 R/M	(DISP-LO),(DISP-HI)	DEC REG8/MEM8
FE	1111 1110	MOD 010 R/M		(not used)
FE	1111 1110	MOD 011 R/M		(not used)
FE	1111 1110	MOD 100 R/M		(not used)
FE	1111 1110	MOD101 R/M		(not used)
FE	1111 1110	MOD 110 R/M		(not used)
FE	1111 1110	MOD 111 R/M		(not used)

Appendix F. Machine Instruction Decoding Guide (continued)

1ST BYTE		2ND BYTE	BYTES 3,4,5,6	ASM-86 INSTRUCTION FORMAT	
HEX	BINARY				
FF	1111 1111	MOD 000 R/M	(DISP-LO),(DISP-HI)	INC	MEM 16
FF	1111 1111	MOD 001 R/M	(DISP-LO),(DISPHI)	DEC	MEM16
FF	1111 1111	MOD 010 R/M	(DISP-LO),(DISP-HI)	CALL	REG16/MEM16(intra)
FF	1111 1111	MOD 011 R/M	(DISP-LO),(DISP-HI)	CALL	MEM16(intersegment)
FF	1111 1111	MOD 100 R/M	(DISP-LO),(DISP-HI)	JMP	REG16/MEM16(intra)
FF	1111 1111	MOD 101 R/M	(DISP-LO),(DISP-HI)	JMP	MEM16(intersegment)
FF	1111 1111	MOD 110 R/M	(DISP-LO),(DISP-HI)	PUSH	MEM16
FF	1111 1111	MOD 111 R/M		(not used)	

Appendix G

Mnemonic Encoding Matrix

HI \ LO	0	1	2	3	4	5	6	7	8	9	A	B	C	D	E	F
0	ADD b,f,r/m	ADD w,f,r/m	ADD b,t,r/m	ADD w,t,r/m	ADD b,ia	ADD w,ia	PUSH ES	POP ES	OR b,f,r/m	OR w,f,r/m	OR b,t,r/m	OR w,t,r/m	OR b,i	OR w,i	PUSH CS	
1	ADC b,f,r/m	ADC w,f,r/m	ADC b,t,r/m	ADC w,t,r/m	ADC b,i	ADC w,i	PUSH SS	POP SS	SBB b,f,r/m	SBB w,f,r/m	SBB b,t,r/m	SBB w,t,r/m	SBB b,i	SBB w,i	PUSH DS	POP DS
2	AND b,f,r/m	AND w,f,r/m	AND b,t,r/m	AND w,t,r/m	AND b,i	AND w,i	SEG =ES	DAA	SUB b,f,r/m	SUB w,f,r/m	SUB b,t,r/m	SUB w,t,r/m	SUB b,i	SUB w,i	SEG =CS	DAS
3	XOR b,f,r/m	XOR w,f,r/m	XOR b,t,r/m	XOR w,t,r/m	XOR b,i	XOR w,i	SEG =SS	AAA	CMP b,f,r/m	CMP w,f,r/m	CMP b,t,r/m	CMP w,t,r/m	CMP b,i	CMP w,i	SEG =DS	AAS
4	INC AX	INC CX	INC DX	INC BX	INC SP	INC BP	INC SI	INC DI	DEC AX	DEC CX	DEC DX	DEC BX	DEC SP	DEC BP	DEC SI	DEC DI
5	PUSH AX	PUSH CX	PUSH DX	PUSH BX	PUSH SP	PUSH BP	PUSH SI	PUSH DI	POP AX	POP CX	POP DX	POP BX	POP SP	POP BP	POP SI	POP DI
6	PUSHA	POPA	BOUND w,f,r/m						PUSH w,i	IMUL w,i	PUSH b,i	IMUL b,i	INS b	INS w	OUTS b	OUTS w
7	JO	JNO	JB/ JNAE	JNB/ JAE	JE/ JZ	JNE/ JNZ	JBE/ JNA	JNBE/ JA	JS	JNS	JP/ JPE	JNP/ JPO	JL/ JNGE	JNL/ JGE	JLE/ JNG	JNLE/ JG
8	Immed b,r/m	Immed w,r/m	Immed b,r/m	Immed is,r/m	TEST b,r/m	TEST w,r/m	XCHG b,r/m	XCHG w,r/m	MOV b,f,r/m	MOV w,f,r/m	MOV b,t,r/m	MOV w,t,r/m	MOV sr,f,r/m	LEA	MOV sr,t,r/m	POP r/m
9	XCHG AX	XCHG CX	XCHG DX	XCHG BX	XCHG SP	XCHG BP	XCHG SI	XCHG DI	CBW	CWD	CALL l,d	WAIT	PUSHF	POPF	SAHF	LAHF
A	MOV m→AL	MOV m→AX	MOV AL→m	MOV AX→m	MOVS	MOVS	CMPS	CMPS	TEST b,i,a	TEST w,i,a	STOS	STOS	LODS	LODS	SCAS	SCAS
B	MOV i→AL	MOV i→CL	MOV i→DL	MOV i→BL	MOV i→AH	MOV i→CH	MOV i→DH	MOV i→BH	MOV i→AX	MOV i→CX	MOV i→DX	MOV i→BX	MOV i→SP	MOV i→BP	MOV i→SI	MOV i→DL
C	Shift b,i	Shift w,i	RET. (i+SP)	RET	LES	LDS	MOV b,i,r/m	MOV w,i,r/m	ENTER	LEAVE	RET. l.(i+SP)	RET l	INT Type 3	INT (Any)	INTO	IRET
D	Shift b	Shift w	Shift b,v	Shift w,v	AAM	AAD		XLAT	ESC 0	ESC 1	ESC 2	ESC 3	ESC 4	ESC 5	ESC 6	ESC 7
E	LOOPNZ/ LOOPNE	LOOPZ/ LOOPE	LOOP	JCXZ	IN b	IN w	OUT b	OUT w	CALL d	JMP d	JMP l,d	JMP si,d	IN v,b	IN v,w	OUT v,b	OUT v,w
F	LOCK		REP	REP Z	HLT	CMC	Grp 1 b,r/m	Grp 1 w,r/m	CLC	STC	CLI	STI	CLD	STD	Grp 2 b,r/m	Grp 2 w,r/m

where:

mod □ r/m	000	001	010	011	100	101	110	111
Immed	ADD	OR	ADC	SBB	AND	SUB	XOR	CMP
Shift	ROL	ROR	RCL	RCR	SHL/SAL	SHR	—	SAR
Grp 1	TEST	—	NOT	NEG	MUL	IMUL	DIV	IDIV
Grp 2	INC	DEC	CALL id	CALL l,id	JMP id	JMP l,id	PUSH	—

b = byte operation
d = direct
f = from CPU reg
i = immediate
ia = immed. to accum.
id = indirect
is = immed. byte, sign ext.
l = long ie. intersegment

m = memory
r/m = EA is second byte
si = short intrasegment
sr = segment register
t = to CPU reg
v = variable
w = word operation
z = zero

Modal Pin States

Appendix H

APPENDIX H
MODAL PIN STATES

The term "modal pin state" refers to the state that a device pin is in while in a particular mode. There are a total of five states for an output pin: driven high, driven low, active (toggling), float, or retain present state (state the pin was in when the current mode was entered). Input pins may be either synchronous or asynchronous. Synchronous pins must meet setup and hold times to guarantee proper device operation. Asynchronous pins must meet setup and hold times to guarantee recognition. Appendix D covers synchronization.

This Appendix includes a list of all 80C186EB/80C188EB pins. With each pin in a description of its function, its type (input, output, or I/O), and its modal pin state. Table H-1 details the nomenclature used.

Table H-1. Pin Description Nomenclature

Symbol	Description
I	Input Only Pin
O	Output Only Pin
I/O	Pin can be either input or output
–	Pin "must be" connected as described
S(..)	Synchronous. Input must meet setup and hold times for proper operation. The pin is; S(E) edge sensitive A(L) level sensitive
A(..)	Asynchronous. Input must meet setup and hold only to guarantee recognition. The pin is; A(E) edge sensitive A(L) level sensitive
H(..)	While the processor's bus is in the Hold Acknowledge state, the pin; H(1) is driven to VCC H(0) is driven to VSS H(Z) floats H(Q) remains active H(X) retains current state
R(..)	While $\overline{RESIN}$ is active, the pin; R(1) is driven to VCC R(0) is driven to VSS R(Z) floats R(WH) weak pullup R(WL) weak pulldown
P(..)	While Idle or Powerdown Modes are active, the pin; P(1) is driven to VCC P(0) is drive to VSS P(Z) floats P(Q) remains active (1) P(X) retains current state
(1) Any pins that specify P(Q) are valid for Idle Mode. All Pins are P(X) for powerdown Mode.	

Appendix H. 80C186EB Pin Description

Name	Modal State	Type	Description
Vcc		–	**Power** connections consist of four pins which must be shorted externally to a Vcc board plane.
Vss		–	**Ground** connections consist of six pins which must be shorted externally a Vss board plane.
CLKIN	A(E)	I	**CLocK INput** is an input for a external clock. An external oscillator operating at two times the required 80C186EB operating frequency can be connected to CLKIN. For crystal operation, CLKIN (along with OSCOUT) are the crystal connections to an internal Pierce oscillator.
OSCOUT	H(Q) R(Q) P(1)	O	**OSCillator OUTput** is only used when using a crystal to generate the external clock. OSCOUT (along with CLKIN) are the crystal connections to an internal Pierce oscillator. This pin is not to be used as 2X clock output for non-crystal applications (i.e. this pin is N.C. for non-crystal applications).
CLKOUT	H(Q) R(Q) P(1)	O	**CLocK OUTput** provides a timing reference for inputs and outputs of the processor, and is one-half the input clock (CLKIN) frequency. CLKOUT has a 50% duty cycle and transitions every falling edge of CLKIN.
$\overline{\text{RESIN}}$	A(L)	I	**RESet IN** causes the 80C186EB to immediately terminate any bus cycle in progress and assume an initialized state. All pins will be driven to a known state, and RESOUT will also be driven active. The rising edge (low-to-high) transition synchronizes CLKOUT with CLKIN before the 80C186EB begins fetching opcodes at memory location 0FFFF0H.
RESOUT	H(0) R(1) P(0)	O	**RESet OUTput** that indicates the 80C186EB is currently in the reset state. RESOUT will remain active as long as $\overline{\text{RESIN}}$ remains active.
PDTMR	A(L) H(Z) R(Z) P(WH)	I/O	**Power-Down TIMeR** pin (normally connected to an external capacitor) that determines the amount of time the 80C186EB waits after an exit from Powerdown before resuming normal operation. The duration of time required will depend on the startup characteristics of the crystal oscillator.
NMI	A(E)	I	**Non-Maskable Interrupt** input causes a TYPE-2 interrupt to be serviced by the CPU. NMI is latched internally.
$\overline{\text{TEST}}$/BUSY	A(L)	I	**TEST** is used during the execution of the WAIT instruction to suspend CPU operation until the pin is sampled active (LOW). $\overline{\text{TEST}}$ is alternately knows as BUSY when interfacing with an 80C187 numerics coprocessor.
AD15:0	S(L) H(Z) R(Z) P(Z)	I/O	These pins provide a multiplexed ADDRESS and DATA bus. During the address phase of the bus cycle, address bits 0 through 15 are presented on the bus and can be latched using ALE. 8- or 16-bit data information is transferred during the data phase of the bus cycle.
A18:16 A19/$\overline{\text{ONCE}}$	H(Z) R(W1) P(Z)	I/O	These pins provide ADDRESS information during the address phase of the bus cycle. Address bits 16 through 19 are presented on these pins and can be latched using ALE. These pins are driven to a logic 0 during the data phase of the bus cycle. During a processor reset ($\overline{\text{RESIN}}$ active), A19/$\overline{\text{ONCE}}$ is used to enable ONCE™ mode. A18:A16 must not be driven low during reset or improper 80C186EB operation may result.

Name	Modal State	Type	Description
$\overline{S2:0}$	H(Z) R(1) P(Z)	O	Bus cycle **Status** are encoded on these pins to provide bus transaction information. $\overline{S2:0}$ are encoded as follows: **$\overline{S2}$ $\overline{S1}$ $\overline{S0}$ — Bus Cycle Initiated** 0 0 0 — Interrupt Acknowledge 0 0 1 — Read I/O 0 1 0 — Write I/O 0 1 1 — Processor HALT 1 0 0 — Queue Instruction Fetch 1 0 1 — Read Memory 1 1 0 — Write Memory 1 1 1 — Passive (no bus activity)
ALE	H(0) R(0) P(0)	O	**Address Latch Enable** output is used to strobe address information into a transparent type latch during the address phase of the bus cycle.
$\overline{BHE}$	H(Z) R(Z) P(X)	O	**Byte High Enable** output to indicate that the bus cycle in progress is transferring data over the upper half of the data bus. $\overline{BHE}$ and A0 have the following logical encoding: **A0 $\overline{BHE}$ — Encoding** 0 0 — Word transfer 0 1 — Even Byte transfer 1 0 — Odd Byte transfer 1 1 — Refresh operation
$\overline{RD}$	H(Z) R(Z) P(1)	O	**ReaD** output signals that the accessed memory or I/O device should drive data information onto the data bus.
$\overline{WR}$	H(Z) R(Z) P(1)	O	**WRite** output signals that data available on the data bus are to written into the accessed memory or I/O device.
READY	A(L) S(L)	I	**READY** input to signal the completion of a bus cycle. READY must be active to terminate an 80C186EB bus cycle, unless it is ignored by correctly programming the Chip-Select Unit.
$\overline{DEN}$	H(Z) R(1) P(1)	O	**Data ENable** output to control the enable of bi-directional transceivers when buffering an 80C186EB system. $\overline{DEN}$ is active only when data is to be transferred on the bus.
DT/$\overline{R}$	H(Z) R(Z) P(X)	O	**Data Transmit/Receive** output controls the direction of a bidirectional buffer when buffering an 80C186EB system. DT/R is only available on the PLCC package (80C186EB).
$\overline{LOCK}$	H(Z) R(W1) P(1)	I/O	**LOCK** output indicates that the bus cycle in progress is not to be interrupted. The 80C186EB will not service other bus requests (such as HOLD) while $\overline{LOCK}$ is active. This pin is configured as an weakly held high input while $\overline{RESIN}$ is active and must not be driven low.

Name	Modal State	Type	Description
HOLD	A(L)	I	**HOLD** request input to signal that an external bus master wishes to gain control of the local bus. The 80C186EB will relinquish control of the local bus between instruction boundaries not conditioned by a LOCK prefix.
HLDA	H(1) R(0) P(Q)	O	**HoLD Acknowledge** output to indicate that the 80C186EB has relinquish control of the local bus. When HLDA is asserted, the 80C186EB will (or has) floated its' data bus and control signals allowing another bus master to drive the signals directly.
NCS	H(1) R(1) P(1)	O	**Numerics Coprocessor Select** output is generated when accessing a numerics coprocessor. NCS is not provided on the S80C186EB.
ERROR	A(L)	I	**ERROR** input that indicates the last numerics coprocessor operation resulted in a exception condition. An interrupt TYPE 16 is generated if ERROR is sampled active at the beginning of a numerics operation. ERROR is not provided on the S80C186EB.
PEREQ	A(L)	I	**CoProcessor REQuest** signals that a data transfer between an External Numerics Coprocessor any Memory is pending. PEREQ is not provided on the S80C186EB.
UCS	H(1) R(1) P(1)	O	**Upper Chip Select** will go active whenever the address of a memory or I/O bus cycle is within the address limitations programmed by the user. After reset, UCS is configured to be active for memory accesses between 0FFC00H and 0FFFFFH.
LCS	H(1) R(1) P(1)	O	**Lower Chip Select** will go active whenever the address of a memory or I/O bus cycle is within the address limitations programmed by the user. LCS is inactive after a reset.
P1.0/GCS0 P1.1/GCS1 P1.2/GCS2 P1.3/GCS3 P1.4/GCS4 P1.5/GCS5 P1.6/GCS6 P1.7/GCS7	H(X)/H(1) R(1) P(X)/P(1)	O	These pins provide a multiplexed function. If enabled, each pin can provide a **Generic Chip Select** output which will go active whenever the address of a memory or I/O bus cycle is within the address limitations programmed by the user. When not programmed as a Chip-Select, each pin may be used as a general purpose output **Port**. As an output port pin, the value of the pin can be read internally.
T0OUT T1OUT	H(Q) R(0) P(Q)	O	**Timer OUTput** pins can be programmed to provide single clock or continuous waveform generation, depending on the timer mode selected.
T0IN T1IN	A(L) A(E)	I	**Timer INput** is used either as clock or control signals, depending on the timer mode selected.
INT0 INT1 INT4	A(E,L)	I	Maskable **INTerrupt** input will cause a vector to a specific Type interrupt routine. To allow interrupt expansion, INT0 and/or INT1can be used with INTA0 and INTA1 to interface with an external slave controller. INT4 is edge triggered only.

Name	Modal State	Type	Description
INT2/$\overline{\text{INTA0}}$ INT3/$\overline{\text{INTA1}}$	A(E,L)/H(1) R(Z)/P(1)	I/O	These pins provide a multiplexed function. As inputs, they provide a maskable **INTerrupt** that will cause the CPU to vector to a specific Type interrupt routine. As outputs, each is programmatically controlled to provide an INTERRUPT ACKNOWLEDGE handshake signal to allow interrupt expansion.
P2.7 P2.6	A(L) H(X) R(Z) P(X)	I/O	BI-DIRECTIONAL, open-drain **Port** pins.
$\overline{\text{CTS0}}$ P2.4/$\overline{\text{CTS1}}$	A(L)	I	**Clear-To-Send** input is used to prevent the transmission of serial data on the TXD signal pin. $\overline{\text{CTS1}}$ is multiplexed with an input only port function.
TXD0 P2.1/TXD1	H(X)/H(Q) R(1) P(X)/P(Q)	O	**Transmit Data** output provides serial data information. TXD1 is multiplexed with an output only **Port** function. During synchronous serial communications, TXD will function as a clock output.
RXD0 P2.0/RXD1	A(L) R(Z) H(Q) P(X)	I/O	**Receive Data** input accepts serial data information. RXD1 is multiplexed with an input only **Port** function. During synchronous serial communications, RXD is bi-directional and will become an output for transmission of data (TXD becomes the clock).
P2.5/BCLK0 P2.2/BCLK1	A(L)/A(E)	I	**Baud CLocK** input can be used as an alternate clock source for each of the integrated serial channels. BCLKx is multiplexed with an input only **Port** function, and cannot exceed a clock rate greater than 1/2 the operating frequency of the 80C186EB.
P2.3/SINT1	H(X)/H(Q) R(0) P(X)/P(Q)	O	**Serial INTerrupt** output will go active to indicate serial channel 1 requires service. SINT is multiplexed with an output only **Port** function.

DOMESTIC SALES OFFICES

ALABAMA

†Intel Corp.
5015 Bradford Dr., #2
Huntsville 35805
Tel: (205) 830-4010
FAX: (205) 837-2640

ARIZONA

†Intel Corp.
11225 N. 28th Dr.
Suite D-214
Phoenix 85029
Tel: (602) 869-4980
FAX: (602) 869-4294

Intel Corp.
7225 N. Mona Lisa Rd.
Suite 215
Tucson 85741
Tel: (602) 544-0227
FAX: (602) 544-0232

CALIFORNIA

†Intel Corp.
21515 Vanowen Street
Suite 116
Canoga Park 91303
Tel: (818) 704-8500
FAX: (818) 340-1144

†Intel Corp.
2250 E. Imperial Highway
Suite 218
El Segundo 90245
Tel: (213) 640-6040
FAX: (213) 640-7133

Intel Corp.
1 Sierra Gate Plaza
Suite 280C
Roseville 95678
Tel: (916) 782-8086
FAX: (916) 782-8153

†Intel Corp.
9665 Chesapeake Dr.
Suite 325
San Diego 92123
Tel: (619) 292-8086
FAX: (619) 292-0628

†Intel Corp.*
400 N. Tustin Avenue
Suite 450
Santa Ana 92705
Tel: (714) 835-9642
TWX: 910-595-1114
FAX: (714) 541-9157

†Intel Corp.*
San Tomas 4
2700 San Tomas Expressway
2nd Floor
Santa Clara 95051
Tel: (408) 986-8086
TWX: 910-338-0255
FAX: (408) 727-2620

COLORADO

Intel Corp.
4445 Northpark Drive
Suite 100
Colorado Springs 80907
Tel: (719) 594-6622
FAX: (303) 594-0720

†Intel Corp.*
650 S. Cherry St.
Suite 915
Denver 80222
Tel: (303) 321-8086
TWX: 910-931-2289
FAX: (303) 322-8670

CONNECTICUT

†Intel Corp.
301 Lee Farm Corporate Park
83 Wooster Heights Rd.
Danbury 06810
Tel: (203) 748-3130
FAX: (203) 794-0339

FLORIDA

†Intel Corp.
6363 N.W. 6th Way
Suite 100
Ft. Lauderdale 33309
Tel: (305) 771-0600
TWX: 510-956-9407
FAX: (305) 772-8193

†Intel Corp.
5850 T.G. Lee Blvd.
Suite 340
Orlando 32822
Tel: (407) 240-8000
FAX: (407) 240-8097

Intel Corp.
11300 4th Street North
Suite 170
St. Petersburg 33716
Tel: (813) 577-2413
FAX: (813) 578-1607

GEORGIA

Intel Corp.
20 Technology Parkway, N.W.
Suite 150
Norcross 30092
Tel: (404) 449-0541
FAX: (404) 605-9762

ILLINOIS

†Intel Corp.*
300 N. Martingale Road
Suite 400
Schaumburg 60173
Tel: (708) 605-8031
FAX: (708) 706-9762

INDIANA

†Intel Corp.
8777 Purdue Road
Suite 125
Indianapolis 46268
Tel: (317) 875-0623
FAX: (317) 875-8938

IOWA

Intel Corp.
1930 St. Andrews Drive N.E.
2nd Floor
Cedar Rapids 52402
Tel: (319) 393-1294

KANSAS

†Intel Corp.
10985 Cody St.
Suite 140, Bldg. D
Overland Park 66210
Tel: (913) 345-2727
FAX: (913) 345-2076

MARYLAND

†Intel Corp.*
10010 Junction Dr.
Suite 200
Annapolis Junction 20701
Tel: (301) 206-2860
FAX: (301) 206-3677
(301) 206-3678

MASSACHUSETTS

†Intel Corp.*
Westford Corp. Center
3 Carlisle Road
2nd Floor
Westford 01886
Tel: (508) 692-3222
TWX: 710-343-6333
FAX: (508) 692-7867

MICHIGAN

†Intel Corp.
7071 Orchard Lake Road
Suite 100
West Bloomfield 48322
Tel: (313) 851-8096
FAX: (313) 851-8770

MINNESOTA

†Intel Corp.
3500 W. 80th St.
Suite 360
Bloomington 55431
Tel: (612) 835-6722
TWX: 910-576-2867
FAX: (612) 831-6497

MISSOURI

†Intel Corp.
4203 Earth City Expressway
Suite 131
Earth City 63045
Tel: (314) 291-1990
FAX: (314) 291-4341

NEW JERSEY

†Intel Corp.*
Parkway 109 Office Center
328 Newman Springs Road
Red Bank 07701
Tel: (201) 747-2233
FAX: (201) 747-0983

†Intel Corp.
280 Corporate Center
75 Livingston Avenue
First Floor
Roseland 07068
Tel: (201) 740-0111
FAX: (201) 740-0626

NEW YORK

Intel Corp.*
850 Cross Keys Office Park
Fairport 14450
Tel: (716) 425-2750
TWX: 510-253-7391
FAX: (716) 223-2561

†Intel Corp.*
2950 Expressway Dr., South
Suite 130
Islandia 11722
Tel: (516) 231-3300
TWX: 510-227-6236
FAX: (516) 348-7939

†Intel Corp.
Westage Business Center
Bldg. 300, Route 9
Fishkill 12524
Tel: (914) 897-3860
FAX: (914) 897-3125

NORTH CAROLINA

†Intel Corp.
5800 Executive Center Dr.
Suite 105
Charlotte 28212
Tel: (704) 568-8966
FAX: (704) 535-2236

Intel Corp.
5540 Centerview Dr.
Suite 215
Raleigh 27606
Tel: (919) 851-9537
FAX: (919) 851-8974

OHIO

†Intel Corp.*
3401 Park Center Drive
Suite 220
Dayton 45414
Tel: (513) 890-5350
TWX: 810-450-2528
FAX: (513) 890-8658

†Intel Corp.*
25700 Science Park Dr.
Suite 100
Beachwood 44122
Tel: (216) 464-2736
TWX: 810-427-9298
FAX: (804) 282-0673

OKLAHOMA

Intel Corp.
6801 N. Broadway
Suite 115
Oklahoma City 73162
Tel: (405) 848-8086
FAX: (405) 840-9819

OREGON

†Intel Corp.
15254 N.W. Greenbrier Parkway
Building B
Beaverton 97005
Tel: (503) 645-8051
TWX: 910-467-8741
FAX: (503) 645-8181

PENNSYLVANIA

†Intel Corp.*
455 Pennsylvania Avenue
Suite 230
Fort Washington 19034
Tel: (215) 641-1000
TWX: 510-661-2077
FAX: (215) 641-0785

†Intel Corp.*
400 Penn Center Blvd.
Suite 610
Pittsburgh 15235
Tel: (412) 823-4970
FAX: (412) 829-7578

PUERTO RICO

†Intel Corp.
South Industrial Park
P.O. Box 910
Las Piedras 00671
Tel: (809) 733-8616

TEXAS

Intel Corp.
8911 Capital of Texas Hwy.
Austin 78759
Tel: (512) 794-8086
FAX: (512) 338-9335

†Intel Corp.*
12000 Ford Road
Suite 400
Dallas 75234
Tel: (214) 241-8087
FAX: (214) 484-1180

†Intel Corp.*
7322 S.W. Freeway
Suite 1490
Houston 77074
Tel: (713) 988-8086
TWX: 910-881-2490
FAX: (713) 988-3660

UTAH

†Intel Corp.
428 East 6400 South
Suite 104
Murray 84107
Tel: (801) 263-8051
FAX: (801) 268-1457

VIRGINIA

†Intel Corp.
1504 Santa Rosa Road
Suite 108
Richmond 23288
Tel: (804) 282-5668
FAX: (216) 464-2270

WASHINGTON

†Intel Corp.
155 108th Avenue N.E.
Suite 386
Bellevue 98004
Tel: (206) 453-8086
TWX: 910-443-3002
FAX: (206) 451-9556

Intel Corp.
408 N. Mullan Road
Suite 102
Spokane 99206
Tel: (509) 928-8086
FAX: (509) 928-9467

WISCONSIN

Intel Corp.
330 S. Executive Dr.
Suite 102
Brookfield 53005
Tel: (414) 784-8087
FAX: (414) 796-2115

CANADA

BRITISH COLUMBIA

Intel Semiconductor of
Canada, Ltd.
4585 Canada Way
Suite 202
Burnaby V5G 4L6
Tel: (604) 298-0387
FAX: (604) 298-8234

ONTARIO

†Intel Semiconductor of
Canada, Ltd.
2650 Queensview Drive
Suite 250
Ottawa K2B 8H6
Tel: (613) 829-9714
FAX: (613) 820-5936

†Intel Semiconductor of
Canada, Ltd.
190 Attwell Drive
Suite 500
Rexdale M9W 6H8
Tel: (416) 675-2105
FAX: (416) 675-2438

QUEBEC

Intel Semiconductor of
Canada, Ltd.
620 St. Jean Boulevard
Pointe Claire H9R 3K2
Tel: (514) 694-9130
FAX: 514-694-0064

†Sales and Service Office
*Field Application Location

DOMESTIC DISTRIBUTORS

ALABAMA

Arrow Electronics, Inc.
1015 Henderson Road
Huntsville 35805
Tel: (205) 837-6955

†Hamilton/Avnet Electronics
4940 Research Drive
Huntsville 35805
Tel: (205) 837-7210
TWX: 810-726-2162

Pioneer/Technologies Group, Inc.
4825 University Square
Huntsville 35805
Tel: (205) 837-9300
TWX: 810-726-2197

ARIZONA

†Hamilton/Avnet Electronics
505 S. Madison Drive
Tempe 85281
Tel: (602) 231-5140
TWX: 910-950-0077

Hamilton/Avnet Electronics
30 South McKiemy
Chandler 85226
Tel: (602) 961-6669
TWX: 910-950-0077

Arrow Electronics, Inc.
4134 E. Wood Street
Phoenix 85040
Tel: (602) 437-0750
TWX: 910-951-1550

Wyle Distribution Group
17855 N. Black Canyon Hwy.
Phoenix 85023
Tel: (602) 249-2232
TWX: 910-951-4282

CALIFORNIA

Arrow Electronics, Inc.
10824 Hope Street
Cypress 90630
Tel: (714) 220-6300

Arrow Electronics, Inc.
19748 Dearborn Street
Chatsworth 91311
Tel: (213) 701-7500
TWX: 910-493-2086

†Arow Electronics, Inc.
521 Weddell Drive
Sunnyvale 94086
Tel: (408) 745-6600
TWX: 910-339-9371

Arrow Electronics, Inc.
9511 Ridgehaven Court
San Diego 92123
Tel: (619) 565-4800
TWX: 888-064

†Arrow Electronics, Inc.
2961 Dow Avenue
Tustin 92680
Tel: (714) 838-5422
TWX: 910-595-2860

†Avnet Electronics
350 McCormick Avenue
Costa Mesa 92626
Tel: (714) 754-6071
TWX: 910-595-1928

†Hamilton/Avnet Electronics
1175 Bordeaux Drive
Sunnyvale 94086
Tel: (408) 743-3300
TWX: 910-339-9332

†Hamilton/Avnet Electronics
4545 Ridgeview Avenue
San Diego 92123
Tel: (619) 571-7500
TWX: 910-595-2638

†Hamilton/Avnet Electronics
9650 Desoto Avenue
Chatsworth 91311
Tel: (818) 700-1161

†Hamilton Electro Sales
10950 W. Washington Blvd.
Culver City 20230
Tel: (213) 558-2458
TWX: 910-340-6364

Hamilton Electro Sales
1361B West 190th Street
Gardena 90248
Tel: (213) 217-6700

†Hamilton/Avnet Electronics
3002 'G' Street
Ontario 91761
Tel: (714) 989-9411

†Avnet Electronics
20501 Plummer
Chatsworth 91351
Tel: (213) 700-6271
TWX: 910-494-2207

†Hamilton Electro Sales
3170 Pullman Street
Costa Mesa 92626
Tel: (714) 641-4150
TWX: 910-595-2638

†Hamilton/Avnet Electronics
4103 Northgate Blvd.
Sacramento 95834
Tel: (916) 920-3150

Wyle Distribution Group
124 Maryland Street
El Segundo 90254
Tel: (213) 322-8100

Wyle Distribution Group
7382 Lampson Ave.
Garden Grove 92641
Tel: (714) 891-1717
TWX: 910-348-7140 or 7111

Wyle Distribution Group
11151 Sun Center Drive
Rancho Cordova 95670
Tel: (916) 638-5282

†Wyle Distribution Group
9525 Chesapeake Drive
San Diego 92123
Tel: (619) 565-9171
TWX: 910-335-1590

†Wyle Distribution Group
3000 Bowers Avenue
Santa Clara 95051
Tel: (408) 727-2500
TWX: 910-338-0296

†Wyle Distribution Group
17872 Cowan Avenue
Irvine 92714
Tel: (714) 863-9953
TWX: 910-595-1572

Wyle Distribution Group
26677 W. Agoura Rd.
Calabasas 91302
Tel: (818) 880-9000
TWX: 372-0232

COLORADO

Arrow Electronics, Inc.
7060 South Tucson Way
Englewood 80112
Tel: (303) 790-4444

†Hamilton/Avnet Electronics
8765 E. Orchard Road
Suite 708
Englewood 80111
Tel: (303) 740-1017
TWX: 910-935-0787

†Wyle Distribution Group
451 E. 124th Avenue
Thornton 80241
Tel: (303) 457-9953
TWX: 910-936-0770

CONNECTICUT

†Arrow Electronics, Inc.
12 Beaumont Road
Wallingford 06492
Tel: (203) 265-7741
TWX: 710-476-0162

Hamilton/Avnet Electronics
Commerce Industrial Park
Commerce Drive
Danbury 06810
Tel: (203) 797-2800
TWX: 710-456-9974

†Pioneer Electronics
112 Main Street
Norwalk 06851
Tel: (203) 853-1515
TWX: 710-468-3373

FLORIDA

†Arrow Electronics, Inc.
400 Fairway Drive
Suite 102
Deerfield Beach 33441
Tel: (305) 429-8200
TWX: 510-955-9456

Arrow Electronics, Inc.
37 Skyline Drive
Suite 3101
Lake Marv 32746
Tel: (407) 323-0252
TWX: 510-959-6337

†Hamilton/Avnet Electronics
6801 N.W. 15th Way
Ft. Lauderdale 33309
Tel: (305) 971-2900
TWX: 510-956-3097

†Hamilton/Avnet Electronics
3197 Tech Drive North
St. Petersburg 33702
Tel: (813) 576-3930
TWX: 810-863-0374

†Hamilton/Avnet Electronics
6947 University Boulevard
Winter Park 32792
Tel: (305) 628-3888
TWX: 810-853-0322

†Pioneer/Technologies Group, Inc.
337 S. Lake Blvd.
Alta Monte Springs 32701
Tel: (407) 834-9090
TWX: 810-853-0284

Pioneer/Technologies Group, Inc.
674 S. Military Trail
Deerfield Beach 33442
Tel: (305) 428-8877
TWX: 510-955-9653

GEORGIA

†Arrow Electronics, Inc.
3155 Northwoods Parkway
Suite A
Norcross 30071
Tel: (404) 449-8252
TWX: 810-766-0439

†Hamilton/Avnet Electronics
5825 D Peachtree Corners
Norcross 30092
Tel: (404) 447-7500
TWX: 810-766-0432

Pioneer/Technologies Group, Inc.
3100 F Northwoods Place
Norcross 30071
Tel: (404) 448-1711
TWX: 810-766-4515

ILLINOIS

Arrow Electronics, Inc.
1140 W. Thorndale
Itasca 60143
Tel: (312) 250-0500
TWX: 312-250-0916

†Hamilton/Avnet Electronics
1130 Thorndale Avenue
Bensenville 60106
Tel: (312) 860-7780
TWX: 910-227-0060

MTI Systems Sales
1100 W. Thorndale
Itasca 60143
Tel: (312) 773-2300

†Pioneer Electronics
1551 Carmen Drive
Elk Grove Village 60007
Tel: (312) 437-9680
TWX: 910-222-1834

INDIANA

†Arrow Electronics, Inc.
2495 Directors Row, Suite H
Indianapolis 46241
Tel: (317) 243-9353
TWX: 810-341-3119

Hamilton/Avnet Electronics
485 Gradle Drive
Carmel 46032
Tel: (317) 844-9333
TWX: 810-260-3966

†Pioneer Electronics
6408 Castleplace Drive
Indianapolis 46250
Tel: (317) 849-7300
TWX: 810-260-1794

IOWA

Hamilton/Avnet Electronics
915 33rd Avenue, S.W.
Cedar Rapids 52404
Tel: (319) 362-4757

KANSAS

Arrow Electronics
8208 Melrose Dr., Suite 210
Lenexa 66214
Tel: (913) 541-9542

†Hamilton/Avnet Electronics
9219 Quivera Road
Overland Park 66215
Tel: (913) 888-8900
TWX: 910-743-0005

Pioneer/Tec Gr.
10551 Lockman Rd.
Lenexa 66215
Tel: (913) 492-0500

KENTUCKY

Hamilton/Avnet Electronics
1051 D. Newton Park
Lexington 40511
Tel: (606) 259-1475

MARYLAND

Arrow Electronics, Inc.
8300 Guilford Drive
Suite H, River Center
Columbia 21046
Tel: (301) 995-0003
TWX: 710-236-9005

Hamilton/Avnet Electronics
6822 Oak Hall Lane
Columbia 21045
Tel: (301) 995-3500
TWX: 710-862-1861

†Mesa Technology Corp.
9720 Patuxent Woods Dr.
Columbia 21046
Tel: (301) 290-8150
TWX: 710-828-9702

†Pioneer/Technologies Group, Inc.
9100 Gaither Road
Gaithersburg 20877
Tel: (301) 921-0660
TWX: 710-828-0545

Arrow Electronics, Inc.
7524 Standish Place
Rockville 20855
Tel: 301-424-0244

MASSACHUSETTS

Arrow Electronics, Inc.
25 Upton Dr.
Wilmington 01887
Tel: (617) 935-5134

†Hamilton/Avnet Electronics
10D Centennial Drive
Peabody 01960
Tel: (617) 531-7430
TWX: 710-393-0382

MTI Systems Sales
83 Cambridge St.
Burlington 01813

Pioneer Electronics
44 Hartwell Avenue
Lexington 02173
Tel: (617) 861-9200
TWX: 710-326-6617

MICHIGAN

Arrow Electronics, Inc.
755 Phoenix Drive
Ann Arbor 48104
Tel: (313) 971-8220
TWX: 810-223-6020

Hamilton/Avnet Electronics
2215 29th Street S.E.
Space A5
Grand Rapids 49508
Tel: (616) 243-8805
TWX: 810-274-6921

Pioneer Electronics
4504 Broadmoor S.E.
Grand Rapids 49508
FAX: 616-698-1831

†Hamilton/Avnet Electronics
32487 Schoolcraft Road
Livonia 48150
Tel: (313) 522-4700
TWX: 810-282-8775

†Pioneer/Michigan
13485 Stamford
Livonia 48150
Tel: (313) 525-1800
TWX: 810-242-3271

MINNESOTA

†Arrow Electronics, Inc.
5230 W. 73rd Street
Edina 55435
Tel: (612) 830-1800
TWX: 910-576-3125

†Hamilton/Avnet Electronics
12400 Whitewater Drive
Minnetonka 55434
Tel: (612) 932-0600

†Pioneer Electronics
7625 Golden Triange Dr.
Suite G
Eden Prairi 55343
Tel: (612) 944-3355

MISSOURI

†Arrow Electronics, Inc.
2380 Schuetz
St. Louis 63141
Tel: (314) 567-6888
TWX: 910-764-0882

†Hamilton/Avnet Electronics
13743 Shoreline Court
Earth City 63045
Tel: (314) 344-1200
TWX: 910-762-0684

NEW HAMPSHIRE

†Arrow Electronics, Inc.
3 Perimeter Road
Manchester 03103
Tel: (603) 668-6968
TWX: 710-220-1684

†Hamilton/Avnet Electronics
444 E. Industrial Drive
Manchester 03103
Tel: (603) 624-9400

†Microcomputer System Technical Distributor Center

DOMESTIC DISTRIBUTORS (Contd.)

W JERSEY

rrow Electronics, Inc.
ur East Stow Road
nit 11
arlton 08053
l: (609) 596-8000
/X: 710-897-0829

rrow Electronics
Century Drive
rsipanny 07054
el: (201) 538-0900

lamilton/Avnet Electronics
Keystone Ave., Bldg. 36
herry Hill 08003
el: (609) 424-0110
WX: 710-940-0262

Hamilton/Avnet Electronics
0 Industrial
airfield 07006
el: (201) 575-5300
WX: 710-734-4388

MTI Systems Sales
7 Kulick Rd.
airfield 07006
el: (201) 227-5552

Pioneer Electronics
5 Route 46
inebrook 07058
el: (201) 575-3510
WX: 710-734-4382

EW MEXICO

lliance Electronics Inc.
1030 Cochiti S.E.
lbuquerque 87123
Tel: (505) 292-3360
TWX: 910-989-1151

Hamilton/Avnet Electronics
2524 Baylor Drive S.E.
Albuquerque 87106
Tel: (505) 765-1500
TWX: 910-989-0614

NEW YORK

†Arrow Electronics, Inc.
3375 Brighton Henrietta
Townline Rd.
Rochester 14623
Tel: (716) 275-0300
TWX: 510-253-4766

Arrow Electronics, Inc.
20 Oser Avenue
Hauppauge 11788
Tel: (516) 231-1000
TWX: 510-227-6623

Hamilton/Avnet
933 Motor Parkway
Hauppauge 11788
Tel: (516) 231-9800
TWX: 510-224-6166

†Hamilton/Avnet Electronics
333 Metro Park
Rochester 14623
Tel: (716) 475-9130
TWX: 510-253-5470

†Hamilton/Avnet Electronics
103 Twin Oaks Drive
Syracuse 13206
Tel: (315) 437-0288
TWX: 710-541-1560

†MTI Systems Sales
38 Harbor Park Drive
Port Washington 11050
Tel: (516) 621-6200

†Pioneer Electronics
68 Corporate Drive
Binghamton 13904
Tel: (607) 722-9300
TWX: 510-252-0893

Pioneer Electronics
40 Oser Avenue
Hauppauge 11787
Tel: (516) 231-9200

†Pioneer Electronics
60 Crossway Park West
Woodbury, Long Island 11797
Tel: (516) 921-8700
TWX: 510-221-2184

†Pioneer Electronics
840 Fairport Park
Fairport 14450
Tel: (716) 381-7070
TWX: 510-253-7001

NORTH CAROLINA

†Arrow Electronics, Inc.
5240 Greensdairy Road
Raleigh 27604
Tel: (919) 876-3132
TWX: 510-928-1856

†Hamilton/Avnet Electronics
3510 Spring Forest Drive
Raleigh 27604
Tel: (919) 878-0819
TWX: 510-928-1836

Pioneer/Technologies Group, Inc.
9801 A-Southern Pine Blvd.
Charlotte 28210
Tel: (919) 527-8188
TWX: 810-621-0366

OHIO

Arrow Electronics, Inc.
7620 McEwen Road
Centerville 45459
Tel: (513) 435-5563
TWX: 810-459-1611

†Arrow Electronics, Inc.
6238 Cochran Road
Solon 44139
Tel: (216) 248-3990
TWX: 810-427-9409

†Hamilton/Avnet Electronics
954 Senate Drive
Dayton 45459
Tel: (513) 439-6733
TWX: 810-450-2531

Hamilton/Avnet Electronics
4588 Emery Industrial Pkwy.
Warrensville Heights 44128
Tel: (216) 349-5100
TWX: 810-427-9452

†Hamilton/Avnet Electronics
777 Brooksedge Blvd.
Westerville 43081
Tel: (614) 882-7004

†Pioneer Electronics
4433 Interpoint Boulevard
Dayton 45424
Tel: (513) 236-9900
TWX: 810-459-1622

†Pioneer Electronics
4800 E. 131st Street
Cleveland 44105
Tel: (216) 587-3600
TWX: 810-422-2211

OKLAHOMA

Arrow Electronics, Inc.
1211 E. 51st St., Suite 101
Tulsa 74146
Tel: (918) 252-7537

†Hamilton/Avnet Electronics
12121 E. 51st St., Suite 102A
Tulsa 74146
Tel: (918) 252-7297

OREGON

†Almac Electronics Corp.
1885 N.W. 169th Place
Beaverton 97005
Tel: (503) 629-8090
TWX: 910-467-8746

†Hamilton/Avnet Electronics
6024 S.W. Jean Road
Bldg. C, Suite 10
Lake Oswego 97034
Tel: (503) 635-7848
TWX: 910-455-8179

Wyle Distribution Group
5250 N.E. Elam Young Parkway
Suite 600
Hillsboro 97124
Tel: (503) 640-6000
TWX: 910-460-2203

PENNSYLVANIA

Arrow Electronics, Inc.
650 Seco Road
Monroeville 15146
Tel: (412) 856-7000

Hamilton/Avnet Electronics
2800 Liberty Ave.
Pittsburgh 15238
Tel: (412) 281-4150

Pioneer Electronics
259 Kappa Drive
Pittsburgh 15238
Tel: (412) 782-2300
TWX: 710-795-3122

†Pioneer/Technologies Group, Inc.
Delaware Valley
261 Gibralter Road
Horsham 19044
Tel: (215) 674-4000
TWX: 510-665-6778

TEXAS

†Arrow Electronics, Inc.
3220 Commander Drive
Carrollton 75006
Tel: (214) 380-6464
TWX: 910-860-5377

†Arrow Electronics, Inc.
10899 Kinghurst
Suite 100
Houston 77099
Tel: (713) 530-4700
TWX: 910-880-4439

†Arrow Electronics, Inc.
2227 W. Braker Lane
Austin 78758
Tel: (512) 835-4180
TWX: 910-874-1348

†Hamilton/Avnet Electronics
1807 W. Braker Lane
Austin 78758
Tel: (512) 837-8911
TWX: 910-874-1319

†Hamilton/Avnet Electronics
2111 W. Walnut Hill Lane
Irving 75038
Tel: (214) 550-6111
TWX: 910-860-5929

†Hamilton/Avnet Electronics
4850 Wright Rd., Suite 190
Stafford 77477
Tel: (713) 240-7733
TWX: 910-881-5523

†Pioneer Electronics
18260 Kramer
Austin 78758
Tel: (512) 835-4000
TWX: 910-874-1323

†Pioneer Electronics
13710 Omega Road
Dallas 75234
Tel: (214) 386-7300
TWX: 910-850-5563

†Pioneer Electronics
5853 Point West Drive
Houston 77036
Tel: (713) 988-5555
TWX: 910-881-1606

Wyle Distribution Group
1810 Greenville Avenue
Richardson 75081
Tel: (214) 235-9953

UTAH

Arrow Electronics
1946 Parkway Blvd.
Salt Lake City 84119
Tel: (801) 973-6913

†Hamilton/Avnet Electronics
1585 West 2100 South
Salt Lake City 84119
Tel: (801) 972-2800
TWX: 910-925-4018

Wyle Distribution Group
1325 West 2200 South
Suite E
West Valley 84119
Tel: (801) 974-9953

WASHINGTON

†Almac Electronics Corp.
14360 S.E. Eastgate Way
Bellevue 98007
Tel: (206) 643-9992
TWX: 910-444-2067

Arrow Electronics, Inc.
19540 68th Ave. South
Kent 98032
Tel: (206) 575-4420

†Hamilton/Avnet Electronics
14212 N.E. 21st Street
Bellevue 98005
Tel: (206) 643-3950
TWX: 910-443-2469

Wyle Distribution Group
15385 N.E. 90th Street
Redmond 98052
Tel: (206) 881-1150

WISCONSIN

Arrow Electronics, Inc.
200 N. Patrick Blvd., Ste. 100
Brookfield 53005
Tel: (414) 767-6600
TWX: 910-262-1193

Hamilton/Avnet Electronics
2975 Moorland Road
New Berlin 53151
Tel: (414) 784-4510
TWX: 910-262-1182

CANADA

ALBERTA

Hamilton/Avnet Electronics
2816 21st Street N.E.
Calgary T2E 6Z3
Tel: (403) 230-3586
TWX: 03-827-642

Zentronics
Bay No. 1
3300 14th Avenue N.E.
Calgary T2A 6J4
Tel: (403) 272-1021

BRITISH COLUMBIA

†Hamilton/Avnet Electronics
105-2550 Boundary
Burmalay V5M 3Z3
Tel: (604) 437-6667

Zentronics
108-11400 Bridgeport Road
Richmond V6X 1T2
Tel: (604) 273-5575
TWX: 04-5077-89

MANITOBA

Zentronics
60-1313 Border Unit 60
Winnipeg R3H 0X4
Tel: (204) 694-1957

ONTARIO

Arrow Electronics, Inc.
36 Antares Dr.
Nepean K2E 7W5
Tel: (613) 226-6903

Arrow Electronics, Inc.
1093 Meyerside
Mississauga L5T 1M4
Tel: (416) 673-7769
TWX: 06-218213

†Hamilton/Avnet Electronics
6845 Rexwood Road
Units 3-4-5
Mississauga L4T 1R2
Tel: (416) 677-7432
TWX: 610-492-8867

Hamilton/Avnet Electronics
6845 Rexwood Rd., Unit 6
Mississauga L4T 1R2
Tel: (416) 277-0484

†Hamilton/Avnet Electronics
190 Colonnade Road South
Nepean K2E 7L5
Tel: (613) 226-1700
TWX: 05-349-71

†Zentronics
8 Tilbury Court
Brampton L6T 3T4
Tel: (416) 451-9600
TWX: 06-976-78

†Zentronics
155 Colonnade Road
Unit 17
Nepean K2E 7K1
Tel: (613) 226-8840

Zentronics
60-1313 Border St.
Winnipeg R3H 0I4
Tel: (204) 694-7957

QUEBEC

†Arrow Electronics Inc.
4050 Jean Talon Quest
Montreal H4P 1W1
Tel: (514) 735-5511
TWX: 05-25590

Arrow Electronics, Inc.
500 Avenue St-Jean Baptiste
Suite 280
Quebec G2E 5R9
Tel: (418) 871-7500
FAX: 418-871-6816

Hamilton/Avnet Electronics
2795 Halpern
St. Laurent H2E 7K1
Tel: (514) 335-1000
TWX: 610-421-3731

Zentronics
817 McCaffrey
St. Laurent H4T 1M3
Tel: (514) 737-9700
TWX: 05-827-535

†Microcomputer System Technical Distributor Center

EUROPEAN SALES OFFICES

DENMARK

Intel Denmark A/S
Glentevej 61, 3rd Floor
2400 Copenhagen NV
Tel: (45) (31) 19 80 33
TLX: 19567

FINLAND

Intel Finland OY
Ruosilantie 2
00390 Helsinki
Tel: (358) 0 544 644
TLX: 123332

FRANCE

Intel Corporation S.A.R.L.
1, Rue Edison-BP 303
78054 St. Quentin-en-Yvelines
Cedex
Tel: (33) (1) 30 57 70 00
TLX: 699016

WEST GERMANY

Intel Semiconductor GmbH*
Dornacher Strasse 1
8016 Feldkirchen bei Muenchen
Tel: (49) 089/90992-0
TLX: 5-23177

Intel Semiconductor GmbH
Hohenzollern Strasse 5
3000 Hannover 1
Tel: (49) 0511/344081
TLX: 9-23625

Intel Semiconductor GmbH
Abraham Lincoln Strasse 16-18
6200 Wiesbaden
Tel: (49) 06121/7605-0
TLX: 4-186183

Intel Semiconductor GmbH
Zettachring 10A
7000 Stuttgart 80
Tel: (49) 0711/7287-280
TLX: 7-254826

ISRAEL

Intel Semiconductor Ltd.*
Atidim Industrial Park-Neve Sharet
P.O. Box 43202
Tel-Aviv 61430
Tel: (972) 3-548-3222
TLX: 371215

ITALY

Intel Corporation Italia S.p.A.*
Milanofiori Palazzo E
20090 Assago
Milano
Tel: (39) (02) 89200950
TLX: 341286

NETHERLANDS

Intel Semiconductor B.V.*
Postbus 84130
3099 CC Rotterdam
Tel: (31) 10.407.11.11
TLX: 22283

NORWAY

Intel Norway A/S
Hvamveien 4-PO Box 92
2013 Skjetten
Tel: (47) (6) 842 420
TLX: 78018

SPAIN

Intel Iberia S.A.
Zurbaran, 28
28010 Madrid
Tel: (34) (1) 308.25.52
TLX: 46880

SWEDEN

Intel Sweden A.B.*
Dalvagen 24
171 36 Solna
Tel: (46) 8 734 01 00
TLX: 12261

SWITZERLAND

Intel Semiconductor A.G.
Zuerichstrasse
8185 Winkel-Rueti bei Zuerich
Tel: (41) 01/860 62 62
TLX: 825977

UNITED KINGDOM

Intel Corporation (U.K.) Ltd.*
Pipers Way
Swindon, Wiltshire SN3 1RJ
Tel: (44) (0793) 696000
TLX: 444447/8

EUROPEAN DISTRIBUTORS/REPRESENTATIVES

AUSTRIA

Bacher Electronics G.m.b.H.
Rotenmuehlgasse 26
1120 Wien
Tel: (43) (0222) 83 56 46
TLX: 31532

BELGIUM

Inelco Belgium S.A.
Av. des Croix de Guerre 94
1120 Bruxelles
Oorlogskruisenlaan, 94
1120 Brussel
Tel: (32) (02) 216 01 60
TLX: 64475 or 22090

DENMARK

ITT-Multikomponent
Naverland 29
2600 Glostrup
Tel: (45) (0) 2 45 66 45
TLX: 33 355

FINLAND

OY Fintronic AB
Melkonkatu 24A
00210 Helsinki
Tel: (358) (0) 6926022
TLX: 124224

FRANCE

Almex
Zone industrielle d'Antony
48, rue de l'Aubepine
BP 102
92164 Antony cedex
Tel: (33) (1) 46 66 21 12
TLX: 250067

Jermyn-Generim
60, rue des Gemeaux
Silic 580
94653 Rungis cedex
Tel: (33) (1) 49 78 49 78
TLX: 261585

Metrologie
Tour d'Asnieres
4, av. Laurent-Cely
92606 Asnieres Cedex
Tel: (33) (1) 47 90 62 40
TLX: 611448

Tekelec-Airtronic
Cite des Bruyeres
Rue Carle Vernet - BP 2
92310 Sevres
Tel: (33) (1) 45 34 75 35
TLX: 204552

WEST GERMANY

Electronic 2000 AG
Stahlgruberring 12
8000 Muenchen 82
Tel: (49) 089/42001-0
TLX: 522561

ITT Multikomponent GmbH
Postfach 1265
Bahnhofstrasse 44
7141 Moeglingen
Tel: (49) 07141/4879
TLX: 7264472

Jermyn GmbH
Im Dachsstueck 9
6250 Limburg
Tel: (49) 06431/508-0
TLX: 415257-0

Metrologie GmbH
Meglingerstrasse 49
8000 Muenchen 71
Tel: (49) 089/78042-0
TLX: 5213189

Proelectron Vertriebs GmbH
Max Planck Strasse 1-3
6072 Dreieich
Tel: (49) 06103/30434-3
TLX: 417903

IRELAND

Micro Marketing Ltd.
Glenageary Office Park
Glenageary
Co. Dublin
Tel: (21) (353) (01) 85 63 25
TLX: 31584

ISRAEL

Eastronics Ltd.
11 Rozanis Street
P.O.B. 39300
Tel-Aviv 61392
Tel: (972) 03-475151
TLX: 33638

ITALY

Intesi
Divisione ITT Industries GmbH
Viale Milanofiori
Palazzo E/5
20090 Assago (MI)
Tel: (39) 02/824701
TLX: 311351

Lasi Elettronica S.p.A.
V. le Fulvio Testi, 126
20092 Cinisello Balsamo (MI)
Tel: (39) 02/2440012
TLX: 352040

Telcom S.r.l.
Via M. Civitali 75
20148 Milano
Tel: (39) 02/4049046
TLX: 335654

ITT Multicomponents
Viale Milanofiori E/5
20090 Assago (MI)
Tel: (39) 02/824701
TLX: 311351

Silverstar
Via Dei Gracchi 20
20146 Milano
Tel: (39) 02/49961
TLX: 332189

NETHERLANDS

Koning en Hartman Elektrotechniek
B.V.
Energieweg 1
2627 AP Delft
Tel: (31) (0) 15/609906
TLX: 38250

NORWAY

Nordisk Elektronikk (Norge) A/S
Postboks 123
Smedsvingen 4
1364 Hvalstad
Tel: (47) (02) 84 62 10
TLX: 77546

PORTUGAL

ATD Portugal LDA
Rua Dos Lusiados, 5 Sala B
1300 Lisboa
Tel: (35) (1) 64 80 91
TLX: 61562

Ditram
Avenida Miguel Bombarda, 133
1000 Lisboa
Tel: (35) (1) 54 53 13
TLX: 14182

SPAIN

ATD Electronica, S.A.
Plaza Ciudad de Viena, 6
28040 Madrid
Tel: (34) (1) 234 40 00
TLX: 42477

ITT-SESA
Calle Miguel Angel, 21-3
28010 Madrid
Tel: (34) (1) 419 09 57
TLX: 27461

Metrologia Iberica, S.A.
Ctra. de Fuencarral, n.80
28100 Alcobendas (Madrid)
Tel: (34) (1) 653 86 11

SWEDEN

Nordisk Elektronik AB
Torshamnsgatan 39
Box 36
164 93 Kista
Tel: (46) 08-03 46 30
TLX: 105 47

SWITZERLAND

Industrade A.G.
Hertistrasse 31
8304 Wallisellen
Tel: (41) (01) 8328111
TLX: 56788

TURKEY

EMPA Electronic
Lindwurmstrasse 95A
8000 Muenchen 2
Tel: (49) 089/53 80 570
TLX: 528573

UNITED KINGDOM

Accent Electronic Components Ltd.
Jubilee House, Jubilee Road
Letchworth, Herts SG6 1TL
Tel: (44) (0462) 686666
TLX: 826293

Bytech-Comway Systems
3 The Western Centre
Western Road
Bracknell RG12 1RW
Tel: (44) (0344) 55333
TLX: 847201

Jermyn
Vestry Estate
Otford Road
Sevenoaks
Kent TN14 5EU
Tel: (44) (0732) 450144
TLX: 95142

MMD
Unit 8 Southview Park
Caversham
Reading
Berkshire RG4 0AF
Tel: (44) (0734) 481666
TLX: 846669

Rapid Silicon
Rapid House
Denmark Street
High Wycombe
Buckinghamshire HP11 2ER
Tel: (44) (0494) 442266
TLX: 837931

Rapid Systems
Rapid House
Denmark Street
High Wycombe
Buckinghamshire HP11 2ER
Tel: (44) (0494) 450244
TLX: 837931

YUGOSLAVIA

H.R. Microelectronics Corp.
2005 de la Cruz Blvd., Ste. 223
Santa Clara, CA 95050
U.S.A.
Tel: (1) (408) 988-0286
TLX: 387452

Rapido Electronic Components
S.p.a.
Via C. Beccaria, 8
34133 Trieste
Italia
Tel: (39) 040/360555
TLX: 460461

*Field Application Location

INTERNATIONAL SALES OFFICES

AUSTRALIA

Intel Australia Pty. Ltd.*
Spectrum Building
200 Pacific Hwy., Level 6
Crows Nest, NSE, 2065
Tel: 612-957-2744
FAX: 612-923-2632

BRAZIL

Intel Semicondutores do Brazil LTDA
Av. Paulista, 1159-CJS 404/405
01311 - Sao Paulo - S.P.
Tel: 55-11-287-5899
TLX: 3911153146 ISDB
FAX: 55-11-287-5119

CHINA/HONG KONG

Intel PRC Corporation
15/F, Office 1, Citic Bldg.
Jian Guo Men Wai Street
Beijing, PRC
Tel: (1) 500-4850
TLX: 22947 INTEL CN
FAX: (1) 500-2953

Intel Semiconductor Ltd.*
10/F East Tower
Bond Center
Queensway, Central
Hong Kong
Tel: (852) 844-4555
FAX: (852) 868-1989

INDIA

Intel Asia Electronics, Inc.
4/2, Samrah Plaza
St. Mark's Road
Bangalore 560001
Tel: 011-91-812-215065
TLX: 9538452875 DCBY
FAX: 091-812-215067

JAPAN

Intel Japan K.K.
5-6 Tokodai, Tsukuba-shi
Ibaraki, 300-26
Tel: 0298-47-8511
TLX: 3656-160
FAX: 0298-47-8450

Intel Japan K.K.*
Daiichi Mitsugi Bldg.
1-8889 Fuchu-cho
Fuchu-shi, Tokyo 183
Tel: 0423-60-7871
FAX: 0423-60-0315

Intel Japan K.K.*
Bldg. Kumagaya
2-69 Hon-cho
Kumagaya-shi, Saitama 360
Tel: 0485-24-6871
FAX: 0485-24-7518

Intel Japan K.K.*
Mitsui-Seimei Musashi-kosugi Bldg.
915 Shinmaruko, Nakahara-ku
Kawasaki-shi, Kanagawa 211
Tel: 044-733-7011
FAX: 044-733-7010

Intel Japan K.K.
Nihon Seimei Atsugi Bldg.
1-2-1 Asahi-machi
Atsugi-shi, Kanagawa 243
Tel: 0462-29-3731
FAX: 0462-29-3781

Intel Japan K.K.*
Ryokuchi-Eki Bldg.
2-4-1 Terauchi
Toyonaka-shi, Osaka 560
Tel: 06-863-1091
FAX: 06-863-1084

Intel Japan K.K.
Shinmaru Bldg.
1-5-1 Marunouchi
Chiyoda-ku, Tokyo 100
Tel: 03-201-3621
FAX: 03-201-6850

Intel Japan K.K.
Green Bldg.
1-16-20 Nishiki
Naka-ku, Nagoya-shi
Aichi 450
Tel: 052-204-1261
FAX: 052-204-1285

KOREA

Intel Technology Asia, Ltd.
16th Floor, Life Bldg.
61 Yoido-dong, Youngdeungpo-Ku
Seoul 150-010
Tel: (2) 784-8186, 8286, 8386
TLX: K29312 INTELKO
FAX: (2) 784-8096

SINGAPORE

Intel Singapore Technology, Ltd.
101 Thomson Road #21-05/06
United Square
Singapore 1130
Tel: 250-7811
TLX: 39921 INTEL
FAX: 250-9256

TAIWAN

Intel Technology Far East Ltd.
8th Floor, No. 205
Bank Tower Bldg.
Tung Hua N. Road
Taipei
Tel: 886-2-716-9660
FAX: 886-2-717-2455

INTERNATIONAL DISTRIBUTORS/REPRESENTATIVES

ARGENTINA

Dafsys S.R.L.
Chacabuco, 90-6 Piso
1069-Buenos Aires
Tel: 54-1-334-7726
FAX: 54-1-334-1871

AUSTRALIA

Email Electronics
15-17 Hume Street
Huntingdale, 3166
Tel: 011-61-3-544-8244
TLX: AA 30895
FAX: 011-61-3-543-8179

NSD-Australia
205 Middleborough Rd.
Box Hill, Victoria 3128
Tel: 03 8900970
FAX: 03 8990819

BRAZIL

Elebra Microelectronica S.A.
Rua Geraldo Flausina Gomes, 78
7 Andar
04575 - Sao Paulo - S.P.
Tel: 55-11-534-9641
TLX: 55-11-54593/54591
FAX: 55-11-534-9424

CHINA/HONG KONG

Novel Precision Machinery Co., Ltd.
Flat D, 20 Kingsford Ind. Bldg.
Phase 1, 26 Kwai Hei Street
N.T., Kowloon
Hong Kong
Tel: (852) 422-3222
TWX: 39114 JINMI HX
FAX: (852) 426-1602

INDIA

Micronic Devices
Arun Complex
No. 65 D.V.G. Road
Basavanagudi
Bangalore 560 004
Tel: 011-91-812-600-631
011-91-812-611-365
TLX: 9538458332 MDBG

Micronic Devices
No. 516 5th Floor
Swastik Chambers
Sion, Trombay Road
Chembur
Bombay 400 071
TLX: 9531 171447 MDEV

Micronic Devices
25/8, 1st Floor
Bada Bazaar Marg
Old Rajinder Nagar
New Delhi 110 060
Tel: 011-91-11-5723509
011-91-11-589771
TLX: 031-63253 MDND IN

Micronic Devices
6-3-348/12A Dwarakapuri Colony
Hyderabad 500 482
Tel: 011-91-842-226748

S&S Corporation
1587 Kooser Road
San Jose, CA 95118
Tel: (408) 978-6216
TLX: 820281
FAX: (408) 978-8635

JAPAN

Asahi Electronics Co. Ltd.
KMM Bldg. 2-14-1 Asano
Kokurakita-ku
Kitakyushu-shi 802
Tel: 093-511-6471
FAX: 093-551-7861

C. Itoh Techno-Science Co., Ltd.
4-8-1 Dobashi, Miyamae-ku
Kawasaki-shi, Kanagawa 213
Tel: 044-852-5121
FAX: 044-877-4268

Dia Semicon Systems, Inc.
Flower Hill Shinmachi Higashi-kan
1-23-9 Shinmachi, Setagaya-ku
Tokyo 154
Tel: 03-439-1600
FAX: 03-439-1601

Okaya Koki
2-4-18 Sakae
Naka-ku, Nagoya-shi 460
Tel: 052-204-2916
FAX: 052-204-2901

Ryoyo Electro Corp.
Konwa Bldg.
1-12-22 Tsukiji
Chuo-ku, Tokyo 104
Tel: 03-546-5011
FAX: 03-546-5044

KOREA

J-Tek Corporation
6th Floor, Government Pension Bldg.
24-3 Yoido-dong
Youngdeungpo-ku
Seoul 150-010
Tel: 82-2-780-8039
TLX: 25299 KODIGIT
FAX: 82-2-784-8391

Samsung Electronics
150 Taepyungro-2 KA
Chungku, Seoul 100-102
Tel: 82-2-751-3985
TLX: 27970 KORSST
FAX: 82-2-753-0967

MEXICO

SSB Electronics, Inc.
675 Palomar Street, Bldg. 4, Suite A
Chula Vista, CA 92011
Tel: (619) 585-3253
TLX: 287751 CBALL UR
FAX: (619) 585-8322

Dicopel S.A.
Tochtli 368 Fracc. Ind. San Antonio
Azcapotzalco
C.P. 02760-Mexico, D.F.
Tel: 52-5-561-3211
TLX: 177 3790 Dicome
FAX: 52-5-561-1279

PSI S.A. de C.V.
Fco. Villa esq. Ajusco s/n
Cuernavaca – Morelos
Tel: 52-73-13-9412
FAX: 52-73-17-5333

NEW ZEALAND

Email Electronics
36 Olive Road
Penrose, Auckland
Tel: 011-64-9-591-155
FAX: 011-64-9-592-681

SINGAPORE

Electronic Resources Pte, Ltd.
17 Harvey Road #04-01
Singapore 1336
Tel: 283-0888
TWX: 56541 ERS
FAX: 2895327

SOUTH AFRICA

Electronic Building Elements
178 Erasmus Street (off Watermeyet Street)
Meyerspark, Pretoria, 0184
Tel: 011-2712-803-7680
FAX: 011-2712-803-8294

TAIWAN

Micro Electronics Corporation
5/F 587, Ming Shen East Rd.
Taipei, R.O.C.
Tel: 886-2-501-8231
FAX: 886-2-505-6609

Sertek
15/F 135, Section 2
Chien Juo North Rd.
Taipei 10479, R.O.C.
Tel: (02) 5010055
FAX: (02) 5012521
(02) 5058414

VENEZUELA

P. Benavides S.A.
Avilanes a Rio
Residencia Kamarata
Locales 4 AL 7
La Candelaria, Caracas
Tel: 58-2-574-6338
TLX: 28450
FAX: 58-2-572-3321

*Field Application Location

DOMESTIC SERVICE OFFICES

ALABAMA

*Intel Corp.
5015 Bradford Dr., Suite 2
Huntsville 35805
Tel: (205) 830-4010

ALASKA

Intel Corp.
c/o TransAlaska Data Systems
300 Old Steese Hwy.
Fairbanks 99701-3120
Tel: (907) 452-4401

Intel Corp.
c/o TransAlaska Data Systems
1551 Lore Road
Anchorage 99507
Tel: (907) 522-1776

ARIZONA

*Intel Corp.
11225 N. 28th Dr.
Suite D-214
Phoenix 85029
Tel: (602) 869-4980

*Intel Corp.
500 E. Fry Blvd., Suite M-15
Sierra Vista 85635
Tel: (602) 459-5010

CALIFORNIA

†Intel Corp.
21515 Vanowen St., Ste. 116
Canoga Park 91303
Tel: (818) 704-8500

*Intel Corp.
2250 E. Imperial Hwy., Ste. 218
El Segundo 90245
Tel: (213) 640-6040

*Intel Corp.
1900 Prairie City Rd.
Folsom 95630-9597
Tel: (916) 351-6143
1-800-468-3548

Intel Corp.
9665 Chesapeake Dr., Suite 325
San Diego 92123
Tel: (619) 292-8086

**Intel Corp.
400 N. Tustin Avenue
Suite 450
Santa Ana 92705
Tel: (714) 835-9642

**†Intel Corp.
San Tomas 4
2700 San Tomas Exp., 2nd Floor
Santa Clara 95051
Tel: (408) 986-8086

COLORADO

*Intel Corp.
650 S. Cherry St., Suite 915
Denver 80222
Tel: (303) 321-8086

CONNECTICUT

*Intel Corp.
301 Lee Farm Corporate Park
83 Wooster Heights Rd.
Danbury 06810
Tel: (203) 748-3130

FLORIDA

**Intel Corp.
6363 N.W. 6th Way, Ste. 100
Ft. Lauderdale 33309
Tel: (305) 771-0600

*Intel Corp.
5850 T.G. Lee Blvd., Ste. 340
Orlando 32822
Tel: (407) 240-8000

GEORGIA

*Intel Corp.
3280 Pointe Pkwy., Ste. 200
Norcross 30092
Tel: (404) 449-0541

HAWAII

*Intel Corp.
U.S.I.S.C. Signal Batt.
Building T-1521
Shafter Plats
Shafter 96856

ILLINOIS

**†Intel Corp.
300 N. Martingale Rd., Ste. 400
Schaumburg 60173
Tel: (708) 605-8031

INDIANA

*Intel Corp.
8777 Purdue Rd., Ste. 125
Indianapolis 46268
Tel: (317) 875-0623

KANSAS

*Intel Corp.
10985 Cody, Suite 140
Overland Park 66210
Tel: (913) 345-2727

MARYLAND

**†Intel Corp.
10010 Junction Dr., Suite 200
Annapolis Junction 20701
Tel: (301) 206-2860
FAX: 301-206-3677

MASSACHUSETTS

**†Intel Corp.
3 Carlisle Rd., 2nd Floor
Westford 01886
Tel: (508) 692-1060

MICHIGAN

*†Intel Corp.
7071 Orchard Lake Rd., Ste. 100
West Bloomfield 48322
Tel: (313) 851-8905

MINNESOTA

*†Intel Corp.
3500 W. 80th St., Suite 360
Bloomington 55431
Tel: (612) 835-6722

MISSOURI

*Intel Corp.
4203 Earth City Exp., Ste. 131
Earth City 63045
Tel: (314) 291-1990

NEW JERSEY

**Intel Corp.
300 Sylvan Avenue
Englewood Cliffs 07632
Tel: (201) 567-0821

*Intel Corp.
Parkway 109 Office Center
328 Newman Springs Road
Red Bank 07701
Tel: (201) 747-2233

*Intel Corp.
280 Corporate Center
75 Livingston Ave., 1st Floor
Roseland 07068
Tel: (201) 740-0111

NEW YORK

*†Intel Corp.
2950 Expressway Dr. South
Islandia 11722
Tel: (516) 231-3300

*Intel Corp.
Westage Business Center
Bldg. 300, Route 9
Fishkill 12524
Tel: (914) 897-3860

NORTH CAROLINA

*Intel Corp.
5800 Executive Dr., Ste. 105
Charlotte 28212
Tel: (704) 568-8966

**Intel Corp.
2700 Wycliff Road
Suite 102
Raleigh 27607
Tel: (919) 781-8022

OHIO

**†Intel Corp.
3401 Park Center Dr., Ste. 220
Dayton 45414
Tel: (513) 890-5350

*†Intel Corp.
25700 Science Park Dr., Ste. 100
Beachwood 44122
Tel: (216) 464-2736

OREGON

Intel Corp.
15254 N.W. Greenbrier Parkway
Building B
Beaverton 97005
Tel: (503) 645-8051

*Intel Corp.
5200 N.E. Elam Young Parkway
Hillsboro 97123
Tel: (503) 681-8080

PENNSYLVANIA

*†Intel Corp.
455 Pennsylvania Ave., Ste. 230
Fort Washington 19034
Tel: (215) 641-1000

†Intel Corp.
400 Penn Center Blvd., Ste. 610
Pittsburgh 15235
Tel: (412) 823-4970

Intel Corp.
1513 Cedar Cliff Dr.
Camp Hill 17011
Tel: (717) 761-0860

PUERTO RICO

Intel Corp.
South Industrial Park
P.O. Box 910
Las Piedras 00671
Tel: (809) 733-8616

TEXAS

Intel Corp.
8815 Dyer St., Suite 225
El Paso 79904
Tel: (915) 751-0186

*Intel Corp.
313 E. Anderson Lane, Suite 314
Austin 78752
Tel: (512) 454-3628

**†Intel Corp.
12000 Ford Rd., Suite 401
Dallas 75234
Tel: (214) 241-8087

*Intel Corp.
7322 S.W. Freeway, Ste. 1490
Houston 77074
Tel: (713) 988-8086

UTAH

Intel Corp.
428 East 6400 South, Ste. 104
Murray 84107
Tel: (801) 263-8051

VIRGINIA

*Intel Corp.
1504 Santa Rosa Rd., Ste. 108
Richmond 23288
Tel: (804) 282-5668

WASHINGTON

*Intel Corp.
155 108th Avenue N.E., Ste. 386
Bellevue 98004
Tel: (206) 453-8086

CANADA

ONTARIO

Intel Semiconductor of
Canada, Ltd.
2650 Queensview Dr., Ste. 250
Ottawa K2B 8H6
Tel: (613) 829-9714
FAX: 613-820-5936

Intel Semiconductor of
Canada, Ltd.
190 Attwell Dr., Ste. 102
Rexdale M9W 6H8
Tel: (416) 675-2105
FAX: 416-675-2438

CUSTOMER TRAINING CENTERS

CALIFORNIA

2700 San Tomas Expressway
Santa Clara 95051
Tel: (408) 970-1700
1-800-421-0386

ILLINOIS

300 N. Martingale Road
Suite 300
Schaumburg 60173
Tel: (708) 706-5700
1-800-421-0386

MASSACHUSETTS

3 Carlisle Road, First Floor
Westford 01886
Tel: (301) 220-3380
1-800-328-0386

MARYLAND

10010 Junction Dr.
Suite 200
Annapolis Junction 20701
Tel: (301) 206-2860
1-800-328-0386

SYSTEMS ENGINEERING MANAGERS OFFICES

MINNESOTA

3500 W. 80th Street
Suite 360
Bloomington 55431
Tel: (612) 835-6722

NEW YORK

2950 Expressway Dr., South
Islandia 11722
Tel: (506) 231-3300

†System Engineering locations
*Carry-in locations
**Carry-in/mail-in locations